BIOLOGICAL
ANTHROPOLOGY

Other Mayfield titles in Biological Anthropology

Angeloni, *Annual Editions: Physical Anthropology*
Omohundro, *Mystery Fossil*
Park, *Biological Anthropology: An Introductory Reader*
Relethford, *The Human Species*
Stein/Rowe, *Physical Anthropology*
Stein/Rowe, *Physical Anthropology: The Core*

BIOLOGICAL ANTHROPOLOGY

THIRD EDITION

MICHAEL ALAN PARK

CENTRAL CONNECTICUT STATE UNIVERSITY

McGraw-Hill
Mayfield

Boston   Burr Ridge, IL   Dubuque, IA   Madison, WI   New York   San Francisco   St. Louis
Bangkok   Bogotá   Caracas   Kuala Lumpur   Lisbon   London   Madrid   Mexico City
Milan   Montreal   New Delhi   Santiago   Seoul   Singapore   Sydney   Taipei   Toronto

McGraw-Hill Higher Education

*A Division of The **McGraw-Hill** Companies*

For Jan

3 4 5 6 7 8 9 0 BAH/BAH 0 9 8 7 6 5 4 3 2

Library of Congress Cataloging-in-Publication Data
Park, Michael Alan.
    Biological anthropology / Michael Alan Park.—3rd ed.
      p. cm.
    Includes bibliographical references and index.
    ISBN 0-7674-2594-4
    1. Physical anthropology.   I. Title.

GN60 .P35   2001
599.9—dc21   2001030722

Sponsoring editor, Janet M. Beatty; production editor, Melissa Williams; manuscript editor, Andrea McCarrick; design manager and cover designer, Violeta Diaz; text designer, Anna George; art manager, Robin Mouat; illustrators, Joan Carol, Alice and Will Thiede—Carto-Graphics, and John and Judy Waller; cover photo, © Nicholas Nick/National Geographic Society Image Collection; manufacturing manager, Randy Hurst. The text was set in 10.5/12 Goudy Old Style by UG/GGS Information Services and printed on 50# Chromatone Matte LG by Banta Book Group.

Photo and illustration credits appear on pages 469–470, which constitute an extension of the copyright page.

www.mhhe.com

To the Instructor

Contemporary biological anthropology is a dauntingly broad field. It studies humans in the same way that zoologists study their subject species—from a perspective that includes *all* aspects of the species' biology and that emphasizes the interrelationships among those aspects. In addition to the traditional topics of the human fossil record and human biological variation, bioanthropology includes primatology, modern technologies in molecular genetics, human demography, disease and medical issues, development of the individual, life histories, and such applications as forensic anthropology. Bioanthropology also appreciates that our cultural behavior is an integral part of our behavior as a species.

No wonder, then, that I (and others I have spoken to) have had difficulty in covering the entire field in a one-semester course. We have ended up leaving out important aspects (or paying them little more than lip service), or we have sacrificed a sense of bioanthropology as an integrated whole to a rushed and encyclopedic inventory of all the field's current topics.

As modern bioanthropology increased in breadth and complexity over the past several decades, so, too, did the size and detail of introductory texts. Several are now more than 600 pages long. To date, attempts to produce shorter introductory texts have consisted of simply cutting out parts of these existing tomes, resulting in rather uneven, sometimes oddly organized, presentations of the field.

I wrote this text in order to present a diverse scientific field to beginning students. Here are the major assumptions that guided my writing:

- Because this is a text for introductory courses, I have tried to reduce the field to its most basic information. No part of the discipline has been left out; instead I have achieved brevity by managing the amount of detail and including only the information necessary to clearly and accurately convey the basic themes, theories, methods, and facts of bioanthropology.

- The text assumes that students have limited background knowledge of the material and little understanding of what science is and how it works. The text *explains* rather than simply itemizes facts and ideas, and it does so, as much as possible, in a narrative format. A lesson from the study of folklore is that a story is far more easily understood and retained than is a list of facts.

- I want students to feel that they are reading a text written by a real person who has participated in the field. I have tried to achieve a balance between an informal style and formal style, and I have not shied away from the occasional colloquialism or personal comment.

FEATURES

I've included a number of features that I hope will make this text a more useful learning tool for students.

- *I've used the scientific method as a theme throughout the book to demonstrate the integrity and nature of bioanthropology.* I describe the scientific method and then, because this *is* anthropology, compare science to knowledge garnered from belief systems, discussing the relationship of these two spheres of inquiry and knowledge within cultures. I try to show specifically how scientific reasoning has provided us with the knowledge we have about the topics in bioanthropology. For example, I've presented extended discussions of bipedalism and the issue of modern human origins by posing questions, suggesting answers, and then testing the logic of and evidence for those answers.

- *The text is organized to help students navigate their way through what is still a fairly hefty amount of information.* To help students feel a little less at sea in the midst of new facts and ideas, I regularly refer back to previous topics and ahead to topics that will be covered. The headings I use as signposts are as descriptive as possible (for example, "Natural Selection: The Prime Mover of Evolution").

- *Within chapters, a consistent format helps students better understand material new to them.* Each chapter starts with an **introduction** that sets the stage and context for what's to come, which is followed by a series of **questions** that the chapter will answer. Because science proceeds by asking and answering questions, this format is also used within the body of the text. Important **terms** are in boldface and are defined in the margins at their first appearance. Each chapter concludes with a list of key terms and a **summary** that not only recaps the important points of the chapter but also provides some new ideas and thoughts that help put the chapter into context within the whole discipline. A list of **suggested readings,** made up mostly of nontechnical works, tells students where to find more information about the chapter topics.

- New to this edition are questions at the end of each chapter for students to ponder. These "Questions for Further Thought" are designed to help students explore the ramifications of the chapter topics in today's world.

- Also new to this edition is an appendix with four brief exercises in Mendelian genetics, population genetics, taxonomy, and forensics that allow students to try their hands at applying some of the concepts set out in the text.

- *Two glossaries, a bibliography, and a comprehensive index make information more accessible.* A Glossary of Human and Nonhuman Primates, with a pronunciation guide, defines taxonomic names for taxa discussed in the text. In addition to the running glossary within chapters, a comprehensive Glossary of Terms appears at the back of the book. The Bibliography gives complete references for the suggested readings and also lists technical works referred to within the text. The Index helps students access information quickly.

- *The text's visual appeal enhances its readability.* Detailed, colorful charts and drawings, as well as full-color photographs, underscore significant points in the text. Captions for the artwork add information rather than simply label the pictures.

NEW TO THIS EDITION

The book has been updated throughout and the discussions of many topics have been expanded and clarified. Highlights include the following:

- Chapter 3, "Evolutionary Genetics," has an improved discussion of protein synthesis and concludes with a "Contemporary Reflection" on the decoding of the human genome.

- The distinction between phenetic and cladistic taxonomies is expanded and clarified in Chapter 7, "The Primates."

- Chapter 9, "Studying the Human Past," has an updated and expanded discussion of new genetic technologies used to compare and construct phylogenetic trees of the primates.

- Chapter 10, "Evolution of the Hominids," is updated with the latest fossil finds to include *Equatorius, Kenyanthropus platyops*, and the still-controversial *Orrorin tugenensis*. The discussion of the evolution of bipedalism has been expanded to include additional hypotheses about this behavior's adaptive function.

- The debate over modern human origins, the topic of Chapter 12, continues unabated. This chapter has been extensively rewritten to include data such as new Neandertal DNA and the hypothesized fossil hybrid from Portugal and to clarify the schools of thought in the debate and the evidence supporting and arguing against each.

- Chapter 13, "The Study of Living Peoples," includes new technologies for comparing populations, such as the use of single nucleotide polymorphisms (SNPs); new census data; new information on skin color variation; new research into the influence of viruses on human evolution; the latest information on HIV/AIDS; the latest data on "mad cow disease;" expanded discussion of influences on growth and development; new examples of life history studies; and updated information on the population crisis.

- Chapter 14, "Human Biological Diversity," has an expanded discussion of genetic information on sexual differences and biodiversity; a clarified discussion of the scientific reasons for the nonexistence of biological races; and a new examination of claimed connections between race and athletic ability.

- Chapter 15, now called "Biological Anthropology and Today's World," has a new section on bioanthropology and global issues, which focuses on global warming and its many effects from the perspective of biological anthropology.

SUPPLEMENTARY MATERIAL

The **Instructor's Manual** includes a test bank of about 500 multiple choice and short answer/essay questions, as well as chapter overviews, suggested activities, and lists of key terms.

A **Computerized Test Bank** is available free of charge to qualifying adopters. It is a powerful, easy-to-use test generation system that provides all test items on computer disk for IBM-compatible or Macintosh computers. Instructors can select, add, or edit questions, randomize them, and print tests appropriate to their individual classes.

There is a website (www.mhhe.com/bioanth3) that includes an online study guide and other interactive helps, downloadable illustrations, and Breaking News in Anthropology.

ACKNOWLEDGMENTS

I must go back to the very beginning of my career and thank my first teachers in bioanthropology at Indiana University, Robert Meier and Paul Jamison, and the late Georg Neumann.

For the past seventeen years I have had the privilege and pleasure of working with the folks at Mayfield Publishing, now joining forces with McGraw-Hill. They have become friends and colleagues and I look forward to our continued collaboration. Mayfield's dedication to their motto of "finding solutions to teaching problems" not only resulted in high-quality textbooks but was particularly rewarding to me as an educator. For this edition, I would particularly like to thank the following:

Jan Beatty brought me to Mayfield in the first place and has now been the sponsoring editor of ten of my books. Her knowledge of all aspects of publishing, combined with her understanding of anthropology and the needs (and quirks) of us academic types has been a major contribution to the quality of all the books she works on as well as to the authors' enjoyment in working on them.

Linda Toy has ably directed the production staff that has magically (to me) turned my ideas into finished products.

Melissa Williams has been my production editor for many books. Her good humor, her ability to be patient while still demanding, and her skills at managing all the details of the process have been invaluable.

Robin Mouat, art manager, has understood what I'm trying to show with my doodles and has turned them into actual art. Copy editor Andrea McCarrick has understood what I'm trying to say with some of my words and has turned them into actual sentences. Thanks also to Brian Pecko, photo researcher; Anna George, designer; and Violeta Diaz, design manager. They have helped make the book attractive and, therefore, much more useful than unadorned words would be.

I thank the following colleagues in anthropology for various forms of assistance: Ken Feder, Central Connecticut State University; Agustín Fuentes, Central Washington University; Linda Van Blerkom, Drew University; Linda Wolfe, East Carolina University.

The manuscript was reviewed by Mark C. Griffin, San Francisco State University; Samantha Hens, California State University, Sacramento; Patricia M. Lambert, Utah State University; Dianne Smith, Santa Rosa Junior College; and Mark Taylor, Northern Arizona University. I thank them for their helpful and insightful contributions. All final content, decisions, and errors are, of course, my responsibility.

To the Reader

The broad field of biological, or physical, anthropology deals with everything from evolutionary theory to the human fossil record to the identification of human skeletal remains from crime scenes and accidents. A detailed account of this whole field would result in an unwieldy text that would be a tough assignment for a one-semester introductory course, especially if it were assigned in its entirety.

This text is intended to truly be an *introduction* to biological anthropology. It will tell you about the many different kinds of studies bioanthropologists participate in and how they conduct them; you'll also learn about the scientific theories and data they use. All the important aspects of bioanthropology are covered here but with just the essential amount of detail. When you understand an idea from this book, then you should be able to delve more deeply into the subject if you are interested and you will have the basis for an even more profound understanding.

A major theme of this book is the scientific method. Biological anthropology is a science, so an understanding of how science works is essential. Because the field of anthropology studies the human species in its entirety, however, the text will examine science as a human endeavor, seeing where it fits in the realm of human knowledge.

HOW TO USE THIS BOOK

Each chapter starts with an **introduction** that sets the stage and context for what's to come, followed by a series of **questions** that the chapter will answer. Because science proceeds by asking and answering questions, this format is also used within the body of the text. Important **terms** are in boldface and are defined in the margins at their first appearance. Each chapter ends with a **summary** that not only recaps the important points of the chapter but also provides some new ideas and thoughts that help put what you have just learned into the context of the whole discipline of bioanthropology. There are also "Questions for Further Thought" that will help you explore some of the ramifications of the chapter's topics to life in today's world. A list of **suggested readings,** made up mostly of non-technical works, tells you where to find more information if you are interested in a particular topic.

A Glossary of Human and Nonhuman Primates defines taxonomic (scientific) names for species discussed in the text—names like *Homo sapiens* and *Australopithecus afarensis*—and tells you how to pronounce them. In addition to the running glossary within chapters, a comprehensive Glossary of Terms appears at the back of the book. The Bibliography gives complete references for the suggested readings and also lists technical works referred to within the text. The Index will help you more quickly access information.

For an online study guide and a Breaking News in Anthropology feature, see our Online Learning Center: www.mhhe.com/bioanth3.

Contents

I BIOLOGICAL ANTHROPOLOGY   *I*

In the Field: Doing Biological Anthropology   *2*
What Is Biological Anthropology?   *10*
Bioanthropology and Science   *14*
    The Scientific Method   *14*
    Belief Systems   *18*
Contemporary Reflections: *Is Evolution a Fact, a Theory, or Just a Hypothesis?*   *20*
Summary   *21*
Questions for Further Thought   *21*
Key Terms   *22*
Suggested Readings   *22*

2 THE EVOLUTION OF EVOLUTION   *25*

"On the Shoulders of Giants": Explaining the Changing Earth   *26*
"Common Sense at Its Best": Explaining Biological Change   *34*
Contemporary Reflections: *Has Science Dehumanized Society?*   *41*
Summary   *43*
Questions for Further Thought   *44*
Key Terms   *44*
Suggested Readings   *44*

3 EVOLUTIONARY GENETICS   47

How Genes Work   *48*

From Gene to Trait   *54*

How Inheritance Works   *58*

Contemporary Reflections: *What Does the Decoding of the Human Genome Mean?*   *62*

Summary   *62*

Questions for Further Thought   *64*

Key Terms   *64*

Suggested Readings   *65*

4 THE PROCESSES OF EVOLUTION   *67*

Species: The Units of Evolution   *68*

Mutations: Necessary Errors   *71*

Natural Selection: The Prime Mover of Evolution   *73*

Gene Flow: Mixing Populations   *76*

Genetic Drift: Random Evolution   *78*

Sickle Cell Anemia: Evolutionary Processes in Action   *80*

Contemporary Reflections: *Are Humans Still Evolving?*   *84*

Summary   *86*

Questions for Further Thought   *87*

Key Terms   *88*

Suggested Readings   *88*

5 THE ORIGIN OF SPECIES AND THE SHAPE OF EVOLUTION   *91*

New Species   *92*

Adaptive Radiation: The Evolution of Life's Diversity   *96*

The Shape of the Family Tree   *100*

Evolution Questioned: The Pseudoscience of "Scientific Creationism"   *103*

Contemporary Reflections: *Can We See Evolution in Action?*   106

Summary   *108*

Questions for Further Thought   *109*

Key Terms   *110*

Suggested Readings   *110*

6 A BRIEF EVOLUTIONARY TIMETABLE   *113*

From the Beginning: A Quick History   *114*

Drifting Continents and Mass Extinctions:
   The Pace of Change   *120*

Contemporary Reflections: *Are Mass Extinctions a Thing
   of the Past?*   124

Summary   *126*

Questions for Further Thought   *126*

Key Terms   *127*

Suggested Readings   *127*

7 THE PRIMATES   *129*

Naming the Animals   *130*
   Taxonomy   *131*
   An Alternative System   *134*
What Is a Primate?   *137*
   The Senses   *137*
   Movement   *139*
   Reproduction   *140*
   Intelligence   *140*
   Behavior Patterns   *141*
A Survey of the Living Primates   *145*
   Prosimians   *146*
   Anthropoids   *149*
The Human Primate   *155*
   The Senses   *155*
   Movement   *155*

Contemporary Reflections: *Should Nonhuman Primates Have Rights?* 156
   Reproduction 156
   Intelligence 158
   Behavior Patterns 158
Summary 159
Questions for Further Thought 159
Key Terms 160
Suggested Readings 160

8 PRIMATE BEHAVIOR AND HUMAN EVOLUTION 163

Studying Behavior 164
Baboons 168
Chimpanzees 172
Bonobos 177
Contemporary Reflections: *Are Some Human Behaviors Genetic?* 180
Summary 183
Questions for Further Thought 183
Key Terms 184
Suggested Readings 184

9 STUDYING THE HUMAN PAST 187

Bones: The Primate Skeleton 188
Old Bones: Locating, Recovering, and Dating Fossils 194
How Fossils Get to Be Fossils 202
Genes: New Windows to the Past 206
Contemporary Reflections: *Who Owns Old Bones?* 208
Summary 210
Questions for Further Thought 211
Key Terms 212
Suggested Readings 212

10 EVOLUTION OF THE HOMINIDS   *215*

The Origin and Evolution of the Primates   *216*

The First Hominids: The Bipedal Primate   *223*

Bipedalism   *234*
    The Benefits of Bipedalism   234
    Explaining the Emergence of Bipedalism   237

The Hominids Evolve   *242*

The First Members of Genus *Homo*   *248*

Contemporary Reflections: *Where Is the "Missing Link"?*   *252*

Summary   *255*

Questions for Further Thought   *255*

Key Terms   *256*

Suggested Readings   *256*

11 THE EVOLUTION OF GENUS *HOMO*   *259*

Lumpers and Splitters: An Organizing Plan   *261*

To New Lands   *263*

Big Brains, Archaic Skulls   *280*

The Neandertals   *288*

Modern Humans   *298*

Contemporary Reflections: *What Do We Mean by "Human"?*   *306*

Summary   *306*

Questions for Further Thought   *308*

Key Terms   *309*

Suggested Readings   *309*

12 THE DEBATE OVER MODERN HUMAN ORIGINS   *311*

The Models   *313*
    The Recent African Origin (RAO) Model   313
    The Multiregional Evolution (MRE) Model   315

The Evidence   318
   The Fossil Record   318
   Genetics   322
   Evolutionary Theory   331
Contemporary Reflections: *Is There a Connection between Modern Human Origins and Race?*   334
Summary   337
Questions for Further Thought   337
Key Terms   338
Suggested Readings   338

13 THE STUDY OF LIVING PEOPLES   *341*

Genes in Populations   343
Evolution within Populations   346
Describing Populations   351
Human Adaptations   357
Species Adaptations   358
   Variation in Adaptations   358
   Are All Polymorphisms Adaptively Important?   362
Disease and Human Populations   366
The Bioanthropology of Individuals   371
Contemporary Reflections: *Where Is the Population Crisis?*   376
Summary   378
Questions for Further Thought   379
Key Terms   380
Suggested Readings   380

14 HUMAN BIOLOGICAL DIVERSITY   *383*

Sex and Gender   385
Race as a Biological Concept   389
Why Are There No Biological Races within the Human Species?   395
   Human Phenotypic Variation   395

Genetic Variation 397

Evolutionary Theory 398

What, Then, *Are* Human Races? 401

Race, Bioanthropology, and Social Issues 404

Contemporary Reflections: *Are There Racial Differences in Athletic Ability?* 408

Summary 411

Questions for Further Thought 411

Key Terms 412

Suggested Readings 412

15 **BIOLOGICAL ANTHROPOLOGY AND TODAY'S WORLD** *415*

Forensic Anthropology: Reading the Bones 416

Lessons from the Past 423

Contemporary Reflections: *What Can One Do with a Degree in Bioanthropology?* 428

Bioanthropology and Global Issues 428

Summary 431

Questions for Further Thought 432

Suggested Readings 432

Appendix *434*

Glossary of Human and Nonhuman Primates *443*

Glossary of Terms *447*

Bibliography *455*

Credits *469*

Index *471*

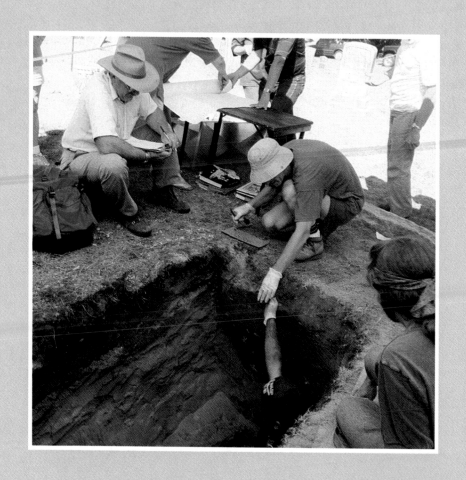

BIOLOGICAL ANTHROPOLOGY

Anthropologists study
spiders, right?
—Anonymous caller

I f you asked twenty different people to define anthropology, you would probably get twenty different answers. Anthropology is such a broad field that many people, understandably, are not sure just what an anthropologist studies. People have brought me rocks to identify and have asked me about the accuracy of the dinosaurs in *Jurassic Park*. One man even called me for information on black widow spiders—and he was referred to me by someone within the university where I teach.

In this chapter, we will define anthropology in general and then focus on the subfield of biological anthropology (also called bioanthropology or physical anthropology). Because fieldwork—where anthropologists make their observations and collect their data—is perhaps the best-known aspect of anthropology and is the part that attracts many students to the discipline, I will begin with a brief description of two of my fieldwork experiences.

As you read, consider the following questions:

What is anthropology, and what are its subfields?

What is biological anthropology?

How does the scientific method operate?

In what way is bioanthropology a science?

What are belief systems, and what is their relationship to scientific knowledge?

IN THE FIELD: DOING BIOLOGICAL ANTHROPOLOGY

The wheat fields on either side of the long, straight road in western Saskatchewan, Canada, stretched as far as the eye could see. I found myself wishing, on that June day in 1973, that the road went on just as far. I was on my way to visit with my first real anthropological subjects, a colony of people belonging to a 450-year-old religious denomination called the Hutterian Brethren, or Hutterites.

Up to this point, I had not felt much anxiety about the visit. Accounts by other anthropologists of their contacts with Amazon jungle warriors and New Guinea headhunters made my situation seem rather safe. The Hutterites are, after all, people who share my European American cultural heritage, number English among their languages, and practice a form of Christianity that emphasizes pacifism and tolerance.

Barns

Seed Cleaning Shed

Cattle Corral

N

Turkey House

Creamery

Garage

Fuel Tanks

Cattle Stable

Storage Shed

Watertank

Machine Shop

Chicken House

Shoemaker Shop

Food Storage

German School

English School (Church)

Kitchen

Sheep Pen

Outhouses

Teacher Residence

Living Quarters

Kindergarten

Cemetery

Duck Lake

100 50 0   100   200   300   400   500 Ft.

FIGURE 1.1
Diagram of Typical Hutterite Colony. The variety of buildings and their functions are indicative of the Hutterites' attempt to keep their colonies self-sufficient and separate from the outside world.

At this point, though, those considerations, no matter how reassuring they should have been, didn't help. Nor did the fact that I was accompanied by the wife of a local wheat farmer who was well known and liked by the people of this colony. I simply had that unnamed fear that affects nearly all anthropologists under these first-contact circumstances.

Finally, the road we traveled—which had turned from blacktop to dirt about 10 miles back—curved abruptly to the right and crested a hill. I saw below us, at the literal end of the road, a neat collection of twenty or so white buildings surrounded by acres of cultivated fields. This was the Hutterite colony, or *Bruderhof*, the "place where the brethren live" (Figure 1.1).

As we drove into the colony, not a soul was to be seen. My companion explained that it was a religious holiday that required all but essential work to cease. Everyone was indoors observing the holiday, but the colony minister and colony boss had agreed to see me.

We entered one of the smaller buildings, which I recognized from pictures and diagrams of "typical" colonies as one of the residential buildings. The interior was darkened in keeping with the holiday. A few minutes later, with my bearings straight and the introductions made, I explained the reason for my visit to two men and a woman.

The men were dressed in the Hutterite fashion—black trousers and coats and white shirts—and they wore beards, a sign of marriage. The older, gray-haired man was the colony minister. The younger man, who happened to be his son, was the colony boss. The woman, the minister's wife, also dressed in the conservative style of the Hutterites and related groups. She wore a nearly full-length sleeveless dress with a white blouse underneath. Her head was covered by a polka-dot kerchief, or "shawl," as they call it (Figure 1.2).

My contacts, the wheat farmer and his wife, had arranged the visit and had already given the Hutterites an idea of what I wanted to do. But if they didn't like me or my planned study, they could still decline to cooperate. The three listened in silence as I went through my well-rehearsed explanation. When I had finished, they asked me only a few questions. Was I from the government? (My study involved using fingerprints as hereditary traits, and they apparently associated fingerprinting with law enforcement and personal identification.) Did I know Scripture? (My equivocal answer created no problem.) What would I use this study for? Was I going to write a book? Did I know so-and-so, who had been there 2 years ago and done medical examinations?

I expected them to confer with one another or ask me to come back when they had decided if they would allow me to conduct the study. Instead, the minister, who was clearly in charge, simply said, "Today is a holiday for us. Can you start tomorrow?"

And so, for the next month I took part in my personal version of fieldwork—taking fingerprints, recording family relationships, observing colony life, and getting to know the Hutterites of this and one other Canadian *Bruderhof* (Park 1979; 14-15Figure 1.3).

What exactly had brought me 1,300 miles from my university to the northern plains, to this isolated community of people whose way of life has changed little over the past 450 years and whose lifestyle and philosophy differ so much from those of North American culture in general? Essentially, it was the same thing that takes anthropologists to such

FIGURE 1.2
Hutterite Women in
Typical Dress.

locations as the highlands of New Guinea, the caves of the Pyrenees, and the street corners of New York City: the desire to learn something about the nature of the human species.

In my case, I was pursuing an interest I had developed early in graduate school—the study of the processes of evolution and how they affect humans. I was curious about two of these processes: gene flow and genetic drift (see Chapter 4 for details). Both topics had been described half a century earlier, but their workings and importance, especially with regard to living human populations, were still poorly understood.

To examine the actions of these processes on human populations and to determine their roles in human evolution, I needed to find a human

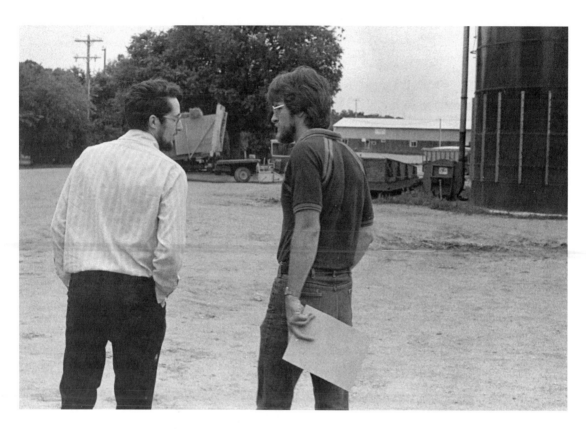

FIGURE I.3
Author (*right*) and Hutterite Informant. I already had the beard, but it was suggested that I keep it so I would look more familiar to the Hutterite children.

group with a few special characteristics. The group had to (1) be genetically isolated, (2) be fairly small as a whole but with large families, and (3) consist of individual populations that resulted from the splitting of earlier populations.

The Hutterites exhibited all these characteristics. (I'll elaborate later.) I discovered them through library research on genetically isolated groups. My opportunity to study them was greatly enhanced by a stroke of luck. A fellow graduate student was the daughter of the wheat farmer and his wife who became my "public relations advisors."

Exactly 20 years after my fieldwork with the Hutterites, I found myself standing over an open grave in an old cemetery in the wooded hills of northwest Connecticut. Our team of anthropologists was hoping to find

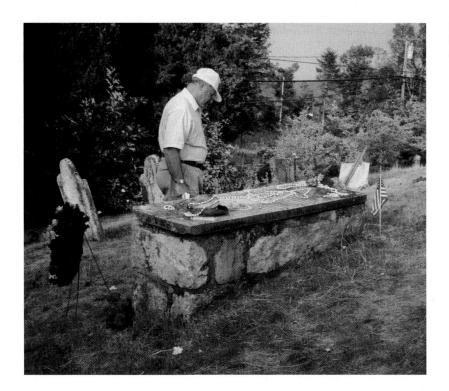

FIGURE 1.4
Headstone of Henry Opuka-haia.

the remains of a native Hawaiian who had been buried here in 1818 and who was now, after 175 years, going home.

A few weeks earlier, Nick Bellantoni, the Connecticut state archaeologist (and a former student of mine) had called me with a fascinating story. In 1808 a young Hawaiian named Opukahaia (pronounced *o-pu-ka-ha-EE-a*) escaped the tribal warfare that had killed his family by swimming out to a Yankee whaling vessel, where he was taken on board as a cabin boy. Two years (and many adventures) later he ended up at Yale University in New Haven, Connecticut. He took the name Henry, converted to Christianity, and became a Congregational minister who helped build a missionary school in Cornwall, Connecticut. His dream was to return to Hawaii and to bring his new faith to the people there (see his portrait in Figure 1.6).

Sadly, Henry's dream was never realized. He died in a typhoid epidemic in 1818 at the age of 26, but his vision inspired the missionary movement that was to change the history of the Hawaiian Islands forever. His grave in Cornwall became a shrine both for the people of his adopted land and for visiting Hawaiians, who would leave offerings atop his platform-style headstone (Figure 1.4).

Nearly two centuries after his death, a living relative of Henry's had a dream that she would honor Henry's final wish to return to his native land. After almost a year of raising funds and making the necessary arrangements, her dream was to come true. And this is where anthropology comes in.

Old New England cemeteries tended to be inexact in the placement of headstones relative to the bodies buried beneath them, and the acidic New England soil is unkind to organic remains. Both logically and legally, this was a job for the state archaeologist, and Nick wanted my help in recovering and identifying whatever remains we might be lucky enough to find. He also wanted my help, it turned out, in moving several tons of stone.

Henry's tomb had been carefully and lovingly assembled by the people of Cornwall. They had placed the inscribed headstone on a pedestal of fieldstone and mortar. We dismantled this with care, labeling each stone and diagramming its position, since it was to be rebuilt by a stone mason. Under the pedestal, and going down about 3 feet into the ground, we uncovered three more layers of fieldstone, which acted as a foundation for the monument and protection for the coffin and the remains we hoped were still below. When all the stones had been removed and we were into a layer of sandy soil, Nick worked alone, delicately scraping away the dirt inch by inch (Figure 1.5).

Late on the second day of our excavation, the remnants of the coffin came into view. In fact, the wooden coffin itself had long since decayed. All that was left was the dark shadow of its outline in the soil. We began to despair of finding much else, but an hour later Nick's trowel grazed something hard, and in a few minutes the apparent remains of Henry Opukahaia saw the light of day for the first time in 175 years.

We soon learned that the skeleton was virtually complete. But was it *Henry*? As Nick slowly freed each bone from the soil and handed it up to me (see chapter-opener photograph), we recorded it and compared it with what we knew of Henry from written descriptions and a single portrait. The skeleton was clearly that of a male and, at first glance, conformed to that of a person in his late 20s of about the right size. Henry had been described as being "a little under 6 feet," and the long bones of the arms and legs appeared to be just a bit shorter than mine, though much more robust. The skull, however, confirmed our identification. As

FIGURE 1.5
Excavating the Grave of Henry Opukahaia. The pattern on the floor of the excavation marks the coffin outline.

the dirt was brushed away, the face of Henry Opukahaia emerged, the very image of his portrait. (The family has requested that, for religious reasons, photographs of Henry's remains not be published.)

We spent 2 more days with the bones, this time in the garage of a Hartford funeral home. We cleaned, photographed, measured, and described each bone. Closer analysis supported our graveside conclusions, and more. On the inside surface of the ribs, we found the telltale ashy texture that can be symptomatic of typhoid. The original diagnosis, done in the days before medicine even understood about microorganisms, had been correct.

Finally, we placed each bone in its proper anatomical position in spaces cut into heavy foam rubber that lined the bottom of a *koa*-wood coffin, specially made and shipped from Hawaii. The following Sunday we attended a memorial service in Cornwall, and then Henry's remains began their long journey back home (Figure 1.6).

FIGURE 1.6
Reverend David Hirano, from Hawaii, speaks over the remains of Henry Opukahaia at his "homegoing" celebration in Cornwall, Connecticut. The *koa*-wood coffin, *ti* leaves, and flowered *lei* all have symbolic meaning in Hawaiian culture.

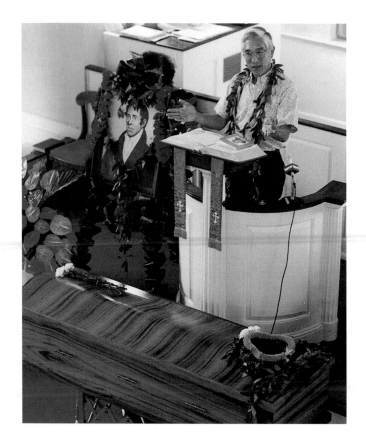

WHAT IS BIOLOGICAL ANTHROPOLOGY?

My experiences as a biological anthropologist range from examining the esoteric detail of evolutionary theory to using my knowledge of the human skeleton for a very personal endeavor. These are just two examples of the many things that biological anthropologists do.

Biological anthropology (or **bioanthropology** or **physical anthropology**) needs to be defined within the context of anthropology as a whole, and doing this is both simple and complex. **Anthropology,** in general, is defined as *the study of the human species*. Simply put, anthropologists study the human species as any zoologist would study an animal **species.** We look into every aspect of the biology of our subject—genetics, anatomy, physiology, behavior, environment, adaptations, and evolutionary history—stressing the interrelationships among these aspects.

This kind of approach—examining a subject by focusing on the interrelationships among its parts—is called **holistic.** The holistic approach is the hallmark of anthropology. We understand that all the facets of our species—our biology, our behavior, our past, and our present—interact to make us what we are. But we need to study some topics separately, since they can be so complex. Thus, you may be taking courses in history, economics, psychology, art, anatomy, and so on. What anthropologists do, though, is seek the connections among these subjects, for in real life they are not absolutely separate.

But here's where it gets complicated. The most characteristic feature of our species' behavior is **culture,** and cultural behavior is not programmed in our genes, as is, for example, much of the behavior of birds and virtually all of the behavior of ants. Human culture is learned. We have a biological potential for cultural behavior in general, but exactly *how* we behave comes to us through all our experiences. Take language, for example. All humans are born with the ability to learn a language. Which language each of us actually speaks is determined by which language is spoken in our family and also in the broader culture in which we live.

Moreover, cultural knowledge involves not just specific facts but, more important, ideas, concepts, generalizations, and abstractions. For example, you were able to speak your native language fairly fluently before you were ever formally taught the particulars of its grammar. You did this by making your own generalizations from the raw data you heard and the rules they followed, that is, from the speech of others and from trying to make yourself understood. Even now when you speak, you are applying those generalizations to new situations. And each situation—every conversation you have, every essay you write, every book you read—is a new situation.

In addition, because culture exists in the context of human social interactions, it must be shared among members of a social group. The complexity of cultural ideas requires this sharing to involve symbols—agreed-upon representations of concepts and abstractions. Human language, of course, is symbolic, as are many visual aspects of our cultures.

In short, culture is highly variable and flexible. It differs from society to society and from one time period to another. It even differs in its details from one individual to another. We continually modify our cultural behaviors to fit the unique circumstances of our lives.

All this variability makes the study of the human species complex and challenging, and so anthropology, the discipline that takes on this challenge, is typically divided into a number of subfields. Biological anthropology looks at our species from a biological point of view. This in-

biological anthropology: A subfield of anthropology that studies humans as a biological species.

bioanthropology: Another name for biological anthropology.

physical anthropology: The traditional name for biological anthropology.

anthropology: The study of the human species.

species: A group of organisms that can produce fertile offspring among themselves but not with members of other groups.

holistic: Assuming an interrelationship among the parts of a subject.

culture: Ideas and behaviors that are learned and transmitted. Nonbiological means of adaptation.

FIGURE 1.7
Major Subfields of Anthropology with Some of Their Topics. The topics of each subfield may be applied to various social issues (see Chapter 15).

cludes all the topics covered in this book. **Cultural anthropology** is the study of culture as a characteristic of our species and of the variation in cultural expression among human groups. This includes human language, although sometimes linguistic anthropology is considered a separate subfield. **Archaeology** is the study of the human cultural past and the reconstruction of past cultural systems. It also involves the techniques used to recover, preserve, and interpret the material remains of the past.

All anthropologists, then, are trying to do the same thing—learn about the human species. The scope and complexity of the subject require several starting points or focuses: These are the subfields of anthropology (Figure 1.7).

Each subfield has many specialties. For biological anthropology, these specialties are best expressed in terms of the questions we seek to answer about human biology:

1. What are the *biological characteristics* that define the human species? How do our *genes* code for these characteristics? Just how much do genes contribute to our traits? How much are traits shaped by the environment? How does *evolution* work, and how does it apply to us? (These were the questions I was pursuing in my study of the Hutterites.)

2. What is the *physical record* of our evolution? This is the specialty referred to as **paleoanthropology,** the study of human *fossils* based on our knowledge of skeletal biology, or **osteology.**

3. What sort of *biological variation* do we see in our species today? How did it evolve? What do the variable traits mean for other aspects of our lives? What do they *not* mean?

4. What can we learn about the biology of our close relatives, the non-human **primates,** and what can it tell us about ourselves? This specialty is called **primatology.**

5. What do we know about **human ecology,** the relationships between humans and their environments?

6. How can we apply all this knowledge to matters of current concern? This is often called **applied anthropology.** (The story of the exhumation of Henry Opukahaia is an example.)

Individual biological anthropologists undertake numerous and diverse studies. I took fingerprints of members of a centuries-old Christian group to learn something about the processes of evolution that have affected our species. Paleoanthropologist Donald Johanson was with the team that discovered and identified the famous fossil of "Lucy," a 3.2-million-year-old human ancestor. Paleontologist Elwyn Simons studies fossils of nonhuman primates that go even further back in evolutionary time—to the dawn of the apes more than 30 million years ago. Other anthropologists study living nonhuman primates. Shirley Strum, Barbara Smuts, and Linda Fedigan, for example, have all observed troops of baboons to understand what their behavior can tell us about our own.

Clyde Snow is a **forensic anthropologist.** He applies his knowledge of the human skeleton to solving crimes and identifying missing persons. He has worked to identify the remains of the victims of death squads in Argentina and has tried (so far without success) to locate the bones of Butch Cassidy and the Sundance Kid in Bolivia.

Melvin Konner has examined the lifestyles of contemporary **hunter-gatherers,** including their diet and exercise, to show how those lifestyles differ (mostly for the better) from those of people in industrial societies.

We'll meet these people and their studies, and many more, as we survey the field of bioanthropology. As we do, keep in mind that what connects these varied activities is their focus on *learning about human beings as a biological species*.

The studies of bioanthropologists are also connected in that they are all scientific. In many cases, they may not seem to fit the common conception of science. Most anthropologists don't wear white lab coats or work with test tubes and chemicals. Many anthropologists study things that can't be directly observed in nature or re-created in the lab because they happened in the past. But bioanthropology *is* a science, just as much as chemistry, physics, and biology. We'll see how this is so, and we'll also look at some nonscientific ways in which people try to understand their world.

cultural anthropology: A subfield of anthropology that focuses on human cultural behavior and cultural systems and the variation in cultural expression among human groups.

archaeology: A subfield of anthropology that studies the human cultural past and the reconstruction of past cultural systems.

paleoanthropology: A specialty that studies the human fossil record.

osteology: The study of the structure, function, and evolution of the skeleton.

primates: Large-brained, mostly tree-dwelling mammals with three-dimensional color vision and grasping hands. Humans are primates.

primatology: A specialty that studies nonhuman primates.

human ecology: A specialty that studies the relationships between humans and their environments.

applied anthropology: Anthropology used to address current practical problems and concerns.

forensic anthropologist: One who applies anthropology to legal matters.

hunter-gatherers: Societies that rely upon naturally occurring sources of food.

BIOANTHROPOLOGY AND SCIENCE

A popular image of a scientist is that of a walking encyclopedia. Science is often seen as fact-collecting. While it's fair to say that scientists know a lot of facts, so do a lot of other people. Champions on the TV quiz show *Jeopardy* are not necessarily professional scientists.

Facts are certainly important to science. They are the raw material of science, the data scientists use. But what scientists really do is *explain* facts, not simply collect them. **Science,** in other words, is *a method of inquiry, a way of answering questions about the world*. But how does science work? Is science the only valid and logical method for explaining the world around us?

The Scientific Method

The world is full of things that need explaining. We might wonder about the behavior of a bird, the origin of the stars in the night sky, the identity of a fossil skeleton, the social interaction of students in a college classroom, or the ritual warfare of a society in highland New Guinea. As people, we strive to understand such phenomena, to know why and how these things occur. As scientists, we must answer these questions according to a special set of rules—the **scientific method.**

The scientific method involves a cycle of steps, and, in reality, one may begin anywhere on the cycle (Figure 1.8). The most basic step is asking the questions we wish to answer or describing the observations we wish to explain. We then look for patterns, connections, and associations so we can generate educated guesses as to possible explanations. These educated guesses are called **hypotheses.** In other words, we try to formulate a *general* explanatory principle that will account for the *specific* pieces of real data we have observed and want to explain. This process of reasoning is called **induction.**

Next comes the essence—indeed the defining characteristic—of science. We must attempt to either support or refute our hypothesis by testing it. Tests may take many forms, depending on what we are trying to explain, but basically we reverse the process of induction and go from the general back to the specific by making predictions: *If* our general hypothesis is correct, *then* what other specific things should we observe? This process is called **deduction.** For example, we look for:

1. *Repetition:* Does the same phenomenon occur over and over?
2. *Universality:* Does the phenomenon occur under all conditions? If we vary some aspect of the situation, will the phenomenon still occur? How might different situations change the phenomenon?

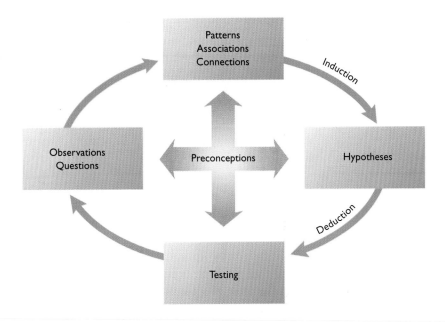

FIGURE 1.8

Steps in the Scientific Method. Science is a cycle of asking questions, finding patterns, generating hypotheses, and testing those hypotheses. Even when a hypothesis is well supported enough to be considered a theory, it still must be subjected to scientific inquiry to check its validity and explain its details. Science should always be skeptical, always open to questioning and self-examination. All science is conducted by individuals within the context of a culture and so is affected by preconceptions. It is an important part of the scientific method to be aware of these preconceptions.

3. *Explanations for exceptions:* Can we account for cases where the phenomenon doesn't appear to occur?

4. *New data:* Does new information support or contradict our hypothesis?

If we find one piece of evidence that conclusively refutes our hypothesis, we consider it disproved. But if the hypothesis passes every test we put it to, we may elevate our idea to the status of a very good hypothesis, which in science is called a **theory.**

Notice that I didn't say we "proved" the hypothesis. Science is skeptical, always looking for new evidence, always open to and even inviting change. The best we can honestly say about a theory is that *so far* no evidence has been found that *disproves* it.

Of course, some theories are so well supported that we are safe in considering them to be facts and in using them as a basis for further investigation. The theories of gravity, evolution, and relativity are all concepts central to many aspects of our thinking because they are ideas supported

science: The method of inquiry that requires the generation, testing, and acceptance or rejection of hypotheses.

scientific method: The process of conducting scientific inquiry.

hypotheses: Educated guesses to explain natural phenomena.

induction: Developing a general explanation from specific observations.

deduction: Suggesting specific data that would be found if a hypothesis were true.

theory: A hypothesis that has been well supported by evidence and testing.

by every test applied to them and refuted by none. As biologist Stephen Jay Gould says, a theory can be taken as fact when it is "confirmed to such a degree that it would be perverse to withhold provisional assent."

We don't stop when we have developed a theory, however. No theory is complete. The theory of gravity establishes that some force we call gravity exists, but we still don't understand exactly what gravity is and how it works. In other words, we still have questions to answer and observations to explain. Scientists are now testing hypotheses that attempt to explain the origin, nature, and operation of gravity.

Another popular conception of science is that it only studies visible, tangible, present-day things—chemicals, living organisms, planets and stars. But notice that gravity is neither visible nor tangible. We can't see gravity, but we know it exists because all our deductive predictions support its existence. We see gravity work every time we drop an object or jump up in the air and come back down to earth instead of flying off into space. We logically predict that if gravity is the property of objects with mass, the bigger the object the more gravity. We saw this clearly when we watched the astronauts walk around on the moon; they were literally lighter (about one-sixth their earthly weight) because the moon, being smaller than the earth, has less gravity. We also see the increased effects of the gravity of very massive objects (Figure 1.9). We can even explain exceptions *within the context of our general idea*. The reason a helium-filled balloon seems to violate gravity can be explained by our theory of gravity: Helium is less dense than the surrounding air and so responds relatively less to the earth's gravity (that is, it is lighter). In other words, the balloon exhibits buoyancy like a boat on water.

Similarly, past events can't be seen or touched. They can't be experimented on directly or repeated exactly. The evolution of plants and animals is an example. But again, we know that evolution occurred because the idea has passed all our tests. The idea of evolution explains observations of the real world. We have observed everything we predicted we would *if* evolution occurred. (We'll look more closely at how science has derived and supported the theory of evolution in Chapter 3.)

Moreover, we often think of the scientific method as applying only to stereotypical scientific matters like gravity, chemistry, and evolution. In fact, however, we all use the scientific method every day for issues somewhat more down-to-earth than gravity. Remember, science is *a way of thinking*. Consider the steps you take to solve some problem—say, how to most efficiently organize all your activities for the day or how to repair a broken household item. You are probably using a version of the scientific method.

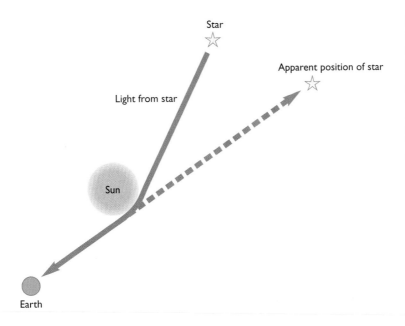

Star

Apparent position of star

Light from star

Sun

Earth

FIGURE 1.9

Light Bent by Gravity. Einstein predicted that a strong gravitational field could bend light. His prediction was verified when light from stars that should have been blocked by the sun could be seen during a solar eclipse. The effect is greatly exaggerated in this drawing.

I noted that scientists may begin their investigations at any point on the cycle diagrammed in Figure 1.8. For instance, we might have a flash of inspiration that presents us with some notion of an overarching concept that might explain many different phenomena. In other words, we might dream up a potential theory. We then, of course, would have to go through all the other steps of making observations, generating individual hypotheses, and testing those hypotheses. As an example, Albert Einstein was working on the nature of light waves when he came up with the idea of the equivalency of matter and energy, his famous formula $E = mc^2$. It was only later that this relationship was experimentally verified and all its implications and applications were understood.

Finally, what about the label "Preconceptions" in the middle of Figure 1.8? Don't scientists search for truths—truths that are objective and not influenced by preconceived notions or prejudices? Ideally, yes. But, in fact, scientists are members of their societies and participants in their cultures, and science is always conducted within the context of a particular culture at a particular point in time. Thus, science—as objective as we try to make it—is always constrained by what we already know, by what we still don't know, by the technology available to us to gather and test data, and even by certain influential social or cultural trends.

For example, I remember back in the mid-1950s, when one of my elementary school teachers pointed out that the east coast of South America and the west coast of Africa seemed to potentially fit together like a giant jigsaw puzzle. Of course, she had said, there's no way the continents could move around, so it must just be a coincidence. In fact, she was reflecting our scientific knowledge of the time. There was plenty of geological and fossil evidence that the continents had moved around, but we knew of no way then that such movement could possibly occur. Although the idea of continental drift had been proposed in 1912, there was no mechanism to explain it. Beginning in the 1960s, however, new technologies gave us new evidence that provided such a mechanism. We now have a well-verified theory of continental drift by the process of plate tectonics.

An interesting example of an influential social trend comes from a hypothesized explanation for the famous Salem witch trials in Massachusetts in 1692, when a group of young girls accused some adults of witchcraft, with the result that a number of people were executed. One idea was that the people of Salem had consumed bread made from grains tainted with ergot, a fungus that contains alkaloids, some of which are derivatives of lysergic acid, which in turn is used in the synthesis of the hallucinogenic drug LSD. In other words, maybe the young girls who made the witchcraft accusations were experiencing substance-induced hallucinations. (I need not tell you in which recent decade this idea arose. By the way, there is no evidence for this explanation.) These examples show us why scientific skepticism is so important and why we should always question and re-examine even our most well supported ideas.

So, science answers questions about our lives and about the world in which we live. For an answer to be defined as scientific, it must be testable—and must be tested. Put another way, it must be impossible to find data that would disprove it. For an answer to be accepted, it must pass all tests and be refuted by none.

Belief Systems

Some questions about the world, even in a technologically complex society like ours, remain beyond the scope of science.

Scientific inquiry, as powerful and important as it is, doesn't answer everything. Though we have some well-established theories about how the universe evolved once it began, the ultimate origin of the universe remains, for the moment at least, outside the realm of science. For most human societies throughout most of our species' history, many questions could not be addressed scientifically.

Nor does science tell us how to behave. In our society, for example, we treat medical matters scientifically. But science does not, and cannot, inform us how best to apply medical knowledge. Who should practice medicine? How are medical practitioners trained and administered by society? How should they be compensated? What should their relationship be with their patients? Is everyone equally entitled to medical care? Society and the medical profession answer these questions through laws and regulations. For example, the Hippocratic Oath, taken by all doctors, says in part, "I will not permit considerations of religion, nationality, race, party politics or social standing to intervene between my duty and my patient."

Finally, there are questions that can never be answered by science—matters like the meaning of life, the existence of a higher power, the proper social relationships among people within a society, or the purpose of one's own life.

All these sorts of questions are addressed by **belief systems**—religions, philosophies, ethics, morals, and laws. Belief systems differ from science in that they cannot be tested, cannot be disproved. Their truths are taken on faith, and that, of course, is the source of their power. They provide stable bases for our behavior, for explanations of what is beyond our science, and for the broad, existential questions of life. Belief systems change, but they only change when *we* decide to change them, either as a society or as individuals.

The existence of a supreme being is an example of a value inherent in one's belief system. Two of us with opposite views on the subject could debate the issue endlessly, but no scientific test could support or refute either view. If I were to change my mind on the matter, it would be because of a personal decision. The supreme being is not to be found in a test tube or through observation using a telescope.

Belief systems don't apply only to these big questions. I had a friend in graduate school from a West African society that was polygynous—men could have several wives. Having more than one wife is normal in his society, whereas in mine, one wife (at least one at a time) is the norm. We discussed the pros and cons of these two systems at length one day, but we never, of course, arrived at any "answer." His belief was the norm for his society as was mine for my society. We each took it on faith that this was so.

belief systems: Ideas that are taken on faith and cannot be scientifically tested.

Contemporary Reflections

Is Evolution a Fact, a Theory, or Just a Hypothesis?

It may at first be surprising that the answer to this box's title is *all of the above*. Evolution, as a broad topic, incorporates theory, fact, *and* hypothesis. This is because the scientific method is not a nice, neat, linear series of steps from first specific observation to final all-encompassing theory. Rather, science works in a cycle (see Figure 1.8), and the inductive and deductive reasoning of science are applied constantly to the different aspects of the same general subject. Data and hypotheses are always being re-examined, and each theory itself becomes a new observation to be questioned, tested, explained, and possibly changed.

A theory is a well-supported idea that explains a set of observed phenomena. Evolution is a theory in that all our observations of life on earth—fossils, the geological formations in which they are found, and the biology of living creatures—make sense and find explanation within the concept of evolution, the idea that living things change through time and that organisms are related as in a huge branching bush, with existing species giving rise to new species.

Moreover, there is so much evidence in support of evolution that this tried and tested theory may reasonably be considered a fact. Of course, new data could conceivably change that, but with an idea as well supported as evolution, it is highly unlikely. A good analogy is the accepted fact that the earth revolves around the sun and not, as people thought for so long, the other way around. But how do we *know* the earth revolves around the sun? It certainly appears upon daily observation to do just the opposite. We accept the heliocentric (sun-centered) theory because there is so much data in its support. It makes so much sense and explains so many other phenomena that we consider it a fact and take it for granted, never giving it much thought on a regular basis. I would be very surprised to read in tomorrow's newspaper that some new evidence refuted the idea. Similarly, that evolution occurs and accounts for the nature of life on earth is, for all intents and purposes, a fact.

But that fact poses more questions. A big one (the one that confronted Darwin) is *how* evolution takes place. The fact of evolution now becomes a new observation that requires explanation through the generation of new hypotheses and the subsequent testing and re-testing of those hypotheses. Darwin proposed a mechanism he called natural selection and then, over many years, examined this hypothesis against real-world data. The mechanism of natural selection is now so well supported that we call it, too, a fact.

But an overall explanation for how evolution works—a theory (or set of theories) to explain the observed fact of evolution—is far from complete. We know that mechanisms in addition to natural selection contribute to evolution. The relative importance of all these mechanisms is still being debated. The broad picture of evolution—the "shape" of the family bush of living things—is a matter of much discussion. The specific genetic processes behind all evolutionary change are really only beginning to be revealed as new technologies are letting us look closer and closer at the very code of life. In other words, we are still examining hypotheses to account for *how* evolution takes place.

Evolution—like any broad scientific idea—involves a complex and interacting web of facts, hypotheses, and theories. It is the never-ending nature of scientific inquiry that can make science so frustrating, but that also makes it so exciting.

Although we often perceive science and belief systems as being eternally and inevitably at odds with one another, nothing could be further from the truth. Conflicts arise among facets of all societies. But it should be apparent that for a society to function, it needs both scientific knowledge and beliefs, because neither by itself addresses all the questions.

▽   ▽   ▽

SUMMARY

Anthropology is the study of the human species. Cultural anthropology studies human culture, cultural systems, and their variation. Our species' most characteristic feature today is our cultural behavior, which is expressed in a great variety of ways among different societies.

Most human cultural systems that ever existed did so in the past and so have left us only meager physical remains of their presence and nature. A second major subfield of anthropology recovers and interprets these remains; this subfield is archaeology.

Biological anthropology studies the human species the way biology studies any species, examining our biological characteristics, our evolution, our variation, our relationship with our environment, and our behavior, including our ability to have culture.

Bioanthropology, as a scientific discipline, asks questions about the human species and then attempts to answer them by proposing hypotheses and by *testing* those hypotheses, looking both for evidence in their support and for anything that would refute them.

Scientific knowledge is important for any society, but it must be mediated by the nonscientific values of belief systems—the untestable ideas of philosophy, law, and religion that are taken on faith. Societies need both, interacting in harmony, to fully function.

QUESTIONS FOR FURTHER THOUGHT

1. Anthropologists have special responsibilities when studying other human beings. What sorts of issues do you think I had to take into account when conducting my research among the Hutterites? What issues would have been involved in the exhumation of Henry Opukahaia? Consider another culture in which you are interested, and

imagine what particular issues would be involved in studying it as an anthropologist.

2. Because of anthropology's wide scope of interests and its overlap with other scholarly disciplines, anthropologists have sometimes been described as "jacks of all trades and masters of none." How would you respond to this label?

3. Our impression that science and belief systems are naturally at odds with one another comes largely from cases in which the two areas are forced into conflict—when, for example, a religious belief is said to refute a scientific idea or a scientific idea is said to undermine a belief. Can you think of an example of one of these cases? How would you resolve the conflict, given what you now understand about these two areas of inquiry?

KEY TERMS

biological anthropology

bioanthropology

physical anthropology

anthropology

species

holistic

culture

cultural anthropology

archaeology

paleoanthropology

osteology

primates

primatology

human ecology

applied anthropology

forensic anthropologist

hunter-gatherers

science

scientific method

hypotheses

induction

deduction

theory

belief systems

SUGGESTED READINGS

For more personal experiences of biological anthropologists, see Part 1 of my *Biological Anthropology: An Introductory Reader*, second edition.

For more information on the Hutterites, see John Hostetler's *Hutterite Society*.

For a longer discussion of the nature of science and the scientific method, see Kenneth L. Feder's *Frauds, Myths, and Mysteries: Science and Pseudoscience in Archaeology*, fourth edition. The relationship between science and belief systems is nicely covered by John Maynard Smith's article, "Science and Myth," in the November 1984 issue of *Natural History*.

A more philosophical discussion can be found in *Rocks of Ages: Science and Religion in the Fullness of Life*, by Stephen Jay Gould.

The field of anthropology in general is covered in my *Introducing Anthropology: An Integrated Approach* and in a collection of contemporary articles edited by Aaron Podolefsky and Peter Brown, *Applying Anthropology: An Introductory Reader*, fifth edition.

I've written an extended version of the story of Henry Opukahaia, "The Homegoing," which appears in *Lessons from the Past: An Introductory Reader in Archaeology*, by Kenneth L. Feder.

THE EVOLUTION
OF EVOLUTION

One touch of Darwin
makes the whole
world kin.
—George Bernard
Shaw

E volution and its application to the human species—how we descended from nonhuman ancestors, how we have changed over time into modern *Homo sapiens*, and how we are still changing—is a central theme of bioanthropology. As noted in Chapter 1, the *fact* of evolution is well supported by scientific examination—the idea has passed every scientific test applied to it. Scientists, however, are still debating the details of evolution and are still refining the *theory* that explains exactly how evolution operates. It took some time, though, for the scientific method to be applied to this idea.

> **How did our knowledge of the history of living organisms move from the realm of belief systems to the realm of science?**

> **How did the scientific evidence for evolution develop?**

"ON THE SHOULDERS OF GIANTS": EXPLAINING THE CHANGING EARTH

The Englishman Charles Darwin (1809–1882) is usually, and correctly, associated with our understanding of biological evolution (Figure 2.1). He is also popularly given credit for the very idea of evolution and for explaining and therefore proving it. This, however, is not entirely correct. Like any great scientific accomplishment, Darwin's was based on the work of many who came before him. He stood, as Isaac Newton said of himself, "on the shoulders of giants." Darwin's genius was in being able to take massive amounts of data and assorted existing ideas and, using an imagination possessed by few humans, put them all together into a logical, cohesive theory that made sense of the world and that could be examined by the methods of science.

The idea of **evolution** is simple enough: Species of living things change over time, and under the right circumstances, this change can produce new species of living organisms. This idea was not new in Darwin's time. Anaximander, a Greek of the sixth century B.C., proposed that humans had arisen from other forms of life. He incorrectly thought we arose directly from fish, but he explained his idea using reason rather than basing it on the supernatural; his reasoning was based on the question of how animals survive in their environments, a question that would form the cornerstone of Darwin's idea (Harris, 1981).

Many others over the next 2,000 years also contemplated the origins of living things, but the modern story of evolutionary theory really began

FIGURE 2.1
Portrait of Charles Darwin in 1869 by Famed Photographer Julia Margaret Cameron.

in seventeenth-century Europe, where the influence of the Bible was felt in all aspects of life, including science. Specifically, the ancient Judeo-Christian creation story—Adam and Eve, the Garden of Eden, the flood and Noah's ark—was generally considered to be literally true. Thus, it was thought that the entire universe was created by supernatural processes over a period of 6 days and that, except for the matter of the great flood, the earth and its inhabitants were pretty much the same now as they were when created. One scholar, Irish archbishop James Ussher (1581–1656), even used the assumption of biblical truth, as well as certain historical records, to help him calculate the date of creation and thus the age of the earth. In 1650 he reckoned that creation began at noon on Sunday, October 23, in the year 4004 B.C. The earth was thus about 6,000 years old.

The literal interpretation of the Bible, in turn, was probably influenced by two old but persuasive ideas that go back to Plato and Aristotle, Greek philosophers of the fourth and fifth centuries B.C. One idea is called *essentialism*—the notion of ideal types. It is the concept that there is an ideal, or essential, form of every natural entity and that the entities we see are largely inexact copies of the ideal. The variations among the members of some species of living organisms—for example, breeds of dogs—are just deviations from the essential form. Applied to biblical creation, essentialism promoted the idea that one ideal form of each living thing had been created and that the present-day variations—breeds of animals or races of people—are mostly departures from those ideals.

The second idea is called the *great chain of being*. It says that since there is an ideal, the various forms of things are not just a list of equals but are arranged in a ladder or chain, from least complex to most complex and from least perfect to most perfect. There are two different creation stories in Genesis, one where humans are created last, after all the animals (Gen. 1), and one where humans are created first (Gen. 2). Whichever order one accepts, however, there is the clear implication that humans are the most perfect form of creation. These two philosophical ideas would also have a strong influence on the later science of evolution, as we will see.

Dependence upon the Bible for knowledge of the natural world was not to last. About the time Ussher was making his calculations, others were beginning to seek knowledge about the earth from the earth itself. What these "natural scientists," or "natural philosophers," saw forced them to begin changing their minds about what seemed to be the obvious lessons from the Book of Genesis.

For example, **fossils** of plants and animals—once thought to be mere quirks of nature—were recognized by another seventeenth-century scientist,

evolution: Change through time; here, with reference to biological species.

fossils: Remains of life forms of the past.

Robert Hooke (1635–1703), as the remains of creatures that had become extinct or that still existed but in different form. Living things, in other words, had changed.

Moreover, Hooke attributed these extinctions and changes to the fact that the earth itself had been continually undergoing change since the creation. He even proposed a naturalistic explanation for Noah's flood; it was, he said, probably caused by earthquakes. So, since the earth is in a continual state of change, so are its inhabitants, changing as their environments are altered or becoming extinct if that alteration is too great.

Evidence for this idea of a changing earth came from the examination of the layers of rock and soil below the earth's present surface. These layers are the earth's **strata** (singular, *stratum*), and their study is called **stratigraphy** (Figure 2.2). One of the earliest scientists to discuss this was a Dane, Nicholas Steno (1638–1686). He suggested that the strata represented layers of sediments deposited by water in a *sequence*, the lower layers earlier and the higher layers later. The nature of the rock and soil of each stratum, and its fossil contents, showed the natural conditions at the time the stratum was deposited: what creatures existed, whether the area was under sea or on land, and so on. It became clear that neither the earth nor its inhabitants were stable and unchanging. It was also clear that the record of past change could be read by observing the present-day world.

Steno and Hooke, however, still believed in a biblical chronology. To Steno, the water-deposited layers of the stratigraphic sequences represented two events—the original water-covered earth on which God created land and plants and animals (Gen. 1) and the waters of Noah's flood (Gen. 6–8). The geological record, however, shows a vast amount of change, and the Bible provides only 6,000 years of the earth's history. To bring about so much change in so short a time, thought Steno and Hooke, required the presence of global catastrophic events—such as earthquakes and volcanos—associated with the creation and the flood. Steno and Hooke and others who subscribed to this explanation are often referred to as **catastrophists.**

One well-known proponent of catastrophism was the French naturalist Georges Cuvier (1769–1832). Cuvier thought that a "prototype" of each creature had been created and that it and its environment had been planned to fit each other. The influence of essentialism is obvious here. Differences in climate, felt Cuvier, could bring about alterations in these prototypes, but such changes were limited, producing minor variations in the created types. He also thought that he could reconstruct the prototypes by

strata: Layers; here, the layers of rock and soil under the surface of the earth.

stratigraphy: The study of the earth's strata.

catastrophists: Those who believe the history of the earth is explained by a series of global catastrophes.

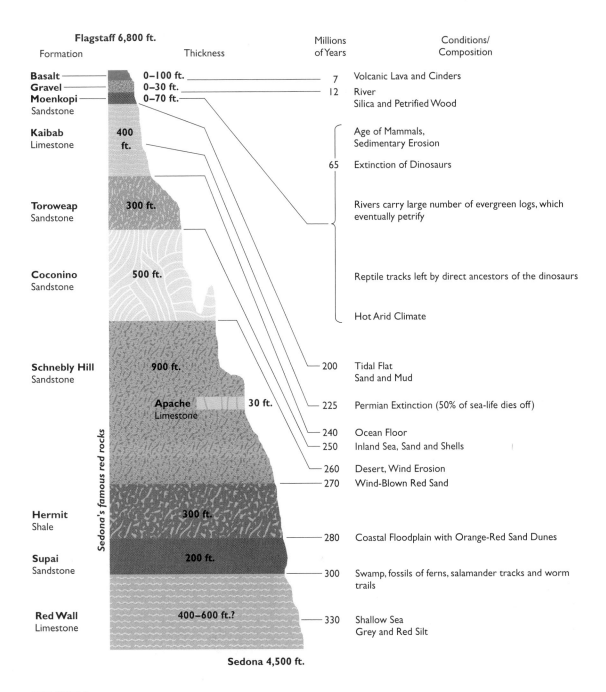

Formation	Thickness	Millions of Years	Conditions/Composition

Flagstaff 6,800 ft.

Basal — 0–100 ft. — 7 — Volcanic Lava and Cinders
Gravel — 0–30 ft. — 12 — River
Moenkopi — 0–70 ft. — Silica and Petrified Wood
Sandstone

Kaibab 400 ft. — Age of Mammals, Sedimentary Erosion
Limestone

65 — Extinction of Dinosaurs

Toroweap 300 ft. — Rivers carry large number of evergreen logs, which eventually petrify
Sandstone

Coconino 500 ft. — Reptile tracks left by direct ancestors of the dinosaurs
Sandstone

Hot Arid Climate

Schnebly Hill 900 ft. — 200 — Tidal Flat / Sand and Mud
Sandstone

Apache 30 ft. — 225 — Permian Extinction (50% of sea-life dies off)
Limestone

240 — Ocean Floor
250 — Inland Sea, Sand and Shells
260 — Desert, Wind Erosion
270 — Wind-Blown Red Sand

Sedona's famous red rocks

Hermit 300 ft. — 280 — Coastal Floodplain with Orange-Red Sand Dunes
Shale

Supai 200 ft. — 300 — Swamp, fossils of ferns, salamander tracks and worm trails
Sandstone

Red Wall 400–600 ft.? — 330 — Shallow Sea / Grey and Red Silt
Limestone

Sedona 4,500 ft.

FIGURE 2.2
This geological cross section of the area around Sedona and Flagstaff, Arizona, shows the variation in composition and thickness of the strata and some of the events represented in those strata.

using fossil remains of creatures. He compared the fragments of ancient creatures to living ones to try to picture what the whole organism looked like. In so doing, he pioneered the method known as **comparative anatomy,** still used today to infer missing parts of fossil organisms.

Cuvier also knew that life on earth had undergone major changes. He believed that the entire plan of creation had been changed several times by the creator and that the changes were manifested in a series of global catastrophes that brought about the extinction of existing forms of life and prepared the way for newly created forms. Thus, as science historian John Greene put it, Cuvier "recognized change but not development" (1959, 130). In other words, he accepted that the world had changed but not that it had evolved, with new forms of life being modifications of older forms. Moreover, since humans were only included in the latest creation (although Cuvier did admit that they might have been around before), there was the implication that humans were somehow the creator's highest, most perfect form of living thing—an idea clearly influenced by the great chain of being concept.

Catastrophism enjoyed a degree of popularity because it seemed to reconcile natural evidence with a biblical timeframe. But strict catastrophism did not stand up to further scientific observation and examination. The French scholar Comte de Buffon (Georges-Louis Leclerc; 1707–1788) concluded that although catastrophic events do occur, they are rare and so "have no place in the ordinary course of nature." Instead, the earth's history is mainly explained by "operations *uniformly* repeated, motions which succeed one another without interruption [emphasis mine]." The motions Buffon spoke of were mainly the motions of the sea—tides and currents—operating to form the earth while the earth was still completely covered by water and while the strata were still being deposited. Phenomena occurring on land, such as wind and water erosion, he thought, were not particularly important. But he did establish a new model: Much of the earth's geological history could be explained by normal, everyday, uniform processes—the things we can see taking place before our eyes. This idea is called **uniformitarianism.** For such processes to account for all the changes recorded in the earth's strata, however, the earth would have to be older than 6,000 years. Buffon was among the first to propose a longer history for the planet.

It was a Scotsman, James Hutton (1726–1797), who brought uniformitarianism onto the land. Hutton said that the history of the earth, as seen in its strata, is the result of three general processes: (1) the deposition of strata under the waters of the oceans; (2) the compacting of these strata by pressure and their uplifting above sea level by subterranean heat; and (3) the erosion of land by water, wind, and decay. Hutton saw these processes as part of a self-regulating system: Erosion produced the soil in which plants grew. Plants, in turn, fed animals and humans (for whom, he thought, all this had been created in the first place). New land was continually being formed under the sea from sediments produced by erosion, which would ultimately provide new sources of soil. And so on. Again, such a system would require far more than 6,000 years, and Hutton suggested that the earth was much older. Indeed, he thought it was virtually timeless, having "no vestige of a beginning—no prospect of an end."

Charles Lyell (1797–1875) was born in Scotland the year Hutton died, and it is his name that is usually associated with uniformitarianism. This is in part because his version of that idea was so extreme. He advocated, as had Hutton, the uniformity of processes throughout time, that is, that present-day processes are the key to explaining the past. He also believed that the rate of geological change was uniform—slow and steady through countless eons, with no need to invoke global catastrophes.

Furthermore, he believed that the earth itself was fairly uniform through time, that the earth has been, and will be, always basically the same. Changes certainly occur, but they occur, said Lyell, just in the details, not in the overall appearance of the earth or in its life forms. Moreover, these changes occur in great cycles. He thought, for example, that dinosaurs, though extinct at the moment, would eventually reappear.

At this point, it would be a good idea to briefly describe where modern scientific knowledge stands on all these issues. We now agree with the major parts of the uniformitarian position, which are as follow:

1. Processes that formed and changed the earth in the past—as seen in its stratigraphic record—are the same processes that take place in the present.

2. By studying the stratigraphic record, we can reconstruct the history of the earth (an idea that goes back to Steno).

3. For known geological processes to account for the changes recorded in the strata, an immense amount of time is required; we know now that the earth is about 4.5 billion years old (Figure 2.3).

We also now understand that Lyell was far too restrictive in his idea about uniform rate. Not all processes are slow and steady. Catastrophic

comparative anatomy: Comparing the anatomical features of various species. Used to reconstruct a fossil species from fragmentary remains.

uniformitarianism: The idea that present-day geological processes can also explain the history of the earth.

FIGURE 2.3
Utah's Bryce Canyon shows the results of geological processes, especially the laying down of strata and subsequent erosion, over millions of years.

events may seem relatively rare to us, but they do take place and have occurred many times during the history of the earth. Even Lyell acknowledged that most are localized events like volcanos and earthquakes that affect the geology and life of a particular area. However, some events are catastrophic on a global scale. At least five times during the 3.5-billion-year history of life on earth, a major catastrophe has taken place—in one case, bringing about the extinction of over 90 percent of the earth's species. The most famous of these cataclysms (though not the biggest) occurred 65 million years ago when an asteroid collided with the earth and caused such radical environmental change that 75 percent of the world's marine species became extinct, along with many terrestrial species, including the dinosaurs. (See Chapter 6.) These are not the series of biblically associated catastrophes of Steno, Hooke, and Cuvier; rather, these catastrophes occur irregularly and are of natural origin. They have, nonetheless, radically altered the history of the planet.

Today we understand that Lyell's idea about the earth changing only in its details and in great cycles is also incorrect. The earth's history is a

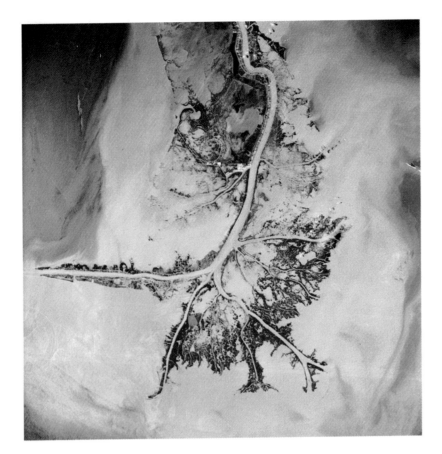

FIGURE 2.4
Aerial View of the Mississippi Delta. By estimating the amount of material deposited in the delta (the delta-shaped [Δ] deposit of sand and soil at the mouth of a river), Charles Lyell concluded (although incorrectly) that it was 100,000 years old.

complex chain of events leading to other events, a continual sequence of changes—major and minor—never to be repeated. The dinosaurs are extinct; they will never return.

Despite what turned out to be some incorrect notions, Lyell's influence was great. Not only did he expand upon the work of Hutton and others, he also began the explicit examination of geological data, bringing it fully into the realm of natural science. For example, he attempted to estimate the age of the Mississippi Delta (Figure 2.4). Because the rate of deposition of sediments at the mouth of the river can be measured and because the size of the existing deposit in the delta can be estimated, the time required for the delta to be formed can be reckoned by assuming a uniform rate of deposition. Lyell arrived at an age of about 100,000 years (1873, 44–47). (Lyell was incorrect; the delta is not that old. Deposition rates are not constant, nor were existing measurement techniques precise enough.)

Through the work of Hooke, Steno, Hutton, and Lyell—and many others—the study of the earth was made natural rather than supernatural. Data about earth's history were sought in the earth itself, not within the presuppositions of belief systems. As a result, by the early nineteenth century, our world was viewed through the interacting perspectives of constant change brought about by observable processes over vast amounts of time.

Lyell put these ideas down in a major scientific work, his three-volume *Principles of Geology*, first published between 1830 and 1833. The book was highly influential. It was enthusiastically received by supporters of the uniformitarian approach, strongly criticized by those who continued to explain earth's history as a series of global catastrophes, and pored over by those still examining the data. Among the latter was a young British naturalist who took the first volume of Lyell's book with him as he embarked, in 1831, on a round-the-world voyage of scientific exploration. This was Charles Darwin.

"COMMON SENSE AT ITS BEST": EXPLAINING BIOLOGICAL CHANGE

The view of life on earth as static and unchanging is exemplified by the work of Carl von Linné (1707–1778), better known to us as Carolus Linnaeus, whom we will discuss in detail in Chapter 7. Linnaeus, who devised the system of scientific names we still use to classify living things, initially thought that all species of plants and animals had been divinely created in their present forms and numbers. But Linnaeus, a keen observer of nature, came to recognize (as had Hooke before him) that some sort of change had taken place—that fossils, for example, represented species that had become extinct and that new species could arise. Still, Linnaeus saw any change as divinely preordained and as taking place within the constraints and limits of the original creation—he thought, for example, that new species arose through hybridization between originally created species. This is another example of essentialism.

Gradually, though, through the observations and interpretations of all the scientists discussed so far, it became clear that life on earth had undergone change, just as had the earth itself, and that this change required scientific explanation using a uniformitarian approach. But this idea—then referred to as the *transmutation of species*—was a somewhat more controversial matter than the idea of a changing earth. For if other forms of life had arisen and changed over eons of time by uniform natural processes, then it followed that the same should apply to humans. It was, in part, in reaction to this idea that Cuvier attempted to apply catastrophism with a divine basis to an explanation of biological change. So, even after it became obvious that life had "evolved" (as we now phrase it), just *how* this had taken place mattered a great deal.

There were many who addressed this issue from a uniformitarian position, including Charles Darwin's grandfather, Erasmus Darwin (1731–1802), but one of the most influential was the French naturalist Jean-Baptiste de Lamarck (1744–1829). Lamarck emphasized Hooke's conclusion that plants and animals are **adapted** to their environments; that is, each kind of living organism has physical traits and behaviors that allow it to survive under a given set of natural circumstances. When environments change—as the stratigraphic record shows they do—organisms must change if they are to continue to exist.

Lamarck was quite correct that organisms underwent "possibly very great" change and that this change is connected to the environment. He erred, however, in his explanation of how this change occurred and in his idea as to the overall direction of evolution. Like others, he could not bring himself to see biological change as lacking a particular direction. Rather, he saw it as **progressive,** going from imperfect to perfect by a process of increasing complexity. This is another example of the influence of the great chain of being concept. It should be obvious which species Lamarck thought was the most perfect and complex. This was the appeal of the idea of progressive evolution: If life itself changed through time, at least *we* were what it was changing toward.

Moreover, Lamarck's mechanism for this progressive change was fairly foolproof. It is called the **inheritance of acquired characteristics,** an old idea that Lamarck formalized in his 1809 *Philosophie zoologique*. He wrote:

> When the *will* guides an animal to any action, the organs which have to carry out that action are *immediately stimulated* to it by the influx of *subtle fluids*. . . . Hence it follows that numerous repetitions of these organised activities strengthen, stretch, develop and *even create* the organs necessary to them. . . . Now every change that is wrought in an organ through habit of frequently using it, is subsequently *preserved by reproduction*. . . . Such a change is thus handed on to *all succeeding individuals* in the same environment, without their having to acquire it in the same way that it was actually created [emphases mine]. (Harris 1981, 116–17)

For example, Lamarck explained the long necks and legs of giraffes in the following way: In the past, giraffes were short, but some environmental

adaptation: The state in which an organism is adjusted to and can survive in its environment through its physical traits and behaviors. Also, the process by which an organism develops this state through natural processes.

progressive: In evolution, the idea that all change is toward increasing complexity.

inheritance of acquired characteristics: The incorrect idea that traits acquired during an organism's lifetime can be passed on to its offspring.

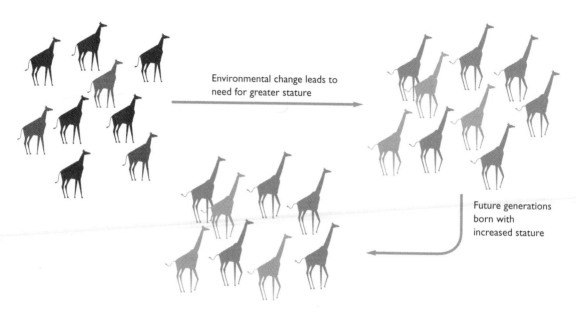

**Environmental change leads to
need for greater stature**

**Future generations
born with
increased stature**

FIGURE 2.5
Lamarck's Model of Evolution
as Exemplified by the In-
creased Stature of Giraffes.

change altered their food source, placing the foliage they ate high up in
the trees. Confronted with this problem, each giraffe was able to stretch
itself enough to reach the leaves. This greater height was automatically
passed on to the giraffes' offspring, who had to make themselves even
taller. And so on (Figure 2.5).

One reason that Lamarck's idea was popular was that it was one of the
first detailed, lengthy, scientific treatments of evolution. Lamarck even
spelled out how he used the scientific method by specifying the data that
would be required to falsify his model. It was also a comfortable explanation for an uncomfortable topic. It had become clear that life had changed
over time. At least, according to Lamarck's hypothesis, life changed in a
particular (and very human-oriented) direction, and it changed by a
process that was unfailing and dependent on something inherent to the
organism—Lamarck called it "will." It even followed that no organisms
ever become extinct. Creatures represented only by fossils are simply creatures that have undergone so much change they now look very different.

But observation and logic produced some major objections to Lamarck's concept. For example, traits acquired during an organism's lifetime cannot be inherited by its offspring. A bodybuilder's children will
not automatically be born with bulging muscles. Further, it was hard to
see how an organism's "will" could change its color or produce a new

organ or even make a giraffe taller. And just what is the "subtle fluid" that is supposed to bring all this about?

Thus, Charles Darwin was born (in 1809, the same year Lamarck's book was published) into a world that accepted the *fact* of biological change but was still in search of a *mechanism* for that change. Although many, like Lamarck, held to a uniformitarian position, others, like Cuvier, still adhered to a catastrophic explanation. It was Darwin who would provide the mechanism that has withstood over a century of scientific examination.

The story of Darwin's life and scientific work is a fascinating one (see, for example, Bowlby 1990). For the purpose of our story, however, we can simply say that Darwin recognized an important fact not fully appreciated by many of his predecessors or contemporaries. In his work in his native England and especially on his famous voyage around the world on the H.M.S. *Beagle* (1831–1836), Darwin realized the incredible degree of variation that exists within each living species (Figure 2.6). If Lamarck were correct, one would expect every member of a particular species to look pretty much the same because they all would have responded identically to the same environmental circumstances. Darwin saw this was clearly not the case. Variation always exists, no matter how well adapted a species might be. What tipped Darwin off to this fact of nature were his observations of domestic species like pigeons, carefully bred for certain features but still showing physical variation every generation. Therefore, in each generation, breeders would have to choose for mating only those individuals possessing the features they desired, using the assumption that offspring tend to resemble parents. The goal was to eliminate undesirable traits and accumulate desirable ones.

Darwin reasoned that the same thing happened in nature. Some of the natural variation within a species would make a difference in the success, or **fitness,** of individuals. The better-adapted individuals would tend to be more reproductively successful. Their traits would be passed on to more offspring than would those of the less well adapted. Over time, then, some traits would accumulate while others would decrease in frequency or even be eliminated. If the environment to which a species is adapted changes, it stands to reason that the fitness value of certain traits might also change, so the process described might proceed in a different adaptive direction—what was once adapted might now be neutral or perhaps even poorly adapted.

So, while Lamarck thought that variation *arose when it was needed*, Darwin understood that variation *already existed*. Because Darwin lived before the processes of genetics were understood, he did not know where

fitness: The relative adaptiveness of an individual organism, measured ultimately by reproductive success.

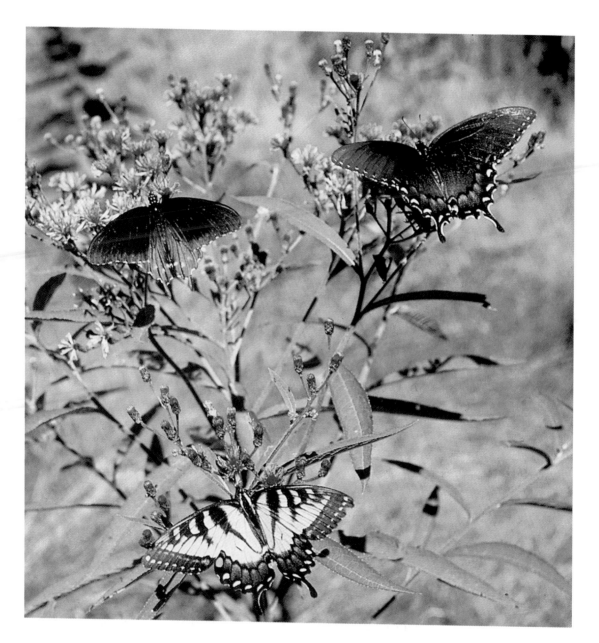

FIGURE 2.6

Variation within a population represents the raw material for natural selection. The tiger swallowtail butterflies *(upper right and bottom)* are members of the same species. The dark one is a mimic of the pipe-vine butterfly *(left)*, which is protected from predation by its foul taste.

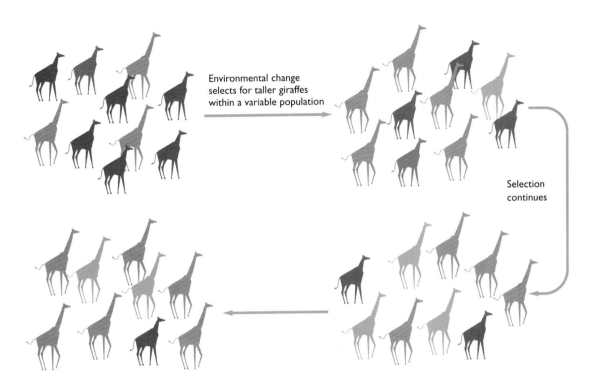

FIGURE 2.7
Darwin's Model of Natural Selection Applied to the Evolution of Long Necks and Tall Bodies in Giraffes. An environmental change, perhaps in the location of food sources, made the taller giraffes within a variable species relatively more reproductively successful. These giraffes thus passed on their tallness to a greater number of offspring, making succeeding generations taller on average.

this variation came from, but his observations showed it was a fact; and he realized that nature, like a plant or animal breeder, "selects" better-adapted individuals for more successful reproduction. Darwin called this process **natural selection** (Figure 2.7).

Several important ideas follow from natural selection:

1. It becomes clear that evolution by natural selection has no particular direction. Organisms do not "progress" to increasingly complex forms, as Lamarck thought, but evolve to simply stay adapted to their environments or, if possible, become re-adapted to changed environments. Variation is not "willed." It results from random processes that we now understand from the study of genetics (see Chapter 3).

natural selection: Evolutionary change based on the differential reproductive success of individuals within a species.

2. It is also clear that such a process, using random rather than directed or "willed" variation, is not foolproof. It doesn't always work. Species do become extinct, usually when the environment changes so extensively or rapidly that none of the existing variation within a species is adaptive. Extinction is, in fact, the norm. Nine-tenths of all species that have ever lived are now extinct.

3. It follows that *new* species can arise from this basic process. If populations within a species become environmentally separated, these populations will exist under different selective pressures—different traits will be differently adapted to each environment. Moreover, different variations will be produced in each population. Natural selection will have different raw materials to work with. Over time, then, a single species may give rise to one or more new species. This, in fact, was what Darwin was ultimately trying to explain, as indicated by the title of his most famous work, *On the Origin of Species by Means of Natural Selection*, first published in 1859.

Darwin's idea generated some controversy, which was perhaps why he delayed publishing his book. We know he understood natural selection sometime in the late 1830s, yet it was not until more than 20 years later that he made it public. Even then, he only did so because a younger, less well known naturalist, Alfred Russel Wallace (1823–1913), independently came up with the same idea, and Darwin was urged by friends to rush his conclusion into print.

The controversy centered not around the idea of uniformitarian evolution itself—which was generally well accepted by that time—but around the fact that Darwin's idea, unlike Lamarck's, did not involve a particular progressive direction nor the direct control or will of the organism. Darwin also acknowledged extinction. These ideas were not always comfortable. But, to Darwin's surprise, by the time his book sold out on its first day of publication, the scientific community and much of the informed public were ready to accept the idea, even with its implications. Natural selection—the mechanism of evolution—was hailed as a major scientific breakthrough and remains today a classic example of scientific reasoning, what Darwin's friend Thomas Henry Huxley called "common sense at its best."

At about the time Darwin was writing *Origin of Species*, a monk in what is now the Czech Republic was answering Darwin's question about the source of variation. After years of undocumented research on several species of plants and animals, Gregor Mendel (1822–1884) derived the basic laws of genetics by experimenting with the pea plants in the garden of his monastery. These laws (which we'll cover in the next chapter) not

Contemporary Reflections

Has Science Dehumanized Society?

To many, the story recounted in this chapter is one of science *versus* belief systems, specifically religious belief. A popular assessment of Darwin's contribution is that by "proving" evolution he "disproved" the Bible. As we will see in Chapter 5, there is still a substantial contingent today who feel that the very idea of evolution is antireligious.

And it's not just the science of evolution. From Mary Shelley's *Frankenstein* (published in 1818) to modern blockbuster movies like *Jurassic Park* and *The Lost World*, science in general is seen as a potential evil, something that is far too easily abused and that, when abused, wreaks havoc on people and their societies. People often use the phrase "playing God" when referring to scientific endeavors—genetics studies in particular—that they perceive as affronts to human spirit and individuality. Science is blamed for many of today's social and environmental ills—and there *are* plenty of them—from global warming to radioactive contamination to the proliferation of high-tech weaponry.

There are three errors in this view of science. First, although science has put forth, and scientists have embraced, ideas that resulted in human suffering, one of the hallmarks of science is its ability for self-correction. The eugenics movement, for example—which held that many human behaviors were hereditary and that therefore selective breeding could improve the species—resulted (even in the United States) in the forced sterilization of many individuals who were deemed less fit because of some characteristic that society felt undesirable (below-average intelligence, for instance, or having borne illegitimate children). This practice is abhorrent, but through scientific progress we now know much more about the nature of human heredity, and such mistakes are at least unlikely in the future.

Second, this view of science ignores the fact that *anything* may be a danger if used incorrectly or for nefarious purposes. One has but to examine world history to see that religious ideals are not always put to positive use. Indeed, many of today's bloody hostilities are the result of religious conflict—often involving religions that specifically prohibit the taking of human life.

Third, in focusing on the negative results of science, we all too easily forget about the positive results. Today's most vocal critics of science still promote their ideas over television, write them down on computers, travel in airplanes, and enjoy all the medical and nutritional benefits of a modern scientific society. The astronomer Carl Sagan (1934–1996) once asked a group of people how many of them would not be alive today if it weren't for modern medical technology. Most raised their hands. (I tried this with a class of undergraduates, average age about 20, and still about half raised their hands.)

But still, didn't Darwin set the stage for this seeming conflict by disproving the Bible with his theory of evolution? Not at all. He *did* show that one literal interpretation of one part of one book of the Bible failed to account for observations of biology in the real world. In no way, however, did his idea of evolution refute a whole religious worldview, nor need it conflict with one's personal sense of the spiritual. Indeed, Darwin himself wrote in the last paragraph of *Origin of Species*, "There is grandeur in this view of life, with its several powers, having been originally breathed *by the Creator* into a few forms or into one [emphasis mine]."

It is not knowledge or ideas, scientific or otherwise, that are dangerous, but how they are used. Ignorance is far more dangerous. It is ignorance that dehumanizes us.

TABLE 2.1
Important People and Ideas Associated with Evolution

	Approx. Date of Publication	Contribution
James Ussher (1581–1656)	1650	Calculation of the age of earth, using biblical data.
Robert Hooke (1635–1703)	1660s–90s	Fossils as evidence of change. Importance of environmental change.
Nicholas Steno (1638–1686)	1669	Stratigraphy.
Carolus Linnaeus (1707–1778)	1758	System of scientific names. Recognition of extinction and possibility of new species.
Comte de Buffon (1707–1788)	1749	Uniformitarianism. Longer timeframe for age of earth.
James Hutton (1726–1797)	1795	Uniformitarianism. Natural cycles. Longer timeframe for age of earth.
Jean-Baptiste de Lamarck (1744–1829)	1809	Adaptation. Inheritance of acquired characteristics. Progressive evolution.
Georges Cuvier (1769–1832)	late 1700s, early 1800s	Ideal prototypes. Climatic alterations. Extinction. Catastrophism.
Charles Lyell (1797–1875)	1830–33	Uniformitarianism. Scientific investigation.
Charles Darwin (1809–1882)	1859	Natural selection. Origin of species.
Gregor Mendel (1822–1884)	1860s	Laws of inheritance.
Alfred Russel Wallace (1823–1913)	1859	Natural selection.

only explained one source of biological variation but also showed why and how offspring tend to resemble their parents. Basic laws of genetics and biological variation are crucial to natural selection and the origin of new species.

Mendel died in relative obscurity (Darwin never learned of his work), and his writings languished in libraries until 1900, when they were rediscovered independently by three European scientists who realized that Mendel's work carried implications far beyond some interesting facts about pea plants. (This had been the reaction to Mendel's work during his life—that he had found some interesting facts about peas.) They understood that genetics filled in those pieces that Darwin acknowledged were missing from his process.

Over the past century, many scientists have added to Darwin's idea of natural selection and Mendel's work on genetics. There have been new details, changes of emphasis, and major discoveries, such as the breaking of the genetic code in the early 1950s. But all the work of the past hundred years has been built upon the thoughts and discoveries of people like Darwin and Lyell and Hooke, and many others. All the men and women whose investigations have led to our modern theory of evolution (which we will cover in the next three chapters) would freely agree that they have stood on the shoulders of these giants (Table 2.1).

▽   ▽   ▽

SUMMARY

The Judeo-Christian belief system, as set down in the Bible, was long seen as both a belief system and a source of literal knowledge. As scholars began looking more objectively at nature itself, however, their observations and the rational conclusions they drew from them showed clearly that knowledge of the heavens, the earth, and the earth's inhabitants required the methods of science. As the scientific method was applied to the study of the earth, scientists gradually learned to give up their presuppositions.

Charles Darwin, adhering faithfully to the spirit of scientific methodology, was able to synthesize his observations and thoughts with those of many others and to formulate a theory that made possible the work that has led to our modern knowledge of the nature and evolution of living things.

QUESTIONS FOR FURTHER THOUGHT

1. The scientific research and ideas of many early biologists and geologists were influenced by philosophical concepts. Do you think such influences ended with people like Darwin? Can you think of a modern example of a scientific matter that may be influenced by beliefs?

2. Whereas biological evolution is not Lamarckian, the evolution of culture is. How so?

3. There are those who say that certain areas of scientific research should be avoided either because their results might be misused or because the facts generated might be unpleasant. What sorts of research do you think these people might be referring to? How would you respond to such cautions?

KEY TERMS

evolution	comparative anatomy	inheritance of acquired characteristics
fossils	uniformitarianism	
strata	adaptation	fitness
stratigraphy	progressive	natural selection
catastrophists		

SUGGESTED READINGS

The history of the study of evolution is covered in C. Leon Harris's *Evolution: Genesis and Revelations*, which contains numerous sections from original works, and in John C. Greene's *The Death of Adam*. The impact of Darwin's work on modern knowledge in general is the theme of Philip Appleman's *Darwin: A Norton Critical Edition*, second edition.

A new biography of Darwin that focuses on the man as well as the scientist, and nicely shows how the two aspects of his life were related, is John Bowlby's *Charles Darwin: A New Life*.

For more on the fascinating life and work of Alfred Russel Wallace, see *Bright Paradise: Victorian Scientific Travellers*, by Peter Raby.

Paleontologist and science historian Stephen Jay Gould has written many wonderful essays about the history of evolution and other scientific topics and the personalities involved. These can be found throughout his books *Ever Since Darwin*, *The Panda's Thumb*, *Hen's Teeth and Horse's Toes*, *The Flamingo's Smile*, *Bully for Brontosaurus*, *Eight Little Piggies*, *Dinosaur in a Haystack*, *Leonardo's Mountain of Clams and the Diet of Worms*, and *The Lying Stones of Marrakech*. These are all highly recommended.

CHAPTER

3

EVOLUTIONARY GENETICS

The laws governing
inheritance are for the
most part unknown.
—Charles Darwin

Two important features of Darwin's natural selection were the seemingly contradictory facts that offspring tend to resemble their parents but that, at the same time, there is continual production of biological variation among members of a species and from generation to generation. Both facts were obvious enough to careful observers like Darwin. But, as Darwin freely admitted, science was largely ignorant of the source of those facts, in other words, of how inheritance worked.

A popular idea of Darwin's time assumed that inheritance was a "blending"—a mixture of some material from both parents. Certainly there are sufficient examples of offspring with combinations of parental traits to make this idea seem logical. For example, new flower colors can be produced by crossbreeding other colors, much like paints are mixed to make new shades. Breeds of dogs can be crossbred to get combinations of the parents' physical and behavioral characteristics in the hybrid offspring. But offspring are often born with characteristics that resemble neither parent's or, as with one's sex, that are definitely *not* mixtures.

Observations of nonblending traits like sex may have led Gregor Mendel to begin experiments to determine just how inheritance operates. The laws he derived are still recognized today as the basis of genetics, although, of course, they have been added to greatly. The most basic and perhaps most important of Mendel's contributions was his conclusion that inheritance does not involve the blending of substances but, rather, is **particulate.** He showed that traits are passed on by individual particles according to very specific principles. Mendel called these particles "factors"; we call them **genes.** We'll now survey the aspects of modern genetics pertinent to bioanthropology by addressing the following questions:

What are genes, and how do they produce the traits that make a pea plant or a human being?

What are the basic laws of inheritance?

What processes bring about the variation we see among members of a species and between parents and offspring?

HOW GENES WORK

We begin to see how genes work with something Mendel could not possibly have understood. Although he concluded that the particulate factors we now call genes produce the features of an organism and he provided us with the basic model for how traits are inherited, Mendel possessed neither the background knowledge nor the technology to figure out just how the genetic code operates at the chemical level.

We now understand that the genetic code is a set of instructions for the production (or synthesis) of **proteins** from **amino acids,** which we obtain from the foods we eat and which are found in the cytoplasm of the cell. Proteins are the basic building blocks of an organism's cells, shaping the cells, supporting the cells' internal structure, linking cells, and building membranes, muscles, and connective tissue. In a form called **enzymes,** proteins are responsible for the cells' chemical reactions. All organisms are composed of cells (Figure 3.1), so it can logically be said that all living things are based on proteins. Even the nonprotein substances found within a living organism—like the calcium in your bones—are regulated by proteins.

The genetic code is found in the nucleus of cells, on long strands called **chromosomes** (see Figure 3.6). A chromosome is made up of a protein core and strands of nucleic acid. It is the nucleic acid—**deoxyribonucleic acid (DNA)**—that carries the code.

DNA is like a ladder with the ends twisted in opposite directions (Figure 3.2). This shape is referred to as a double helix. The sides of the ladder are for structural stability. The rungs of the ladder carry the code. They are made up of pairs of bases (a family of chemicals) joined or bonded in the middle. Each base, along with the portion of the side of the ladder to which it is connected, is called a **nucleotide.** Only four bases are involved: adenine (A), thymine (T), cytosine (C), and guanine (G), and they are only paired in A-T or T-A and C-G or G-C combinations. Thus, if we know the sequence of bases on one side of the DNA helix, we can correctly predict the sequence on the other side.

The first function of this pairing is to enable the DNA molecule to make copies of itself during cell division. During cell division the helix unwinds, and each strand, with its now unpaired bases, picks up the proper complementary bases, which are in solution in the cell. This is called **replication.** Thus, when the whole cell divides, each new *daughter cell* has a complete set of DNA base pairs (see Figure 3.2).

We refer to each consecutive sequence of three DNA bases as a **codon.** Codons are like words made up of three letters. Each word stands for a particular amino acid. A string of words—a genetic sentence—thus stands for a chain of amino acids. A chain of amino acids is a protein. Therefore, a sequence of codons codes for the linking together of amino acids to make a protein. This process is known as **protein synthesis**

particulate: The idea that biological traits are controlled by individual factors rather than by a single hereditary agent.

genes: Those portions of the DNA molecule that code for specific proteins.

proteins: Molecules that make cells and carry out cellular functions.

amino acids: The chief components of proteins.

enzymes: Proteins that control chemical processes.

chromosomes: Strands of DNA in the nucleus of a cell.

deoxyribonucleic acid (DNA): The molecule that carries the genetic code.

nucleotide: The basic building block of DNA and RNA, made up of a sugar, a phosphate, and one of four bases.

replication: The copying of the genetic code during cell division.

codon: The three-base sequence that codes for a specific amino acid. Technically, the sequence on the mRNA.

protein synthesis: The process by which the genetic code puts together proteins in the cell.

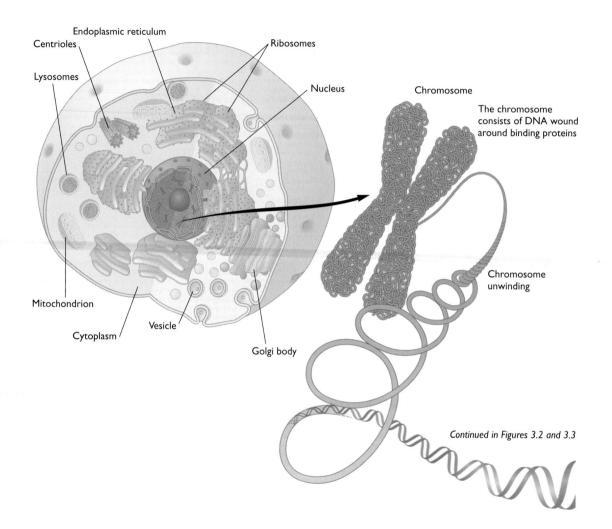

Endoplasmic reticulum

Centrioles

Lysosomes

Ribosomes

Nucleus

Chromosome

The chromosome consists of DNA wound around binding proteins

Chromosome unwinding

Mitochondrion

Cytoplasm

Vesicle

Golgi body

Continued in Figures 3.2 and 3.3

FIGURE 3.1

Typical Cell and Its Important Parts. This cell represents all types of cells, from the more complex single-celled organisms like amoebas to the cells in the human body. The ribosomes are the sites of protein synthesis (see Figure 3.3). The mitochondria are the cells' energy factories, converting energy stored in nutrients into a form the cells can use to perform their various functions.

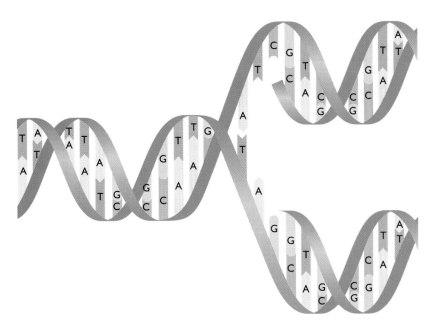

(Figure 3.3). (It is technically correct for *codon* to refer to the three-letter word on the mRNA after it has been transcribed from DNA [see the following discussion]. For clarity we will, as is often done, use the term to refer to the three-letter sequence coding for an amino acid on the DNA as well.)

For our purposes here, then, we will define *gene* in a functional way, that is, as that portion of the DNA molecule that carries the codon sequence for a particular protein. To summarize:

FEATURE	ANALOGUE	MEANING
base (A, T, C, G)	letter	
codon	word	amino acid
gene	sentence	protein

How does protein synthesis work? As you read this description, follow along in Figure 3.3. During protein synthesis only a portion of the DNA molecule is unwound (in contrast to the complete unwinding seen in replication). **Messenger ribonucleic acid (mRNA)** is assembled against one strand of this unwound DNA. (Only one strand carries the code; the other is structural.) The mRNA transcribes the gene by matching complementary bases to those exposed in the coding strand of DNA, except that uracil (U) replaces thymine (T).

messenger ribonucleic acid (mRNA): The molecule that carries the genetic code out of the nucleus for translation into proteins.

1. Section of DNA molecule with base pairs.

2. DNA molecule temporarily separates at bases. mRNA lines up its bases (with U replacing T) with their complements on the coding side of the DNA.

3. mRNA moves out of cell nucleus to ribosomes. As ribosomes move along mRNA, tRNA picks up amino acids and lines up along mRNA according to base complements. Each tRNA transfers its amino acid to the next active tRNA as it leaves, resulting in a chain of amino acids.

4. This chain of amino acids forms a protein.

FIGURE 3.3
Protein Synthesis. In reality, no protein is only four amino acids long, but the process works exactly as shown.

After mRNA has transcribed the code, it leaves the nucleus of the cell and moves to specialized structures in the cell called *ribosomes,* where the message is decoded and translated into an actual protein. Another type of RNA called **transfer RNA (tRNA)** reads the three-letter codes, or codons, as instructions for assembling a chain of amino acids. Each set of three exposed RNA bases codes for one amino acid. Thus, for example, a sequence of 300 bases codes for a sequence of 100 amino acids. A sequence of amino acids is a protein. Although there are only about 20 or so types of amino acids, it is possible to arrange them in a nearly infinite variety of sequences and lengths. In this way, the sequence of DNA bases represents a sequence of amino acids, and it is this sequence that determines the shape and function of the protein.

It's still a long way from a protein to a trait—the observable, measurable physical or chemical characteristics of an organism. Some traits are fairly simple. Hemoglobin, the chemical on red blood cells that carries oxygen, *is* protein. It is made up of two chains of 141 and 146 amino acids. In other words, it is coded for by two genes—two sentences with 141 and 146 words.

Skin color, by contrast, is not a simple trait. It involves three different pigments (including red hemoglobin) and other factors such as skin thickness. The color of a person's skin is thus a trait produced by the complex interaction of many proteins and so is coded for on many genes. Such traits are called **polygenic** (Figure 3.4). Traits coded for by a single gene are called **monogenic.** Most traits of complex organisms are polygenic.

But now, having described the basic process, it must be noted that the genetic code is not as neat and precise as we once thought. New analyses (see the "Contemporary Reflections" box at the end of this chapter) have revealed that only 1 to 1.5 percent of the human **genome** is coding, that is, carries instructions for building proteins. All the rest is noncoding and used to be referred to as "junk DNA." It now appears much of this "junk" has important functions. For example, some of it acts as punctuation, marking the beginnings and ends of coding sequences. Some serves to regulate gene function and activity level. Some jumps around, carrying other DNA with it; this allows the genetic code to reshuffle its own elements, partially explaining why a mere 30,000 genes (the latest estimate) can produce a huge variety of proteins and something as complex as a human being. Moreover, coding sequences are not lined up neatly together but are scattered and interrupted by noncoding sequences. So, the coding pieces of a gene can be read in different ways, thus producing many proteins from the same gene.

transfer ribonucleic acid (tRNA): RNA that lines up amino acids along mRNA to make proteins.

polygenic: A trait coded for by more than one gene.

monogenic: A trait coded for by a single gene.

genome: The total genetic endowment of an organism.

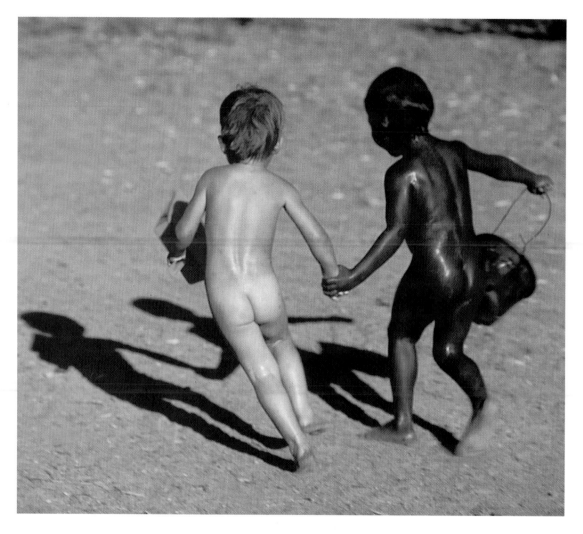

FIGURE 3.4
Skin color variation in humans provides an example of a polygenic trait with a wide range of phenotypic expressions.

FROM GENE TO TRAIT

If Mendel possessed neither the technology nor the background knowledge to understand the structure of the genetic code and the process of protein synthesis, what then did he discover about the processes of genetics? We refer to his contribution as **Mendelian genetics.** It involves the basic laws of inheritance, which we will take up in the next section, and some general principles about the relationship between the genetic code and the traits that are the end product of that code.

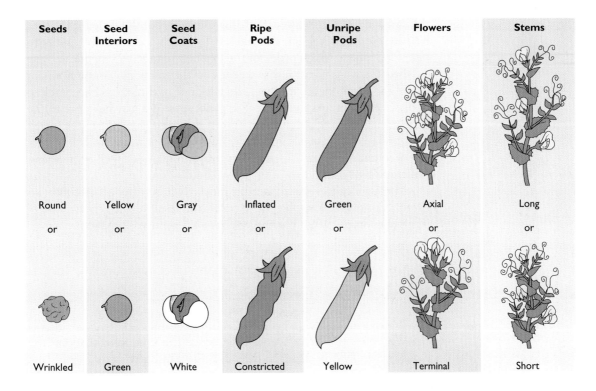

Seeds	Seed Interiors	Seed Coats	Ripe Pods	Unripe Pods	Flowers	Stems
Round	Yellow	Gray	Inflated	Green	Axial	Long
or	or	or	or	or	or	or
Wrinkled	Green	White	Constricted	Yellow	Terminal	Short

FIGURE 3.5
These are the traits of the pea plant that Mendel observed in his famous experiments.

Mendel conducted at least 8 years of extensive breeding experiments, mostly on pea plants. He crossed plants that exhibited different expressions of a trait and then crossed hybrids with each other and back with the original plants.

Mendel used only traits that were monogenic (Figure 3.5). He carefully picked these after considering other traits, many of which were polygenic and so were rejected because, like skin color, they did not appear in simple either/or variation. While no modern scientists would simply leave out what didn't fit their expectations, we forgive Mendel because, in fact, all *genes* work the way he thought even if some *traits* are more complex.

Mendel reached the conclusion that *each organism possesses two genes for each trait—one from each parent*. Not only does each organism possess two of each gene, but genes may come in different versions. We call these **alleles.** Although Mendel used pea plants, it might be more interesting for us to use a human example. There is a chemical called PTC (phenylthiocarbamide) that people can either taste or not. (For those who can, it has a dry, bitter flavor. If you find brussels sprouts bitter, you are tasting a

Mendelian genetics: The basic laws of inheritance, discovered by Gregor Mendel in the nineteenth century.

alleles: Variants of a gene.

thiocarbamide.) This "taster trait" is monogenic, but the gene for the trait has, as you might suspect, two alleles: *T*, which codes for the ability to taste PTC, and *t*, which codes for the inability to taste the chemical.

Because we each possess two genes for the taster trait—one from our father and one from our mother—we have one of three possible combinations. These combinations are called **genotypes.** We may have two of the same allele: *TT* or *tt*, a condition known as **homozygous** (from the Greek root *homo*, "the same"). Or we may have a pair of nonmatching alleles: *Tt*, a condition known as **heterozygous** (from the Greek root *hetero*, "different").

These genotypes are responsible for producing either a taster individual or a nontaster. The observable trait—the result of the genetic code— is the **phenotype.** What phenotype does each genotype produce?

GENOTYPE	PHENOTYPE
TT	taster
tt	nontaster
Tt	taster

Why does the heterozygote *Tt* produce the same phenotype as the homozygote *TT*? Because, as Mendel also reasoned, some alleles are **dominant** and some are **recessive.** In this case, the allele for tasting is dominant (that's why it's written as a capital letter), and so, in the heterozygous genotype, it hides the action of the allele for nontasting. The only way a phenotype can reflect a recessive allele is if the genotype is homozygous for the recessive (*tt*).

It is very important to understand that the words *dominant* and *recessive* have no value attached to them. Dominant alleles are not necessarily better or more common. There are, for example, quite a few human genetic diseases, some lethal, caused by dominant alleles. The terms *dominant* and *recessive* simply mean that if two alleles in this relationship are in a heterozygous genotype, the action of the dominant will be expressed and the action of the recessive will be hidden.

Alleles for most traits do not, in fact, work this neatly. In most cases, heterozygous genotypes result in phenotypes that exhibit some action of both alleles. (This is, in part, what led to the mistaken concept of "blending" inheritance.) Such alleles are said to be **codominant,** and they result in a greater number of possible phenotypes. In addition, many genes have more than two possible alleles, resulting in even more potential phenotypes. (Remember, however, that each individual can only possess a *pair* of alleles.)

A single example can demonstrate both these concepts. Your blood type for the ABO system is coded for by a single gene, the I gene, which has three possible alleles: I^A, I^B, and I^O. So we have six possible genotypes but only four possible phenotypes. (We can designate the genotypes using only the superscript, but remember that these are alleles of a single gene, not separate genes.)

GENOTYPE	PHENOTYPE
AA	
AO	type A
BB	
BO	type B
AB	type AB
OO	type O

It's clear that both A and B are dominant over the recessive O. The AB genotype, however, expresses the action of both alleles. The A and B alleles are codominant. (We will discuss the ABO system in greater detail in Chapter 13.)

Most phenotypic traits are coded for by multiple genes, some of which may have more than three possible alleles. In addition, some alleles are in an even more complex relationship, where the action of both is expressed in the phenotype, but one more so than the other.

Some of the pea plant traits that Mendel rejected were probably traits like these. He rejected them because their phenotypic expressions were too complex for him to easily see any regularities. We still have this problem today, although, of course, we don't simply ignore data we can't explain. The genetic bases for most phenotypic traits have eluded us because there are multiple genes involved and because the alleles of those genes are not in a simple dominant/recessive relationship to one another.

There is a further complication, and it's an important one. The path between the genetic code and the resultant phenotypic expression can be influenced by outside factors, that is, factors that are not directly part of the reading of the genetic code and the synthesis of proteins. We can call these nongenetic influences **environmental.** Certainly, some traits are unaffected by environmental influences. Your ABO blood type is a direct product of your genetic code—there's nothing that can change what those genes code for except a change in the code itself. Such a change is called a **mutation,** literally a mistake in the genetic code. (We will discuss mutations in the next chapter.)

genotypes: The alleles possessed by an organism.

homozygous: Having two of the same allele in a gene pair.

heterozygous: Having two different alleles in a gene pair.

phenotype: The chemical or physical results of the genetic code.

dominant: The allele of a pair that is expressed in the phenotype.

recessive: The allele of a pair that is only expressed if homozygous.

codominant: When both alleles of a pair are expressed in the phenotype.

environmental: Here, any nongenetic influence on the phenotype.

mutation: Any mistake in an organism's genetic code.

Other traits, however, are influenced by environmental factors. Your skin color, for example, is certainly coded for in your genes (there are at least four genes involved and probably more). Your specific skin color phenotype at any point in time, however, is influenced by a number of nongenetic factors: the amount of exposure to ultraviolet radiation from the sun, your health status, even your psychological condition (blushing from embarrassment, for example). In other words, two of us might have exactly the same genes for skin color but still differ in our phenotypic expression of that trait. In fact, different parts of your own body can have different skin colors at the same time depending upon environmental influences, as many of us learn every summer when we're not careful about exposure to the sun. Mendel noticed such variation even in some of the simple traits he worked with in peas, some of which may have been the result of different environmental effects on individual plants.

HOW INHERITANCE WORKS

Genes come in pairs. So do the chromosomes that carry these genes. Thus, the members of a pair of genes are found on a pair of chromosomes. Species differ in number of chromosomes. In humans, there are forty-six chromosomes, which come in twenty-three pairs (Figure 3.6). Chimpanzees have forty-eight chromosomes, wheat plants have forty-two, and dogs have seventy-eight.

When cells divide—as the organism grows or to replace cells that have died or been lost—each chromosome copies itself. It does this by unwinding and splitting at the bond between the bases A, T, G, and C, as in the first step of protein synthesis. Each strand now picks up nucleotides with the proper complementary bases (which are in solution within the cell) and thus replaces its other half. There are now *two* pairs of each chromosome. When the cell divides, each daughter cell receives a full set of chromosome pairs. This process is known as **mitosis** (Figure 3.7).

Some single-celled organisms reproduce in this fashion, but other single-celled organisms and nearly all multicellular organisms reproduce sexually, that is, by the joining of specialized cells from two parents. Such specialized sex cells are called **gametes** (sperm and egg in animals, for example). Now, if each gamete had a full set of chromosome pairs and thus

FIGURE 3.6
The Twenty-Three Pairs of Chromosomes Typically Found in a Human Being. This set of chromosomes came from a man—note the last pair has an X chromosome and a Y chromosome. A woman would have two X chromosomes.

a full set of gene pairs, the resultant fertilized cell, the **zygote,** and all the cells of the offspring, would have *twice* the normal number of chromosomes and *twice* the normal number of genes.

This duplication does not occur, however, because when gametes are produced, the chromosome pairs—and thus the gene pairs—separate. Mendel called this **segregation.** Each gamete, then, has only one member of each chromosome pair and so only one member of each pair of genes. The process of producing gametes is **meiosis** (see Figure 3.7). When the gamete from the male fertilizes the gamete from the female, the zygote once again has two of each chromosome and two of each gene. But, because the members of each pair come from different parents, the combination of alleles for each gene may well be different from that of either parent.

mitosis: The process of cell division that results in two copies of the original cell.

gametes: The cells of sexual reproduction, which contain only half the chromosomes of a normal cell.

zygote: The fertilized egg before cell division begins.

segregation: In genetics, the breaking up of allele pairs in the production of gametes.

meiosis: The process of cell division in which gametes are produced.

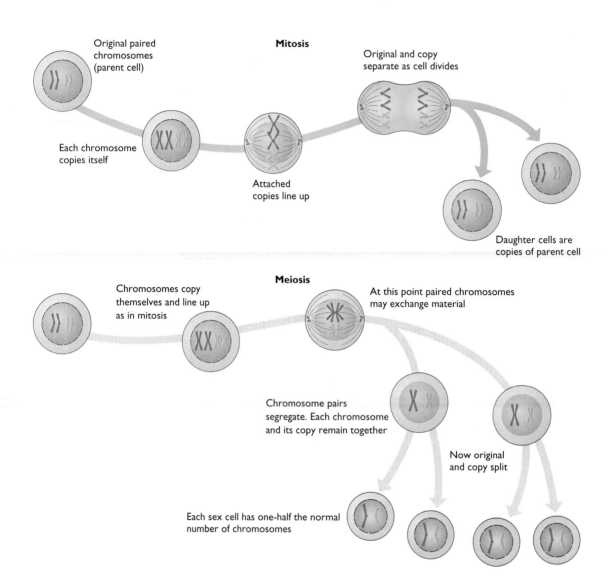

FIGURE 3.7
Mitosis and Meiosis. Cell division occurs in two ways. Mitosis produces exact copies of the parent cell and is the most common form of cell division. Meisosis results in four daughter cells, each with one-half the genetic content of the parent cell. Meiosis is the process by which gametes, or sex cells (sperm and egg), are manufactured. It ensures that when fertilization occurs, the new individual has a complete set of genes, one-half from each parent.

Adding to the differences between parents and offspring that result from fertilization are differences caused by two other phenomena, independent assortment and crossing over. **Independent assortment,** described by Mendel, says that, as long as genes are on different chromosomes, their alleles will segregate independently during the production of gametes. For example, all the traits Mendel observed in pea plants (see Figure 3.5) are on different chromosomes and therefore assort independently. One expression of stem length is not linked to a particular expression of seed texture or to a particular expression of seed color. All combinations are possible. If, on the other hand, two genes are on the same chromosome, they are said to exhibit **linkage;** therefore, their alleles will not assort independently, and variation is reduced.

But sometimes during meiosis portions of chromosome pairs break and are "spliced" back together, but to the *other* member of the pair. This is **crossing over.** Thus, alleles are exchanged between chromosome pairs, and this adds to the possible genotypic combinations that linkage reduces. This phenomenon is called **recombination.**

Independent assortment, crossing over, and recombination, (together with mutations, the mistakes that change the code itself) account for the variation within a species that Darwin observed but could not explain. Recall that without the continuous generation of variation, natural selection—and therefore evolution as we know it—could not take place.

We can demonstrate Mendelian inheritance using the taster trait. Suppose we have two individuals who are both phenotypic tasters and who are both heterozygotes, that is, their genotypes are Tt. Because chromosomes carrying allele pairs segregate during meiosis, each person will produce some gametes that receive the dominant allele and some that receive the recessive. At fertilization, then, depending on which sperm fertilizes which egg, three possible genotypic combinations are possible in the zygote. A device called a Punnett Square, named after an English geneticist, illustrates this (Figure 3.8).

The cells of the Punnett Square represent the possible fertilizations. If a T sperm fertilizes a T egg, the zygote is homozygous dominant. If a T sperm fertilizes a t egg, the zygote is heterozygous, and so on. Notice that two individuals with exactly the same genotype and phenotype can produce offspring with all three possible genotypic combinations and even, in the case of the homozygote tt, a different phenotypic expression. Two tasters, in other words, can give birth to a nontaster. This variation between parents and offspring is the result of the processes of segregation and fertilization. Variation is the raw material of evolution, the topic of the next chapter.

FIGURE 3.8
This Punnett Square illustrates the possible genotypic combinations when two heterozygotes for the taster trait reproduce. Note that because of the hidden recessive, two tasters have a one-quarter chance of producing a nontaster offspring. (The Punnett Square is an important device. There is an exercise on the use of the Punnett Square in Mendelian genetics in the Appendix.)

independent assortment: When genes on different chromosomes segregate to gametes independently of one another.

linkage: When genes occur on the same chromosome and are inherited together.

crossing over: When sections of chromosomes switch between chromosome pairs.

recombination: The genetic change that results from crossing over.

Contemporary Reflections

What Does the Decoding of the Human Genome Mean?

On June 26, 2000—ahead of an originally predicted date of 2003—came the exciting announcement that over 90 percent of the human genome had been decoded. This was a joint effort of the Human Genome Project, a public consortium, and Celera Genomics, a private company. What this means is that we now know the sequence of most of the approximately 3 billion base pairs (A, T, G, and C) of the human genetic code.

One question that immediately comes to mind is Whose genetic code is it? Most of each genome sequence—each of the two groups mentioned above is offering one—comes from one anonymous person, with portions from several other individuals included. In other words, they do not reflect the sequence for every human, because we all differ in the specifics of our code. But they will serve as a reference sequence, against which others may be compared.

What happens now? Quite a bit of work, perhaps enough to take up much of the next century, according to the president of Celera. The sequence will have to be "proofread" to locate errors. (With all those data, there are bound to be some mistakes.) Then some gaps will have to be filled in. (Many of these omitted segments were intentional, because their nature makes them particularly difficult to decode.) Then, the genome will have to be "annotated." This means finding the genes themselves, that is, those portions of the genome that carry instructions for building proteins. So far, about 26,500 human genes have been identified, with the total number estimated at an amazingly low 30,000 to 40,000 (Venter et al. 2001).

The completed sequencing of the genomes of other organisms has contributed greatly to human genome research. We now know the code for yeast, some bacteria, a roundworm, the fruit fly, and the lab mouse. Work on others, including other primates, is under way. One of the interesting facts coming from comparing the genomes of different organisms is that the number of

▽   ▽   ▽

SUMMARY

This brief account of the basic facts of genetics demonstrates two important points relative to evolution:

1. It is important to understand that all phenotypic traits are, initially, the products of the genetic code. Thus, evolutionary change is at its most basic level genetic change. But the pathway from the genetic code to phenotypic traits is a complex one. A gene simply codes for the synthesis of a protein. Proteins build cells, run their chemical reactions, link them together, and help them communicate; cells make

human genes is not as great as expected. The fruit fly has 13,000 genes, the roundworm 19,000. Many of these genes are held in common by humans and these other species. So far only 300 human genes have been found with no counterpart in the mouse. What makes us human is determined by a small number of genes indeed.

Finally, we need to figure out just what the genes *do*. Even after we know what proteins they make, we still have to trace the path from protein to phenotypic trait. Most traits involve multiple proteins that interact with other proteins, as well as with other molecules. Most proteins influence more than one trait. In other words, we have a long way to go before we truly understand how our genome makes each of us a member of our species and an individual human being.

What good is all this knowledge? As an example, we can look at the first nearly complete sequence of a human chromosome, number 22, announced in 1999. This chromosome, the second smallest, includes perhaps 1,000 genes, of which at least 27 have been linked to human diseases and disorders, including a form of brain tumor. Knowledge of the location of genes involved in disease is of obvious value.

We can also better understand individual genetic differences. Humans differ, on average, in about one nucleotide per thousand. Most of these are in noncoding regions, but for those that do have an effect on the body, knowledge of differences will allow us to better individualize medical care—conducting genetic tests to identify those at risk for certain diseases, individualizing drug choice and dose, and devising various genetic therapies and gene-based drugs.

Care and foresight, of course, are required in the use and application of all this new knowledge. We must, for example, consider individual privacy, since the genome carries information that could be used to discriminate against someone in terms of employment or insurance eligibility. There are also issues regarding patents and ownership of genetic knowledge and its products. In the end, as with any knowledge, it is up to us to use and disseminate this knowledge wisely, because the value of knowing our genetic code can far outweigh the potential dangers.

up tissues, which in turn make up the body of a living organism—humans as well as pea plants. Moreover, this complex process is affected by environmental factors, so that the genetic code is most definitely *not* solely responsible for the final form and function of a living being. As we try to explain the phenotypic changes we see in evolution, we must keep these ideas in mind, for if the genetic process itself is complex, so, then, are the processes of evolution that act to change it.

2. The very process by which organisms pass on traits from parent to offspring also accounts for the variation seen between generations and among members of a species. If inheritance produced offspring that were exact copies of their parents, no change would ever take place and there would be no evolution—no adaptation, no change through time, and

no new species. But segregation, independent assortment, crossing over, and recombination mix existing genetic combinations (sort of like shuffling a deck of cards), and mutation produces new genetic variation.

We will look more closely at sources of variation and the processes of evolution in the next chapter.

QUESTIONS FOR FURTHER THOUGHT

1. New information about the specific nature of the human genome indicates, among other things, that we are, from several perspectives, not all that different from other organisms. We have far fewer genes than would be expected given our complexity. We share a great many of those genes with other organisms, from mice to bacteria. What philosophical issues might follow from these facts? Of what practical applications might these facts be?

2. Some concerns generated by all our new and intimate knowledge of the human genome were noted. How do you feel about these? Would your privacy be violated if your entire genome were known and on record somewhere? Should important health information about a person be considered by potential employers or by insurance companies? One of the groups that sequenced the human genome was a private company. Should it "own" the information it derived? Should it "own" applications of that information?

KEY TERMS

particulate

genes

proteins

amino acids

enzymes

chromosomes

deoxyribonucleic acid (DNA)

nucleotide

codon

protein synthesis

messenger ribonucleic acid (mRNA)

transfer ribonucleic acid (tRNA)

polygenic

monogenic

genome

Mendelian genetics

alleles

genotypes

homozygous

heterozygous

phenotype

dominant

recessive

codominant

environmental

mutation

mitosis

gametes	meiosis	linkage
zygote	independent	crossing over
segregation	assortment	recombination

SUGGESTED READINGS

For additional details on the workings of genes and inheritance, try the genetics chapter of John H. Relethford's *The Human Species: An Introduction to Biological Anthropology*, fourth edition, or the genetics section of any good introductory biology text, for example, *Focus on Human Biology*, by Carl E. Rischer and Thomas A. Easton.

A nicely illustrated article on the basics of genetics, with information about genetic engineering, is "Changing Life's Genetic Blueprint," by Robert F. Weaver, in the December 1984 *National Geographic*. For a more recent piece on new discoveries in genetics and their applications, see "Secrets of the Gene," by James Shreeve, in the October 1999 *National Geographic*.

For a brief discussion of Mendel and an excerpt from his writing, see C. Leon Harris's *Evolution: Genesis and Revelations*.

For more information on the Human Genome Project's map of chromosome 22, with a fold-out diagram, see "The DNA Sequence of Human Chromosome 22," by I. Dunham et al., in the December 1999 issue of *Nature*, or look at www.sanger.ac.uk/HGP/Chr22. The "Science Times" section of the *New York Times* for June 27, 2000, has several informative articles on the genome project, along with good, clear diagrams. For detail on the uses of the genome information, see a collection of articles, "The Business of the Human Genome," in the July 2000 *Scientific American*.

For the exciting results of the human genome project so far, see the "Science Times" section of the *New York Times* for February 3, 2001, and the 15 February 2001 issue of *Nature* and the 16 February issue of *Science* (in the latter publications, see page 1163 for a list of websites on the genome project and data).

CHAPTER

4

THE PROCESSES
OF EVOLUTION

I am convinced that
Natural Selection has
been the most
important, but not the
exclusive, means of
modification.
—Charles Darwin

One of the scientists who "rediscovered" Mendel's work in 1900 was the Dutch botanist Hugo de Vries (1848–1935). De Vries had been trying to explain the variations that sometimes spontaneously appeared in plants (and, of course, in animals)—such as a single flower of the wrong color or an individual that was far smaller or larger than other members of its species. At that time breeders called these oddities "sports." De Vries called them mutations. When he read about Mendel's experiments, De Vries realized that these mutations were the results of sudden changes in Mendel's "factors." We now say that a mutation is any change in the genetic mechanism.

With De Vries's contribution, all the major pieces were in place to articulate a *basic theory of evolution*, which may be stated as follows:

A particulate genetic code is initially responsible for the form and function of an organism. Mutations in the coding portion of DNA continually add genetic, and therefore phenotypic, variation to a species. Segregation, independent assortment, recombination, and crossing over shuffle existing genotypic combinations at reproduction and thus provide additional genetic and phenotypic variation. Phenotypic variation is affected by the process of natural selection, where the better-adapted individuals will be more reproductively successful and will thus disproportionately pass on their phenotypic traits to future generations. The results of natural selection are the maintenance of a species' adaptive relationship to existing environmental conditions, the potential alteration of a species' phenotypic variation under circumstances of changing environmental conditions, and, ultimately, the development of new species.

As research continued throughout this century, scientists realized that other processes also play roles in the production of the variation on which natural selection acts. Research still goes on into the relationships and relative importance of all these processes in the evolution of species.

In this chapter, we will address the following questions:

What are species?

What are the processes of evolution?

How do these processes interact to bring about evolution as we understand it today?

SPECIES: THE UNITS OF EVOLUTION

We observe evolution as the change in species over time and the development of new species. Evolution does not take place in individuals. You and I don't evolve in this sense. Evolution takes place in *populations* of organisms, and the basic population in nature is the species.

A species is *a population of organisms whose members can, under natural circumstances, freely interbreed with one another and produce fertile offspring.* Humans and chimpanzees, despite our 98.5-percent genetic similarity, cannot (even under *un*natural circumstances) interbreed and produce offspring because our two species have different numbers of chromosomes. But any two normally healthy humans of opposite sexes, no matter how different they may appear phenotypically (see, for example, Figure 14.1), can reproduce and generate fertile offspring. Thus, humans and chimps are different species, but all human beings are members of a single species, *Homo sapiens*.

Horses and donkeys can mate and produce offspring, known as mules. But mules are nearly always sterile. Two mules can't reproduce and make more mules. Thus, horses and donkeys are considered separate species that are unable to share their genetic endowments.

In captivity, lions and tigers have been known to produce hybrid offspring that are, in many cases, fertile. But lions and tigers don't interbreed in the wild. Though their ranges overlap (in India), the specific environmental **niche** of each animal is different, as are their behaviors, including mating behavior. Thus, lions and tigers are separate species.

Domestic dogs and wolves can and will mate and produce hybrid offspring that are fertile. To be sure, such hybridization is not common. And humans have produced some breeds of dogs that because of their small size could not possibly mate with a wolf (or with some other dog breeds for that matter), nor could they carry and give birth to the fetuses from such matings. But the reality of hybridization and the genetic similarity between dogs and wolves have recently led authorities to lump the dog into the wolf species. Formerly *Canis familiaris*, your family pooch is now *Canis lupus*, technically a wolf.

It is not surprising to us that humans and chimps are separate species because, very simply, we don't *look* like the same species, although we do differ in only 1.5 percent of our genes. Horses and donkeys, on the other hand, do look pretty similar and yet are different species. Lions and tigers look like different species but can still produce fertile offspring, although only under artificial conditions. And some breeds of dogs look so similar to wolves as to obviously belong to the same species, although other breeds only faintly resemble their wild ancestors (Figure 4.1).

If the species is the natural basic unit of evolution, then why is the distinction among various species sometimes so vague? Why aren't all species equally distinct—separate from one another to the same degree and for the same reasons? And why are scientists who specialize in

niche: The environment of an organism and its adaptive response to that environment.

FIGURE 4.1
Wolflike and Very Un-
wolflike Dogs. The German
shepherd dog (*top*) closely
resembles the wolf, the ancestor of all dog breeds. The
West Highland terrier (*bottom*) bears little resemblance
to that ancestor. Both breeds,
however, are genetically the
same as wolves and could
potentially interbreed with
them.

classifying species (called **taxonomists** or **systematists**) sometimes at odds
with one another over which populations belong to the same species?

The answer to all these questions is that while the origin of new
species from existing species usually happens relatively quickly, it does
not happen instantly. It is a *process* that takes place over time (a subject
we'll examine in Chapter 5). Thus, there is usually a period when an
emerging species still can interbreed with its ancestral species and is
therefore difficult to define.

In addition, all species did not emerge at the same time. They appeared at different times, they evolve at different rates, and they continue
to evolve. Species thus change in relation to one another as time goes on.

We established in the last chapter that although evolution results in phenotypic change, it must also involve genetic change. So, if species change over time, we need to characterize populations within a species in genetic terms in order to fully examine their evolution. We do so by using the concept of **gene frequency,** which is also more accurately called **allele frequency.**

Going back to our example in Chapter 3 of the taster trait, suppose every human on earth were homozygous for the dominant (T) allele. The allele frequency would be $T = 1.0$ (or 100 percent). The phenotypic result of this would be that every member of the species would be a taster.

Now, suppose that a mutation occurred somewhere that changed a T allele to a t allele and that, over time, the mutated allele was passed on over many generations of offspring so that at some point 25 percent of the alleles of the taster gene were recessives (t). Now the allele frequencies for this gene would be .75 (75 percent) T and .25 (25 percent) t.

This alteration in frequency would, of course, have a phenotypic effect. Most individuals would still be tasters since T would still be the most frequent allele—and, as you recall, heterozygotes are phenotypically tasters. But there would be some homozygous recessives (tt) who would be nontasters. The species would have changed phenotypically over time as a result of a genetic change. Thus, evolution operates by *changes in allele frequency through time.* Anything that changes allele frequency is therefore a process of evolution.

We will now describe those processes that produce evolutionary change within species and that, ultimately, bring about the origin of new species.

MUTATIONS: NECESSARY ERRORS

A mutation is any change in the genetic code. Some mutations involve a single incorrect base in a codon (one letter of one word). These are known as **point mutations.** Some point mutations are inconsequential, but some result in the wrong amino acid in a protein, which could have disastrous results for the organism. (An example is sickle cell anemia, a genetic disease, which we'll cover at the end of this chapter.)

Other mutations involve a whole chromosome or a large portion of one. These are called **chromosomal mutations.** They are almost always deleterious because many genes are involved. For example, humans who have three copies of chromosome 21, instead of the usual pair, have Down syndrome, or Trisomy 21, which results in mental retardation and

taxonomists: Those who classify and name living organisms.

systematists: Another name for taxonomists.

gene frequency: The percentage of times a particular allele appears in a population.

allele frequency: Another name, and the preferred term, for gene frequency.

point mutations: Mutations of single codons.

chromosomal mutations: Mutations of a whole chromosome or a large portion of a chromosome.

FIGURE 4.2
This child with Down syndrome, has the characteristic facial features that are some of the multiple phenotypic effects of the presence of the extra chromosome. This girl has just won medals in swimming at a Special Olympics event.

other phenotypic effects (Figure 4.2). This mutation most commonly takes place as a result of a failure of a pair of parental chromosomes to segregate in the production of gametes.

Mutations are random; that is, a specific mutation doesn't occur at a specific time or for a specific reason. In other words, mutations don't occur because they are needed. They occur continually, but exactly *what* mutation occurs is totally unpredictable. Some mutations are the results of environmental influences like cosmic radiation, other forms of radioactivity, or chemical pollutants. Most, however, are simply mechanical errors that occur during the complex process of gene replication at cell division or during the even more complex process by which the genetic code is read, translated, and transcribed into proteins.

As you might imagine, then, mutations are frequent. They are occurring in the cells of your body as you read this sentence. The mutations that occur during the reading of the code affect just the individual since they cannot be passed on. The process of aging, for example, is partly a result of the accumulation of cells with mutations that make them in some way abnormal, though they are still alive and able to divide.

The only mutations that concern us in an evolutionary sense are those that occur in the gametes or in the specialized cells that produce gametes. These mutations are the ones that are passed on to future generations and thus bring about genetic change through time. Therefore, mutations change allele frequency through time by making new versions of a gene (as in the taster trait example above) or by otherwise altering the details of the genetic code. Mutation is a process of evolution.

Because mutations are mistakes—deviations from the normal genetic code—many are deleterious. They produce a phenotypic result that is abnormal and therefore, to one degree or another, maladaptive. Individuals with such traits may not be as reproductively successful as most members of their species, and so the mutant gene or genes will not be passed on as often, if at all. In other words, natural selection will *select against* those genes. But mutations may also produce alleles that are neutral, making no difference to an individual's fitness, or they may produce alleles that result in even *better-adapted* phenotypes and are thus *selected for* by being passed on more often.

Mutation, in other words, changes allele frequency and, as it does so, adds genetic variation to a species' **gene pool.** Mutations are the price living things pay for the process of evolution. Without mutation—if the first life forms had reproduced themselves absolutely without error—nothing would have changed, and the first living things would be the *only* living things. Mutations are thus one of the basic processes of evolution. They are necessary errors.

NATURAL SELECTION: THE PRIME MOVER OF EVOLUTION

By now, you should have a pretty good idea how natural selection operates. The genetic variation produced by mutation, segregation, independent assortment, and recombination results in phenotypic variation within a species. Much of a species' phenotypic variation may make little difference to the fitness and reproductive success of individuals. We have come to see that nature is more tolerant of variation than Darwin thought. He felt that *every* variation made a difference. We now know this is not the case.

At the same time, however, some phenotypic variation *does* make a difference. How much of a difference, of course, depends upon what traits are important for the adaptation of a particular species to a particular environment at a particular time. What's adaptive for one species—say, large size or a certain color—will not necessarily work for another species. As environments change, a trait that *was* adaptive for a species may no longer be adaptive, or a trait that was once neutral, or even nonadaptive, may now be adaptive.

A striking example of natural selection in changing environments comes from the pioneering work of Rosemary and Peter Grant and their colleagues (Weiner 1994). These scientists have studied the famous birds of the Galápagos Islands collectively known as Darwin's finches (Figure 4.3; see also Figure 5.3). Among the important adaptive features of this group of birds are their beaks, which have evolved to help each species of finch exploit particular food sources. In 1977 there was a severe and nearly yearlong drought on one of the small islands that the Grants' team was using as a study area. Insects virtually disappeared, and the only plant seeds available were larger than average and had tougher than average exteriors to preserve their moisture. The finches on the island suffered a serious food shortage.

The next year, when the rains returned, the researchers found that just one finch in seven (a mere 14 percent) had made it through the drought. Moreover, the surviving birds of one species common to the island (the medium ground finch) were 5 to 6 percent larger than those that had perished and had beaks that were slightly (in fact, less than a millimeter) longer and deeper than the average before the drought. These are not big differences on a human scale, but the beak-size difference allowed some of the finches to more easily crack open the larger, tougher seeds during the drought, enabling them to survive. As a result, many more males survived than females because they are about 5 percent larger overall than females.

gene pool: All the alleles in a population.

FIGURE 4.3
The medium ground finch, *Geospiza fortis,* was one of the species of Darwin's finches studied by Rosemary and Peter Grant and their colleagues.

Now, however, because evolution takes place across generations, it had to be seen if this change would be passed on to the offspring of the surviving finches. This was, indeed, the case. It is the female finches who select males for mating. The males that the few surviving females selected were the largest and had the deepest beaks. As a result, the finches of the next generation were both larger and had beaks that were 4 to 5 percent deeper than the average before the drought. Moreover, when conditions, and thus food sources, returned to normal for a time, the average beak size decreased over several generations toward its previous dimensions. Larger beaks were no longer a district advantage and so were no longer selected for. These changes showed natural selection in action. Because of the severity of the situation, it took place rapidly enough for human observers to measure and record it.

It is important to note that in this case, as in any example of natural selection, the variation that proved useful under changed circumstances was already present. It did not appear when it was needed or because it was needed. The finches that survived *already* had larger bodies and beaks; they did not develop these after the drought altered their food source. It was, in other words, already an aspect of their variation, although only a small number of finches possessed large beaks and bodies because under usual conditions they conferred no distinct advantage and may even have been disadvantageous. This is the essential difference between Lamarck's inheritance of acquired characteristics and Darwin's natural selection.

It follows from these points that natural selection is not always successful in maintaining a species' adaptation and survival in the face of environmental change. If a change is too rapid or too extensive, the natural variation within a species simply may not be enough to provide any individuals with sufficient reproductive success to keep the species going. When that asteroid hit the earth 65 million years ago and radically altered the earth's climate, perhaps hundreds of thousands of species, the dinosaurs and many others, were unable to adapt and thus became extinct. Natural variation within a species cannot predict what environmental change may take place in the future. Adaptation to change is a matter of luck. Indeed, for over 90 percent of all species that have ever existed, their luck did run out; they are extinct.

Recognition that extinction is commonplace was another reason for Charles Darwin's delay in making his idea of natural selection known to the public. Natural selection does not produce change in a particular direction, nor is it always successful in ensuring the survival of a species. Darwin thought, perhaps correctly at first, that these implications were too uncomfortable for most people to accept. By 1859, however, the Victorian world of rapid social, industrial, economic, and political transformation had come to accept change as the norm, for nature as well as for itself. Moreover, the logic of *Origin of Species* was so lucid and well presented that its conclusions were seen as obvious. Darwin's book was a best-seller, and his idea was, except for a few holdouts, well accepted, at least within science.

Mutation and natural selection are the major processes of evolution. Mutation provides new genetic variation. Natural selection selects phenotypes for reproductive success based on their adaptive relationship with the environment. But because evolution is technically defined as change in allele frequency, two other processes must also be considered as processes of evolution: gene flow and genetic drift (Figure 4.4).

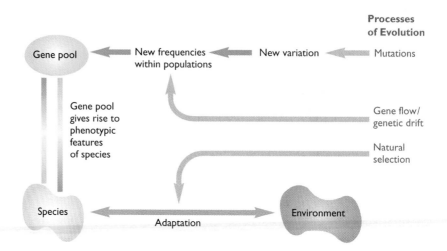

FIGURE 4.4

Processes of Evolution. A species is in an adaptive relationship with its environment. This relationship is maintained by natural selection. Environments, however, are constantly changing, so the adaptive characteristics of species change through time. In addition, the gene pool of a species is always changing, altering the phenotypes on which selection acts. Processes that alter a species' gene pool are also, by definition, processes of evolution because they change allele frequency. Mutation provides new genetic variation by producing new alleles or otherwise altering the genetic code. Gene flow and genetic drift mix the genetic variation within a species, continually supplying new combinations of genetic variables.

GENE FLOW: MIXING POPULATIONS

By definition, members of a species can and do interbreed with one another. The members of a species, however, are usually unevenly distributed over that species' range. Populations within a species can be to some degree separated from other populations by environmental barriers, geographic distance, or, in the case of our species, social and cultural distinctions like political, religious, and ethnic boundaries. Such populations are called **breeding populations,** or **demes.** Individuals tend to find mates within their own deme (Figure 4.5).

Although belonging to the same species, demes may exhibit genetic differences. There are two reasons for this. First, demes may exist in somewhat different environmental circumstances from each other, as illustrated in Figure 4.5. Natural selection will have been favoring different phenotypes, and thus different allele frequencies, in adaptive response to these environments.

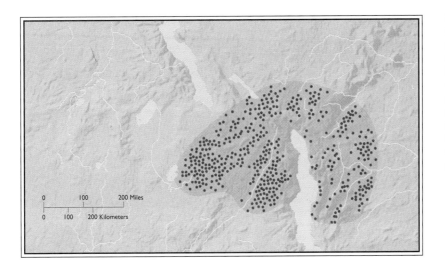

FIGURE 4.5

Demes. The members of a species of lowland, non-aquatic animal (represented by the dots) are unevenly distributed within that species' range because of mountain and water boundaries. The separate population concentrations—the demes—may show genetic and phenotypic differences.

Second, other genetic events (such as mutations and the evolutionary processes we're about to discuss) tend to be concentrated within demes because that is where breeding is concentrated. What happens genetically in one deme will differ from what happens in another.

However, because demes *are* still members of one species, interbreeding between them does take place as populations and individuals migrate and as neighboring populations exchange genes. This is called **gene flow.** When members of different demes interbreed, new genetic combinations may be produced in the offspring. In other words, genes within a species "flow" among the populations of that species, altering the allele frequencies in those populations and adding still more genetic—and thus phenotypic—variation to the species as a whole (Figure 4.6).

This process of evolution is particularly effective in a mobile species like ours, with populations that are continually moving around and mixing genes. For example, half of the Hutterite marriages take place between colonies, the bride moving to the colony of her husband. The woman thus brings her genes into the population and contributes them to subsequent generations. In one of the colonies I visited, 70 percent of the female parents came from other colonies, and marriages involving these women produced nearly 60 percent of the children of the next generation. In the other colony, 75 percent of female parents "flowed" in, and their marriages produced 47 percent of the next generation. Changes from one generation to the next in a Hutterite colony are greatly affected by this continual mixing or flowing of genes among populations, and it is the same for the human species as a whole.

breeding populations: Populations within a species that are genetically isolated to some degree from other populations.

demes: Another name for breeding populations, but sometimes implies physical distinctions.

gene flow: The exchange of genes among populations through interbreeding.

FIGURE 4.6
Simple Example of Gene Flow. The dots represent the relative frequencies of two alleles.

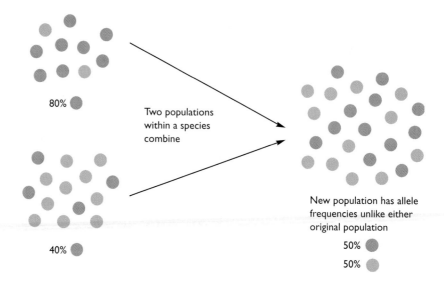

80%

Two populations within a species combine

40%

New population has allele frequencies unlike either original population

50%

50%

GENETIC DRIFT: RANDOM EVOLUTION

The several processes that fall under *genetic drift* can be demonstrated by the following experiment: Take 100 coins and arrange them so you have 50 heads and 50 tails. Mix them up and without looking (that is, at random) select 10 coins. They will probably *not* be 5 heads and 5 tails, 50 percent of each as in the original group. The odds are against it (about 4:1). Your sample of 10 will probably not be representative of the whole population of coins. It will probably be a nonrepresentative sample, and this effect is called **sampling error.**

Similarly, when a population within a species splits, each new population will exhibit a nonrepresentative sample of the genes, and therefore the phenotypes, of the original. The splitting of a population is called **fission** and is the opposite of gene flow (Figure 4.7). When one of the new populations is drawn from a small sample of the parental population, it will be strikingly different genetically (as with the coins above). This phenomenon is called the **founder effect.**

The Hutterites again provide an example. Hutterites have one of the highest recorded birth rates, an average of about ten children per family. After such rapid population growth for about 15 or 20 years, a colony becomes so large (130 to 150 people) that social and administrative problems arise, and there is increasing duplication of labor specialists. The colony will then fission or, as they call it, "branch out." Half the colony families will stay in the original location, and half will found a new

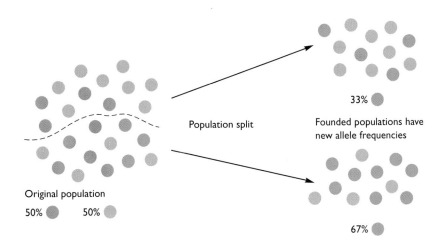

Population split

Founded populations have
new allele frequencies

33%

Original population

50%   50%

67%

FIGURE 4.7
Fission and the Founder Effect. Notice that this diagram is basically the reverse of that representing gene flow (Figure 4.6).

colony. As a result, the 3 original North American Hutterite colonies, founded in 1874 and 1875, have now increased to more than 380, and the original 300 Hutterite immigrants now number 35,000.

In fact, the situation is more pronounced than that. Of the 300 original North American Hutterites, only 90 contributed genes to future generations. So most of the 35,000 present-day Hutterites can trace most of their genes back to fewer than 100 ancestors. (Some people have joined the group from the outside in the past 120 years.) When a founder population is a small percentage of an original group, it is referred to as a **bottleneck.** Other bottlenecks may take place as a result of an epidemic disease, natural disaster, or overexploitation by humans.

The founder effect can have interesting and sometimes tragic results. In a population of 333 Pennsylvania Dutch, nearly one-third (98) were found to have the gene for Tay-Sachs disease, a fatal condition that kills recessive homozygotes by their fourth year of life (see also Chapter 15). The high frequency of this lethal recessive allele can be explained by the fact that these 333 people were all descended from one couple who founded the group in the nineteenth century. One of them, no doubt, by sad circumstance, carried the gene (Diamond 1991).

Fission, the founder effect, and gene flow are particularly important in the evolution of our species. For most of human history we have been divided into many populations, defined by such things as religion, politics, and ethnicity; and, of course, we have been separated by our ability to live all over the globe in nearly all natural environments. Our populations, however, have always mixed genes, and they have often split up to found new populations. Cultural boundaries, in addition, are temporary, so the definitions of populations change. Gene flow and fission are

sampling error: When a sample chosen for study does not accurately represent the population from which the sample was taken.

fission: Here, the splitting up of a population to form new populations.

founder effect: Genetic differences between populations produced by the fact that genetically different individuals established (founded) the populations.

bottleneck: A severe reduction in the size of a population such that only certain genes survive and come to characterize the descendant population.

processes caused by population movement, and our species is among the most mobile. This is the essential reason why our species cannot be divided into biologically meaningful racial groups (see Chapter 14).

Another form of genetic drift is called **gamete sampling.** Just as genes are not sampled representatively when a population fissions, they are not sampled representatively when two individuals produce offspring. An organism passes on only one of each of its pairs of genes at a time, and only chance dictates which one will be involved in the fertilization that produces a new individual.

For example, two humans who are each heterozygotous for the taster trait (see Figure 3.8) will possess one of each allele of the taster gene (*Tt*). But they will not necessarily, in their reproductive lifetimes, pass on an equal number of each allele. It's a matter of chance. It's possible that they could pass on only their dominant allele or only their recessive—or both, but in a proportion other than fifty-fifty. In other words, the very act of reproducing—with the genetic processes of segregation and fertilization—can change allele frequency from one generation to the next.

This example refers to a single set of parents, but the combined effects of this phenomenon on a whole population can bring about a great deal of change between generations. This is especially true in small populations of 100 or fewer (about the size of the average Hutterite colony). Here, the change produced by one set of parents is not likely to be balanced by change in the opposite direction produced by another set.

Allele frequencies, then, may change at random across generations, "drifting" in whatever direction chance takes them. The change may be great enough that certain alleles may be completely lost, while others may reach a frequency of 100 percent—all with no necessary relationship to natural selection based on the fitness of those alleles.

SICKLE CELL ANEMIA: EVOLUTIONARY PROCESSES IN ACTION

We can now take the ideas covered in Chapters 2 and 3 and see how they work in a real example. Sickle cell anemia is a genetic blood disorder; it is often associated with Africans and African Americans because it is found in high frequency in a band across central Africa. It is also found in North Africa, Southwest Asia, India, and Southeast Asia (Figure 4.8).

Sickle cell anemia is the result of a mutation affecting hemoglobin, the protein on the red blood cells that carries oxygen from the lungs to the body's tissues. Hemoglobin, as you recall, is made up of two pairs of

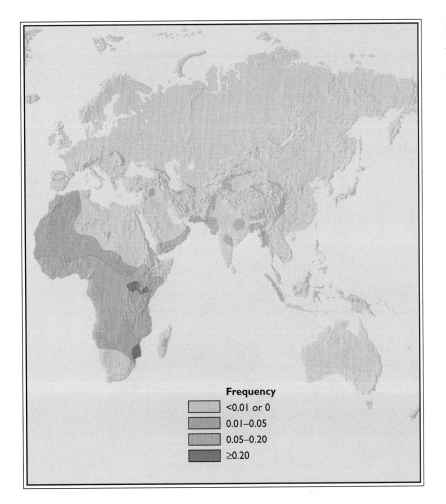

FIGURE 4.8
Distribution of Frequencies of the Sickle Cell Allele. Compare this with the map of endemic malaria (Figure 4.10).

Frequency
<0.01 or 0
0.01–0.05
0.05–0.20
≥0.20

amino acid chains, the alpha chain of 141 amino acids and the beta chain of 146. Mutations no doubt occur all along the codes for these proteins. But if the codon CTC for glutamic acid mutates to CAC for valine in the sixth position of the beta chain—one particular wrong word in a sentence of 287 words—an abnormal form of hemoglobin results.

When this abnormal form is present and stress, high altitude, or illness lowers an individual's oxygen supply, the red blood cells take on peculiar shapes, some resembling sickles (Figure 4.9). These misshapen cells cannot carry sufficient oxygen to nourish the body's tissues and can also block capillaries. The results include fatigue, retarded physical development in children, increased susceptibility to infection, miscarriage, fever, and severe pain. Sickle cell kills about 100,000 people a year, 85 percent of whom die before their 20s. Those who live longer experience constant pain and have

gamete sampling: The genetic change caused when genes are passed to new generations in frequencies unlike those of the parental generation. An example of sampling error.

FIGURE 4.9
Shown here are normal red blood cells and one with the abnormal shape (*bottom left*) that results from the presence of hemoglobin with one incorrect amino acid. Such cells fail to transport oxygen properly to the body's tissues.

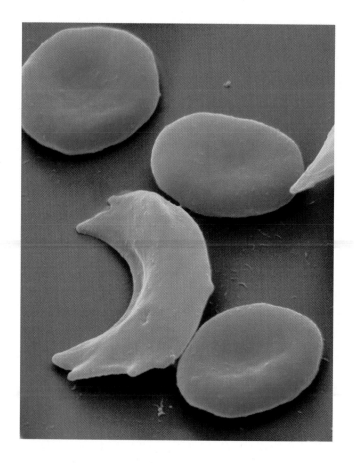

very low reproductive rates. In terms of evolutionary fitness—that is, reproductive success—sickle cell anemia may be considered nearly 100 percent fatal. (It should be noted that there have been recent breakthroughs in the treatment of this disease, including a new means of repairing the messenger RNA so that it produces normal hemoglobin. This new technique remains out of reach, of course, for most people suffering from the disease.)

The abnormal allele for sickle cell is an example of a codominant allele. An individual who is homozygous for the allele will have sickle cell anemia. A heterozygote, who inherits one sickle cell allele and one allele for normal hemoglobin, will possess only about 40 percent abnormal hemoglobin. These people are said to have the sickle cell *trait*. In extreme conditions of low oxygen, they may experience symptoms of the disease, but usually not as severe as homozygotes and with a great deal of variation from person to person. The heterozygous condition is not normally fatal.

FIGURE 4.10
Distribution of Endemic (consistently present) Malaria. Compare with the map showing high frequencies of the sickle cell allele (Figure 4.8).

For a disease that kills its victims, usually without allowing them to pass on their genes, sickle cell is found in unexpectedly high frequencies in parts of the world (see Figure 4.8), in some areas as high as 20 percent. One would expect such an allele to be selected against and to virtually disappear.

The answer to this puzzle is a perfect example of the complexity of natural selection. Not only do heterozygotes experience less severe episodes of the disease, they also have a resistance to malaria, an often fatal infectious disease caused by a parasitic single-celled organism and transmitted by mosquitos. Malaria, though now treatable, still kills 1 million to 3 million people a year. Red blood cells with abnormal hemoglobin (recall that heterozygotes have about 40 percent of this) take on abnormal shapes when infected by the malaria parasite and die, thus failing to transport the parasite through the body. Sickle cell is found in highest frequencies where malaria is found in highest frequencies (Figure 4.10).

Contemporary Reflections

Are Humans Still Evolving?

As asked by most people, the question posed in this box's title has two meanings. Perhaps the most common refers to the direction of future human evolution; in other words, how will we look in so many millions of years? As our minds do more and more of our work—and our bodies do less and less—will we eventually be great big heads atop short, spindly bodies? (This is the image we are often given of aliens from more advanced civilizations. Think of *Close Encounters of the Third Kind*, *E.T.*, or *The X-Files*.)

The answer to this first meaning of the question is, obviously, who knows? Evolution is so complex, so dependent upon multiple, interacting series of events, that there is really no way of predicting the evolutionary future of any species, especially our species, with its ability to control its behavior, the environment, and, indeed, its genes through culture. If we could take a time machine back to the Cambrian Period 543 million years ago and look at its animal life (see Figure 6.5), made up mostly of primitive arthropods (ancestors of modern insects, spiders, and crustaceans), who would predict that a rare little wormy creature only about 2 inches long, called *Pikaia*, would be the earliest-known representative of the chordates, the important group of organisms now represented by fish, amphibians, reptiles, birds, and mammals (Gould 1989; Gore 1993)?

A second, more sophisticated meaning of the question concerns whether we humans have stopped our evolution by so controlling our environment that natural selection is no longer in operation, that genetic variation is no longer an important factor in reproductive success.

There are two parts to the answer. First, as we discussed, there are processes other than natural selection that bring about genetic change from generation to generation in a species. Our control over our environment certainly won't halt the processes of mutation, gene flow, and genetic drift. Indeed, one might argue that we have increased mutation rates through some of our environmental

In no environment is there any advantage to being homozygous for sickle cell. In most environments, being heterozygous also confers a disadvantage. But in malarial areas, heterozygotes do have an advantage. They are resistant to malaria, and they exhibit a variable and nonfatal form of the anemia. If heterozygotes are the healthiest in such environments and thus are relatively more successful at passing on their genes, then more sickle cell alleles will be inherited than would be expected if sickle cell had no benefit in any environment. Whenever two heterozygotes mate, they stand a one-quarter chance of producing an individual with normal hemoglobin, a one-quarter chance of producing an offspring who will die from sickle cell, and a one-half chance of producing an offspring who will die neither from sickle cell nor from malaria but who will possess one sickle cell allele that can be passed on (Figure 4.11). This shows dramatically how adaptive fitness is related to specific environmental conditions. Even a lethal allele may be adaptive under certain circumstances.

manipulations and that our increasing mobility makes gene flow ever more powerful. So, by its genetic definition, evolution will always be taking place in our species.

But have we buffered ourselves against natural selection? For some genetically based characteristics, yes, we have. Remember that fitness is measured against a particular environment. If, through culture, we change the environment, we then change the adaptive fitness of certain phenotypes and thus of the genes that code for them. If I had lived in, say, *Homo erectus* times (1.8 million to 100,000 years ago), I'd no doubt be dead by now. If my infected appendix hadn't killed me (which it would have), my nearsightedness would have prevented me from being a very effective hunter or gatherer. Our present environment, however, has available all sorts of techniques and devices to improve one's eyesight. I wear glasses and see my optometrist once a year, so my poor vision (which, for the sake of the example, we'll say has a genetic basis) does not put me at any survival or reproductive disadvantage. You can probably think of dozens of other examples.

We have not, however, completely eliminated all relevant genetic variation. There are plenty of genes for diseases that place severe, or absolute, limits on a person's ability to reproduce and thus pass on those genes. Tay-Sachs disease, for example, is lethal well before reproductive age. Sickle cell anemia lowers reproductive rates in the few individuals who live long enough to reproduce.

And let's end on a hypothetical note (keeping in mind my precaution about predicting future evolution). There could well be some genetic variables that will make some difference in reproductive success in the near future. Suppose there is genetically based variation in humans' abilities to withstand less-than-optimal air quality, or severely crowded living conditions, or high levels of noise pollution. As these conditions worsen, it is certainly conceivable that genes for such tolerances would become more frequent as their possessors are less reproductively affected by the modern environment.

FIGURE 4.11
Punnett Square for Sickle Cell Anemia Showing the Potential Offspring of Two Heterozygotes. Because heterozygotes have an adaptive advantage in malarial areas but stand a one-quarter chance of producing an offspring with sickle cell anemia, the allele for sickle cell is maintained and passed on in such populations, and the disease exhibits high frequencies.

The connection between sickle cell and African Americans is an example of the founder effect. African Americans can trace at least some of their ancestry back to the populations from West Africa that provided much of the slave trade to North America. The African American population was thus, in part, founded by individuals from an area where sickle cell already existed in high frequencies.

But sickle cell is less frequent among African Americans than it is in Africa. Moreover, sickle cell is not limited to persons of African descent in this country. One only has to have the alleles to have the disease. Persons of largely European American background can also have sickle cell. Both these facts can be explained partly as a result of gene flow. There has been a good deal of genetic mixing between European Americans and African Americans over the past several hundred years. The addition of European genes would have lessened the frequency of the sickle cell allele in African Americans because Europe is largely free of the disease. The presence of the disease among a small number of persons of largely European descent might be the result of their having an ancestor of African descent who carried the allele. Of course, the mutation that produces the sickle cell allele can occur in people of any geographic or ethnic background, European Americans included.

Moreover, because malaria is less common in the United States and Canada than in central Africa (although it was a problem in the southern United States until about 20 years ago), there has been less of an adaptive advantage in possessing the sickle cell trait. Natural selection has thus been producing lower frequencies of the sickle cell allele, even in persons whose ancestors are from one of the areas of highest frequency.

Finally, while we're on the subject, there is evidence (Relethford 2000) that the frequency of malaria increased when people began farming in Africa several thousand years ago. Clearing and planting the land provides the sunlight and the pools of stagnant water that are ideal breeding grounds for the mosquitos that carry the malaria parasite. An increase in malaria would result in an increase in selection for the sickle cell allele, which, in heterozygotes, confers an immunity to the infectious disease.

Thus, the full story of this lethal disease shows the interaction of the forces of evolution and involves not only the genetics behind the cause of the disease but also a single-celled parasite, an insect, and human demographic and cultural practices. The story of sickle cell is a perfect example of the holistic perspective of anthropology.

▽   ▽   ▽

SUMMARY

A basic theory of evolution involves the production of new genetic variation by mutation and the continual mixing of that variation at reproduction. Gene flow and the forms of genetic drift (fission, the founder effect that results from fission, and gamete sampling) act to randomly change allele frequencies within populations of a species. The resulting phenotypic variation becomes the raw material for natural selection that selects individuals for reproductive success, thus accumulating adaptive traits across generations and decreasing the frequency of poorly adapted traits.

The basic unit of evolution is the species, an interbreeding population that is reproductively isolated from other populations. Because the evolution of new species is a process that occurs over time and at differing rates, species are not always equally distinct from one another and can often be difficult to define. Species are characterized genetically by allele frequency, the percentage of times each possible allele of a gene occurs. Evolution is thus technically defined as a change in allele frequency over time.

The processes of evolution, based on this definition, are:

1. *Mutation*—mistakes in the genetic mechanism that add new variation to a species' gene pool.

2. *Natural selection*—the differential reproduction of individuals based on the relative adaptive value of their traits.

3. *Gene flow*—the mixing of genes as populations within a species move about and interbreed.

4. *Genetic drift*—the splitting of populations to found new populations with new sets of allele frequencies (fission and the founder effect) and the nonrepresentative sampling of genes as each new generation is produced (gamete sampling).

Sickle cell anemia is not only an example of the processes of evolution at work but is also an example of anthropology's holistic approach—the search for connections among the various aspects of its subject.

QUESTIONS FOR FURTHER THOUGHT

1. Domestic dogs are now classified in the same species as wolves, but we humans have been able to produce hundreds of different dog breeds, each with its own phenotype and behavioral attributes—many decidedly unwolflike. Given what you know about the processes of evolution, how do you think we've accomplished this?

2. Severe bottlenecks can pose a serious problem for a species. We are seeing this now among such species as cheetahs and elephant seals. What do you think the problem is with a severe bottleneck, in some

cases even after the species regains a fairly large population? Why is it actually threatening some species with extinction?

3. If I were an African American planning on having children, I might want to be screened to see if I were heterozygous for sickle cell. (I could be without ever having exhibited noticeable symptoms.) But since I am a European American, there is virtually no need for me to do so. Some people have found such reasoning objectionable, saying that since it makes an assumption about one's health based on one's race, it is potentially racist. What do you think about this? Do you know of any other diseases that are statistically linked to certain populations?

KEY TERMS

niche	chromosomal mutations	sampling error
taxonomists		fission
systematists	gene pool	founder effect
gene frequency	breeding populations	bottleneck
allele frequency	demes	gamete sampling
point mutations	gene flow	

SUGGESTED READINGS

An extended discussion of genetics and evolutionary processes within the context of anthropology can be found in John H. Relethford's text, *The Human Species: An Introduction to Biological Anthropology*, fourth edition. It includes a chapter that covers sickle cell and many additional examples of evolution in action within human populations.

A highly technical but very readable text on all aspects of evolution is *Evolution*, second edition, by Mark Ridley. The nature of species and the evolutionary processes that affect them are nicely covered in Edward O. Wilson's *The Diversity of Life*, a book about the importance of maintaining the biological diversity of the planet.

The reseach on Darwin's finches and the people who conducted it are the subjects of Jonathan Weiner's Pulitzer Prize–winning *The Beak of the Finch: A Story of Evolution in Our Time*. For an update, see Peter and Rosemary Grant's article "Non-Random Fitness Variation in Two

Populations of Darwin's Finches," in the *Proceedings of the Royal Society of London: Biological Sciences* 267:131.

For a discussion of the definition and origin of species, which also relates to the next chapter, see Stephen Jay Gould's article, "What Is a Species?" in the December 1992 issue of *Discover*.

CHAPTER

5

THE ORIGIN OF SPECIES AND THE SHAPE OF EVOLUTION

... endless forms most
beautiful and most
wonderful have been,
and are being evolved.
—Charles Darwin

The examples of evolution in action that we discussed in the previous chapter—the finches responding to climatic changes on the Galápagos and populations of our own species interacting with malaria—have focused on changes within single species. Darwin's book, however, was called *Origin of Species*. What Darwin was ultimately trying to explain was how new species arise, the "mystery of mysteries," as he called it in his introduction.

We will address the following questions in this chapter:

How do existing species give rise to new species?

How do the processes of evolution contribute to the origin of new species?

How do species diversify?

What does the "family tree" of species look like?

Are there any challenges to the idea of evolution? Are they valid?

NEW SPECIES

Species are, by definition, reproductively isolated from other species. Members of two species cannot mate and produce fertile offspring. Members of the same species can. What prevents interbreeding between species?

Any difference that prevents the production of fertile hybrid offspring between two populations under natural conditions is called a **reproductive isolating mechanism.** These isolating mechanisms fall into several general categories (based on Dobzhansky 1970):

1. *Ecological.* Members of the populations are adapted to different environmental niches. Even though their ranges may overlap, their specific environments don't—as is the case with lions and tigers in India. Ecological isolation probably explains the origin of the **hominids,** the group to which our species belongs (see Chapter 10).

2. *Seasonal.* Mating within each population or the flowering of plants of two related species takes place at different times of the year.

3. *Sexual.* Behaviors that attract one sex to the other (called *courtship behaviors*) are different in the two populations.

4. *Mechanical.* The organs of reproduction (genitalia or flower parts) are incompatible.

5. *Different pollinators.* In flowering plants, different species, even though closely related, attract different insects, birds, or bats to facilitate pollination.

6. *Gamete isolation.* The cells of reproduction may be incompatible or may not be able to survive within the body of a member of the other species, thus preventing fertilization even if mating takes place.

7. *Hybrid inviability.* Fertilization may occur, but the hybrid zygotes do not survive.

8. *Hybrid sterility.* Hybrids survive but do not produce functional gametes. Mules are normally an example, although in some cases they are fertile.

The origin of new species, then, is the evolution of *any* of these differences between populations that prevent the production of fertile offspring. As biologist Edward O. Wilson puts it, "In order to spring forth as a species, a group of breeding individuals need only acquire *one* difference in *one* trait in their biology. . . . When that happens, a new species is born [emphases mine]" (1992, 68).

How do such differences arise? It is important to understand that reproductive isolating mechanisms do not evolve *in order* to produce a new species. It is an accident when the differences in traits are isolating mechanisms. The differences themselves evolve through the processes of mutation, gene flow, genetic drift, and natural selection acting differently on different populations.

To take the simplest model, a species inhabits a wide geographic range, and populations (demes) at opposite ends of the range exhibit slightly different adaptive responses to the particular environmental circumstances found there (Figure 5.1). Now, some environmental change—say, a river changing its course, the destruction of some important resource, or the advance of a glacier—splits the species, geographically isolating one deme from another. Over time, each population will continue to adapt to its environment but without being able to exchange genes with the other deme. In other words, there will be no gene flow. Each population will accumulate different genetic and phenotypic traits. Quite possibly one or more of these will, by chance, be a reproductive isolating mechanism. If at some later point the geographical barrier were removed and the two populations *could* mix, they would not be able to interbreed. They would be separate species, and we would say that **speciation** had occurred.

Even if there are no district geographical barriers separating portions of a species, speciation can still take place. For example, in Nicaraguan lakes there are two closely related species of cichlid fishes

reproductive isolating mechanism: Any difference that prevents the production of fertile offspring between members of two populations.

hominids: Modern human beings and our ancestors, generally defined as the primates who habitually walk erect.

speciation: The evolution of new species.

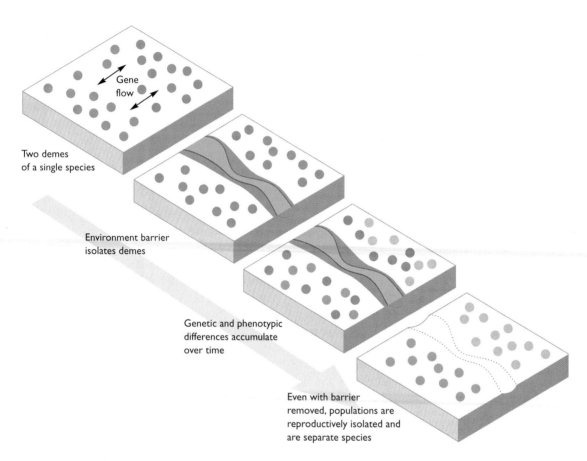

Gene flow

Two demes
of a single species

Environment barrier
isolates demes

Genetic and phenotypic
differences accumulate
over time

Even with barrier
removed, populations are
reproductively isolated and
are separate species

FIGURE 5.1

Simple Example of Speciation through Environmental Isolation.

(see the "Contemporary Reflections" box in this chapter) that are distinguished by color. Since cichlids mate according to color, these two groups don't hybridize. They apparently evolved from an original species when a new color arose through mutation, and because of the importance of color in mate choice, those with the new color were reproductively isolated (Kirkpatrick 2000).

Speciation may be accelerated when a breeding group within a species shares a mutation with extensive phenotypic effects. Such mutations are called **macromutations.** Most macromutations are, as you would expect, deleterious. But, by chance, some macromutations might be neutral or even beneficial. In such a case, they would be retained by natural selection, and they might serve to very rapidly make a small population within a species adaptively isolated from the rest of the species. Speciation is given a "head start" by the macromutation.

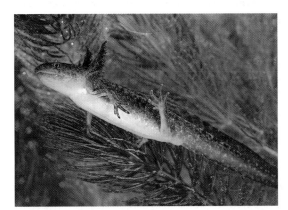

FIGURE 5.2
Axolotl (*upper left*), Larval Salamander (*lower left*), and Adult Salamander (*upper right*). Note the similarity between the axolotl and the immature salamander. The axolotl is, in a sense, a salamander that never completely matured.

As an example, there are genes that influence the development of an individual during its life. A mutation of one of these genes could have important consquences for the structure and function of the adult organism. There's a well-known illustration of such a mutation. Salamanders begin life as aquatic larvae, much like tadpoles. Eventually they develop functioning lungs and legs and spend their adult life on land. The axolotl from Mexico (Figure 5.2) is a salamander that never grows up. Because its pituitary gland fails to supply its thyroid with a certain hormone, the axolotl becomes sexually mature but does not finish developing physically and retains into adulthood the external gills and fully aquatic lifestyle of salamander larvae. It is a separate species. If injected with the missing hormone, the axolotl will mature and live on land. The difference, in other words, is a simple one—the presence of a hormone—but the mutation that brought about the difference served to immediately reproductively isolate its possessors

macromutations: Mutations with extensive and important phenotypic results.

from the rest of their species. The speciation that produced the axolotl was nearly instant. (Obviously, more than one salamander would have had to share the mutation. Perhaps the mutation occurred during the production of a group of eggs, and so all the salamanders that developed from those eggs were actually axolotls.)

The processes of evolution that bring about genetic and phenotypic variation are constantly in action (see Figure 4.4). So are the processes that alter environmental circumstances. It stands to reason, then, that the conditions that produce new species are ever-present and that speciation must be a very common occurrence indeed.

ADAPTIVE RADIATION: THE EVOLUTION OF LIFE'S DIVERSITY

No one is sure how many species of living things inhabit the earth, and we have no idea how many have *ever* lived on this planet. There are about 1.5 million *named* species living today; the total is certainly many times that number.

Even in modern times, new species are still being discovered. In 1997, for example, a new species of marmoset (a type of monkey) was discovered in Brazil—the seventh new monkey species found in that country over the past decade. New species of small mammals, mostly rodents and bats, are described at an average rate of sixteen per year. New species of bacteria are being found by the thousands, some recently discovered ones living in small spaces within rocks nearly 2 miles below the surface of the earth and at temperatures of more than 235°F.

Indeed, some microbes (single-celled organisms) that live at extreme conditions in superheated water near volcanic vents on the ocean floor, for example, or in water so salty it would kill most creatures, have been shown to be far more common than previously thought. Genetic tests of these and other microbes have shown them to belong to a whole new branch of life and have indicated that microbes compose the bulk of the world's *biomass*—a measure of the weight of organic matter (Gould 1996a). The actual number of species in the world must be, as one scientist put it, "staggering."

Despite the great array of living creatures, however, there is a high degree of similarity among them all. All living things, for example, use the same genetic code; they are built from the proteins that are the products of that code, using the same basic twenty amino acids. We assume, then, that life on earth had a single origin. This being the case, all those millions upon millions of species have descended from a common ancestor and have come about by the process of speciation.

For a potential new species to persevere, it must survive the adaptive trials of natural selection. Put another way, it must have a place to go, an environment to which its traits are adapted, an *ecological opportunity*. When such opportunities are extensive, speciation may take place numerous times, and a group of related species may spread into a number of niches. This spread of related species is called **adaptive radiation.** Evolution has been a story of the adaptive radiation of species into different environments and the subsequent actions of the processes of evolution on those species.

Ecological opportunities come about and can foster adaptive radiation under these three general circumstances:

1. When an environment supports no similar and therefore competing species

2. When extensive extinction empties a set of environments of competing species

3. When the new group of related species are adaptively **generalized** (as opposed to **specialized**) and are able to disperse successfully into different niches and displace species already there

An example of the first circumstance is the famous case of Darwin's finches (introduced in Chapter 4), a group of thirteen related species that inhabit the Galápagos, the volcanic archipelago of some nineteen islands in the Pacific about 600 miles west of Ecuador (Figure 5.3). This was one of Darwin's stops on his voyage around the world. There is a fourteenth related species that lives on Cocos Island, north of the Galápagos.

From a small group of original migrants of an ancestral species, blown out to the islands from the mainland of Central or South America no more than 3 million years ago, these birds have radiated into niches that were pretty much unoccupied by other birds.

Today there are species of ground-dwelling finches that feed on seeds of different sizes and have bills shaped accordingly. There are several species that feed on cactus and several that live in trees and eat insects. Their beaks, too, as noted in Chapter 4, are adapted for the specific foods they eat. One species is a tool-user, holding a cactus spine or twig in its bill and using it to probe for insects in tree trunks. The ground finches on two of the smaller islands peck the skin of larger birds and drink the blood that results. Not surprisingly, they are referred to as "vampire finches."

Moreover, there is new evidence that beak form influences the songs the various finch species sing, which could also affect species distinction (Podos 2001).

adaptive radiation: The evolution and spreading out of related species into new niches.

generalized: Here, species that are adapted to a wide range of environmental niches.

specialized: Here, species that are adapted to a narrow range of environmental niches.

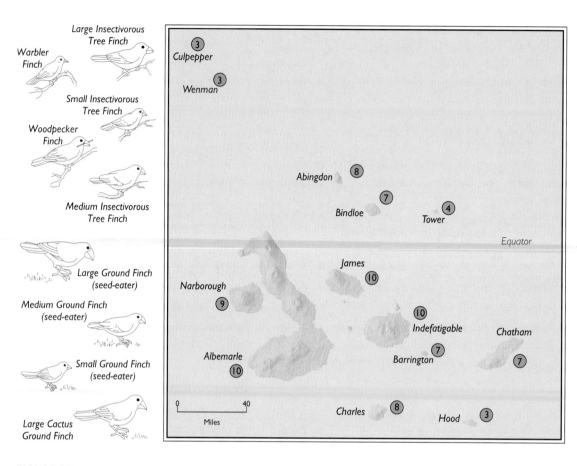

FIGURE 5.3

The various species of Darwin's finches evolved when small groups from an original species underwent adaptation to the varying environmental conditions found throughout the Galápagos Islands. The numbers on the map represent the number of finch species found on each major island. The bird drawings illustrate some of the variation observed among the species of Darwin's finches.

In fact, birds in general are an example of adaptive radiation into empty niches. Birds first evolved some 150 million years ago from dinosaurs (Figure 5.4). There was little competition for species possessing the new attributes of feathers and, for some, flight. This evolutionary novelty radiated into a wide variety of niches, resulting currently in about 9,000 species of birds of incredible diversity. All are variations on the same basic theme.

Mammals are an example of a group of species that were able to take advantage of the niches opened up by a major extinction—the one that killed off all the dinosaurs and many other species 65 million years ago. Mammals were among the survivors. At the time they were mostly small, **nocturnal** shrewlike or rodentlike creatures, but they now had a world of niches open to them that were free of many previous competitors. The mammals radiated rapidly, and by about 40 million years ago most major

FIGURE 5.4
Shown here are the fossil remains of *Archaeopteryx* ("ancient bird"), about 150 million years old. It is actually a small, bipedal dinosaur with feathers. These feathers, modifications of dinosaurian scales, are an example of a sudden but sizable alteration in a species' genetic makeup that eventually gave rise to a whole new group of organisms.

types of mammals we know today had evolved. (The ancestors of all modern birds, too, survived this extinction.)

We can look to our own group of mammals, the primates, for examples of species that were able to radiate because they were generalized and could fairly easily disperse into diverse niches. When monkeys first evolved, about 40 million years ago, they proved more generalized than their **prosimian** ancestors, the so-called primitive primates. The monkeys were larger-brained, **diurnal,** and well adapted to an active **arboreal** life, eating a mixed diet of leaves, fruits, and insects. As the monkeys underwent speciation and radiated into new niches, they displaced the prosimians. In the New World (Central and South America; the North American prosimians apparently became extinct), there are only monkeys. In the Old World (Europe, Africa, and Asia), prosimians were pushed into marginal areas. A few species live on the mainland of Africa and the mainland of Southeast Asia, but most inhabit isolated islands of Southeast Asia and the island of Madagascar, which had separated from mainland Africa prior to the monkeys' evolution (see Chapter 10 for more detail).

On the scale of a single species, we will see this pattern repeated when we look more closely at our own evolution. At least once during

nocturnal: Active at night.

prosimian: A primate with primitive features, most closely resembling the ancient primates.

diurnal: Active during the day.

arboreal: Adapted to life in the trees.

the evolution of our group of primates, a new and more generalized species of hominid spread geographically and ecologically, displacing an existing hominid species (see Chapters 10, 11, and 12).

THE SHAPE OF THE FAMILY TREE

What is the pattern of speciation, and what, as a result, is the shape of the evolutionary family tree of species?

Charles Darwin felt that natural selection was directly responsible for speciation and that it was a process of almost unlimited power. He said that natural selection brought about "the accumulation of innumerable slight variations, each good for the individual possessor," and he added:

> What limit can be put to this power, acting during long ages and rigidly scrutinizing the whole constitution, structure, and habits of each creature,—favoring the good and rejecting the bad? I can see no limit to this power, in slowly and beautifully adapting each form to the most complex relations of life. (1898, 267)

In other words, Darwin saw natural selection as "fine-tuning" each species to its environment, constantly favoring or rejecting any difference among individuals, no matter how "slight." This constant selection eventually changes one species so much it may be considered a new species. In addition, such constant selection, Darwin said, will also produce variation among populations within a species in response to slight differences in their environments. He referred to these populations as "varieties." Eventually, selection brings about such marked distinctions in varieties that two or more new species branch from the old one. These species, said Darwin, "are only well-marked varieties, of which the characters have become in a high degree permanent"(1898, 285).

According to this model, referred to as **Darwinian gradualism,** the family tree of species has relatively few, gracefully diverging branches (Figure 5.5). These represent the slow but steady pace at which individual species change through time and at which populations within species slowly become distinct from one another under the "scrutiny" of natural selection. The tree of evolution represents, in Darwin's words, "an interminable number of intermediate forms . . . linking together all the species . . . by [fine] gradations" (1898, 271–72).

Here, however, Darwin's model may be challenged. For one thing, the fossil record has failed to show intermediate forms with fine gradations for all evolutionary lines. Instead, fossil species often tend to remain relatively stable for long periods of time, and changes—new species—

Darwinian gradualism:
The view, held by Darwin, that evolution is slow and steady with cumulative change.

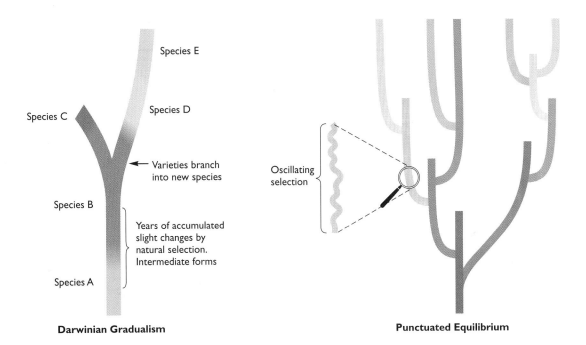

Darwinian Gradualism

Species E

Species C

Species D

← Varieties branch into new species

Species B

Years of accumulated slight changes by natural selection. Intermediate forms

Species A

Punctuated Equilibrium

Oscillating selection

FIGURE 5.5

Models of Evolution. According to Darwinian gradualism, the evolution of species through time is a slow, steady process. By contrast, according to the punctuated equilibrium model, major evolutionary change is the result of speciation, the branching of new species from existing ones. Individual species change relatively little through time, although natural selection still acts constantly to maintain a species' adaptation to its environment.

show up rather suddenly. For example, one of the first birds we know of for sure in the fossil record is not a mix of birdlike and dinosaurlike traits, a fifty-fifty combination, as one might expect if evolution were slow, gradual, and steady. Rather, *Archaeopteryx* (see Figure 5.4) is a perfectly good dinosaur with perfectly good feathers. Clearly, evolution here was not a slow, steady accumulation of many small changes, but was focused on the evolution of feathers and may have occurred fairly quickly. (It is important to remember that "quickly" in evolutionary perspective is, of course, a relative term and may mean *tens* of thousands of years or more.)

Similarly, the origin of our own group, the hominids, did not occur slowly and steadily, gradually producing a humanlike form from an apelike one. The first fully accepted hominid fossils, from over 4 million years ago, are, to exaggerate only slightly, apes that stood upright (see Chapter 10). The change was not gradual but was focused on bipedalism and was quick enough so that few other evolutionary changes had time to occur.

Another problem is more theoretical. If, as according to Darwin, each "slight variation" that natural selection favors is "good for the individual possessor," then we have to assume an adaptive benefit for *each small step* in the development of some trait. But could one-tenth of a wing, or one-hundredth of an eye—like a millimeter in those finches' beaks—*always* convey to its possessor a reproductive advantage over the members of its species that lack this trait?

It would seem, then, that evolutionary change over great spans of time is not the result of gradual change *within* species (individual species changing so much they become a new species) but, rather, the result of new species *branching from* existing species. Indeed, natural selection is not the creative "scrutinizing" force that Darwin envisioned but a more conservative force, simply eliminating what doesn't work adaptively and allowing to reproduce what does. Change *within* a species is limited.

This does not mean that natural selection has *no* effect on a species over time. Traits that are important may change back and forth as environmental conditions change. Recall the changes in beak size among the Darwin's finches studied by the Grants and their team. The data indicate that a slight difference in beak size among members of one species—as little as a millimeter or two—can be of adaptive importance during sudden, prolonged, or radical environmental changes such as droughts. In fact, small differences made the difference between life and death, and so, after such an environmental episode, the average beak size of an affected finch species could be significantly altered. When conditions—and thus food sources—returned to normal, the average beak size returned to its previous measurement. The average expression of important traits of a species, then, may change back and forth as environmental conditions change. This is called **oscillating selection.** But it is adaptive variation around a norm, rather than continual change in a particular direction—a sort of nondirectional fine-tuning.

So, natural selection is a conservative force, rejecting what doesn't work and allowing whatever does to reproduce. The role of natural selection is basically to maintain the adaptation of a species to its environment. Natural selection is not the author of evolution so much as the editor. Thus, species normally change little over the course of their tenure on earth, and new species seem to arise fairly quickly as a result of the isolation of populations within species through geographic separation, mutation, or a combination of both. Natural selection, of course, *then* plays an important role in screening the isolated population in terms of adaptive fitness.

We may describe this model of evolution as follows: The adaptive equilibrium of species with their environments is punctuated (interrupted) by the evolution of a new species from a population of the parent species. The parent species, in the meantime, may remain unchanged, at least for a time. This model is called **punctuated equilibrium** and is represented not by a tree with gracefully diverging branches but by a bush with many twigs (see Figure 5.5). These twigs are evolution's experiments, potential new species. Many twigs are short, since the species they represent became extinct over a short time. Some are longer, however, and give rise to yet more new species.

So, the evolution of life on earth cannot be depicted as a ladder or a chain representing the steady march of progress toward complexity, as Lamarck and other early scientists believed. Nor is it a gracefully branching tree, as Darwin pictured it. Instead, it is, in the words of Stephen Jay Gould (1994a, 91), a "luxuriant bush," more complex than we will probably ever know—a "blooming and buzzing confusion" (1985,355).

EVOLUTION QUESTIONED: THE PSEUDOSCIENCE OF "SCIENTIFIC CREATIONISM"

All the information about the theory of evolution presented in Chapters 3 and 4 has been developed and tested, using the methods and principles of science, over the past several hundred years by many people and from many different perspectives. Evolution is so well supported we consider the basic idea to be a fact, and it is the central concept of all biology, although we continue to apply the scientific method to our investigation of specific details. Our ideas about the generation of genetic variability, adaptation by natural selection, and the origin of species from existing species—all nicely explain everything we observe and understand about the living world.

We benefit from this knowledge every day of our lives. We eat foods from species of plants and animals bred according to the principles of genetics and selection. We know the causes of many of the illnesses that beset us because we understand the genetic operations of our cells, and we have insight into how some organisms (like viruses and bacteria) are adapted to other organisms (like us), and vice versa. Many of the antibiotics and other medicines that help us treat those illnesses work only because of the interrelatedness of all life. And this interrelatedness has also allowed us to manipulate the genes of other organisms, like bacteria, to "trick" them into producing, say, human insulin for the treatment of diabetes. This same techcnique is used in producing human growth hormone and interferon, a chemical found in our body's immune system. Moreover, recent advances in decoding the genome (see the "Contemporary

oscillating selection:
Adaptive variation around a norm, rather than in one direction, in response to environmental variation in a species' habitat.

punctuated equilibrium:
The view that species tend to remain stable and that evolutionary changes occur fairly suddenly.

Reflections" box in Chapter 3) have shown remarkable genetic similarities among even distantly related species. The basic genetic code for the development of eyes, for example, is pretty much the same in organisms from humans to fruit flies. Genes that control cell division in baker's yeast (a single-celled fungus) are matched by abnormal genes in human cancer cells.

So it is truly astounding that some people, even today, question the fact that evolution actually occurred, and many of these people base their questioning on religious belief. Why is this a problem? Think back to our discussion of science from Chapter 1. Science and belief systems are both important for the operation of any society, and, ideally, they operate in harmony with one another. They are still, however, distinct realms of knowledge, distinguished by the *testability* of science and the *faith* of belief.

But what about ideas that have characteristics of both? Suppose someone holds a scientific idea (an idea that is testable) but treats it as a belief by taking it on faith and by not testing it or recognizing the results of tests that have been applied to it, even if those tests refute it. Here's an example: There are people who believe that the lines in the palms of your hands and on your fingers hold information about your personal character and even, perhaps, about your future. This belief is called palmistry, and its precepts are quite scientifically testable. In fact, I examined them scientifically (Park 1982–83) and they failed. But will palmists all over the country close up shop because some anthropologist says their ideas are false? Hardly. Palmists take their ideas on faith. In other words, they treat a scientifically testable idea like a belief system. Thus, palmistry is a **pseudoscience,** or "false science."

Although pseudoscientific ideas like palmistry, astrology, or the power of crystals may be harmless enough, other examples have implications that may not be so benign. Some pseudoscientific ideas find support within established belief systems. There are—believe it or not—still people who want to think the earth is flat and who refuse to acknowledge the masses of scientific evidence to the contrary (Schadewald 1981–82). It turns out that a major source for this belief comes from literal interpretations of several biblical passages, for example, Matthew 4:8: "Again, the devil taketh him [Jesus] up into an exceedingly high mountain, and sheweth him all the kingdoms of the world. . . ." How, the flat-earthers ask, could Jesus have seen all the kingdoms of the earth unless the earth were flat?

Although most people recognize the allegorical sense of this and similar passages in both testaments of the Bible, there is a danger that some might find the issue terribly confusing. On the one hand, scientific evi-

pseudoscience: Scientifically testable ideas that are taken on faith, even if tested and shown to be false.

scientific creationism: The belief in a literal biblical interpretation regarding the creation of the universe, with the connected belief that this view is supported by scientific evidence.

FIGURE 5.6

Strata of the Grand Canyon in Arizona. Scientific creationists contend that these strata and all the fossils they contain are the results of the biblical flood. Scientific data show that the canyon's strata represent geological and biological events that took place over nearly 2 billion years. (See also Figure 2.2.)

dence—not to mention photographs taken from space—tells us unequivocally that the earth is a sphere. On the other hand, an interpretation of the chronicles of two major religions seems to say the earth is flat. Must one choose between science and religion? There are those who think so, and in the process, both science and belief suffer.

The idea of a flat earth is utterly ridiculous, but there is another pseudoscience, relevant to our topic here, that is far more complex and difficult to evaluate. It's called **scientific creationism.** It proposes that the entire universe, including the earth and all its inhabitants, were created spontaneously by untestable supernatural forces around 10,000 years ago. Except for minor changes within "kinds" of plants and animals (breeds of dogs, for example, or regional varieties of a wild species), no changes in living organisms have occurred. Certainly no *new* species have arisen. But, we might ask, what about the layers of rock and soil and the fossils they contain? According to supporters of scientific creationism, those are the results of "a primeval watery cataclysm" (Morris 1974, 22), a great flood, in other words (Figure 5.6).

Contemporary Reflections

Can We See Evolution in Action?

When we look around us, it seems as if the world is a fairly stable place, biologically speaking any-way. Certainly we hear of species becoming extinct at a rapid rate (see the "Contemporary Reflec-tions" box in Chapter 6), but otherwise we don't see much change. There doesn't seem to be any evolution still going on. But there is, of course.

The problem is one of scale. We tend to see the world from our perspective—as large mam-mals with large brains that afford us a great deal of control over our environments. We have an amazing ability to live in a wide variety of environmental conditions and to withstand a wide range of environmental extremes. But most creatures are a lot smaller than we are, and most are far more at the mercy of their environments. And we rarely see things from the point of view of our genes.

By definition, evolution is phenotypic change across generations, involving at the most basic level genetic change. Much genetic change is brought about by the processes of mutation, gene flow, and genetic drift (fission, the founder effect, and gamete sampling). These processes are *always* taking place. Indeed, given the mobility of our species and our proclivity for exchanging genes, gene flow and the forms of genetic drift might be seen as particularly powerful processes of evolu-tion for us. The human species is evolving all the time, by these processes alone.

What about natural selection? As noted in the "Contemporary Reflections" box in Chapter 4, natural selection is certainly still taking place in our species, although, again because of scale—es-pecially our long life spans—we might not always perceive it. But look to some other species.

In the woods in back of my house there are numerous small stands of young pine trees. Where the trees are very young, a foot tall or less, they can grow in quite dense concentrations. I counted six small trees growing in a 1-square-foot area of forest floor. A square foot, however, is hardly enough space for six full-grown pines. There will be fewer plants there next year, fewer still the

Sound familiar? It should. This argument derives directly from one literal interpretation of the first eight chapters of the Book of Genesis, and it is clearly in direct opposition to all the data and ideas accumulated and tested by science. More than 200 years of scientific inquiry tell us that the universe, including the earth and its inhabitants, arose through knowable, natural processes. The universe is at least 12 billion years old, the earth 4.5 billion years old, and life on earth nearly 4 billion years old. Living organisms do change through time, and species give rise to new species. The geological and fossil records are the records of these billions of years of change. We're been covering the evidence, data, and argu-ments for evolution in these last few chapters.

next year, and fewer the next. Many years from now, with luck, there will be one adult tree in that space. Only one will have the characteristics that will allow it to out-compete the others—greater height to catch more sun, greater ability to withstand insects, cold, and drought—whatever makes successful pine trees successful. Only one will be left to reproduce and pass on those traits that made it successful. Natural selection right in my backyard. Evolution in action.

But evolution in its broadest sense involves the origin of new species. Can we see this? Think about how new species evolve, but *don't* think on our human scale. There must be new species of small organisms evolving all the time. Speciation in microbes must be very common indeed. And even with larger organisms, whose generation times are longer, we can see distinct evidence of evolution. Although we recognize and name thirteen species of Darwin's finches on the Galápagos, the Grants and their team noted that some of those species can interbreed when altered environmental circumstances cause their niches to overlap. In other words, they are still in the process of becoming completely separate species. With several species of Darwin's finches, we have caught speciation in the act.

In another striking example, a recent study (Johnson et al. 1996) has indicated that the basin of Lake Victoria in East Africa was completely dry only 12,000 years ago. And yet there are 300 distinct but closely related species of cichlid fishes in the lake, species found *nowhere else*. (Cichlids are common fishes in home aquariums.) Clearly all these species have arisen over the past 12,000 years from, according to DNA studies, a single ancestral species. Apparently, cichlids are poor swimmers that prefer certain habitats and don't move around much. They may also have a tendency not to select mates outside their local group. So small populations could quickly become isolated, and this could account for what seems to be the world's record for speciation rate in a vertebrate (Yoon 1996a).

Evolution—even the origin of new species—is happening all around us. We just have to look carefully enough.

Scientific creationism is thus a pseudoscience—a testable set of ideas that even in the face of contrary evidence are accepted on faith. But scientific creationism goes further. Its proponents claim its ideas are, indeed, supported by scientific evidence that also refutes the accepted theory of evolution. That the creation model coincides with one interpretation of Genesis merely shows, they say, the scientific accuracy of the Bible. Because advocates of scientific creationism claim both models are scientific, they feel both should be taught in science classes as viable alternative explanations for the origin and diversity of life.

The argument is persuasive, especially in a society like ours, concerned with religious freedom and with our American senses of fair play and equal time. *But equal time is for equivalent things.* There is not a single shred of scientific evidence in support of the creation model.

To teach scientific creationism alongside evolution would be to violate the religious freedoms of those who do not subscribe to a strict creationist interpretation. It would also badly confuse those trying to learn how science really operates and what conclusions about our world science has arrived at. The distinction between science and belief would be blurred, interfering with the harmonious and important relationship between the two.

The quality of our lives now and in the future depends on the continued progress of our testable scientific knowledge, mediated by the values of our belief systems. We need to understand what these two areas of knowledge are and how they interact, and we must promote free access to, and sharing of, all knowledge.

▽   ▽   ▽

SUMMARY

The evolution of new species is an obvious result of the interacting processes of genetic variation, natural selection, and environmental change. New species arise when a population within an existing species becomes isolated. Isolation is usually geographic but may also be the result of a macromutation. In isolation, this new population experiences the processes of genetic variation and phenotypic adaptation separate from the parent species. Among the differentiating traits that result may be characters that act as reproductive isolating mechanisms, meaning that even if the populations once again have the opportunity to interbreed, they will probably not be able to do so. They will have become separate species.

The process of speciation, occurring countless times over the billions of years of life's history, has produced the incredible array of living forms we know today and see in the fossil record. The species we know about only hint at the variety that exists today and has existed in the past. When species have the opportunity, they are able to adaptively radiate into new niches, and the increased diversity of living forms is the result. It must be remembered, however, that all these forms are variations on the single theme of life that originated on this planet. All life, through speciation and adaptive radiation, is descended from a single origin.

We can depict evolution as a luxuriant bush, dense with innumerable twigs, each representing a new species. We use the bush as a metaphor for evolution for two reasons. First, we realize that the conditions for speciation are continuously being produced, so that speciation has probably taken place more often than we can imagine. Second, we understand that Darwin's model of the origin of species, driven by the steady, gradual "fine-tuning" of natural selection, is not accurate. Natural selection is a conservative force, acting largely to maintain a species' adaptation. What produces new species is geographic or genetic isolation, and these processes act relatively quickly.

The evidence for evolution is overwhelming. We are still examining the specific details of evolutionary theory, but the idea of evolution and our knowledge of the essential processes involved are hypotheses that have passed numerous scientific tests and failed none. They are *theories* in the scientific sense of the word. The evidence for evolution is as strong as, say, the evidence for the theory that the earth revolves around the sun. Nonetheless, some people, for reasons that have nothing to do with science, claim that evolution did not occur. These claims have been examined scientifically, and they have been shown to be scientifically invalid. Their proponents, however, continue to insist on their accuracy. These claims are thus pseudoscience, and they confuse the important relationship between science and belief systems; for, in fact, there is no necessary conflict between the two.

QUESTIONS FOR FURTHER THOUGHT

1. Does the conflict between scientific creationism and mainstream evolutionary science mean that we must choose between science and religion? Are the two realms of knowledge, with regard to this subject, incompatible?

2. Consider the processes of evolution and speciation. Can you think of any examples of these processes in action today? How are human influences on the world part of these processes? Or are they? Do these processes still affect our species? If so, how?

3. The result of adaptive radiation is biodiversity. Human actions are threatening the rich biodiversity of the planet. Is there a real problem with this, beyond the loss of some interesting or attractive species? How might diversity in and of itself be vital to the health of the planet?

KEY TERMS

reproductive isolating
  mechanism

hominids

speciation

macromutations

adaptive radiation

generalized

specialized

nocturnal

prosimian

diurnal

arboreal

Darwinian gradualism

oscillating selection

punctuated
  equilibrium

pseudoscience

scientific creationism

SUGGESTED READINGS

You should certainly have a look at the book that began our modern understanding of evolution, Darwin's *Origin of Species*. The last chapter, "Recapitulation and Conclusion," nicely summarizes his arguments and provides a good idea of his style.

A wonderful book on evolutionary processes, the origin of new species, and the variety of living things is Edward O. Wilson's *The Diversity of Life*.

For more on Darwin's finches, see Jonathan Weiner's *The Beak of the Finch*.

One of the originators of the model of punctuated equilibrium is biologist Stephen Jay Gould, and many of his articles concern that model. Try "The Episodic Nature of Evolutionary Change" and "Return of the Hopeful Monster," both in *The Panda's Thumb*.

Gould has also addressed the shape of the evolutionary bush. See his informative books *Wonderful Life* and *Full House* and his article in the October 1994 *Scientific American*, "The Evolution of Life on the Earth."

For an idea of the arguments of the scientific creationists, try *Evolution: The Fossils Say No!* by Duane T. Gish. For a refutation of scientific creationism, go once again to Stephen Jay Gould and a series of articles on the subject in *Hen's Teeth and Horse's Toes*.

The National Center for Science Education, Inc. (NCSE) works to support the teaching of evolution and to increase public understanding of evolution and science. They publish "Reports of the NCSE," which contain interesting and useful articles on all aspects of this topic. Their website is www.natcenscied.org.

The relationship between science and philosophical ideas, brought out so powerfully by the issue of scientific creationism, is addressed in Kenneth Miller's "Finding Darwin's God," and in Stephen Jay Gould's *Rocks of Ages*; for a very broad discussion, see *Consilience*, by Edward O. Wilson.

A BRIEF EVOLUTIONARY TIMETABLE

... and there is no new
thing under the sun.
—Ecclesiastes 1:9

Anthropology focuses on one group of organisms, the hominids, and deals mostly with a single species of hominid, *Homo sapiens*. Hominids have been around for 5 or 6 million years. Depending upon one's interpretation (see Chapter 12), our species has inhabited the earth for 2 million years at most. Although this seems like a long time to us, it is really just the last tick of the earth's evolutionary clock, four-hundredths of 1 percent (0.04 percent) of the history of our planet, and one-hundredth of 1 percent (0.01 percent) of the estimated history of the universe. If the history of the universe were reduced to a single year, our species would not show up until after 11:30 P.M. on December 31.

So, although we focus on *us*, we need to appreciate the fact that all the processes of evolution apply to all forms of life on earth and that the idea of evolution—change through time—applies to the whole history of the universe.

Before we focus on ourselves, our close relatives, and our immediate ancestors, we need to put human evolution in context, to see it as part of a long and ongoing series of changes that began some 15 billion years ago.

Following are two questions we will consider in this chapter:

What is the history of the universe, the earth, and life on earth?

What processes and events have affected the overall history of the earth and life on earth?

FROM THE BEGINNING: A QUICK HISTORY

The origin of the universe is shrouded in mystery. We don't, in all honesty, really know exactly how old it is, although 15 billion years is an average of recent estimates. We do know, however, that the universe is expanding in all directions. All the galaxies in the universe (an estimated 50 billion) are constantly traveling farther away from each other. A logical conclusion from this fact is that the universe began at a single location, and evidence indicates that it started as an incredibly tiny, dense, and hot speck (the proper term is a *singularity*) composed of pure energy that would one day become all the energy and space and matter—including us—of the universe we know.

At the beginning of time—we'll use 15 billion years ago—this speck began to expand, an event commonly called the Big Bang, although it wasn't really an explosion. It was more like a balloon being rapidly inflated—a balloon that contained both energy and space. It is hypothe-

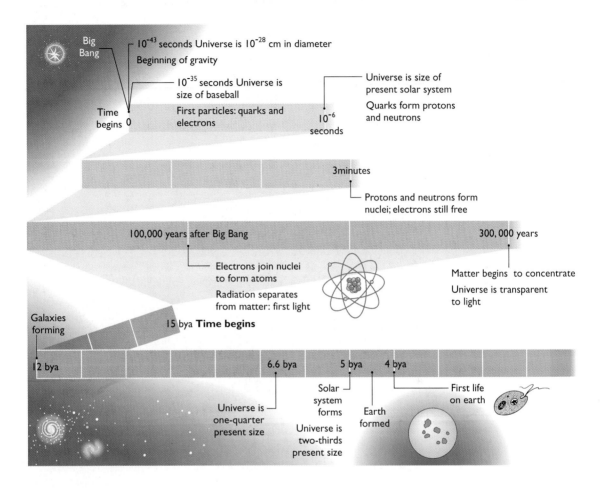

FIGURE 6.1
History of the Universe, from the Big Bang to the Origin of Life on Earth. The scale of the timeline changes because some events are condensed into incredibly small periods and others are stretched over unimaginable spans.

sized that this inflation was caused by the accumulation of a material that produced a repulsive force—the opposite of gravity's attracting force. The details of the Big Bang are still a matter of intense debate and are among the most complex issues in science. For our purposes here, suffice it to say that as the newborn universe expanded, it cooled, and matter quickly condensed from energy (Figure 6.1). Within 3 minutes after the beginning, protons and neutrons had formed and had joined to make atomic nuclei, but it took another 100,000 years for electrons to join the nuclei to form atoms. At about the same time, radiation separated from matter and there was light, but for the next 200,000 years the universe was still too dense for that light to travel through it.

By 12 billion years ago (bya), galaxies had begun to form as gravity pulled matter together into huge clusters. These were made up of stars

FIGURE 6.2

Stromatolites in Australia, (*top*), are formed when mats of blue-green algae (single-celled organisms), are covered with sand, silt, and mud, which the algae cement down and then grow over. Fossil stromatolites (*bottom*), and thus the organisms that made them, have been dated to 3.5 bya.

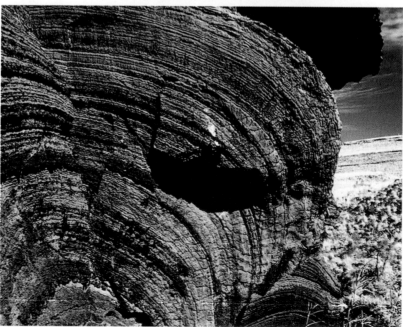

that were mainly hydrogen, the simplest element. As a result of the nuclear reactions in these stars, heavier, more complex elements formed. When these early stars died in tremendous supernova explosions, their elements were scattered into space, some eventually to contribute to the formation of new galaxies with all their stars and, in several known cases, planets. (Planets have recently been discovered orbiting other stars in our galaxy.)

About 5 bya, when the universe was two-thirds its present size, our solar system formed around a medium-sized star in the Milky Way galaxy. Earth, the third of nine planets orbiting that star, came into being 500 million years later. Amazingly, in less than a billion years—3.8 bya—life on earth was established. We know this indirectly from fossils found in Greenland, southern Africa, and Australia (Figure 6.2). In Australia there are also actual fossils, preserved in stone, of single-celled organisms from at least 2.8 bya, many of which were probably already capable of **photosynthesis.**

Just how life came about on the earth is also a matter of debate. For over 40 years, scientists have been able to produce carbon-rich **organic** compounds from **inorganic** compounds with a fairly simple laboratory procedure, showing that the process could have occurred quite easily. In fact, they have been able to produce amino acids, which, as you recall, are the building blocks of proteins. But, as you also recall, proteins cannot be built without a nucleic acid code. Evidence now suggests that RNA formed very early in earth's history. RNA was able to replicate itself and act as a code for the synthesis of proteins. Later, DNA took over this role (Orgel 1994). It is still, of course, a long way from amino acids and RNA to a living organism, and the details of this path remain unclear.

Whatever happened, it happened fast (about 700 million years from the formation of the earth to life *is* fast, in the geological time scale), but once established, life at first evolved slowly. The world's first identifiable organisms were simple single cells like bacteria (Figure 6.3). It wasn't until about 2 bya that complex single-celled organisms containing nuclei and organelles evolved (see Figure 3.1). Multicellular organisms first appeared about 1.7 bya. The earliest evidence for life on land—bacteria or perhaps fungi—dates to 1.2 bya.

All these early single-celled organisms reproduced **asexually** by splitting and making copies of themselves. Evolutionary change relied entirely on mutations. Then about 1 bya, some organisms began to reproduce **sexually.** Sexual reproduction may have begun as a mechanism of genetic exchange to replace defective genes. Soon, however, it proved to be an accelerator of evolution. Now, in addition to mutation, fertilization also provided genetic and phenotypic variation, and evolutionary change

FIGURE 6.3
This typical bacterium represents some of the earliest forms of life on earth and what are still—in terms of time and numbers—the dominant forms of life today.

photosynthesis: The process by which plants manufacture their own nutrients from carbon dioxide and water, using chlorophyll as a catalyst and sunlight as an energy source.

organic: Molecules that are part of living organisms. They are based on the chemistry of carbon and contain mostly hydrogen, oxygen, carbon, and nitrogen. Even carbon-based molecules that are not found in living things are sometimes referred to as organic.

inorganic: A molecule not containing carbon.

asexually: Reproducing without sex, by fissioning or budding.

sexually: Reproducing by combining genetic material from two individuals.

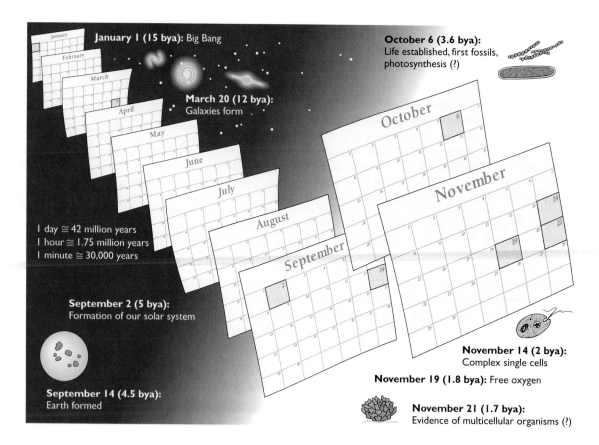

January 1 (15 bya): Big Bang

March 20 (12 bya): Galaxies form

October 6 (3.6 bya): Life established, first fossils, photosynthesis (?)

1 day ≅ 42 million years
1 hour ≅ 1.75 million years
1 minute ≅ 30,000 years

September 2 (5 bya): Formation of our solar system

September 14 (4.5 bya): Earth formed

November 14 (2 bya): Complex single cells

November 19 (1.8 bya): Free oxygen

November 21 (1.7 bya): Evidence of multicellular organisms (?)

FIGURE 6.4

Astronomer Carl Sagan likened the history of the universe to a single calendar year in his 1975 Pulitzer Prize–winning book *The Dragons of Eden*. This calendar has been recalculated to show the currently accepted dates for important events.
(Adapted from Sagan, 1977)

vertebrates: Organisms with backbones.

quickly started to gain speed. Figure 6.4 summarizes what is known about the timing of important events in the evolution of life on earth.

About 543 million years ago (mya), in the Cambrian period, complex multicellular organisms burst on the scene. Some even possessed hard parts like shells. So sudden and rapid was this event that it is referred to as the Cambrian Explosion. In a mere 5 million years, all major body plans of multicellular animals had evolved, including ancestors of the **vertebrates,** animals with backbones (Figure 6.5). So far, there are no explanations for this "explosion" that everyone agrees upon, but it is clearly a major event in the history of life. The evolution of animals since the Cambrian has been, essentially, variations on the themes set during that relatively brief time (Gould 1989, 1995b).

By 425 mya, fish had evolved, and plants and animals began to colonize the land. Insects appeared about 400 mya; by 350 mya, some of them had evolved wings. Reptiles showed up around 350 mya as well, and the reptilian form that is thought to have given rise to the mammals was

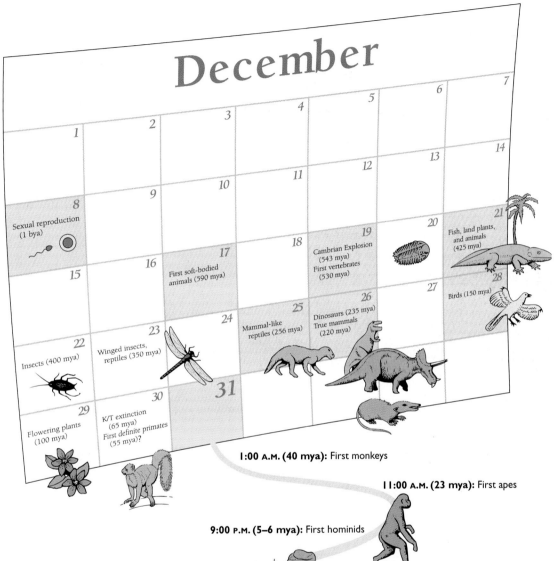

December

1

2

3

4

5

6

7

8
Sexual reproduction
(1 bya)

9

10

11

12

13

14

15

16

17
First soft-bodied
animals (590 mya)

18

19
Cambrian Explosion
(543 mya)
First vertebrates
(530 mya)

20

21
Fish, land plants,
and animals
(425 mya)

22
Insects (400 mya)

23
Winged insects,
reptiles (350 mya)

24

25
Mammal-like
reptiles (256 mya)

26
Dinosaurs (235 mya)
True mammals
(220 mya)

27

28
Birds (150 mya)

29
Flowering plants
(100 mya)

30
K/T extinction
(65 mya)
First definite primates
(55 mya)?

31

1:00 A.M. (40 mya): First monkeys

11:00 A.M. (23 mya): First apes

9:00 P.M. (5–6 mya): First hominids

10:30 P.M. (2.5 mya): First stone tools

11:22 P.M. (0.5 mya): First use of fire

11:59 P.M. (30,000 ya): Cave paintings

11:59:35 P.M. (12,000 ya): Farming

11:59:55 P.M. (2,000 ya): Common Era begins

11:59:59 P.M. (500 ya): Renaissance

FIGURE 6.5
Cambrian fauna consisted mostly of arthropods, ancestors of modern-day insects, spiders, and crustaceans. The large creature in the center grew to 3 feet long. The flowerlike animals on the right are unclassified.

found at about 256 mya. Dinosaurs began evolving around 235 mya, with true mammals appearing about 220 mya. Sometime around 150 mya, a small dinosaur with feathers signaled the beginning of the evolution of birds (see Figure 5.4). Flowering plants appeared only a little more than 100 mya, and the primates, the group to which humans belong, showed up about 55 mya, perhaps earlier.

DRIFTING CONTINENTS AND MASS EXTINCTIONS: THE PACE OF CHANGE

plate tectonics: The movement of the plates of the earth's crust, caused by their interaction with the molten rock of the earth's interior. The cause of continental drift.

During all this time, life was not the only thing evolving on earth. The earth itself was also evolving as the continents changed shape and position, a phenomenon known as *continental drift,* which operates through the process of **plate tectonics.** The outer layer of rock on the earth, the *crust,* is in a constant state of change. It is broken into some sixteen *plates* of various sizes that fit together like a huge spherical jigsaw puzzle. The motion of the molten rock, *magma,* below the crust causes the plates to

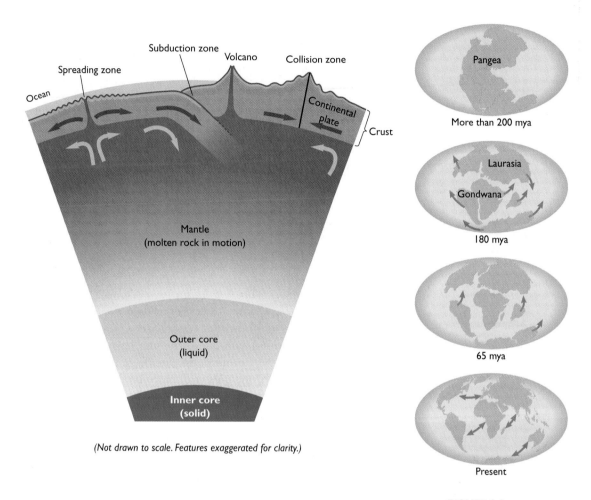

(Not drawn to scale. Features exaggerated for clarity.)

FIGURE 6.6
This cross section of the earth shows the process of plate tectonics and the resultant drift of the continents over the past 200 million years. Continental drift, of course, occurred prior to 200 mya and will continue into the future as well.

change shape and location. In some areas, magma seeps up between the plates and solidifies, pushing the plates apart. Something has to give, and at other boundaries called *subduction zones*, one plate is pushed under another and plunges deep within the earth, where it melts and adds to the magma. Clearly, then, the continents—those parts of the plates that protrude above sea level—have shifted over time and will continue to do so (Figure 6.6). It should also be noted that plate tectonics accounts for important geological phenomena. Where the plates meet and move against one another, tremendous forces are produced that cause earthquakes, volcanos, and mountain building.

By the time the dinosaurs and early mammals had appeared, all the continents had drifted together to form a huge supercontinent we call

FIGURE 6.7
This painting, by the late Rudolph Zallinger, reflects some now outdated ideas about the appearance and behavior of the dinosaurs. It does show, however, some of the variety of these creatures as they existed over 170 million years of time (from left to right in the mural). The dinosaurs once dominated the earth's environments. (The mural is shown here reversed from its original orientation).

Pangea, literally "all lands." This is why, for example, we find fossils of the same type of dinosaur in what are now such widely separated places as China, North America, and Antarctica. Around 200 mya, Pangea began to break up, and the resulting landmasses—the ancestors of our present-day continents—drifted over the globe, producing a diversity of environments and geographical boundaries that has profoundly affected the nature of life on earth as we know it today.

From all we've discussed so far, it would seem that the evolution of the earth and of life—influenced by continental drift and the environmental changes it brings about—has been a steady process. And basically, it has been—relative to the immense amount of time involved. But the fossil record shows that at least five times in the planet's history, some change has taken place that was so rapid and extensive that it radically altered the course of biological evolution by causing a mass extinction.

For example, about the time the continents were drifting together to form the supercontinent of Pangea—at the end of the Permian period (250 mya)—over 95 percent of all species of marine and terrestrial organisms suddenly became extinct. Some changes occurred to which none of the variants within all those species were adapted. The cause for this greatest of all mass extinctions is not known for sure, but a new hypothesis suggests it was the result of massive volcanic eruptions in what is now Siberia that altered the planet's climate. At any rate, such a catastrophe certainly had a major effect on the future course of life's evolution.

Other mass extinctions do not have such a "down-to-earth" explanation, and one of these directly affected the evolution of our small section of the evolutionary bush. About 65 mya, the dinosaurs were a dominant form of land animals. There were large reptiles in the seas and close relatives of the dinosaurs in the air (Figure 6.7). Mammals were also around, and had been for nearly as long as the dinosaurs. In terms of ecological niches, however, mammals didn't have many places to go because other niches were already occupied.

Then one day—literally—an asteroid, thought to measure 6 miles across, crashed through the earth's atmosphere and into the crust where the north coast of the Mexican Yucatán is now. The impact made a crater 200 miles in diameter. The asteroid may have broken apart on impact with the atmosphere, and pieces may have hit in other locations as well.

This collision created a blast like that of a nuclear explosion. Thousands of cubic miles of vaporized rock, water vapor, and small particles and dust were shot into the atmosphere, where they were carried around the world. Heat from the impact caused massive forest fires that created smoke and ash. One hypothesis suggests that the impact produced shock waves that bounced inside the earth and were focused on the opposite side of the planet, causing large-scale volcanic activity that put even more smoke and ash into the air. It has recently been noted that the Yucatán is rich in sulfur, suggesting that the impact might have produced sulfuric acid in the atmosphere, causing acid rain. All this matter would have created a blanket that blocked sunlight, cooling the earth and preventing green plants from carrying out photosynthesis.

These extensive environmental changes proved disastrous (a word that means, appropriately, "bad star"). Dinosaurs became extinct, along with every other species of land animal weighing more than about 55 pounds, many plants, and much of the ocean's plankton, the small

Pangea: The supercontinent that included parts of all present-day landmasses.

Contemporary Reflections

Are Mass Extinctions a Thing of the Past?

Extinction is part of evolution. For one reason or another, species become extinct all the time. An estimated 95 percent of all species that have ever existed are now extinct.

But the idea of some intense event that can bring about the extinction of up to 90 percent of the earth's living forms over a short period of time seems inconceivable to us. And yet, at least five such events have occurred over the 3.8-billion-year history of life on this planet. The best known of these wiped out the dinosaurs—a long-lived and very successful group of species—65 million years ago. Surely, we think, these events were part of the earth's "formative" years and could not happen again. Sadly, this view is incorrect—for two reasons.

First, we know that the mass extinction that included the dinosaurs was initiated by the impact of a huge asteroid, and impacts are associated with some of the other mass extinctions as well. Although impacts were more common in the past, asteroids, comets, and fragments of them are far from used up. Lots of them still orbit through our solar system. Go outside on any clear night, look up long enough, and you're bound to see one of the smaller ones burn up as it hits the earth's atmosphere. These are so-called shooting stars. Bigger ones, parts of which survive the atmosphere, hit the earth regularly (although most are neither seen nor found).

And, on occasion, we encounter very large ones. A few years ago, an asteroid large enough to do serious damage missed the earth by a mere 250,000 miles—the distance between the earth and the moon, a near miss on the cosmic scale. It was not seen until it had already passed us!

In 1908, a large portion of an asteroid or a fragment of a comet nucleus exploded 6 miles up in the atmosphere over Siberia. The shock waves were heard 600 miles away and flattened trees over

organisms that provide a great deal of the world's oxygen and that act as an important source of food at the base of the food chain. This event is the famous *Cretaceous/Tertiary (K/T) extinction.*

But, many of the mammals survived. Perhaps, by a stroke of luck, they already were adapted to withstand adverse, changing conditions. Now, with the dinosaurs suddenly gone, a whole world of new niches was open to them and to many other creatures that had made it through the catastrophe. This group included some of the birds, thought by many to be the dinosaurs' only living direct descendants (Figure 6.8).

So rapid was the mammals' adaptive radiation that within about 20 million years, all the major types of mammals we know today had appeared—everything from bats to whales to a group of tree-dwelling creatures possessed of acute eyesight, dexterous hands, and large, inquisitive brains. These were the primates, and it is this group that we shall focus on in the next chapters.

770 square miles. It's altogether possible, then, that our planet will be hit by another large object from space in the future, and, if it's big enough, devastating consequences will follow, including the extinction of many species.

But there is a second reason why mass extinctions are not things of the past—a reason even more disturbing since (unlike the situation with asteroids) we *could* do something about it. There is, in fact, a sixth mass extinction in earth's history, and it is happening right now.

Starting about 10,000 years ago, species began becoming extinct at a rate faster than usual. At present, species are disappearing at a rate at least as fast as, and probably faster than, during any of the previous five mass extinctions (Eldredge 1991, 1995; Leakey and Lewin 1995). Estimates vary, but the earth may be losing species at a rate of 27,000 a year—that's 3 every hour. Now, one might argue that given what we know of earth's history, extinctions—even mass ones—are "natural." Well, they have been; but this one is different. Unlike the other extinctions, where the conditions causing the problem eventually went away, this situation is unlikely to get better because, as biologist Niles Eldredge says, "the irritant . . . remains on the scene" (1995, 128). That "irritant," of course, is us.

Since we figured out how to control natural food sources through farming and animal husbandry some 12,000 years ago, our species' population has grown at an ever-increasing rate. Our need for resources, energy, and space has grown along with our numbers. We have pushed other species into marginal areas, destroyed their habitats and resources, and hunted or otherwise exploited them to extinction. We are well into the process of changing the very climate of the earth as our emissions into the atmosphere are causing the world's climate to warm.

Although we may or may not experience the catastrophic death and destruction of an asteroid impact, we are—*right now*—in the midst of what may be the biggest, fastest of all mass extinctions. Decidedly *not* a thing of the past.

FIGURE 6.8
The wild turkey shows a striking similarity to bipedal dinosaurs, further evidence of the evolutionary relationship between dinosaurs and birds.

▽   ▽   ▽

SUMMARY

This narrative of the history of the universe has been necessarily brief, but it does point out three themes that are important to remember as we continue.

First, it could be said—by virtue of human numbers (over 6 billion) and our impact on the planet—that we are the dominant species on the earth today. But our evolutionary history makes up a small fraction of the whole history of the universe and even of the earth. We are the new kids on the evolutionary block, and we have not as yet even proved ourselves successful by the criterion of longevity. Cockroaches have been around hundreds of times longer than we have; bacteria have been around since the beginning of the fossil record. By these standards, our species is in its infancy.

Second, as the Bible says, "there is no new thing under the sun." Indeed, although we often speak of the "origin of the earth" or the "origin of life," the only *real* origin is that of the universe itself. All the events listed above have been *rearrangements* of what already existed: matter condensing from energy as it cools; large atomic particles forming from smaller ones; stars coming together from cosmic dust; heavy elements being created from lighter ones in the nuclear furnaces of those stars; the elements of inorganic molecules being rearranged to form the molecules of life; and the shuffling of the genetic code, producing the extraordinary multitude of living things that have inhabited this planet.

Third, and perhaps most humbling, the specific history of the universe, including the earth and its life, could have happened in countless other ways. Each event in our story is contingent upon preceding events. Even our evolution is dependent upon the specific sequence of events that came before it. If those events had been different, *we* might be different— or we might not be here at all. Imagine if that asteroid had *not* hit the earth 65 million years ago. In other words, the evolution of humans—or anything else for that matter—was not inevitable. We're lucky we're here.

QUESTIONS FOR FURTHER THOUGHT

1. Consider a question from Chapter 5, from a more specific perspective: We humans may be bringing about the extinction of a large number of other species, but for some of them, what real difference does it make? We hear about such endangered species as the snail darter (a small North American fish), the spotted owl, and the Texas blind salamander. Would it really matter, beyond an ethical or an aesthetic consideration, if any of these became extinct?

2. The astronomer Carl Sagan once referred to human beings as "star stuff." He meant it literally. How so? What does this say about the nature of evolution, both on a biological as well as a cosmic level?

KEY TERMS

photosynthesis	asexually	plate tectonics
organic	sexually	Pangea
inorganic	vertebrates	

SUGGESTED READINGS

For an update on the latest thinking in cosmology—the history of the universe—see the February 2000 issue of *Natural History*, especially "Genesis: The Sequel," by Alan Guth. For a good discussion of the science behind our understanding of the history of the universe, I recommend *Coming of Age in the Milky Way*, by Timothy Ferris.

The evolution of life is covered in the lavishly illustrated *The Book of Life*, edited by Stephen Jay Gould. For a good narrative approach, see *Life*, by Richard Fortey, and for a more technical but still readable work, see *History of Life*, second edition, by Richard Cowen. *National Geographic* has a series of articles called "The Rise of Life on Earth" in the March 1998, April 1998, May 1999, February 2000, and September 2000 issues.

The Cambrian Explosion is the subject of an article by R. Gore in the October 1993 *National Geographic*, "Explosion of Life: The Cambrian Period." It is also the focus of Stephen Jay Gould's *Wonderful Life* and Simon Conway Morris's *The Crucible of Creation*. These two well-respected authorities disagree on the meaning of the Cambrian fossils and the nature of evolution as a series of contingent events. For a summary of their debate, see "Showdown on the Burgess Shale," by Morris and Gould, in the December 1998/January 1999 *Natural History*.

The subject of mass extinctions is discussed in Edward O. Wilson's *Diversity of Life* and in an article in the June 1998 *National Geographic*, "The March Toward Extinction," by R. Gore.

To see animations of continental drift, go to www.scotese.com/pangeanim.htm. A good site on the geology of North America is tapestry.usgs.gov/Default.html. It's called "Tapestry of Time and Terraine" and features a section called "Rocks of Ages" that discusses the different geological divisions of earth history.

CHAPTER

7

THE
PRIMATES

I confess freely to you,
I could never look long
upon a monkey,
without very mortifying
reflections.
—William Congreve
(1695)

"The proper study of mankind is man," said the poet Alexander Pope. The last few chapters should have convinced you that even biological anthropologists, who by definition focus on the study of mankind (or, more properly, humankind), cannot limit their interests to just our own species. The processes that have produced modern *Homo sapiens* are the processes that have produced every single species that has ever inhabited this planet. Additionally, all those species are part of an integrated whole, composed of all environments and all living things in complex interaction with one another across geographical space and through evolutionary time.

Moreover, were we to limit our study just to our species, or even to the hominids in general, we would lose a great deal of perspective. We need to compare ourselves to other forms of life to see in what ways we are similar and in what ways we differ. This comparison is made all the more important because we *are* the species we are studying, and so it can be difficult to be objective about ourselves. Thus, primatology is an important part of anthropology.

In this chapter we will address several important questions:

What is our place in nature; that is, where do we fit—from a scientifically objective point of view—in the world of living things?

What are the characteristics of the primates—the group of animals of which we are a part?

In what ways are humans like the other primates? In what ways are we unique?

NAMING THE ANIMALS

We have already discussed the concept of the species, the natural unit of classification. Each organism belongs to a *specific species* (the words come from the same root), a group of potentially interbreeding individuals that are reproductively isolated from other groups.

The most cursory examination, however, shows clearly that there are larger units of classification of living things. Some species are more similar to one another than they are to other species. The Book of Genesis, for example, does not name each species that God creates, but it lists general categories: "the fish of the sea," "the fowl of the air," "every herb of the field," "every beast of the earth."

TABLE 7.1
Taxonomy of Five Familiar Species

	Human	*Chimpanzee*	*Bonobo*	*Gorilla*	*Orangutan*
Kingdom	Animalia	Animalia	Animalia	Animalia	Animalia
Phylum	Chordata	Chordata	Chordata	Chordata	Chordata
Class	Mammalia	Mammalia	Mammalia	Mammalia	Mammalia
Order	Primates	Primates	Primates	Primates	Primates
Family	Hominidae	Pongidae	Pongidae	Pongidae	Pongidae
Genus	Homo	Pan	Pan	Gorilla	Pongo
Species	sapiens	troglodytes	paniscus	gorilla	pygmaeus

Taxonomy

The idea that species had similarities so struck Swedish botanist Carolus Linnaeus (introduced in Chapter 2) that he devised a taxonomic system to name and thus categorize all living creatures. A **taxonomy** is a classification based on similarities and differences. I have, for example, accumulated thousands of notes, articles, and other important individual pieces of paper in my years as a bioanthropologist. If I simply stored all these together randomly, I'd never find anything when I needed to refer to it. Instead, I file my papers according to general categories and subcategories nested within them. For instance, I have a file cabinet marked "Biological Anthropology." One of its drawers is marked "Evolution," and within that drawer is a file folder marked "Taxonomy," where I keep notes and copies of articles on Linnaeus and the related matters I'm now writing about.

Similarly, Linnaeus (who used Latin names and even latinized his original name, Carl von Linné) devised a system, published in final form in 1758, that used four nested categories—class, order, genus, and species. Modern taxonomy recognizes seven basic categories but may use additional categories when needed. Table 7.1 shows a traditional Linnaean taxonomy for five familiar species. We'll detail the taxonomy of our species to show what Linnaeus's system accomplishes.

It should be noted that a species is never referred to by just the species name, listed in the bottom row of the table. The species name is

taxonomy: A classification based on similarities and differences.

FIGURE 7.1

Shown here is an amphioxus, a chordate with a notochord but no bony spine (shown about four times life size).

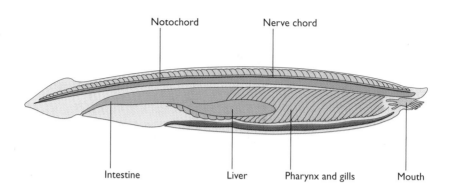

Notochord   Nerve chord

Intestine   Liver   Pharynx and gills   Mouth

usually descriptive, and so there may be many species that share the same name. Many African animals have the species name *africanus*, for example. The chimpanzee shares its species name, *troglodytes*, with the winter wren, a small North American bird (the name conveying the erroneous assumption that these species are cave dwellers). It takes *both* the genus and species names to denote a particular species. We are, for instance, *Homo sapiens*.

Humans are members of the kingdom called Animalia. We share this grouping with the other four species in Table 7.1 by virtue of the fact that we all ingest our food, have sense organs and nervous systems, and are capable of intentional movement. We are not members of any of the other three kingdoms of eukaryotes (organisms whose cells have nuclei): complex single-celled organisms (amoebas and the like), fungi (mushrooms, mildews, molds), or plants (roses, ferns, broccoli, pine trees). There are, in addition, two main groups of prokaryotes, single-celled organisms that lack nuclei: bacteria and archaea. These are the microbes, referred to in Chapter 5, that may make up the bulk of the earth's biomass.

Within kingdom Animalia are about thirty *phyla* (singular, *phylum*), groups such as sponges, jellyfish, starfish, three types of worms, mollusks, arthropods (insects, spiders, crustaceans), and chordates. We are members of phylum Chordata because we have a bony spine, the evolutionary descendant of a **notochord,** a long cartilaginous rod running down the back to support the body and protect the spinal chord, the extension of the central nervous system (Figure 7.1). Chordates with a bony spine are grouped into a subphylum, Vertebrata. All five species in Table 7.1 are chordates and, more specifically, vertebrates.

There are seven classes within the vertebrates: the jawless fishes (an ancient group represented by only a few existing species), cartilaginous fishes (sharks and rays), bony fishes (guppies, tunas, and so on), amphibians (frogs and salamanders), reptiles (snakes, lizards, and alligators), birds, and mammals. All our sample species are members of class Mammalia because they maintain a constant body temperature (commonly called *warm blooded*), have hair, give birth to live young, nourish the young with milk from mammary glands, and have relatively large, complex brains.

We need to stop here for an important point. You may have noticed that some of the traits listed for mammals are also possessed by other classes. Birds, for example, are also warm-blooded; so, according to many, were some of the dinosaurs, and so are a number of other creatures, including great white sharks. Some sharks, some bony fishes (like guppies), and some snakes give birth to live young. By the same token, you might know two mammals that do not possess all the mammalian traits. The spiny anteater (or echidna) and the duckbill platypus, both from Australia, lay eggs. Obviously, though, birds, dinosaurs, and great white sharks are *not* mammals, while the spiny anteater and platypus *are*. What's the resolution to this seeming contradiction?

The answer is that inclusion into a taxonomic category is more than simply a matter of possessing a list of traits. The traits of an organism make possible that organism's *adaptation,* and it is adaptation, measured by reproductive success, that is the criterion of natural selection. Thus, taxonomic categories become statements about adaptation, as well as biological relationships, with each taxonomic level becoming more specifically focused. Mammals, whether they lay eggs or not, are animals that are adapted through active lifestyles and a reliance on learned behavior facilitated by a set of shared traits. Mammalian young, therefore, require a great deal of direct care and nurturing. And mammals require a constant body temperature to sustain their level of activity, and they require hair (or in the case of whales, a thick layer of fat) to maintain that temperature. That's not a very concise definition of a mammal, but the real world doesn't always make things easy for those of us who try to describe it.

Within class Mammalia are about nineteen existing orders—nineteen rather specific adaptive strategies and resulting sets of characteristics. There are, for example, the flying bats; the fully aquatic whales and dolphins; the partially aquatic seals, sea lions, and walruses; two orders of hoofed plant eaters (the difference being a skeletal feature of the feet); the rabbits and hares; the rodents; the meat eaters; the insect eaters; the pouched marsupials (kangaroos and opposums); and a group of large-brained tree-dwellers with three-dimensional vision and dexterous hands. These last mammals are the members of order Primates.

All the species in Table 7.1 are primates, but they differ at the level of family. Humans are classified in family Hominidae, while the other four are members of family Pongidae. Within the pongids we recognize

notochord: The evolutionary precursor of the vertebral column.

three *genera* (singular, *genus*). The only Asian species, the orangutan is placed in genus *Pongo*. The African gorilla, although similar to the other African apes, is different enough to be placed in a separate genus, *Gorilla*. The chimp and bonobo are recognized as two species within the same genus, *Pan*. A Linnaean taxonomy thus indicates the relative relationships among named organisms.

Linnaeus's goal was to describe the system that, as he believed, God had in mind when he created all the earth's living things. Linnaeus was a creationist, as were just about all scientists of his time. But as you can probably see, to modern scientists his taxonomy indicates not only present-day similarities and differences but evolutionary relationships as well. For example, the reason the chimp is more similar to the bonobo than to a human is that the chimp and bonobo diverged from each other more recently than they did from humans. The chimp and bonobo are thought to have had a common ancestor from which they split less than 1 million years ago. Humans and the chimp/bonobo line had branched about 5 million years ago. Humans and chimps have had a longer time to evolve in different ways than have the bonobo and chimp, which is why they are more different and why they are placed in different taxonomic families.

So, a Linnaean taxonomy, or **phenetic taxonomy** (one based on existing phenotypic features and adaptive focuses), can be directly translated into an evolutionary tree, showing when the classified species and other **taxa** (categories; singular, *taxon*) branched from one another. Of course, such a tree can't tell us the exact dates of divergence. Evolutionary rates differ in different evolutionary lines and at different times. But it can tell us the *relative* times of branching. Figure 7.2 shows an evolutionary tree derived from the classification of the five species in Table 7.1.

An Alternative System

The tree in Figure 7.2 demonstrates the basis of a current debate within taxonomy. The tree was *inferred* from phenetic categories—physical comparisons of living species. Many such evolutionary trees prove quite accurate with regard to relative branching times and, thus, the overall pattern of branching. But as we learn more about the fossil ancestors of living species and as we improve our techniques of genetic comparison, we also learn more about the details of the evolutionary relationships among those species—particularly about the exact times and patterns of their evolutionary divergences.

Current knowledge from the fossil record and from genetic comparisons indicates that the orangutan line diverged earliest and that the

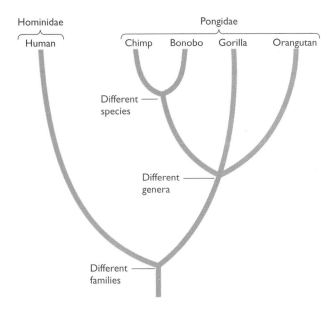

FIGURE 7.2
Evolutionary Tree Based on Phenetic Analysis. We infer the evolutionary relationships from the taxonomic classifications.

human, chimp/bonobo, and gorilla lines diverged from one another at about the same time or the gorilla line may have diverged a bit earlier. (The difference depends on the specific analysis of genetic similarities used as a basis of comparison.) In other words, the tree inferred from the phenetic taxonomy (see Figure 7.2) is inaccurate. The actual evolutionary tree should look like Figure 7.3 Thus, there is a contradiction between the traditional taxonomic names and categories for these species and their evolutionary relationships.

An alternative taxonomic system attempts to resolve this problem. It is called **cladistics** (from *clade*, meaning "branch"). It works the opposite way from phenetics by starting with the evolutionary tree and placing organisms in taxonomic categories based on their order of branching, regardless of how their present-day appearances might assort them into groups.

Branching order is determined in two ways. First, we use **shared derived characteristics.** If two groups share phenotypic features not found in other groups and if it can be supported that those features were derived from a common ancestor, the groups must be lumped into the same category at whatever taxonomic level is appropriate. For example, lumping birds with dinosaurs in the same order and placing reptiles in a different order is justified by cladistics because birds and dinosaurs share a feature of the pelvis not found in any other group, including reptiles. Second, branching order is determined by genetic comparison, now done at the

phenetic taxonomy: A classification system based on existing phenotypic features and adaptive focuses.

taxa: Categories within a taxonomic classification.

cladistics: A classification system based on order of evolutionary branching rather than on present similarities and differences.

shared derived characteristics: Phenotypic features shared by two or more groups that are derived from a common ancestor and that are not found in other groups.

FIGURE 7.3

Accurate Evolutionary Tree Based on Cladistic Analysis (using the model of an earlier branching of the gorilla clade). The family names reflect one of several suggested classification schemes. An exercise on classification can be found in the Appendix.

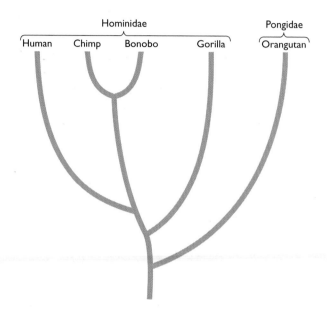

level of the base sequence of the genetic code itself. (See the "Contemporary Reflections" box in Chapter 3 and the genetics section of Chapter 9 for more detail.)

What are the implications for the primates? Under a phenetic scheme (see Figure 7.2), there is a family division between hominids and pongids—in other words, between humans and apes. This is intuitively obvious since the four ape species resemble one another in some basic phenotypic features and adaptations more than they do us humans.

But in cladistics (see Figure 7.3), there is no such thing as an "ape." There is no clade that *includes* the four great apes and *excludes* humans. Cladists have proposed a number of different taxonomies to reflect this. In one taxonomy, family Pongidae includes only the orangutan, and humans and the African apes are lumped into family Hominidae. Subfamily and other new categories are then added to make further distinctions, depending on exactly how one draws the evolutionary tree of those species (gorillas branching first or the three clades equally related).

Is a phenetic or a cladistic system better? Phenetics captures obvious phenotypic and adaptive relationships but may fail to accurately reflect actual patterns of branching. Cladistics is evolutionarily accurate but requires redefinition of taxonomic categories that make sense in terms of obvious adaptive focuses. For instance, if we accept the preceding cladistic taxonomy, *hominid* is no longer restricted to "the **bipedal** primate" but now includes the **quadrupedal** chimps, bonobos, and gorillas. Its definition then becomes much more complex.

The debate continues, with no agreed-upon resolution in sight. My own preference is to classifty taxa by branching order (that is, cladistically) and then, although it can get wordy, describe the phenotypic and adaptive differences that may have arisen within a taxon and figure out why they arose. Having said that, however, we will stick with the traditional phenetic classification for the primates in this text. My focus is to show how primate species, especially the so-called higher primates, look and behave and how those looks and behaviors have evolved. It is simpler to use phenetic categories because they are based on looks and adaptive behaviors. And it's easier to start with phenetic categories and *then* see how categories change under cladistic analysis.

Now, let's focus on the adaptive strategy and the phenotypic traits that characterize the members of order Primates.

WHAT IS A PRIMATE?

There are about 200 living species of primates. We're not sure how many have existed during the order's evolutionary history of more than 55 million years. Primates range from the very small, such as the mouse lemur of Madagascar, which weighs less than 3 ounces, to the gigantic—*Gigantopithecus,* an extinct ape from China, Vietnam, and India that may have stood 12 feet tall and tipped the scales at half a ton (Figure 7.4). Some primates inhabit small, very specific environmental ranges and spend their lives slowly moving through the trees, eating fruits, leaves, or insects; one species of primate lives in nearly every environment and produces its own food.

This wide variety makes it a bit difficult to define the primate order in a simple sentence. The primates are best defined by looking at the characteristics that they have in common and in seeing how these traits facilitate the primate adaptive strategy. We'll look at the primate traits by using the following categories: (1) the senses, (2) movement, (3) reproduction, (4) intelligence, and (5) behavior patterns.

The Senses

Bats and dolphins live in worlds of sound. Dogs live in a world of smells. The primates live in a visual world. Vision is the predominant sense for the primates.

bipedal: Walking on two legs.

quadrupedal: Walking on all four limbs.

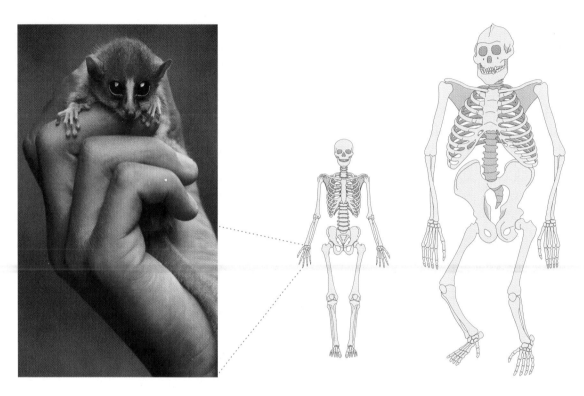

FIGURE 7.4

Here we compare a mouse lemur, the smallest living primate, with a human and with *Gigantopithecus,* now extinct, the largest primate ever (see Chapter 10).

Most primates see in color, and all primates see in three dimensions. They have true depth perception, technically called **stereoscopic vision**— possible because the eyes face forward and see the same scene from slightly different angles (Figure 7.5). The nerves and muscles of most primate eyes are protected by being enclosed within a bony socket. Look at your surroundings. What you are able to see is what the majority of primates could see if they were in your place.

Other primate senses are not as acute as in many mammals. Primates lack the auditory (hearing) and olfactory (smell) sensitivity of such familiar animals as dogs, cats, and cattle. Furthermore, and obviously related to the less acute sense of smell, primates tend to lack a snout and so are relatively flat-faced in profile. There is, as you might expect for a group of 200 species, some variation among primates. Many members of one group of primates (the prosimians, which we'll discuss in the next section) are nocturnal and lack color vision, but they have better senses of smell and hearing than do monkeys, apes, and humans.

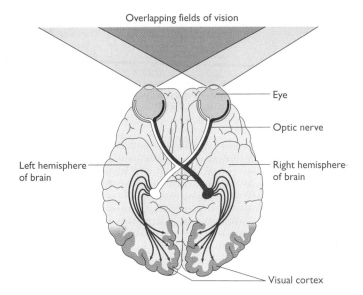

Overlapping fields of vision

Eye

Optic nerve

Left hemisphere of brain

Right hemisphere of brain

Visual cortex

FIGURE 7.5
Stereoscopic Vision. The fields of vision overlap, and the optic nerve from each eye travels to both hemispheres of the brain. The result is true depth perception.

Movement

Like most mammals, primates are, with one exception, quadrupedal. Although many primates can stand or even walk on two legs for short periods, humans are the only habitually bipedal primates. Unlike most mammals, the limbs of primates are extremely flexible, and the hands (and in many cases the feet) of primates have the ability to grasp objects. That is, they are **prehensile** (Figure 7.6). Primates use this trait for several forms of locomotion. Some primates, called vertical clingers and leapers, jump from branch to branch or trunk to trunk, using the grasping ability of all four limbs. The apes are suspensory climbers with the ability to hang and climb by the arms (see Figure 7.17). An extreme form of this mode of movement is **brachiation,** swinging arm-over-arm through the trees. When on the ground, most primates use all fours. Asia's orangutans walk on their fists. The African apes have a unique quadrupedalism, supporting themselves on the knuckles of their hands instead of the palms. Primate species may use one or more of these locomotor methods, depending on their anatomy and the situation.

In addition, most primates are able to touch their thumbs to the tips of the other fingers on the same hand, allowing them to pick up and manipulate small objects. This capacity is called **opposability.** Finally, most primates have nails rather than claws on the tips of the fingers and toes.

stereoscopic vision: Three-dimensional vision; depth perception.

prehensile: Having the ability to grasp.

brachiation: Locomotion by swinging arm-over-arm.

opposability: The ability to touch the thumb to the tips of the other fingers on the same hand.

FIGURE 7.6
Prehensile Grip. An orang-utan holding its trainer's hand demonstrates the prehensile grip shared by nonhuman and human primates.

These provide support for the sensitive tactile sense receptors of the fingers. In short, primates have manual dexterity. Some have a great degree of dexterity in the feet as well (see Figure 7.13).

Reproduction

Most primate species give birth to one offspring at a time. Several primates, such as some of the marmosets from South America and some of the lemurs from Madagascar, normally produce twins or triplets. As is typical of mammals, primate parents take an active role in the protection, nurturing, and socialization of their young. Mostly because of their large, complex brains and because of the importance of learning, young primates are dependent upon adults and take a long time to mature. How long, of course, varies according to the size of the primate species. The primates, relative to size, have the longest period of **postnatal dependency** of any mammal.

Intelligence

Intelligence can be defined as the relative ability of an organism's brain to acquire, store, retrieve, and process information. These abilities are related to brain size and brain complexity. A bigger brain has more room for

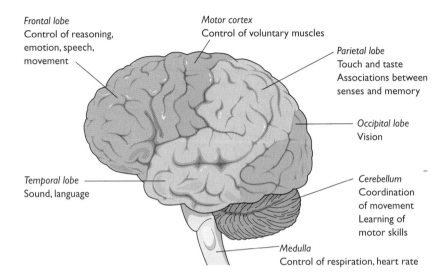

Frontal lobe
Control of reasoning, emotion, speech, movement

Motor cortex
Control of voluntary muscles

Parietal lobe
Touch and taste
Associations between senses and memory

Occipital lobe
Vision

Temporal lobe
Sound, language

Cerebellum
Coordination of movement
Learning of motor skills

Medulla
Control of respiration, heart rate

FIGURE 7.7
The Human Brain with Major Parts and Their Functions. The lobes and the motor cortex are all part of the neocortex.

all the complex nerve connections that make it work, just as a very sophisticated computer must necessarily be larger than a simple one. (Brain size variation *within* a species is another matter, which we'll cover in Chapter 14.) But brain size must also be looked at in a relative way: How big is the brain compared to the body it runs? A sperm whale, with its 20-pound brain, has a brain size ten times that of the average human's. A sperm whale's body, however, is over *five hundred* times the size of ours. We have bigger brains than whales have *relative to* the size of our bodies; we run less body with more brain, which is true of the primates in general. Of all land mammals, the primates have the largest relative brain sizes. The human brain, however, is three times the size one would expect for a primate of our body weight (Passingham 1982, 78).

In addition, the primate brain is complex, especially in the neocortex, that part of the brain where memory, abstract thought, problem solving, and attentiveness take place (Figure 7.7). In short, the primates are smart.

Behavior Patterns

Primates are social animals. Most primate species live in groups. Many other animals do too, but even those few primate species—like orangutans—that usually remain solitary still interact with other members of their species in ways that are far more complex than are the ways that, say, antelopes in a herd or even wolves in a pack interact. The difference

postnatal dependency: The period after birth during which offspring require the care of adults to survive.

intelligence: The relative ability of the brain to acquire, store, retrieve, and process information.

FIGURE 7.8
We see here some colorful primate faces, including that of one primate that purposely enhances the color. Colorful faces are evidence of the importance of individual recognition within primate societies. Shown here (*clockwise from upper left*) are a Chinese white-handed gibbon, mandrill, human, and bald uakari.

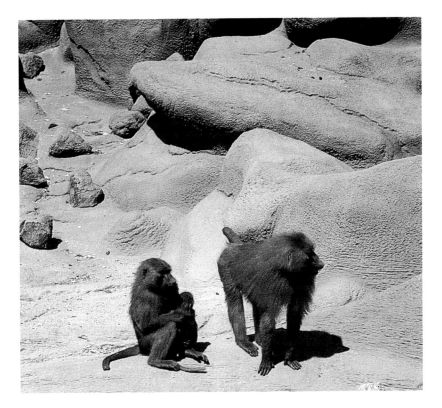

FIGURE 7.9
Male Baboon Protecting Mother and Young. The female holding her baby at left was being threatened by the boisterous play of a group of adolescent males, out of the picture to the right. The adult male in the center stepped in and barked at the group, which quickly took its play elsewhere. (These baboons are part of a captive troop.)

is that primates recognize individuals, and the individual primate holds a particular status relative to others in its group and to the group as a whole. A primate group is made up of the collective relationships among all its individual members. We will see these relationships in action when we examine primate behavior more closely in Chapter 8.

As physical evidence of the importance of these relationships, it may be noted that primates are among the most colorful of mammals, and most of the color patterns of many primates, especially monkeys, are on their faces (Figure 7.8). The attention of one primate to another is drawn to the face, to the primate's identity as an individual.

In some primates—baboons and chimpanzees, for example—each individual may have rather specific status within the group. Some have more social power and influence than others. They are said to be dominant, and the structure of the relative power and influence of all a group's individuals is called a **dominance hierarchy.** In addition, most primate species recognize a special status for females with infants, and these mother–child units are well protected by other members of the group, even those who are not directly related to them (Figure 7.9). Among

dominance hierarchy: Individual differences among group members in terms of power, influence, and access to resources and mating.

FIGURE 7.10
Primate Communication and Grooming. (*Top*) A chimp exhibits a "*pant-hoot*," a call used when a food source is found, when two groups join together, or to communicate over distances. (*Bottom*) Grooming serves not only to rid these Francois's langurs (monkeys from Southeast Asia) of parasites and dirt but also helps maintain group unity and harmony.

chimpanzees and baboons we even see lasting relationships that can only be described as friendship.

Primate social groups are maintained through communication. Primates have large repertoires of vocalizations, facial expressions, and body gestures. Touch is also an important form of communication among primates and often takes the form of **grooming,** an activity that serves not only the practical purpose of removing dirt and parasites but also as a source of reassurance to maintain group harmony and unity (Figure 7.10).

How, then, may we characterize the primate adaptive strategy? It is important to acknowledge the environment that the primates are adapted *to*. The basic primate environment is arboreal—primates live in trees. To be sure, several species—gorillas, for instance—spend more time on the ground than in the branches, and we humans are thoroughly terrestrial. But the majority of primates spend most of their time in the trees, and the primate traits in the preceding discussion all evolved in response to an arboreal environment. Even the partially and completely terrestrial primates possess features that are variations on the arboreal adaptive theme. So, we can define primates in the following way:

> The primates are mammals adapted to an arboreal environment through well-developed vision, manual dexterity, and large, complex brains that rely on learned behavior; the latter is aided by the birth of few offspring at a time and the direct and extensive care of those offspring during a long period of dependency while they are socialized into groups based upon differential relationships among individuals.

Such a complex group of organisms requires a lengthy description.

A SURVEY OF THE LIVING PRIMATES

Figure 7.11 is a simplified phenetic taxonomy of the approximately 200 species of living primates. For the sake of space, some groups are indicated only by the number of those groups within a category; for instance, there are six families of prosimians. One of the first things you should notice is that there are new categories here as compared to those shown in Table 7.1. *Suborder, infraorder,* and *superfamily* have been added between the traditional Linnaean categories of *order* and *family*. A cladistic taxonomy may add more. Sometimes a taxon of organisms has many species adapted to a wide variety of geographical locations and environmental niches; consequently, additional taxonomic categories need to be added to accurately capture what seem to be natural divisions. (A complete taxonomy of insects, for example, a class with over three-quarters of a million *known* species, is, as you can well imagine, incredibly complex.)

grooming: Here, cleaning the fur of another animal, which promotes social cohesion.

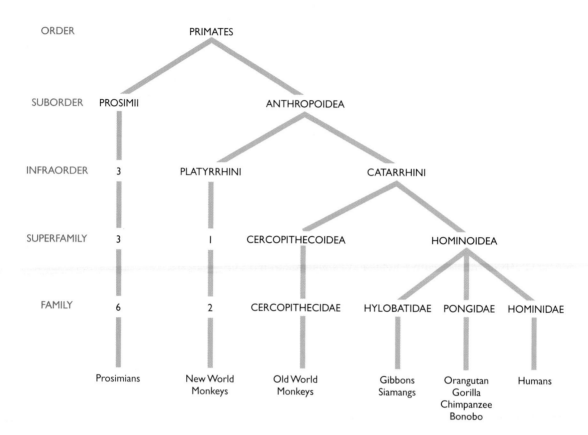

FIGURE 7.11
Primate Taxonomy Using Traditional Phenetic Categories. Numbers refer to living primate groups in that category when the specific group names are not given.

Prosimians

The order Primates is traditionally divided into two major suborders, Prosimii and Anthropoidea. Prosimians ("pre-apes") represent the most primitive primates, that is, those that most closely resemble the earliest primates. At first widespread, prosimians were pushed into marginal areas as newer, more adaptively flexible primates evolved. Some modern prosimians live on the mainlands of Africa, India, and Southeast Asia and on the isolated islands of Southeast Asia, but the majority inhabit the island of Madagascar (Figure 7.12).

The forty or so living species of prosimians exhibit a number of differences from the general primate pattern. About half of the prosimian species are nocturnal and so lack color vision. They have large eyes that can gather more light and better than average senses of smell and hearing (Figure 7.13). To aid their olfactory sense, they have a protruding snout

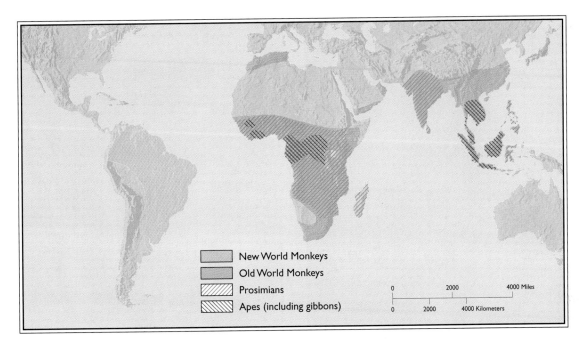

FIGURE 7.12
Distribution of Living Nonhuman Primates.

with a large smell receptor area (the mucous membranes within the nose) and a moist, naked outer nose (like a dog or cat) to help pick up the molecules that make up olfactory signals. Prosimians do have the stereoscopic vision characteristic of primates because they need to judge distances in bushes and trees, and their three-dimensional vision helps them catch insects, a favorite food of many prosimian species.

Prosimians have prehensile hands and feet, but the opposability of their thumbs is limited. Many can only touch the thumb with the other four digits together; their digits don't move independently. Some prosimians have claws instead of the typical primate nails on a couple of fingers or toes. These are known as *grooming claws* and are used both for that purpose and to help acquire food.

A few species of lemurs from Madagascar give birth to twins or even triplets on a regular basis. Transporting them through the trees, however, is no problem because an adult male or an older brother or sister often helps the mother carry and care for her infants. At other times, the infants are kept in a nest.

A particularly interesting prosimian is the tarsier of Southeast Asia (Figure 7.14). Weighing just 4 or 5 ounces, this little insect eater has powerful hind limbs for jumping, enlarged fingertips and toetips for added

FIGURE 7.13

Two Prosimians. The slender loris of India and Sri Lanka (*left*) has the large eyes and moist, naked nose characteristic of this suborder. Note also the prehensile hands and feet and the grooming claw on one toe of the foot at the top of the picture. The crowned lemur of Madagascar (*right*) displays a posture that is typical of the locomotor pattern called "vertical clinging and leaping." All the Madagascar primates are endangered.

friction, and the ability to turn its head 180 degrees in either direction, like an owl. Its name comes from its elongated ankle, or tarsal, bones, which make its legs look like they bend too many times.

The tarsier is at the center of another debate within primate taxonomy. Because of its flat face, upright posture when clinging to trunks and branches, lack of the moist, naked nose of other prosimians, and some recent genetic comparisons, some authorities suggest placing the tarsier in the second primate suborder, Anthropoidea. Cladists go further. Focusing on the fact that all prosimians have the moist nose but that no anthropoids do, they suggest dividing order Primates into suborders based on that trait. The former prosimians would thus be in suborder Strepsirhini ("nose with curved nostrils"), and the anthropoids would become suborder Haplorhini ("simple nose"). The latter group would include the tarsier because of its nose, color vision, and other traits. Both versions are found in the literature; here we will use the traditional classification.

FIGURE 7.14
Philippine Tarsier. Note the huge eyes (each eyeball is as big as the entire brain) for nocturnal vision, the enlarged finger- and toetips, and the powerfully built legs.

Anthropoids

The anthropoid ("humanlike") primates include monkeys, apes, and humans. Suborder Anthropoidea is further divided into two infraorders, Platyrrhini and Catarrhini. This division is based on a geographical separation of early primates into a Western Hemisphere, or New World, group and an Eastern Hemisphere, or Old World, group. All the New World platyrrhine primates are monkeys. The Old World catarrhine primates are made up of monkeys, apes, and humans. Despite the fact that humans now inhabit the entire globe, the hominids first evolved in the Old World, in Africa.

Several features distinguish New World from Old World primates. The most obvious is the nose. Platyrrhine means "flat nose," and the noses of the Central and South American monkeys have widely spaced nostrils separated by a broad septum (Figure 7.15). Compare this with a typical Old World catarrhine nose ("with nostrils close together and facing downward") by looking in the mirror.

New World and Old World anthropoids also have different dental formulas, that is, the number of each type of tooth in each quadrant of the mouth. Old World anthropoids have two incisors, one canine, two

FIGURE 7.15
Northern Woolly Spider Monkey, a Platyrrhine Primate from Brazil. Note the prehensile tail with the bare strip of skin on the inner surface to enhance grasping ability. Note also the typical platyrrhine nose (see also Figure 7.8 bottom left).

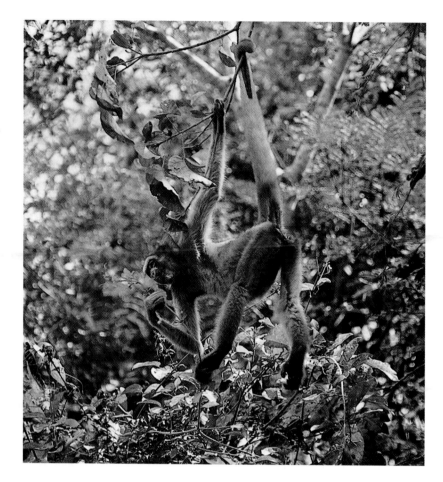

premolars (bicuspids), and three molars. This is written as $\frac{2.1.2.3}{2.1.2.3} \times 2 = 32$. Some New World anthropoids have four extra premolars: $\frac{2.1.3.3}{2.1.3.3} \times 2 = 36$. Other New World anthropoids have four fewer molars: $\frac{2.1.3.2}{2.1.3.2} \times 2 = 32$.

Moreover, because New World monkeys are almost entirely arboreal, they have evolved long limbs, and some have clawlike nails. Several species also have evolved prehensile tails and thus effectively have five grasping limbs. No Old World monkey evolved this adaptation. Finally, two groups of platyrrhines, the marmosets and tamarins, normally give birth to twins.

The Old World primates are divided into two superfamilies. The monkeys of Europe (now limited to Gibraltar), Africa, and Asia make up superfamily Cercopithecoidea. Apes and humans are in superfamily Hominoidea, divided into three families.

FIGURE 7.16
Rhesus Monkey, a Catarrhine Primate from Asia. Note the more closely spaced nostrils as compared to the platyrrhine (New World) monkey in Figure 7.15. (See also Figure 7.8, *top left and right and bottom right,* and Figure 7.10, *bottom.*) The rhesus has been important in medical and behavioral experimentation. The Rh blood factor was named after it.

There are about seventy-five species of cercopithecoids (Figure 7.16). They have the nasal shape and tooth number of all Old World primates, and most have tails. Males tend to be larger than females, a trait not common in New World species. Also unlike the platyrrhines, the Old World monkeys have fully opposable thumbs. The monkeys of the Eastern Hemisphere seem more adaptively flexible than those of the New World. At home in the trees, many cercopithecoids are equally comfortable on the ground. They live everywhere from the deserts of Africa and the Middle East to the mountains of northern Japan.

Superfamily Hominoidea contains the larger, tailless primates. The hominoids—the apes and hominids—are generally larger than the monkeys and have larger brains, both relatively and absolutely. Their brains also have larger neocortexes, meaning that the hominoids are more intelligent, as we have defined that term. Finally, a series of traits make the hominoids good suspensory climbers and hangers; they are adapted to an arboreal environment through the ability to climb and hang from branches with their arms. The traits behind this ability are a flexible shoulder joint, a shoulder blade that is farther back than in monkeys, and a stronger collarbone (clavicle) for added support. Although modern humans do not display this ability as often or as well as the apes, we still possess it, as is evident by watching gymnasts on the high bar or rings.

FIGURE 7.17
White-Handed Gibbon from Southeast Asia. Note the long, hooklike fingers and the grasping feet.

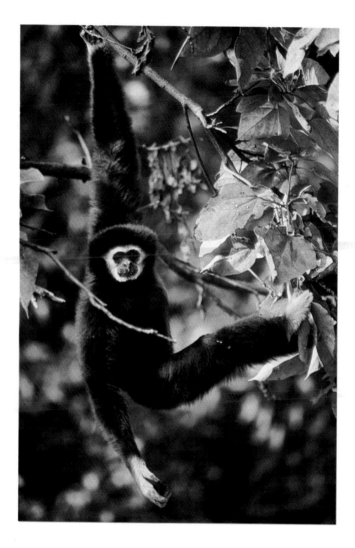

Family Hylobatidae includes the gibbons and siamangs of Southeast Asia and Malaysia. Sometimes referred to as *lesser apes*, they are noted for their brachiating mode of locomotion (Figure 7.17). They also have an unusual social organization for primates. Male and female hylobatids form a monogamous pair, though not neccessarily a permanent one.

There are four species within family Pongidae, known collectively as the *great apes*: the orangutan of Southeast Asia and the gorilla, chimpanzee, and bonobo of Africa (Figure 7.18).

The pongids are large (a male gorilla in the wild may weigh 450 pounds), with heavy, powerful jaws used for eating a wide range of fruits,

FIGURE 7.18
The Great Apes. Shown here (*clockwise from top left*) are the orangutan of Southeast Asia and the gorilla, bonobo, and chimpanzee of Africa.

FIGURE 7.19
Chimps use tools they have made to extract termites from their mound.

nuts, and vegetables. Chimps and bonobos also eat meat on occasion. The apes are quadrupeds, although chimps, gorillas, and especially bonobos are fairly good at upright walking for short distances. Orangutans are solitary, but the other apes live in social groups marked by some degree of dominance but otherwise with fairly loose organization and changeable group membership.

The apes have relatively large brains; a large chimp may have a brain half the size of the smallest modern human brain. Apes are intelligent. They have, for example, an intimate knowledge of a large number of food sources, many of which ripen seasonally or grow in limited areas.

Some chimpanzees can make simple tools, the best known of which is their termite "fishing stick," a modified twig or blade of grass they insert into a hole in a termite mound and wiggle around to stimulate an attack by the insects. The termites cling to the "invader," and the chimps draw out a tasty meal (Figure 7.19). Other chimps have been seen to use rocks to break open hard-shelled nuts. Chimps are also known to cooperatively hunt small animals, including other primates, and meat is the one food source that chimps will share with one another (see Chapter 8).

Finally, apes have a large repertoire of calls, facial expressions, and body gestures with which they communicate information, mostly about emotional states. Though this form of communication is nothing like human language, some individuals from all the great ape species have been taught to use nonvocal versions of human languages, most notably American Sign Language (AMESLAN), developed for the hearing impaired. It is said by some researchers that with this skill they can communicate at the level of a 4- or 5-year-old human.

The third hominoid family is Hominidae, the hominids. This includes all living and extinct species of habitually bipedal primates. We need, of course, to detail the traits of this group.

THE HUMAN PRIMATE

Each of the 200 living primate species has its own unique expression of the primate adaptive strategy. Humans are no exception. Let's describe hominids by using the same categories with which we characterized primates in general.

The Senses

Our senses are essentially the same as those of the anthropoid monkeys and the apes. There may be some minor differences, but basically all these species hear, smell, and, especially, see the same world.

Movement

Bipedalism is the characteristic that in broad evolutionary perspective defines the hominids. We are the only primate that is habitually bipedal, and we have been for over 4 million years. (Our big brains came along much later.) The bones and muscles of our back, pelvis, legs, and feet are all structured to balance us and hold us upright. Because our legs are the limbs of locomotion, they are longer and more muscular than our arms—just the opposite of the arms and legs of the apes. Completely freed from locomotor functions, our hands have become organs of manipulation. We have the most precise opposability of any of the primates and the relatively longest and strongest primate thumb.

Contemporary Reflections

Should Nonhuman Primates Have Rights?

The question posed in this box's title is part of a larger question that has become one of today's most contentious issues: Do animals share with us any of our basic rights, and do they, consequently, deserve considerations equal to those accorded humans? Opinions on this issue vary enormously. One animal rights advocate (Francione 1996) argues that we should not consider animals as property and so should treat them as independent, autonomous individuals and not in any way exploit them. At the other extreme is a letter that appeared in a local newspaper in which the writer seriously claimed that God put animals on earth to sustain people, assist them in work, entertain them at circuses, and provide fur coats for women to "uplift" men's spirits.

Ideas on the subject vary even more when put into actual practice. Many supporters of some form of animal rights adamantly refuse to eat mammals or birds but continue to eat seafood—drawing some sort of ethical line between warm-blooded and cold-blooded creatures. Many who are sickened at the sight of a fur coat still wear leather shoes. Hunters easily justify killing wild creatures for sport while at the same time treating their hunting dogs as family members. Veterinary researchers, interested in promoting the health of animals, will subject other animals to experimentation and practice surgery. Clearly, this is a complicated issue for any thinking person, involving many aspects of one's moral, emotional, and material life.

The question is perhaps most profound and intense with regard to our closest relatives, especially the apes. These species have always struck us as being very much like our own, and we know now that these apes share with us 98.5 percent of our genes. The African apes and we share a recent common ancestor. Some 5 or 6 million years ago, we and they were the same creature.

Reproduction

Like most primates, we usually have one offspring at a time. Though we are not the largest primate (the gorilla is), we have the longest period of postnatal dependency, and we take the longest time to mature. Chimps, for example, reach sexual maturity at about 9 years and physical maturity at about 12. For humans, the averages are 13 and 21. In addition, we are born even more helpless than other primates.

Our sexual behavior, too, is different. Most other primates, like most mammals, engage in sexual activity, for the most part, only when it can lead to reproduction. Thus, mating tends to occur most often when a female has ovulated, that is, produced an egg that is ready to be fertilized. She undergoes hormonal changes that make her sexually receptive and lead her to solicit male attention, and she gives off signals that sexually stimulate males. During this time, the female is said to be in **estrus** (pop-

CHAPTER

8

PRIMATE BEHAVIOR AND HUMAN EVOLUTION

Often I have gazed
into a chimpanzee's
eyes and wondered
what was going on
behind them.
—Jane Goodall (1990)

Just as we look to the anatomy of our close relatives to get some idea about the basic set of phenotypic traits from which we evolved, we may also look at the behavior of the other primates to gain some insight into why we behave the way we do. Because we share common ancestors, some of our behavior patterns—just like some of our physical features—may be variations on the same evolutionary theme.

In this chapter we will look at several nonhuman primates, particularly the several species collectively called baboons (genus *Papio*) and the two species of genus *Pan*, the common chimpanzee and the "pygmy chimp," or bonobo. The reasons for choosing these primates will be explained as well.

We will address the following questions:

How do we organize a study of something as complex as behavior?

What are some of the scientific cautions that must be exercised in doing so?

What are some of the relevant behaviors of our close relatives?

What light do they shed on the evolution of the behavior of the hominids?

STUDYING BEHAVIOR

The idea of studying nonhuman primate behavior is based on the same premise as is our use of physical comparisons with other primates: We share a common heritage with the other primates and so have inherited our shared features from the same source, a common ancestor. It is not a coincidence, for example, that all the primates have prehensile hands. Our common prehensile ability is a shared, derived characteristic, coming from the same ancient ancestor and, in this case, serving the same basic function. Such traits, shared by multiple species through inheritance from a common ancestor, are called **homologies.** Thus, we gain some perspective on our prehensile hands by fully examining the prehensile appendages of species with whom we share an ancestor from whom we all derived the trait.

It should be noted that homologous traits need not share a common function. Your arms and the wings of a bat, though they are used for different things, are homologies. The traits are similar by virtue of having evolved from the same source, an early mammal.

(a)

(b)

(c)

FIGURE 8.1
Homology and Analogy. The arm of a human (*a*) and the wing of a bat (*b*) are homologous—they have different functions but share the same evolutionary source. The wing of a bat (*b*) and the wing of an insect (*c*) are analogous—they share a function but are evolutionarily different.

The wings of a bat and the wings of an insect, however, though they share a similar function, have evolved independently and are not at all similar in structure. These functionally similar but evolutionarily unrelated traits are known as **analogies.** We can certainly learn something about the physics of flight by comparing bats and insect wings, but there is a limited amount of information we can get about the wings of bats by studying the wings of insects because they evolved quite separately from one another (Figure 8.1).

homologies: Traits shared by two or more species through inheritance from a common ancestor.

analogies: Traits shared by two or more species that are similar in function but unrelated evolutionarily.

Just as organisms pass on anatomical and physiological features in their genes, they also pass on behavioral characteristics. In some groups— ants, for example—whole behavioral repertoires are passed on. Ants rely completely on built-in instinct; they don't really think or, in fact, have much of anything to think *with*. So, even though ants live in highly complex societies and act in elaborate ways, all their behaviors are coded in their genes, to be triggered by outside stimuli but with little or no flexibility or variation in their response.

Other organisms with larger and more complex brains can vary their behavior as needed to cope with specific situations. Their behavior is flexible. They have behavioral *potentials* or *themes* carried in their genetic codes, and they respond to their environments by building on these potentials—taking in information from the outside, remembering it, retrieving stored information, and utilizing it in appropriate circumstances. In other words, they *think*.

The nature of the inborn behavioral potentials in complex organisms is still a matter of debate, especially when humans are the topic. Some have argued that we are born as "blank slates" or, in a more modern image, as computers with internal hardware but nothing programmed. The extreme opposite view says that our brains come equipped with specific behaviors that are only modified to a small degree by our individual experiences—like a computer with many application programs already in the system.

The reality is no doubt somewhere in the middle. Certainly we come into this world with some basic behavioral responses built in. Facial expressions like smiling, nursing behavior among infants, the bond between a mother and her offspring, the drives to walk upright and learn language—these are all recognized as universal in our species and as preprogrammed in our biology. But just as certainly, we are not programmed for *particular* ways of expressing these and other behaviors. Language ability, for example, may be instinctive, but the specific language you speak is learned within a specific cultural and individual context.

There is a scientific study that looks for evolutionary explanations for behaviors, especially social behaviors. It is called **sociobiology,** and two of its ideas are particularly relevant here. The first, **inclusive fitness,** refers to the fact that your close relatives share many of your genes. As a result, the adaptive fitness of your genes is not just a matter of your own adaptive success (the usual definition of fitness); it also includes the adaptive success of your relatives. Thus, any behavior that has evolved through time that causes you to aid your close relations also serves to help your genes get passed on.

A good example is the case of **altruistic** behavior. If, for instance, I perform some action that saves my sister's life but costs me mine in the process, *I* might not pass on any more genes, but I have helped increase the possibility that *some of my genes* will get passed on, because my sister and I share, on average, 50 percent of our genetic endowment.

Of course, humans have moral reasons for altruistic actions, but altruistic behaviors are seen in many other species where there could be no cultural motivation. It may not seem logical that a behavior that might endanger the individual could have evolved by natural selection. But, if we look at the genes rather than just the "packages" they come in, we can see how this could be the case. The altruistic behavior was selected for because it helped a group of individuals possessing genes for that behavior to be reproductively successful, even if a few individuals were sacrificed in the process.

The second idea from sociobiology relevant to our discussion concerns **reproductive strategies.** Put simply, individuals have evolved behaviors that maximize their reproductive success. Male and female mammals, however, differ in their contributions to reproduction, so their evolved behaviors may differ as well. Females, of course, carry, nurture, and raise offspring—largely by themselves in most mammalian species, including most primates. Males, on the other hand, contribute sperm. Thus, behaviors have evolved that help females raise healthy offspring and that allow males to try to impregnate as many females as possible.

If it is the case that at least behavioral themes can be inherited, then we can shed light on our behaviors by looking into those of other creatures. In doing so, however, we need to take into account the concepts of homology and analogy. In comparing the behaviors of humans and chimpanzees or bonobos, it is highly likely that a behavior is shared because it is the *same* behavior, derived by all three species from our common ancestor of 5 or 6 mya. Understanding the nature and function of that behavior in chimpanzees or bonobos is likely to provide insight into the origin of the behavior in humans because the behavior in question is homologous.

By contrast, a specific behavior similar in humans and baboons is less likely to be homologous. Our two species have evolved independently for over 20 million years, so there is a greater chance that the behaviors evolved separately, under separate environmental circumstances and perhaps for different adaptive reasons. Still, the behavior may be a variation on some *general behavioral pattern* common to the primates and inherited from an early common ancestor.

The chance of two similar behaviors being analogous increases as we compare species that are less and less closely related. Some investigators

sociobiology: The scientific study that examines evolutionary explanations for social behaviors within species.

inclusive fitness: The idea that fitness is measured by the success of one's genes, whether possessed by the individual or by that individual's relatives.

altruistic: Benefiting others without regard for one's own needs or safety.

reproductive strategies: Behaviors that evolve to maximize an individual's reproductive success.

have compared the behavior of humans with that of social carnivores like lions, wolves, and African wild dogs. There are strikingly "human" behaviors in these species: All three hunt cooperatively. Lions from the same pride will eat from the same carcass, and mothers, of course, will bring food—sometimes still alive—back to their young. Wolves and wild dogs have complex social relationships, they use vocal and gestural signs to maintain these relationships, and both actively feed their young. Wolves, especially, are territorial. These collections of similarities, however, are probably not derived from a common ancestor but have, at most, evolved quite independently from some general mammalian traits of social interaction, care of young, and relatively large, complex brains that allow for flexibility of behavior. What we do learn from the behavior of such species is that one possible route to adaptive success for mammals is through complex social behavior and that this behavior is common in species that include meat in their diet, especially meat from large animals. But it is only one route; other carnivores—the fox and leopard, for example—are solitary hunters. And lions, although they hunt cooperatively, do not share food in the sense that one actively gives a portion of a kill to another.

Comparing analogous behaviors, then, can be informative and can point out possible clusters of adaptive traits. But analogies must be used with the understanding that the more evolutionarily distant the species, the less useful the comparison. Ants live in highly complex societies, which investigators often describe in human terms (*slave, caste, queen, nurse, soldier*), but studying the social behavior of ants probably tells us nothing directly about our own societies.

We can now look at the behavior of some other species that have, to varying degrees, been used as models for the origin and evolution of our own behavior. For years, nearly all our information about the behavior of other species came from studies conducted in the artificial environments of zoos and laboratories. Only when the science of **ethology**—studying creatures in the wild, under natural conditions—became popular and possible could we see how they were *really* adapted. And only then did we begin to learn some of the truly remarkable adaptations that our fellow primates possess.

BABOONS

There are five distinguishable types of baboon that live in the African woodland, desert, and **savanna,** all grouped within genus *Papio*. (Some

FIGURE 8.2
Baboons on the African Savanna. Our early ancestors might have seen scenes like this.

authorities consider them to be subspecies of a single species because where their ranges overlap, they can and do interbreed and produce fertile offspring. Other taxonomists think that the physical and behavioral differences are sufficient to warrant giving them five different species names.) These primates have long been of interest to anthropologists because of the complexity of their social organization and because of their savanna habitat—an important habitat for our early hominid ancestors (Figure 8.2).

Baboon groups range in size from 20 to 200 individuals. One of the most striking aspects of baboon behavior is the aggressive competition for dominance among the males, who may be nearly twice the size of females and who are endowed with huge, sharp canine teeth (Figure 8.3). The male who is the largest, strongest, most aggressive, smartest (whatever

ethology: The study of the natural behavior of animals under natural conditions.

savanna: The open grasslands of the tropics.

FIGURE 8.3
Baboon Threat. A male baboon shows his long canine teeth and flashes his white eyelids in a "threat gesture," probably directed at a less dominant male.

traits are important to baboons) becomes, for a time, the dominant animal, a position recognized and acknowledged by the whole group. The dominant male is the group's leader and decision maker. He has first rights to food and often to females. He may produce the most offspring, perpetuating those traits that allowed him to achieve dominance. It is also the role of the dominant male and his immediate subordinates to protect the more vulnerable members of the group—the females and infants—from danger (see Figure 7.9).

Males are also, in general, dominant over females. In the hamadryas baboon of Ethiopia, males gather a group of females with whom they have exclusive mating rights. Such a group is referred to as a *harem*, and the proximity of and sexual access to the females in a harem is maintained by male aggression and violence. Many harem females show the literal scars of such treatment.

Observations of these behaviors led early investigators to depict baboon social organization as almost militaristic—centered around and totally dominated by a hierarchically arranged group of males and maintained through violent (though not always bloody) confrontations. Indeed, baboon groups have traditionally been called *troops*. A female's role was seen as the bearing and raising of offspring, her individual identity being defined by that role, and her position in baboon society was seen as subordinate to that of all males and specifically determined by the position of the male with whom she mated.

More recent studies have shown, however, that baboon societies are far more complex and variable (Fedigan and Fedigan 1988; Smuts 1985, 1995; Strum 1987). While male baboons do vie for dominance, achieve differential social power and influence, and protect the group from other baboons and from predators—and while hamadryas males do maintain harems through violent coercion—a formal, permanent, tightly structured dominance hierarchy among males does not seem to be at the center of social organization in all cases. Among other types of baboons—for example, the olive baboons of equatorial Africa—social structure is based on "a network of social alliances" (Fedigan and Fedigan 1988, 14), including friendships between females and between females and males. These friendships may be so strong that a male will aid his female friend's infants even though he may not be their father. Such friendships, rather than the social position of the males, may be what determines who mates with whom.

Differential social positions exist, but they are based not on those "masculine" traits mentioned previously but more on an individual's "experience, skill, and . . . ability to manipulate others [and] mobilize allies" (Fedigan and Fedigan 1988, 15). If there is any subgroup that is central to a troop and that ties generations together, it is that made up of related females; the males, being more mobile, are a less stable part of the troop than was previously supposed. In fact, the competition that may be most important to the troop is not that among males but that among females, who compete with one another "over access to the resources necessary to sustain them and their offspring" (Fedigan and Fedigan 1988, 5). Finally, it appears that mate choice is more a female prerogative. Males make overtures toward estrus females, but it is the females who decide with whom they will mate.

The behaviors described in the preceding paragraphs are examples of inclusive fitness and male reproductive strategy. The male baboons have evolved protective behaviors toward females and offspring in their troop because those offspring *may* be theirs and perhaps because those females may one day bear their offspring. Moreover, they try to keep away males from other troops to enhance their own reproductive success. At the same time, males are more mobile than females and will also try to contribute sperm to females in other troops.

The females, on the other hand, by forming alliances with related females and by selecting the males with whom they will mate, are helping ensure their own reproductive and child-rearing success, as well as the success of their genes via the reproductive success of their close relatives. Keep in mind, however, that the baboons don't have these results consciously in mind. The behaviors have evolved over time because they increase the inclusive fitness of the genes of the individuals who perform them. We don't really know what is going on in the minds of the baboons—what motivates them to act in these ways.

The earlier version of baboon social organization indicated that to survive on the savanna, the primates needed a tightly organized, male-oriented and -dominated, almost militaristic society. The obvious conclusion was that the early hominid savanna dwellers probably had a similar set of behaviors and that our modern social systems are, to one extent or another, variations on this theme.

Again, however, we must remember that we can share with baboons only the most general primate homologous traits. Similarities between humans and baboons exist because we have evolved variations of the same basic primate behavioral themes. Our specific expressions of those themes, though, are the results of separate and independent evolutionary histories.

Nevertheless, those separate histories have produced results that are similar in baboons and humans and, as we shall see, in chimpanzees and bonobos: the adaptive focus of a social structure built around a family unit, friendships, mutual aid within the group, defense of the group, and recognition of individuals. This social structure at least tells us that such a focus is one possible adaptive path among primates, and so it is reasonable to assume that something like it was the key to the survival of the early hominids. Given that our closest relatives, the chimpanzees and bonobos, exhibit this cluster of adaptive traits, it seems an even more reasonable assumption.

CHIMPANZEES

Some of the most remarkable results of ethological observations have come from three landmark studies of the great apes: Jane Goodall's study of the chimpanzee, Dian Fossey's of the gorilla, and Biruté Galdikas's of the orangutan. Subsequent studies as well have contributed to our understanding of these primates. Each study is interesting in its own right and tells us something of the variations possible on the basic primate pattern of social organization.

The orangutan (*Pongo pygmaeus*) is an Asian ape and is separated from us by 12 million years or more. The gorilla (*Gorilla gorilla*) is nearly, if not as, close to us genetically as the chimp; while it exhibits many of the same basic social behaviors as the chimpanzee, it is a rather specialized ape. Unlike the chimpanzee, it spends much of its time on the ground, and its almost exclusively vegetarian diet consists largely of ground plants. This species is not known to make or use tools. (Orangutans, however, have recently been observed using simple tools.) The species most relevant to our present subject are the chimpanzee and bonobo.

Much of what we know of the ethology of the chimp (*Pan troglodytes*) comes from the more than 30 years of research at Gombe Stream National Park in Tanzania led by Jane Goodall (1971, 1986, 1990). Goodall's studies have shown that in addition to physical and physiological traits, we share with chimps a number of behavioral characteristics. These center on aspects of social interaction and are thus instructive for our understanding of our own behavior.

The bond between mother and infant is strong in chimps, as it is in most mammals. These apes, though, have large, complex brains, and infants have a lot to learn about their world before they can become functioning adults. Thus, the mother–infant bond is particularly long-lived and important, and the nature of that interaction can have a lasting effect on the rest of a chimp's life. Poor treatment by its mother, for example, often makes a chimp a poor mother herself when she bears young. Chimps have been seen to help their mothers with younger siblings, and siblings often remain close into adulthood. Chimps, in other words, *raise* their young, and the family bonds that result may last a lifetime.

The chimps in a group are arranged in a dominance hierarchy. Males are generally dominant over females, but among females a loose hierarchy also exists. Males compete with one another in an attempt to achieve the highest position possible. The rewards are access to feeding places and to females, the latter being another example of male reproductive strategy. Social position, though attained in males through violent-looking but seldom injurious actions (Figure 8.4), is maintained via a series of expressions, gestures, and vocalizations. One of the most important actions is grooming (see Figure 7.10), which maintains social cohesion and on occasion is a sign of dominance when a subordinate male grooms his superior. Other expressions of social interaction include kissing, hugging, bowing, extending the hand, sexual gestures, grinning, and various vocalizations—and we can freely use these terms because the meanings of these actions in chimp society seem to be precisely what they are in human societies.

A chimp society, however, is in no way some sort of dictatorship. Instead, it is marked by cooperation and mutual concern, which is seen

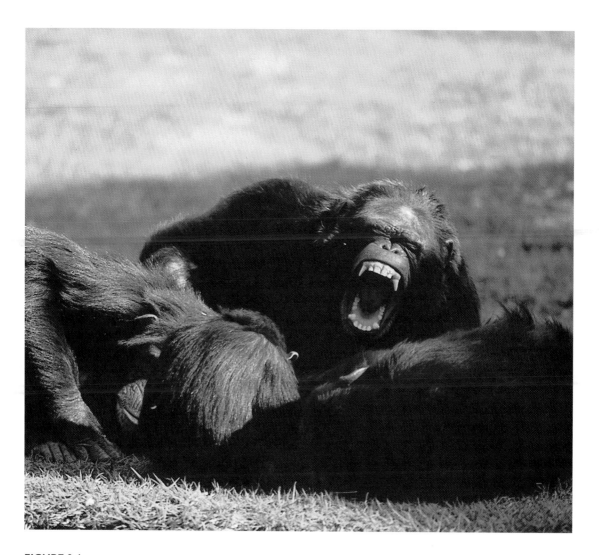

FIGURE 8.4

A Male Chimpanzee Showing a "Full Open Grin." This is a sign of excitement, often used by a high-ranking chimp when in close contact with a subordinate. Compare this with the expression of the baboon in Figure 8.3.

mostly within the family unit of mother and offspring (because chimps are sexually promiscuous—a female may mate with a dozen males during estrus—the biological father is unknown). Throughout their lives, members of this family unit will protect and care for each other, especially during illness and injury. Males have even been known to help brothers in their competition for dominance.

Care also extends outside the family unit. Offspring are important to the group as a whole, and adults will come to the aid or protection of a youngster threatened with some harm, possibly risking their own welfare, even if the youngster is not necessarily theirs. Goodall once observed an adolescent male adopt an unrelated youngster who had been orphaned (1990, 202). This protectiveness may be another example of inclusive fitness, where genes contributing to a behavior have been selected for because they confer adaptive fitness to individuals, both to the protectors and the protected, who may share genes.

Group membership is somewhat fluid. Chimps, for various reasons, will leave a group, and outsiders will occasionally enter it. Despite this fluidity, there is a sense of group identity and territory. Small bands of males will sometimes patrol the boundaries of their group's range, and when they encounter members of other groups, they react to them as outsiders. This is another case of males performing a behavior that serves to protect their reproductive investment.

With chimps, however, we may reasonably wonder about more conscious motivation for some of these behaviors. In one chilling series of events, for example, males from Goodall's main study group attacked and killed a female and all the males of a group that had broken away to establish their own territory. Goodall thinks the motivation may have been to reclaim the area. Although other examples of similar behavior have been reported, there is still debate over whether it is typical of the species. It has been suggested (Power 1991, for example) that because the researchers at Gombe interfered with the chimps' normal activities by providing food, they may have influenced the apes' behavior, including this event. Others (Sussman 1997) question how convincing the evidence is for similar occurrences.

Among the chimpanzee's wide range of food sources is meat. Chimps from some groups, including those studied by Goodall and associates at the Gombe, are hunters (Stanford 1995, 1999). Males, and occasionally females, will hunt and kill small pigs, antelopes, and monkeys, including young baboons (Figure 8.5). The Gombe chimps, sometimes hunting in cooperative groups, kill over 100 red colobus monkeys a year, nearly a fifth of the members of that species within the chimps' range. Meat is the one food that chimps will share, and male chimps are more likely to share with friends than with rivals—they will even withhold meat from rivals. There is evidence, too, that a male will hunt in order to get meat to give as an offering to a female in estrus.

Much of our information about this species comes from Goodall's research, but work on other chimp groups amply bears out her general observations and conclusions and lends support to the idea that chimp behavior is flexible, adaptable, and the result of intelligence and reasoning.

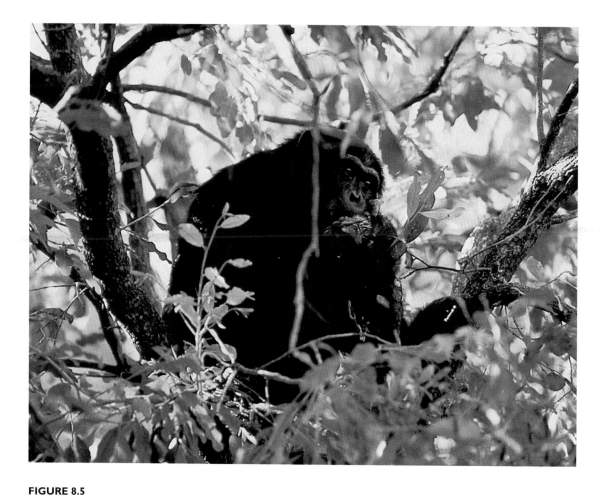

FIGURE 8.5

A chimp in Tanzania eats the carcass of a baboon he has recently hunted and killed. He may share some of his prize with close friends in his group.

It is thus variable from group to group. For example, a chimp group in the forests on the west coast of Africa uses hammerstones to crack open nuts, something the Gombe chimps don't do, though the Gombe chimps are famous for their termite sticks (see Chapter 7). The West African chimps also have different hunting techniques, relying more on cooperation between hunting males than do the Gombe chimps (Boesch and Boesch-Achermann 1991).

W. C. Mc Grew (1998) has suggested that this and other observations are evidence of cultural differences. And a recent synthesis of data from seven well-established chimpanzee field sites across Africa, comprising an accumulated 151 years of observation, has shown variation in thirty-nine different behavior patterns, not including those for which there are obvious ecological explanations (such as not nesting on the ground where leopards and lions are common). These patterns include tool use, grooming, and courtship behavior, and the nature of the variation points to the chimps' ability to invent new behaviors and pass them on socially—in which case the behaviors might be thought of as "customs" (Whiten et al. 1999; Whiten and Boesch 2001).

BONOBOS

Even more intriguing information has come to light about the third species of African ape, the bonobo (*Pan paniscus*; de Waal 1995; Ingmanson and Kano 1993; Kano 1990; White 1996). The bonobo lives in the lowland forests of the Democratic Republic of the Congo and has been estimated by genetic studies (see Chapter 9) to have been separate from the chimp for 930,000 years.

As mentioned earlier, bonobos are sometimes referred to as pygmy chimpanzees. But bonobos are not pygmies at all; they are as large as chimps, though more slender, with smaller heads and shoulders. They walk upright more often than chimps (Figure 8.6). Like chimps, bonobos do some hunting (though rarely) but show no evidence of cooperative hunting; further, females are sometimes the hunters, and the game is small (flying squirrels or a tiny antelope; Ingmanson and Ihobe 1992). Also like chimps, bonobos use tools, but never to acquire food. Rather, the bonobos use leaves as rain hats and drag branches to serve the social purposes of initiating group movement and indicating direction of movement (Ingmanson 1996).

The bonobos are more peaceful and gregarious than chimps. There is a dominance hierarchy among males, but unlike the case with chimpanzees, the hierarchy is easily established with brief aggressive chases. Female hierarchies appear to be based on seniority. Also unlike the chimps, female bonobos may dominate males (de Waal and Lanting 1997).

Bonobos more readily share food with one another, and the food shared is not limited to luxury items like meat (Figure 8.7). They have never been observed to kill another of their kind, and their sexual behaviors play important roles in group cohesion. In contrast, sexual coercion, as seen in the hamadryas baboons, has been observed among the chimps of Gombe.

FIGURE 8.6
Bonobo Standing Bipedally. This bonobo is collecting and carrying stalks of sugar cane in his hands, now freed from locomotor activities.

FIGURE 8.7
Bonobo society is characterized by peaceful relationships, with sexual activity and—as seen here on the left—food sharing as mechanisms to maintain harmony, ease tensions, reassure other members, and show reconciliation.

Bonobos, especially when feeding, constantly posture toward one another, rubbing rumps or "presenting" themselves as if initiating sexual activity. When sex does follow, it is usually face-to-face, a behavior uncommon in other primates but common in humans. Sexual activity is not limited to opposite-sex partners. Females commonly rub genitalia with other females, and males will mount each other.

Contemporary Reflections

Are Some Human Behaviors Genetic?

Since Darwin's time, people have speculated about the possible biological bases of some human behaviors. Over the past thirty years especially, a huge number of books have been written suggesting biological bases for human aggression, social practices such as marriage patterns, altruistic acts, morality, territoriality, and many more. The more extreme versions of such ideas claim that we have a genetic program for such behaviors and that these programs evolved in the past and are maintained today because they confer a reproductive advantage on those who express them. In other words, they have been, and many continue to be, naturally selected for. According to opponents of this idea, a logical—and dangerous—implication of this claim is that variation in the specific expression of a behavior might reflect genetic variation among populations of our species.

Addressing this issue is complicated (and there are just as many books that take some opposing viewpoint), but there are a few guiding concepts we may use to think about it. We must remember that genes are instructions for making proteins. It's a long way from the gene to the phenotypic trait, and the more complex the phenotypic trait, the longer the path and the more genes involved. Behaviors are *very* complex phenotypes. In short, just as there is no single "stature gene" that determines my height, there is no "aggression gene," or "marriage gene," or "altruism gene." Even in creatures with less complex nervous systems—ants, for example—whose behaviors *must* be biologically programmed, those behaviors are still complex responses of the whole organism to a whole host of environmental stimuli. There must be very many genes involved.

A behavior's biological program, then, is just a program for a potential or a general theme. Its expression requires some environmental stimulus (that is, something outside the genes themselves) and will vary as the exact nature of the stimulus varies. A biological basis for a human

Moreover, the signs of fertility, the estrus signals, seem nearly always present in bonobo females. In both chimps and bonobos, the fertile and therefore sexual period is marked by a swelling and coloration of the skin of the genital area, which stimulates sexual interest on the part of the males. In chimps, the swelling only occurs when the female has ovulated and is fertile. In bonobos, however, there is some swelling almost all the time, and they seem almost constantly sexually receptive. Sexual activity in this species has become separate from purely reproductive activity and is responded to on a conscious level. The motivation for sex may be as much psychological and social as it is reproductive.

The function of this friendly posturing and sexual receptiveness seems to be the same as that of grooming and as that of some expressions behavior can only be for the most general potential. Our cultural environment, which pervades every aspect of our individual and social lives, is immensely complex, and so the expressions of a behavioral potential must be varied indeed. Thus, the variation in a human behavior from society to society (or even from individual to individual) is largely a result of different cultural environments—different systems of belief and knowledge that mark the variety of humans' ways of life.

Language is a perfect—and fairly uncontroversial—example. All normal humans come equipped with the ability to take in raw data—the speech of the people around them and the responses to their attempts to communicate—and turn it into a working knowledge of their native language. Think about it: You spoke your native language fluently before you ever were formally taught all the grammatical rules in school. And you did it by yourself, using some built-in "software" in your nervous system into which data were fed by your senses. The ability to learn language is biological and thus, at its base, genetic. The genetic basis for this ability was selected for during our evolution (see Chapters 11 and 12). Linguistic ability conferred a reproductive advantage on our ancestors.

However, *what* language you speak, how well you speak it, what words you know, what accent you have—these particulars are cultural. They vary from society to society and even within societies—not because of genetic differences among populations but because of variation in the cultural contexts of which they are a part.

Similarly, the social system, with its sexual consciousness, that we see in bonobos may represent a common behavioral theme that we humans have translated into various sets of learned cultural norms like sexual ethics and marriage patterns. Nature has given us behavioral potentials, ultimately coded in our genes, that we inherited from our evolutionary ancestors and that evolved over the course of our species' history. Culture has given rise to our specific expressions of those behaviors. In this way, yes, some of our behaviors may be said to have a genetic basis—but only in this limited way.

and gestures among chimps: to prevent violence, to ease tension, (especially while feeding), to serve as a greeting, to signal reconciliation, or to reassure another group member. Sex or some form of sexual activity, between opposite- or same-sex partners, has even been seen to precede food sharing.

While on the subject of bonobos, we should mention Kanzi, a teenage male bonobo at the Language Research Center at Georgia State University (Savage-Rumbaugh and Lewin 1994). Kanzi is one of the most successful apes at communicating through a language with the characteristics of human communication. He uses symbols on a computer keyboard; he can even recognize and, using his computer, respond to a large number of spoken English words. In addition to his linguistic skills, he has been taught to make and use simple stone tools. Although not resembling even the earliest known hominid stone tools (see Chapter 10), Kanzi's tools are, nonetheless, true artifacts, and so may show us what the *very* earliest stone tools of our lineage might have looked like. Neither of these behaviors—using a humanlike language or stone toolmaking—is seen among wild bonobos, but they do give us an idea as to the cognitive potentials of the brains of these apes.

Now, if all the behaviors of the chimp and bonobo sound more than vaguely human, the reason may be simple. We share certain general behavioral patterns because we inherited them from a common ancestor. To be sure, our evolutionary line and that of the chimps and bonobos have been going their separate and independent ways for 5 or 6 million years, and even shared features have had the chance to become modified by all the processes of evolution—to be changed, eliminated, enhanced, and differently adapted to our species' different niches. Chimps and bonobos are not "living fossils" stuck in some 5-million-year-old rut while our ancestors continued to evolve. But because our common ancestor is relatively recent and there is striking similarity between their bodies and behaviors and ours, we can argue that our shared behavioral themes are homologous.

This does *not* mean that humans have specific genes for friendship, food sharing, territoriality, or continual sexuality. These are complex behaviors, and humans and apes are complex species. It does, however, hint that, as with the chimps and bonobos, the focus of the human adaptation—what adapted our earliest hominid ancestors and what has been the adaptive theme of our line—is social interaction based on individual recognition, a strong bond centered around family relationships (generally mothers and their offspring), long-term friendships, sexual consciousness, mutual care within the group, and recognition of and defense of the group. It seems reasonable to assume that our hominid ancestors behaved in similar ways. As Jane Goodall says,

> The concept of early humans poking for insects with twigs and wiping themselves with leaves seems entirely sensible. The thought of those ancestors greeting and reassuring one another with kisses or embraces, cooperating in protecting their territory or in hunting, and sharing food with each other, is appealing. The idea of close affectionate ties within the Stone Age family, of brothers helping one another, of teenage sons hastening to the protection of their old mothers, and of teenage daughters minding the babies, for me brings the fossilized relics of their physical selves dramatically to life. (1990, 207)

▽   ▽   ▽

SUMMARY

As we noted in the last chapter, one way to guide us as we look at our own species is to understand the context from which our species evolved. This approach works for behavior as well as for physical adaptations. The importance of a well-defined social organization is seen among one savanna primate, the baboon, and is a good hint that an analogous behavior was a key to the survival of early savanna hominids.

More useful to understanding our own behavior is to examine the behavior of close evolutionary relatives, especially the chimpanzee and bonobo. Chimp and bonobo behaviors differ in specifics from ours and have been evolving separately from ours for 5 or 6 million years. All three species have adapted to different niches. The basic patterns for the behavior of all three species, however, are homologous. They are the same because we inherited them from a common ancestor. It is highly likely, then, that our remote hominid ancestors also manifested these patterns in some way.

Such studies indicate to us that the early hominids of Africa may very well have been highly social creatures and that their social organization was built around differing interpersonal relationships, a family unit, conscious sexuality, recognition of group membership and territory, and mutual care at both the individual and the group level.

QUESTIONS FOR FURTHER THOUGHT

1. Consider the debate over the biological bases of human behaviors. Much of the debate in both the scientific and popular presses has focused on such things as human aggression, intelligence, and sexual orientation. What are the ramifications of the extreme points of view ("blank slate" versus "preprogrammed behaviors") with regard to these topics? How might each be seen in terms of an intermediate model, as described in the chapter?

2. In fields as diverse as particle physics and cultural anthropology, it has been noted that the very act of scientific observation affects that which is being observed. Certainly this would also be the case for the ethological observation of nonhuman primates. What are

the scientific as well as the ethical implications of this idea? Are some of our scientific ideas potentially inaccurate? Has studying other primates in the wild been in any way detrimental to them? benefical to them?

KEY TERMS

homologies	inclusive fitness	ethology
analogies	altruistic	savanna
sociobiology	reproductive strategies	

SUGGESTED READINGS

The latest thinking on baboon behavior can be found in Shirley Strum's *Almost Human* and in Barbara Smuts's *Sex and Friendship in Baboons.* Jane Goodall's latest work on the chimps and her experiences studying them is *Through a Window: My Thirty Years with the Chimpanzees of Gombe.*

For more technical information on primate behavior, see *The Evolution of Primate Behavior,* by Alison Jolly; *Patterns of Primate Behavior,* by Claud A. Bramblett; and *The Nonhuman Primates,* by Phyllis Dolhinow and Agustín Fuentes.

Dian Fossey recounts her study of gorillas in *Gorillas in the Mist;* her own story, in turn, including her murder, is told by Farley Mowat in *Woman in the Mists* and in the 1988 movie *Gorillas in the Mist.* Biruté Galdikas tells about orangutans in *Reflections of Eden: My Years with the Orangutans of Borneo.*

Chimpanzee hunting behavior and the possible influence of meat eating on human evolution are the topic of Craig B. Stanford's *The Hunting Apes: Meat Eating and the Origins of Human Behavior.* His position—that the quest for meat was what helped select for our big brains and gave rise to many human social behaviors—is controversial. For a critique, see the review of Stanford's book by Christophe Boesch in the June 17, 1999, issue of *Nature,* page 653.

For information on the cultural customs of chimpanzees, see "The Cultures of Chimpanzees," by Andrew Whiten and Christophe Boesch, in the January 2001 issue of *Scientific American.*

Bonobos are described in Frans de Waal's *Bonobo: The Forgotten Ape*, which has outstanding photographs by Frans Lanting. For more on the amazing Kanzi and other bonobos, see *Kanzi: The Ape at the Brink of the Human Mind*, by Sue Savage-Rumbaugh and Roger Lewin, and *Apes, Language, and the Human Mind*, by Savage-Rumbaugh et al.

CHAPTER

9

STUDYING
THE HUMAN
PAST

The present contains
nothing more than the
past, and what is found
in the effect was already
in the cause.
—Henri Bergson

The study of the human past—our evolutionary history—is a central part of biological anthropology. To understand the human species today, we need to know where, when, how, and from what we evolved. But the past *is* the past. We can't see past events as they were happening. We can't make them happen again. All we have are the present-day results of series of past events, like the living species of primates we discussed in Chapters 7 and 8. In some cases, we have the physical remains of past events, such as the fossils of extinct species, but these have themselves undergone change since they were part of a living creature.

The present, however, can be a powerful tool. Recall from Chapter 2 how Hooke and Steno used fossils and stratigraphy to plot the events of the past and how Hutton and Lyell used the idea of uniformitarianism— that the past can be explained by present-day processes—to understand how past events took place.

In this chapter, we will address the methods used by bioanthropologists to answer these questions about our past:

What are the features of the primate skeleton, and how can knowledge of them help us identify fossil remains?

How do we locate, recover, and date fossil remains?

How are fossils formed, and what affects the condition of the fossils we find?

What can we learn about our past from new technologies in the study of genetics?

BONES: THE PRIMATE SKELETON

Most of the physical remains we find of the evolutionary past are in the form of preserved bone. Only in rare cases are we lucky enough to discover soft tissue remains of an ancient organism (see Chapter 15). Therefore, knowledge of the skeletal structure, or **osteology,** is vital. The first thing we need to do, of course, is determine what species the skeletal remains are from. The human skeleton is a variation on the basic mammalian skeletal theme and, more specifically, on the primate skeletal theme. Figure 9.1 compares the skeletons (with the major bones labeled) of a modern human, a gorilla, and a domestic cat.

The bones are not separate from the muscles, nerves, blood vessels, and other soft tissues of the body. Rather, they all develop together and are adapted to function together. For example, the skull serves to protect

osteology: The study of the skeleton.

FIGURE 9.1
Skeletons of a Modern Human, a Gorilla, and a Domestic Cat. (As a learning exercise, label the gorilla skeleton yourself.)

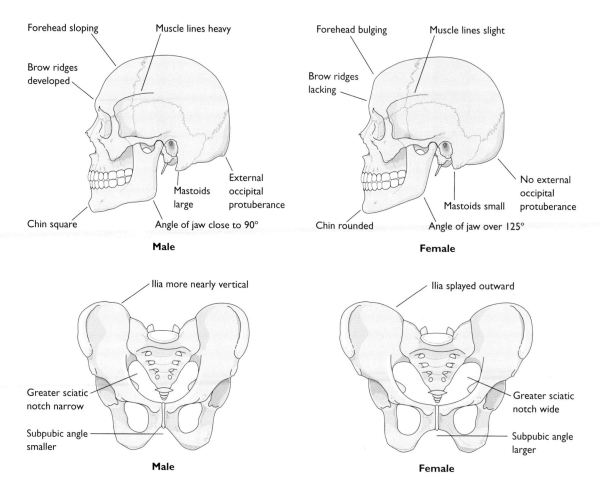

Forehead sloping
Muscle lines heavy
Brow ridges developed
External occipital protuberance
Mastoids large
Chin square
Angle of jaw close to 90°
Male

Forehead bulging
Muscle lines slight
Brow ridges lacking
No external occipital protuberance
Mastoids small
Chin rounded
Angle of jaw over 125°
Female

Ilia more nearly vertical
Greater sciatic notch narrow
Subpubic angle smaller
Male

Ilia splayed outward
Greater sciatic notch wide
Subpubic angle larger
Female

FIGURE 9.2
Sex Differences in the Human Skull and Pelvis.

the brain; therefore, the skull is a good indicator of the size and shape of the brain it once protected. Muscles are attached to bones, and so the location, size, and shape of the point where the muscle attaches to a bone will provide some indication of the size and shape of the muscle, even though the muscle itself may have decayed long ago. We can tell a lot about a creature from the bones it leaves behind.

One of the more obvious and important things we can tell about a human skeleton is its sex. Humans belong to a species that exhibits **sexual dimorphism,** notable physical differences between the sexes that are not related to reproductive traits. In general, human males tend to be larger and more heavily muscled than females, a fact that also applies to the apes and to extinct hominid species. The skull and, for obvious reasons, the pelvis are the best features for identifying the sex of a skeleton (Figure 9.2).

Age at death may also be determined from skeletal remains. The body, including the bones, goes through many physical changes as it develops, matures, and ages, and many of these changes take place at a fairly predictable rate. By determining on a skeleton which changes have already taken place and which have yet to take place, we may approximate the age at which these changes ceased, that is, the age at which the individual died (Figure 9.3).

The skeleton acts as a framework for the body, and thus the size and shape of the bones can reveal something of the appearance of the entire living person. We know, for example, from the sheer size and ruggedness of their bones, that a group of humans from Ice Age Europe (the *Neandertals*, whom we will discuss in Chapter 11) were big, brawny, and extremely strong. Several investigators have attempted to reconstruct the faces of our ancestors from the shapes of skulls and facial bones. Using their knowledge of human anatomy, they artistically add missing bones, eyes, fatty tissue, cartilage, muscle, and skin to casts of ancient skulls, "fleshing out" our picture of early humans (Figure 9.4; see also Figure 15.2). (This technique is also used in law enforcement to try to identify skeletal remains. We will discuss the application of human osteology to legal matters in Chapter 15.)

The skeleton can also tell us something about the behavior of the deceased organism. We have mentioned the importance of bipedal locomotion in our evolution and that this behavior was the first hominid trait to evolve. We know it was first because the nature of the bones of the pelvis and femur, along with the position of the skull atop the spine, suggests posture and movement. Thus, our analysis of the bones of our most ancient ancestors provides indications of how they walked (Figure 9.5; see also Chapter 10 for the evolution of this behavior).

Moreover, we can discern information about diet from dental and skeletal remains. Look at the dentition of a **carnivore** in your dog or cat, and compare it to the teeth of an **omnivore** in your own mouth. The teeth of the dog or cat, although they show some differentiation, are all pointed and sharp, adapted for grasping, piercing, cutting, and crushing meat. Our teeth are adapted for a greater variety of operations and, thus, a greater variety of food types. In addition, certain wear patterns on the teeth, when examined microscopically, can reveal whether the diet was made up of soft foods like fruits, or more abrasive, gritty foods like grains and roots (see Figure 10.20). We can even examine the chemical content of ancient bones for the proportion of strontium, calcium, carbon isotopes, and other elements to determine whether plants or meat made up the bulk of the diet of certain populations.

sexual dimorphism: Physical differences between the sexes of a species not related to reproductive features.

carnivore: An organism adapted to a diet of mostly meat.

omnivore: An organism with a mixed diet of animal and vegetable foods.

Average ages for cranial suture closure (years)

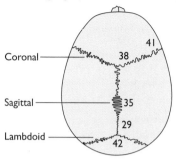

Coronal — 41
38

Sagittal — 35

29

Lambdoid — 42

Cranial Suture Closure. The bones of the cranial vault are separate at birth and gradually fuse during a person's lifetime. The numbers indicate the average age (in years) of complete closure at different points along the lines of attachment, the sutures. There are other dates as well, on locations not shown in this view. Because of the great degree of individual variation, this is not a particularly reliable technique, but it is still used.

Eruption dates of deciduous and permanent teeth

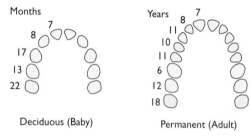

Months

7
8
17
13
22

Years

7
8
11
10
11
6
12
18

Deciduous (Baby)   Permanent (Adult)

Dental Eruption. Humans have two sets of teeth: deciduous, or "baby" teeth, and permanent, or adult teeth. Each tooth erupts through the gum line at a certain average age. We determine age by seeing which tooth was the last to erupt and which unerupted tooth would have erupted next. We recognize this method in our use of the term "six year molar" for the first adult tooth to erupt. The degree of development of each tooth below the gum line (seen in broken bone or in x-rays) can also be used.

Pubic symphysis

Ages of epiphyseal union (years)

Elbow	14
Hands and feet	15
Ankle	16
Thigh (top)	17
Knee	18
Wrist	19
Shoulder	20
Hip	21
Clavicle	28

28 years
20 years

14 years
21 years
17 years
19 years
15 years

18 years

Epiphysis (cap)

Diaphysis (shaft)

Epiphyseal disk

16 years
15 years

Epiphyseal Union. The bones of the arms, legs, hands, feet, and other bones grow in sections: a shaft, or diaphysis, and caps, or epiphyses. When growth is complete, the cartilaginous disks between caps and shaft turn to bone and a single bone results. Ages for epiphyseal union are uniform enough to provide a reliable aging method. The ages shown indicate that all the sites at any one location fuse at about the same time. For example, at the elbow, the far (distal) end of the humerus and the near (proximal) ends of the radius and ulna all fuse at approximately 14 years.

Pubic Symphysis. The inner surface of the bones where the pelvis meets in front is called the pubic symphysis. Between the ages of 18 and 50+, the appearance of this surface undergoes characteristic changes. By assessing the phase to which a specimen belongs, we can approximate the age of a specimen at death. The symphyseal face shown is a Phase VIII, giving an age of 40 to 44 years. (Redrawn from Todd 1920.)

FIGURE 9.3
Major Techniques Used to Determine the Age of Hominid Bones.

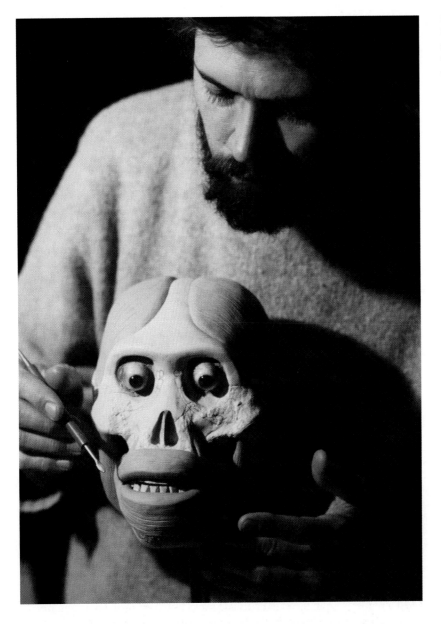

FIGURE 9.4
Using a cast of a fossil skull, modeling clay is added to flesh out the face of an ancient human ancestor.

Finally, we may acquire information about the health status of our ancestors, a field known as **paleopathology.** Many diseases leave characteristic marks on the skeleton. These include such important disorders as arthritis, tumors and other cancers, tuberculosis, leprosy, anemias, syphilis, osteoporosis, typhoid (as in Henry Opukahaia, discussed in

paleopathology: The study of disease and nutritional deficiency in prehistoric populations, usually with reference to the use of skeletal material.

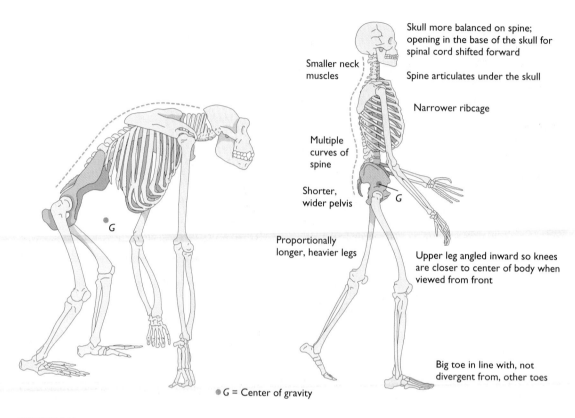

Skull more balanced on spine; opening in the base of the skull for spinal cord shifted forward

Smaller neck muscles

Spine articulates under the skull

Narrower ribcage

Multiple curves of spine

Shorter, wider pelvis

G

Proportionally longer, heavier legs

Upper leg angled inward so knees are closer to center of body when viewed from front

Big toe in line with, not divergent from, other toes

● G = Center of gravity

FIGURE 9.5
Note the anatomical changes and, thus, the physical evidence associated with bipedalism in the human primate. Compare human features with corresponding ones in the gorilla. G represents the center of gravity when standing bipedally. The ape expends much more energy to keep from falling forward.
(Modified from John Napier, *The Antiquity of Human Walking,* ©1967 Scientific American. Drawing by Enid Kotschnigo)

trephination: The cutting of a hole in the skull, presumably to treat some illness.

Chapter 1), and various infections. Injuries, too, leave their marks, as do other cultural behaviors, including scalping and **trephination,** a prehistoric surgical procedure that involved cutting a hole in the skull (Figure 9.6).

OLD BONES: LOCATING, RECOVERING, AND DATING FOSSILS

Most creatures that have ever lived, including humans, have left no remains. Fossilization (which we'll discuss in the next section) is a rare occurrence. A fossil, therefore, is really a priceless treasure, and finding one is an uncommon event—even in those **sites** that because of their geological history and nature yield many remains. Olduvai Gorge in Tanzania (Figure 9.7) has provided us with some of the most important hominid fossils, yet Louis and Mary Leakey lived and worked there for more than 20 years before finding one. How then, do we even decide where to begin looking?

FIGURE 9.6

Ancient Disease and Injury. (*Left*) The effects of advanced syphillis are evident on the bones of the face, skull, arms, and legs of this skeleton. Note the extensive lesions on the skull and at the ends of the humeri and tibias. (*Above*) The arrow shows the outer margin of the surgery on this trephined skull. The edge of the hole indicates that healing had taken place before the individual died.

A lot, of course, depends upon just *what* we're looking for. If it's dinosaurs we're interested in, we look in rock strata that date from the time of the dinosaurs. For hominid fossils, we need strata that were deposited in the past 5 or 6 million years.

It helps, too, if those strata are exposed by geological processes. Layers that are far under the surface might contain important fossils, but

sites: Locations that contain fossil evidence of human presence.

FIGURE 9.7
Olduvai Gorge, Tanzania. This location is one of the world's most productive sites for paleoanthropologists. The strata represent more than 2 million years of evolution.

purely practical considerations would make it difficult, time-consuming, and expensive to dig them up. A place like Olduvai Gorge is ideal. There, an ancient river cut a canyon 300 feet into the earth, exposing layers of soil and rock that go back about 2 million years. At Omo, in Ethiopia, another important early hominid site, the strata have been tilted by geological forces, so that layers from 1 million to 4 million years old are all on the surface. Walking back and forth at such sites as these is like walking through time. In addition, in such places, natural water and wind erosion help expose new soil and whatever fossils it may contain.

Of course, just because a location *looks* like it might easily yield fossils doesn't mean that the conditions there were always conducive to fos-

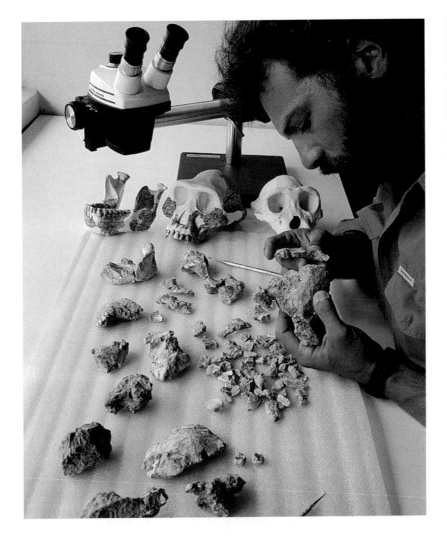

FIGURE 9.8
Paleoanthropologist Bill Kimbel of the Institute of Human Origins uses dental tools, a small drill, and a binocular microscope to chip stone from bone on nearly sixty fragments of a fossil hominid from Ethiopia. The results of his efforts are shown in Figure 10.14.

silization. Paleoanthropologists might inquire as to whether fossils of *any* sort have been found in a potential area of investigation in strata from the time period they are interested in. Both Olduvai and Omo already had reputations as rich fossil areas before the search for hominid fossils began there.

Recovering fossils once they are located can be a tricky business. Fossils are old and often very fragile. Many old bones are **petrified**—turned to stone—and so are hard to distinguish from the stone in which they were found (Figure 9.8). Raymond Dart, the discoverer of one of the most famous hominid fossils (both of whom we shall meet in the next chapter),

petrified: Turned to stone.

FIGURE 9.9

Hypothetical Stratigraphic Sequence. The humanlike remains are between two layers of volcanic rock that can be dated using the K/Ar (potassium/argon) method. They must be younger than the volcanic deposit below and older than the one above.

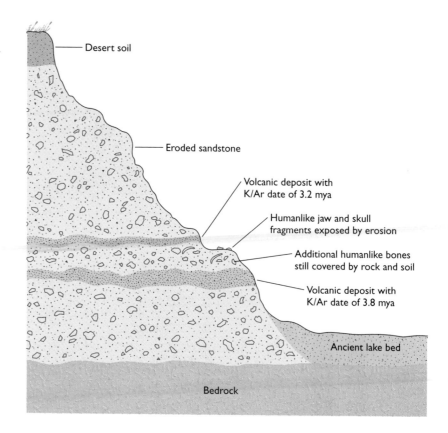

Desert soil

Eroded sandstone

Volcanic deposit with K/Ar date of 3.2 mya

Humanlike jaw and skull fragments exposed by erosion

Additional humanlike bones still covered by rock and soil

Volcanic deposit with K/Ar date of 3.8 mya

Ancient lake bed

Bedrock

took 73 days to separate the tiny fossil from the limestone in which it was encased (see Figure 10.7). The excavation tools of the paleoanthropologist, then, are not so much the backhoe or even the shovel but rather the mason's trowel, the dentist's pick, and the artist's brush.

A fossil sitting on a shelf in a lab or on display in a museum may be beautiful, intriguing, and provocative, but it is scientifically useless unless we know precisely where it was found, its **provenience.** To keep track of the proveniences of fossils, recovery is carried out with the utmost care directed at detailed and accurate record keeping. After all, once fossils are removed, a site is destroyed, and we must have records of the relative locations of all the important items contained in that site.

Many early hominid fossils are simply found on the surface of the ground, exposed by wind and water erosion. Many, however, are dug out of the ground or are found associated with particular strata.

The depth at which a fossil is found in the natural strata of the soil or rock is, of course, an indication of relative age. This is the principle of **superposition**—the deeper a layer is the older it is. It is an important dating method and is referred to as a **relative dating technique;** that is, it indicates the age of one fossil in comparison to that of another (Figure 9.9). In the absence of any natural stratigraphy, the excavator of fossils must establish one. For example, the investigator may dig down by regular increments, perhaps only centimeters at a time, recording the precise depth of any item of interest.

Fossils can also be dated relative to their stratigraphic correlation with other fossils of known age. This is the principle of **biostratigraphy.** It has been used in some of the early hominid sites in South Africa. Many of these are in limestone caves, which are difficult to date by the techniques discussed in the following paragraphs. But when nonhominid fossils of known age are found in association with hominid fossils, we may infer the age of the hominids.

Similarly, the horizontal location of each fossil is important. Often a paleoanthropologist—like the archaeologist looking for human cultural remains—uses a grid system. A site is divided into squares, or grids, and each grid is excavated separately (Figure 9.10). The precise location of a fossil, relative to that of others at the same level, is recorded through photographs and maps.

Besides relative dating, there are also **absolute dating techniques** (also called **chronometric techniques**). These tell us the actual age of a fossil. Among the best known are **radiometric** techniques, such as **radiocarbon dating,** which can be used to date fossils back to about 60,000 ya and so is relevant to the later period of human evolution. It works as follows: Carbon, in the form of carbon dioxide, is found in all living things, which continuously exchange it with the environment through respiration and metabolism. Most carbon is ^{12}C, indicating that there are twelve particles in the nucleus (six protons and six neutrons). Some carbon, however, is called *carbon 14*, or ^{14}C, because it has two extra neutrons. It is formed when swifty moving neutrons hit nitrogen atoms in the atmosphere. We know the proportion of each form (*isotope*) of carbon in a living organism. Once an organism dies, however, it no longer takes in new carbon, and so its ^{14}C—an unstable, or radioactive, isotope—begins to decay back into nitrogen, and it does this at a constant rate called a **half-life.** The half-life of ^{14}C is 5,730 years. In that time, one-half of the ^{14}C will have decayed. In another 5,730 years, half of the remaining half will decay, leaving a quarter of the original. And so on.

provenience: Here, the precise location where a fossil or artifact was found.

superposition: The principle of stratigraphy that, barring disturbances, more recent layers are superimposed over older ones.

relative dating technique: A dating method that indicates the age of one item in comparison to another.

biostratigraphy: The study of fossils in their stratigraphic context. Used as a relative dating technique.

absolute dating techniques: Dating methods that give a specific age, year, or range of years.

chronometric techniques: Another name for absolute dating techniques.

radiometric: Referring to the decay rate of a radioactive substance.

radiocarbon dating: A radiometric dating technique using the decay rate of a radioactive form of carbon found in organic remains.

half-life: The time needed for one-half of a given amount of a radioactive substance to decay.

FIGURE 9.10

Grid System Diagram. Illustrated here is a portion of an excavation from Ambrona, Spain, dated at around 350,000 ya (see Chapter 11). The grid helps record the precise location of each bone and artifact. Notice how much less information is conveyed by the solid part of the drawing, which does not show the grid.

Now, if we find some organic remains—bone, for example, or even burnt wood from a fire—we can test it to see how much ^{14}C is left compared to how much the organism contained when alive. We know how much ^{14}C a living organism should contain, and we test the amount left as we would test any radioactive substance, with a device that measures the amount of radiation emitted. Suppose that our specimen has one-quarter of the living amount. Two half-lives have passed, or $5{,}730 \times 2$, or 11,460 years. In fossils older than about 50,000 years there is not enough ^{14}C left to accurately measure. So how do we date the really old fossils, like those of the early hominids?

We could use another important method called **potassium/argon,** or **K/Ar, dating.** Radioactive potassium (^{40}K), found in volcanic rock, decays into stable argon gas over time; its half-life is 1.31 billion years. Organic matter contains ^{40}K as well but loses the argon gas that it decays into. Volcanic rocks, formed during eruptions, have a crystalline structure that traps the argon. Using the same reasoning as for carbon dating, we test volcanic rock for the amount of argon, work backward, and date the eruption. Then, organic remains may be dated relatively: Any fossils found in a layer of volcanic rock are as old as that rock. Fossils found just above are younger; those found just below are older (see again Figure 9.9). Recently, a technique called **argon/argon dating,** which uses the decay of radioactive ^{40}Ar into argon gas (^{39}Ar), has provided more accuracy in dating volcanic rock. With the use of lasers, it can be performed on a sample as small as a single crystal.

Two other techniques have recently become more widely used and have provided new dates for some fossil sites (see Chapters 11 and 12). One is called **electron spin resonance (ESR) dating.** Natural radioactivity can excite electrons in crystalline material to higher energy levels, where they are "trapped." The number of trapped electrons in such material is related to the nature of the material, the amount of natural background radiation, and, most important, the amount of time since the material formed. By measuring the number of trapped electrons, we can calculate the age of materials such as tooth enamel, mollusk shells, cave deposits, corals, and volcanic rock. This technique has been particularly useful for sites too old (more than 50,000 years) to be dated with radiocarbon. It does not, however, work well on bone.

Luminescence dating, like ESR dating, measures electrons that have been trapped at higher energy levels by background radiation. The more energy trapped, the older the material. Here, the trapped energy is released in the lab using heat (a process called *thermoluminescence,* or *TL*) or light (*optically stimulated luminescence,* or *OSL*) and is seen in the form of a light glow (*luminescence*). It is useful to about 800,000 ya. This technique has been used to date mostly artifacts like fired clay, pottery, bricks, and burned rock, such as would be found lining a hearth. This technique has also been applied to soil sediments, but there is still some debate over the accuracy of this application.

Other dating techniques also exist (these are listed in Table 9.1, along with the preceding methods). Several date volcanic rock; others can be used directly on organic remains. In many cases, more than one of these methods may be applied, and when they agree, we have a well-established date for a geological stratum or a fossil. Most of the dates that will be presented in the following chapters are reasonably well confirmed through the use of one or more of these techniques.

potassium/argon (K/Ar) dating: A radiometric dating technique using the rate that radioactive potassium, found in volcanic rock, decays into stable argon gas.

argon/argon dating: A radiometric dating technique that uses the decay of radioactive argon into stable argon gas. Can be used to date smaller samples and volcanic rock with greater accuracy than does K/Ar dating.

electron spin resonance (ESR) dating: An absolute dating technique that measures the number of electrons excited to higher energy levels by natural radiation and trapped at those levels. Can be used to date tooth enamel, shells, corals, mineral cave deposits, and volcanic rock, but does not work well on bone.

luminescence dating: An absolute dating technique that measures trapped electrons by releasing their energy in the form of light. Can be used to date fired clay, pottery, brick, and burned stones. It may have some application in soil dating.

TABLE 9.1
Absolute Dating Techniques

Dating Method	Age Range	Material Dated	Basis
Accelerator mass spectrometry	100s–70,000 B.P.*	Organic remains	Counts actual number of ^{14}C atoms
Amino (aspartic) acid racemization	1,000,000–2,000 B.P.	Bone	Measures shift in polarity of amino acids
Electron spin resonance	100s–10 million B.P.	Teeth, cave deposits	Measures electrons produced by natural radiation that become trapped in crystalline materials at a regular rate
Fission track dating	1,000,000–100,000 B.P.	Volcanic rock	Measures radioactive decay that leaves microscopic damage "tracks" in rock at a regular rate
Obsidian hydration	800,000 B.P.-present	Obsidian (volcanic glass)	Measures regular buildup of a "hydration layer," caused by the chemical reaction of obsidian to water over time
Paleomagnetism	2,000 B.P.-present	Material with magnetic minerals	Determines movement of earth's magnetic pole against known dates of its position
Potassium/argon and argon/argon	100,000–billions B.P.	Volcanic rock	Measures decay of radioactive potassium (or argon isotope) to stable argon gas
Radiocarbon	100s–60,000 B.P.	Organic remains	Measures decay of radioactive carbon isotope to stable nitrogen
Thermoluminescence	To 800,000 B.P.	Fired clay, pottery, bricks, burned rock	Measures amount of energy captured in material from the decay of radioactive elements in surrounding soil; amount of energy captured is the proportional to age
Uranium series	350,000–1,000 B.P.	Calcium carbonate	Measures decay of radioactive uranium to a series of other elements

*B.P. = "before present."

HOW FOSSILS GET TO BE FOSSILS

As mentioned earlier, most animals and plants that have inhabited the earth have left no fossil remains. There may be whole taxonomic groups that we have no idea of because we've found no clues to their existence. Why is this so?

The conditions under which an organism, or some of its parts, can be preserved are quite specific. In New England, where I live, the soil is very acidic, due largely to the annual fall of leaves and pine needles. Organic remains tend to disappear very quickly. This is why we were surprised to find the intact skeleton of Henry Opukahaia (see Chapter 1). His bones were preserved because he was buried on a hill in sandy soil, so water, with all its related chemical and biological decaying activity, could not accumulate around him, and probably because the cemetery was regularly cleared of leaves.

Organic remains tend to be preserved under several conditions. In cases of extreme dryness, even soft tissues—usually eaten by everything from bacteria to insects to scavengers—may mummify. Natural mummies were created in normal burials in the desert sands of ancient Egypt, even before the Egyptians began artificial mummification. In 1995, near the summit of the 20,760-foot volcano Nevando Ampato in Peru, the naturally mummified remains of a young Inca girl were found (Figure 9.11). Sacrificed to the gods of the mountains some 500 ya, her body was preserved by the cold and dry conditions of the high altitude (Reinhard 1996). More recently, at another and even higher site in the Andes, the bodies of three more children were discovered (Reinhard 1999). (See Chapter 15 for another famous example—the "Ice Man" from the Alps.)

Lack of oxygen also contributes to preservation. Such conditions are found in the thick sediment at the bottom of some lakes and ponds. With no oxygen, there is little bacterial action, and organic remains decay very slowly. Many important fossils have been found in places that were once lake bottoms.

Of course, the longer ago an organism lived, the less likely we are to find remains, simply because there is more chance that they will have been crushed, dissolved, eaten, washed away, and so on. But in some cases, minerals may crystallize out of water around the bones or shells of a creature, or in rare cases around slowly decaying soft tissue, and may fill in the spaces left by the decay of organic matter. In this case, the fossil becomes petrified; it literally turns to stone and so is harder, more resistant to processes of decay, and no longer edible—although, naturally, some anatomical detail is lost. The dinosaur fossils with which we are so familiar, as well as the remains of the earliest hominids, are all stone. Luckily for us, the creatures that left these remains perished in just the right situations. Most creatures, however, aren't so considerate.

A fossil is more than just an indication of the type of organism of which it was once a part. A fossil also contains clues as to how the animal died and what happened to it after its death. The study of these factors is

FIGURE 9.11
The Inca "Ice Maiden" is one of several naturally preserved mummies of sacrificial victims found in the Andes.

called **taphonomy** (from the Greek word *taphos*, "dead"), and it has been important in our understanding of our own evolution.

For example, some early hominid bones have been found in limestone caves in South Africa along with the bones of other mammals. These finds led investigators to believe that our early ancestors inhabited those caves and were hunters who brought their kills back home. More recent taphonomic analysis, however, reveals that the hominids were the hunted, not the hunters. The bones were the leftovers of leopard kills. Here's how scientists believe it happened: Leopards often drag their prey up into a tree, where no other predator or scavenger can get at it. Although much of South Africa is dry, trees are able to grow around the mouths of limestone caves, which hold moisture. As leopard kills hanging

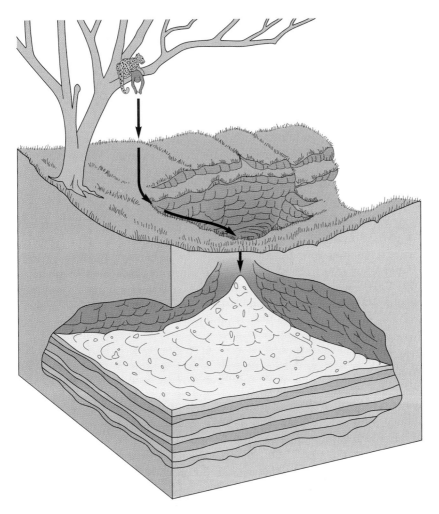

FIGURE 9.12
This artist's reconstruction shows a leopard with the remains of an early hominid in a tree above the entrance to a cave. This behavior probably accounts for the accumulation of bones, including bones of our ancestors, in South African caves.

in the trees fell apart—after being eaten over several days or decaying over time—the bones fell into the caves. Those bones were of antelopes, baboons, and other animals leopards eat. Apparently, our ancestors were on the menu as well (Figure 9.12). One early hominid skull shows twin puncture wounds that appear to have been the cause of death. The lower canine teeth of a leopard fit exactly into these punctures, providing evidence for the preceding analysis. Taphonomy, although the study of the dead, has thus told us important things about how our distant ancestors *lived*. We will describe another important conclusion from taphonomy in the next chapter, when we see how microscopic scratches on bones and teeth reveal something about the diet of the early hominids.

taphonomy: The study of how organisms become part of the paleontological record.

GENES: NEW WINDOWS TO THE PAST

Just as we can reconstruct evolutionary relationships by comparing the anatomical traits of living creatures, we may do the same by making comparisons at the genetic level. In some ways, genetic comparisons are more accurate. Phenotypic traits are normally controlled by a complex interaction of multiple genes, evolutionary processes, and environmental factors. As a result, a trait may look the same in two species, but the expressions of that trait in each species may be based on very different genetics, developmental processes, and environmental interactions, and the two traits may have different adaptive functions.

Stephen Jay Gould (1980) notes the example of the panda's "thumb," which looks like the thumb of primates and is used for grasping. It is actually, however, not a finger at all but an elongated wrist bone that is used solely to strip bamboo stalks of their leaves, just about the panda's only food. One might conclude from this striking similarity in a rather unique feature that pandas are closely related to primates, but the similarity is purely a coincidence. The thumbs of primates and the "thumb" of the panda are analogous, not homologous (see Chapter 8). The panda is a bear, in order Carnivora, and is not closely related to primates, as an examination of the genes themselves would clearly show.

However, any two species may look very different, but their differences may be the result of extensive phenotypic effects of a very small number of genes, and the species may actually be quite closely related. Humans and chimps are an example.

Comparing genetic differences among individuals, species, and higher taxa (genera, families, and so on) reveals actual biological relationships, no matter what the species look like or how seemingly similar or different some of their traits are. In the 1960s, Vincent Sarich and the late Allan Wilson of the University of California at Berkeley pioneered research that used genetic comparisons to determine evolutionary relationships. Because the technology for comparing actual genes was still unknown when they carried out their work, they compared the chemistry of blood proteins. These are large proteins, easily obtained and easy to work with and, most important, the direct products of the genetic code. This research provided some startling conclusions.

It had been assumed at the time that humans and our closest relatives, the great apes, were separated by 12 to 15 million years of evolution. This estimate was based on the degree of phenotypic difference between us and them and on some 12-million-year-old fossils that *appeared* to show the beginnings of hominid traits. Wilson and Sarich's research showed that the blood proteins of humans and chimps are almost

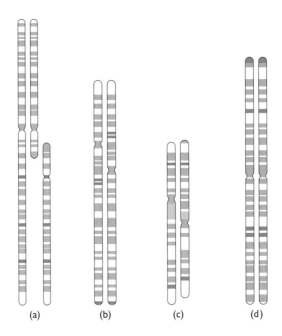

(a)   (b)   (c)   (d)

FIGURE 9.13

Comparison of Human and Chimpanzee Chromosomes. Human chromosomes appear on the left in each pair and chimpanzee chromosomes on the right. The similarities in banding pattern are clear. In the far-lefthand pair, the pattern of human chromosome 2 is similar to that of two chimp chromosomes. The far-righthand pair are virtually identical. Banding patterns are the results of different concentrations of the four bases that make up the genetic code. Light bands are rich in noncoding sequences with mostly C's (cytosine) and G's (guanine; see Chapter 3). These tend to be associated with areas of high gene concentration. This is one piece of evidence for the 98.5-percent genetic similarity between our two species.

identical. In other words, our genes, at least for those traits, are almost the same. Comparing this difference with that between species whose evolutionary divergence time was known, Wilson and Sarich calculated that our two species had branched apart a mere 5 mya. These 12-million-year-old fossils, they concluded, were not hominids, no matter what they appeared to be. They were right, as we will see in Chapter 10.

Other methods for making comparisons closer to the genetic level verified this hypothesis. A protein, you recall, is a genetically coded sequence of amino acids. Proteins may thus be compared for the sequence of amino acids that constitute them. Again, research demonstrated that humans and chimpanzees show less than 2 percent difference in the amino acid structure of certain blood proteins—we are nearly identical. Comparison of a chemical reaction of the DNA of chimps and humans and of the pattern of bands on chromosomes of chimps and humans (an indication of the nature of their sequence of genes) revealed the same lack of difference (Figure 9.13).

Contemporary Reflections

Who Owns Old Bones?

In 1990, the nearly complete skeleton of a *Tyrannosaurus rex*, nicknamed "Sue," was found in South Dakota and soon became the center of a controversy over ownership. After some complex legal haggling, the owner of the land on which the bones were found was granted permission to sell them. The skeleton went up for public auction in October 1997 and was purchased (with corporate help) by the Field Museum of Natural History in Chicago—for $8.36 million! It will now be available for research and is currently on public display. In this case, everybody won, but scientists worry that this could set a precedent that would remove important evidence of the past from free scientific inquiry.

The issue of ownership and availability to science becomes even more complex when the remains of the past are human. In these cases, ownership may be a matter not only of landholding but also of direct biological or cultural descent. The extreme cases are easy enough to sort out. I don't think anyone would object to the excavation and study of early African hominids, even though they are the ancestors of us all. They are simply too far removed in time, and their potential scientific value is too great. On the other hand, I would object if some anthropologist wanted to dig up my grandparents, examine their bones, and put them in a museum case—and the law would clearly be on my side. Not all situations, however, are as clear-cut.

For years, otherwise well-meaning scientists have enjoyed the freedom to recover, study, and store the skeletal remains of the remote and not-so-remote ancestors of living peoples. In North America, thousands of Native American skeletons have been recovered—many of which were exhumed from the graves into which they had been placed by members of their societies. Although these remains have provided much information about the original inhabitants of this continent, Native American groups have voiced objections, for obvious reasons. In 1990, the Native American Graves Protection and Repatriation Act (NAGPRA) was passed. It says that lineal descendants have a right to the remains of their ancestors housed in institutions or discovered on federal or tribal territory. This legislation has led to the removal of large collections of human remains and associated artifacts from museums and labs and has made new excava-

Now, recent technology (see the "Contemporary Reflections" box in Chapter 3) has allowed us to look at and compare the most basic genetic components—the sequence of base pairs that make up the codons, which in turn make up the genes. This is the same technology that has made great strides in such matters as personal identification in criminal and missing persons cases. For example, blood samples from crime scenes can be genetically compared with samples from suspects, virtually ensuring accurate identifications. DNA sequencing also helps in locating genes involved in various diseases. And, relative to our topic here, we can now precisely compare the genetic makeup of primate species, establishing just how genetically similar or different they are, and, using the logic detions of Native American remains difficult, if not impossible. Indeed, before "naturally shed" remains were excluded from NAGPRA regulations, two local tribes demanded the return of some 10,000-year-old human hair found at a site in Montana, hair that could provide information on the DNA of early Americans (see Feder 1997 and references therein for a more complete discussion of this and related issues). A well-known example involves the skeletal remains discovered in 1996 in Washington State and commonly known as "Kennewick Man." A coalition of Native American tribes from the area laid claim to the 9,000-year-old bones under the terms of NAGPRA. Despite scientific testimony to the contrary, Secretary of the Interior Bruce Babbitt declared in September 2000 that the remains were culturally affiliated with the coalition and that the bones should be turned over to them. A suit by a group of scientists to gain access to the remains for study has been reinstated. As of this writing, the bones are in the custody of the Army Corps of Engineers.

Is there a compromise between honoring the cultural laws and heritage of peoples and providing science with important data—data that may even shed light on the history of the people in question? Each case, in the end, must be examined and judged on its own merits. Much evidence of early America is in the form of abandoned and naturally covered-over objects and bones, not intentional burials. Much cannot be reasonably affiliated with any specific living group. Such things should be freely open to legitimate scientific investigation. Alternatively, scientists should not go into clearly identified burial areas armed with shovels and trowels. As is most often the case, where ancient bones are uncovered by natural processes or accident (say, during a construction project), the group with which those bones are affiliated might allow scientific information to be gathered before the bones are reburied. This is the situation with the well-known African Burial Ground in New York City. A model example for me is the case of Henry Opukahaia (Chapter 1), where the family kindly allowed us to fully examine Henry's bones before preparing and returning them for burial.

Whatever the individual cases, however, there is one overriding consideration that should guide our actions in these matters—no matter how old or from what species, bones were once integral parts of living, breathing, feeling beings. Even when we can use them as scientific specimens, they deserve respectful treatment.

scribed above, estimate how long ago their evolutionary lines deverged. There has even been an attempt to reconstruct the ancestral genome of all living primates (O'Brien and Stanyon 1999).

To be sure, until we can compare *all* the base pairs of the species in which we're interested, there will be some differences in the estimated relationships. Comparisons of different sections of genomes may yield slightly different results. But this new technology is accurate enough that we are, for example, confident in the 1.5 percent genetic difference identified between humans and chimpanzees and of the evolutionary branching pattern that has been genetically determined for the hominoids (see Chapter 7).

An interesting question that has resulted from these studies is the matter of just *which* genes differ between humans and chimpanzees and *what* those genes do. In other words, what genetic differences make chimps chimps and humans humans? Recent studies suggest that the difference may be as few as 50 coding genes (out of an estimated 100,000); (Wade 1998) and that one of those differences—a 92-base pair section of a single gene—leads to our lacking a certain chemical on the surface of all body cells that all other mammals, including the apes, possess (Gibbons 1998b; Muchmore et al. 1998). The results of this difference are still being investigated, but it is known that the chemical acts as a receptor for messages from other cells, is used by pathogens to attach to a cell and, importantly, may be involved in cellular communication during brain development and function, something that could influence the timing and extent of brain growth. This last function has obvious implications for the story of human evolution.

In addition to these specific differences, it has also been established that 5 chromosomes in our two species show significant differences in the arrangement of the same genes. Some sequences, for example, have been flipped (or inverted) in one species as compared to the other. These changes could lead to different roles for those genes. Identifying their functions is a current goal, as is the establishment of a nonhuman primate genome project to provide a complete sequence of the genomes of our closest relatives (Gibbons 1998b).

In the next three chapters, we will outline the story of hominid evolution. All the above scientific techniques have been applied to studying this story and have allowed us to achieve what knowledge we have of our evolutionary history. As we will see, these new technologies have also been applied to the relationships between modern humans and various groups of our ancestors (Chapter 12) and to comparisons among modern human populations (Chapter 14).

▽   ▽   ▽

SUMMARY

Often, when we read a necessarily brief article in the popular press about a new fossil find, we get the impression that the scientists conducted some sort of magic to arrive at their stated conclusions. In the October 3, 1994, issue of *Time*, for example, we read that a small fossil tooth and a few other fragmentary bones from Ethiopia had been discovered and heralded as "a new chapter in the history of human evolution" (Lemonick 1994). On the basis of these bones, a new species of hominid was established, and it is described as having been about 4 feet tall and probably bipedal, having been "ravaged by carnivores," and having lived 4.4 mya in the forests. That's pretty specific information from a handful of bones turned to stone.

You should now understand that arriving at such conclusions is not magic at all. Though data like these bones are from a creature millions of years old, we may still use scientific methodology to interpret them. We know what modern mammalian skeletons look like and what previous fossil finds look like, so we can compare our new fossils to them in order to give them at least a provisional taxonomic assignment. As the fossils were being recovered in Ethiopia, exhaustive data were recorded about their provenience, allowing us to generate hypotheses about their environment and, using technologies from physics, their date. We understand how fossils are formed and what their specific condition can tell us about how the creature died and became part of the fossil record. We know, for example, what bones that have been "ravaged by carnivores" look like.

Finally, combining the preceding techniques with new methods from genetics, we have been able to piece together a tentative family tree of the hominids and related primates. When a new set of fossils is found, we have a context into which it may be placed and a taxonomic system that can supply it with a name. We will meet this 4.4-million-year-old fossil species and many others in the next chapter, as we see exactly how these fact-finding techniques are applied.

QUESTIONS FOR FURTHER THOUGHT

1. Recently, the Parliament of Iceland gave a private company the right to create and maintain a database on the health records, genealogies, and DNA profiles of nearly all living and many decreased Icelanders. The intent is to better understand links between diseases and genes. But there are concerns over matters of privacy and the fact that the company may sell its information to pharmaceutical and insurance companies. What issues must be taken into account so that we might benefit from such a study while still respecting the rights of individuals?

2. Read the latest information about Kennewick Man on the websites listed in this chapter's "Suggested Readings." What do you think

about the motives of the scientists who want to use the remains for study as opposed to those of the Native Americans who want to rebury the bones with no further study? Is a compromise possible? How should we approach remains that have definite cultural affiliations but that might hold important scientific information? How far back into history must we go to find human or archaeological remains that preclude such controversy?

KEY TERMS

osteology	superposition	half-life
sexual dimorphism	relative dating technique	potassium/argon (K/Ar) dating
carnivore	biostratigraphy	argon/argon dating
omnivore	absolute dating techniques	electron spin resonance (ESR) dating
paleopathology	chronometric techniques	
trephination		
sites	radiometric	luminescence dating
petrified	radiocarbon dating	taphonomy
provenience		

SUGGESTED READINGS

A detailed and beautifully photographed book on the human skeleton, with life-sized pictures, is *Human Osteology*, second edition, by Tim White and Pieter Folkens. Analysis of the human skeleton in anthropological context is also covered nicely in William Bass's *Human Osteology: A Laboratory and Field Manual of the Human Skeleton*; in *Skeleton Keys*, by Jeffrey H. Schwartz; and, for comparative osteology among the primates, in *An Introduction to Human Evolutionary Anatomy*, by Leslie Aiello and Christopher Dean.

Techniques of excavation, interpretation, and dating are covered in more detail in Ken Feder and Michael Park's *Human Antiquity*, fourth edition, and in even more detail in *Archaeology: Discovering Our Past*, by Robert Sharer and Wendy Ashmore, and *In the Beginning*, by Brian Fagan.

Taphonomy is covered by Pat Shipman in *Life History of a Fossil: An Introduction to Taphonomy and Paleoecology* and by Lewis Binford in *Bones: Ancient Men and Modern Myths*.

For information on the new techniques and discoveries regarding human genetics, see *Genome: The Autobiography of a Species in 23 Chapters*, by Matt Ridley.

More on the Ice Maiden and other mummies uncovered in the Andes can be found in three articles by Johan Reinhard in the June 1996, January 1997, and November 1999 issues of *National Geographic*.

The African Burial Ground is the topic of "Archaeology as Community Service: The African Burial Ground Project in New York City," by Warren Perry and Michael Blakey, in Kenneth Feder's *Lessons from the Past*. For the latest on Kennewick Man, see the following websites: www.cr.nps.gov/aad/kennewick/; www.kennewick-man.com/news/index.html.

The Iceland genetics study is covered in "Decoding Iceland," by Micheal Specter, in the January 18, 1999, *New Yorker*.

CHAPTER

10

EVOLUTION
OF THE
HOMINIDS

...there are no final
words. Human origins
will always be
enigmatic.
—Donald Johanson

P hysicists observe and measure the universe as we see it today in an attempt to understand its origin and evolution. Their methods of observation and measurement are highly technical and are considered essentially accurate. Therefore, we know the distances to the stars, the speed with which those stars are moving away from us, and even their chemical makeup.

When these individual pieces of data are put together, however, the story is often confusing and puzzling. Recently, for example, some new estimates of the age of the universe seemed to indicate that the universe is *younger* than some of the stars it contains. This obviously couldn't be. Either some of the observational or measurement techniques were wrong, or they were less accurate than we thought, or perhaps different groups of scientists have interpreted the data differently, or—just maybe—the universe is more complicated than we imagined.

Similarly, paleoanthropologists observe present-day species and the fossilized remnants of other species to try to reconstruct the biological past. The study of human evolution is also a complicated venture. We have many thousands of individual pieces of data, each observed, measured, dated, and analyzed according to the very latest technologies. But when we try to put them all together, we come up with inconsistencies, contradictions, and often several equally plausible interpretations. This chapter and the two that follow will give you the most current ideas about our evolution, including all the missing pieces and alternative interpretations—at least the ones based on scientific inquiry. We will address the following questions:

What is the evolutionary history of the primates?

When and under what circumstances did the hominids evolve, and why was bipedalism so important?

What do we know about the first members of the genus *Homo*?

THE ORIGIN AND EVOLUTION OF THE PRIMATES

There are a large number of fossil specimens of primates, but the fossil record is still spotty. Our identifications of over half of the extinct primate species are based on fragmentary remains, mostly pieces of jaw or sometimes just teeth. Although a particular extinct species may be represented by many specimens, fossils of its contemporaries are often lacking, giving us no basis for comparison. There are large gaps in the primate fossil record. Some periods are represented by many fossils, but they all come

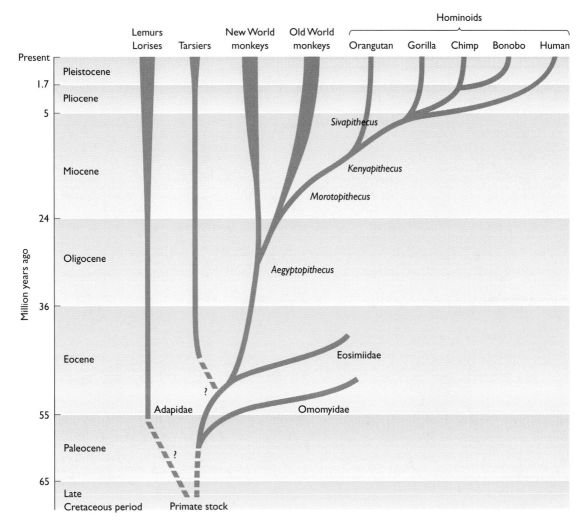

FIGURE 10.1

Simplified Evolutionary Tree for the Primates, with Major Geological Epochs and Dates. Question marks and dashed lines indicate insufficient data to establish evolutionary relationships. This tree represents one of several possible interpretations.

from one or two sites. Still, we can put together a general, if tentative, picture of the course of primate evolution (Figure 10.1).

We have few fossils that tell us about the earliest stages of primate evolution. Some genetic comparisons, such as those described in Chapter 9, point to the origin of the primates as far back as 86 mya, well into the time of the dinosaurs (Gibbons 1998a). In terms of hard evidence, there are a few primatelike teeth from Montana dated at 65 mya and some bones from Wyoming dated at 60 mya that have primate features related to climbing behavior. Remember that, at the time, North America and Eurasia were still very close together and possibly still connected in

FIGURE 10.2
Skeleton and Reconstruction of Early Adapid, *Smilodectes*. The form was similar to that of some modern prosimians. Compare to Figure 7.13.

some locations (see Figure 6.6), so the primates probably originated on the large northern landmass called Laurasia, not on what is now North America.

Undisputed primates appear about 55 mya. The traits that we associate in modern primates with an arboreal environment (see Chapter 7) may not have first evolved specifically to facilitate that adaptation. After all, other mammals that do not possess these traits are also arboreal. Anthropologist Matt Cartmill (1992) suggests that prehensile extremities and stereoscopic vision may have evolved to aid leaping as a means of locomotion in the forest canopy or the shrub-layer undergrowth and to promote fruit-eating and "visually directed predation" on insects. Modern mouse lemurs, lorises, and tarsiers, for example, all track insects by sight

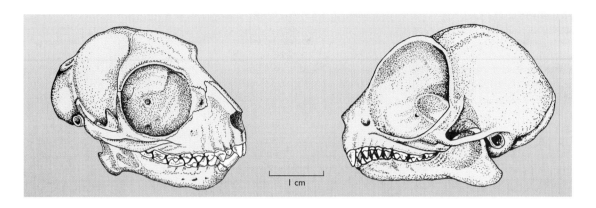

1 cm

FIGURE 10.3
Fossil Omomyid, *Necrolemur* (*left*), Compared with Modern Tarsier (see Figure 7.14).

and seize them by hand. As the primates evolved, these basic traits proved a useful adaptive theme for life in the trees.

The early primates come in two groups, both found in North America, Europe, Asia, and Africa. One group, the Adapidae, are lemurlike and so are thought to be ancestral to modern lemurs and lorises (Figure 10.2). The other group, the Omomyidae, are tarsierlike; they may date back as far as 60 mya and may be ancestral to both tarsiers and anthropoids (Figure 10.3, and see Figure 7.14). A recently discovered group, the Eosimiidae from Asia, may represent the more direct ancestors of monkeys, apes, and hominids (Gebo et al. 2000; Jaeger et al. 1999; Kay et al. 1997). Important evolutionary shifts that marked the origin of the anthropoids included changes to (1) a diurnal lifestyle from a nocturnal one, (2) less leaping and more climbing through the trees with all fours, and (3) a more herbivorous diet with less emphasis on insects.

By the time the omomyids were moving into Asia, the Eastern and Western Hemispheres were completely separate. We know that all modern New World primates are monkeys, but there are very few monkey fossils from the New World, mostly because the jungle environment leads to quick and complete scavenging or decay of dead animals. Thus, we don't know for sure how the evolution of the primates proceeded in the Western Hemisphere. There are two views on the subject. The first is that the early New World prosimians moved into Central and South America when those areas joined together with North America and that the prosimians subsequently evolved into modern platyrrhines, the New World monkeys.

The second view is that early monkeys from the Old World "rafted" over to the Americas, floating on logs and branches or "island hopping" over a chain of volcanic islands when the two hemispheres were closer together. These early monkeys replaced any prosimians that still inhabited the New World, and they eventually evolved into the modern New

FIGURE 10.4

Skull of *Aegyptopithecus* from the Fayum in Egypt. This fossil is considered an early monkeylike form that may be ancestral to later Old World anthropoids.

World monkey species. Although there are some distinct differences (see Chapter 7), the basic similarity between the Old World and New World monkeys argues for a single origin and thus for the second scenario. In addition, although most of the fossils from the New World are incomplete and therefore hard to evaluate, a recent find of a 25- to 27-million-year-old monkey from Bolivia (Takai et al. 2000), whose teeth are very similar to an older fossil form from Egypt, suggests that the New World monkeys originated and diversified first in Africa. That this scenario is plausible was shown by a recent report (Yoon 1998) of fifteen iguanas (large lizards) floating on a huge raft of trees 200 miles from their native Caribbean island of Guadeloupe to the island of Anguilla, where they had not previously been found. They are established and reproducing in their new habitat.

We are most interested in primate evolution in the Old World. Much of the history of the Old World anthropoids comes from a single site, the depression formed by an ancient lake in the desert southwest of Cairo, Egypt, called the Fayum. Paleontologist Elwyn Simons began extensive investigations there in the early 1960s that continue today (Simons and Rasmussen 1994). From this valuable site come a number of monkeylike forms dated from 40 to 25 mya. The most important, perhaps, is *Aegyptopithecus*, from about 34 mya (Figure 10.4). This 10-pound primate shows anthropoid traits as well as several features of the teeth, braincase, and skull that resemble later hominoids (apes and hominids). It may be ancestral, then, to all the modern Old World anthropoids.

As the early anthropoids expanded, they outcompeted the prosimians and pushed these more primitive primates into marginal areas. Most prosimians now live—as endangered species—on the island of Madagascar, which they probably reached by rafting, possibly aided by a land bridge. No other primates invaded Madagascar until humans got there.

Apes appear in the fossil record about 23 mya. We refer to these earliest apes as *dental apes* because it is their teeth, rather than their overall anatomy, that resemble those of modern apes. Especially important is a feature of the molar teeth found only in hominoids and no other primates. It is called the *Y-5 cusp pattern* (Figure 10.5).

Between 23 and 5 mya, there were an estimated thirty or more different types of apes—larger-bodied, tailless, larger-brained primates. Only one lineage, however, gave rise to the modern apes and hominids. Evidence is scanty, but new fossil finds point to two African forms as candidates for the earliest hominoid. *Kenyapithecus*, from around 15 mya, had some modern ape features of the jaw, face, and teeth. Newer fossils, placed by some into a new genus, *Equatorius* (S. Ward et al. 1999), indicate similarities in the arm and ankle bones that are related to the modern chimpanzee's abilities to hang in trees and to rotate the foot, which also permits walking flat-footed on the ground and grasping (McCrossin 1997).

A more ancient and more arboreal form, *Morotopithecus* from Uganda, dated at 20 mya, also shows similarities. It had a mobile shoulder joint that would have aided in hanging from trees by the arms, as chimps and orangutans do, and vertebrae that suggest a short, stiff spine, a feature of modern apes that allows them occasional upright posture (Gebo et al. 1997).

Starting about 12 mya, we find fossils of more ground-dwelling, open-country apes, whose larger back teeth with thicker enamel point to a more mixed vegetable diet that included harder foods such as nuts. Fossils of these apes have been found in Africa, India, Pakistan, China, Turkey, Hungary, and Greece. First evidence consisted of teeth and partial jaws, and an early interpretation claimed they possessed hominid traits (see Chapter 9). We know now they are too old to be hominids, and as more complete fossils have been recovered, it has become clear they are indeed apes. One group from India and Pakistan, *Sivapithecus*, shares features with the modern orangutan and so is most likely an ancestor of that species (Figure 10.6). A new form from Turkey, *Ankarapithecus*, dated at 9.8 mya, also shows similarities to this group.

Another form, however, *Ouranopithecus*, so far only found in Greece and dated at 10 to 9 mya, shares some features with hominids. Though

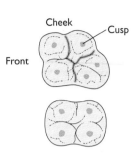

FIGURE 10.5
The Y-5 cusp pattern is found only in hominoids, and the four-cusp pattern is found in *all* anthropoids. The chewing surface is shown here. A look in the mirror will probably give you a glimpse of a Y-5 tooth, but note that not all hominid molars show this feature.

FIGURE 10.6

Skull of *Sivapithecus* (left) Compared to That of a Modern Orangutan. They are essentially identical.

clearly an ape, about the size of a female gorilla, it is thought by some to be a good candidate for a member of the ape line that eventually led to the hominids (De Bonis and Koufos 1994).

We can't leave this discussion without noting perhaps the most famous, and the biggest, sivapithecid—indeed, the biggest primate ever. This giant ape, whose fossils have been found in China, northern India, and Vietnam is called, appropriately, *Gigantopithecus* (see Figure 7.4). So far, only jaws and teeth have been found, but estimates from these indicate this primate may have been 10 to 12 feet tall when standing upright and may have weighed from 700 to 1,200 pounds. Evidence from the teeth indicate that it was, like the gorilla, a vegetarian and linked to the sivapithecid group. Gigantopithecus lived from about 7 mya to perhaps as recently as 300,000 ya, recently enough to have possibly encountered modern humans. (One can't help but wonder if these creatures, or at least their bones, may have given rise to legends of the famous "abominable snowman," or yeti, from the Himalayas. In any case, there is absolutely no indication that this primate still exists.)

Current evidence indicates that apes evolved in Africa and Europe about 20 mya and diverged subsequently into a number of evolutionary

FIGURE 10.7
The "Taung Baby," the First
Specimen of *Australopithecus*.
Note the naturally formed
cast of the brain toward the
back of the skull.

lines all over the Old World. Gradually, these lines decreased, leaving relatively few forms to evolve into the modern hominoids. One line that we are fairly sure of is that from *Sivapithecus* to modern orangutans. Some African form or an African population of that form gave rise to the line leading to modern African apes and hominids.

THE FIRST HOMINIDS: THE BIPEDAL PRIMATE

The first evidence from the dawn of hominid evolution came in 1925. South African anatomist Raymond Dart was given a fossil found in a limestone quarry at a site called Taung (Figure 10.7). It took Dart seventy-three

FIGURE 10.8

Comparison of the Placement of the Foramen Magnum and Orientation of the Spinal Column Relative to the Skull in a Nonprimate Quadruped and Three Primates. The wolf, with equally long fore and hind limbs, has a foramen magnum toward the back of the skull with an almost horizontal orientation of the spine. The chimp, still a quadruped but with longer arms than legs, has a more forward placement with the spine extending at an angle. In the bipedal hominids we see a trend toward even more forward placement and a vertical orientation of the spine.

Wolf

Chimpanzee

Australopithecus

Modern human

days to separate the fossil from the limestone around it. When freed, it revealed the face, braincase, and brain cast of a young primate, apelike but for two important differences. First, the canine teeth, long and large in apes with gaps to accommodate them when the jaws are shut, were no bigger than those of a human child. Second was the position of the **foramen magnum.** This is the hole in the base of the skull through which the spinal cord extends from the brain and around the outside of which the top vertebra articulates. In the Taung specimen, this hole was well underneath the skull rather than toward the back, as in apes, indicating an upright, bipedal posture rather than a quadrupedal one (Figure 10.8). Dart hypothesized that the "Taung Baby," as it came to be known, was an intermediate between apes and hominids. Nevertheless, he named it *Australopithecus africanus,* the "southern ape of Africa"; because of its many apelike traits, he wasn't ready to formally classify it in the human family.

Further finds in Africa substantiated Dart's assessment of the anatomy of his fossil and his opinion that it represented a new type of primate. Those finds also made it clear that *Australopithecus,* rather than being an intermediary, was in fact a hominid, a bipedal primate. (The rules of scientific nomenclature, or taxonomic names, however, require that first-used names stick even if they later prove to be descriptively inaccurate. Thus, these hominids are still named "southern apes.")

The story of the discoveries and various interpretations of the fossil hominids from the first years of hominid evolution is fascinating in itself. Several of the books listed at the end of the chapter tell that story. Here, we'll look at the story as it stands today. There is still no general agreement on exactly how this part of our evolutionary tree looks, but anthropologists have found fossils with well-established dates (Table 10.1) at various locations (Figure 10.9).

First, a general orientation. All the fossils discussed here belong to family Hominidae. Within that family anthropologists now recognize four defined genera: *Ardipithecus, Australopithecus, Paranthropus,* and *Homo.* Only the last genus still exists; the other three are extinct. These groups may be distinguished by the following definitions, on which I'll elaborate:

> Family Hominidae: the bipedal primates (by the traditional definition we'll use here)
>
>> Genus *Ardipithecus:* most apelike hominids
>>
>> Genus *Australopithecus:* small-brained, gracile (slender) hominids with a mixed vegetable diet
>>
>> Genus *Paranthropus:* small-brained, robust hominids with a grassland vegetable diet
>>
>> Genus *Homo:* large-brained, omnivorous hominids

foramen magnum: The hole in the base of the skull through which the spinal cord emerges and around the outside of which the top vertebra articulates.

TABLE 10.1
Summary of Major Early Fossil Hominid Species*

	A. anamensis	A. afarensis	A. africanus	P. robustus	P. boisei	Early Homo
Dates	4.2–3.8 mya	3.7–3 mya	3–2.3 mya	2.2–1.5 mya (?)	2.2–1 mya	2.4–1.6 mya
Sites	Lake Turkana	Hadar Omo Laetoli Maka Lake Turkana	Taung Sterkfontein Makapansgat Lake Turkana (?) Omo (?)	Kromdraai Swartkrans Drimolen	Olduvai Lake Turkana Omo	Olduvai Lake Turkana Omo Sterkfontein (?) Swartkrans (?) Uraha
Cranial capacity (in ml)	(no data)	380–500 mean = 440	370–515 mean = 440	520 (based on one specimen)	500–530 mean = 515	500–800 mean = 680
Estimated size (average, in lb)	114	110	100	105	101	89
Skull	Canines large, but hominidlike canine roots More apelike chin than A. afarensis Tooth rows parallel as in apes	Very prognathous Receding chin Large teeth Pointed canine with gap Shape of tooth row between ape and human Hint of sagittal crest	Less prognathous than A. afarensis Jaw more rounded Large back teeth Canines smaller than P. robustus, larger than A. afarensis No sagittal crest	Heavy jaws Small canines and front teeth Large back teeth Definite sagittal crest	Very large jaws Very large back teeth Large sagittal crest	Flatter face Less sloping forehead Teeth similar to A. africanus No sagittal crest
Postcranial skeleton	Bipedal knee and ankle joints Fibula intermediate between ape and hominid	Long arms Short thumb Curved fingers and toes Bipedal	Similar to A. afarensis but possibly with longer arms and shorter legs	Hands and feet more like modern humans Retention of long arms	Similar to P. robustus	Limited evidence Retention of long arms Maybe retention of primitive features of hand and foot

*Excludes less well-established or more recent proposed species still under study, which are discussed in the text.

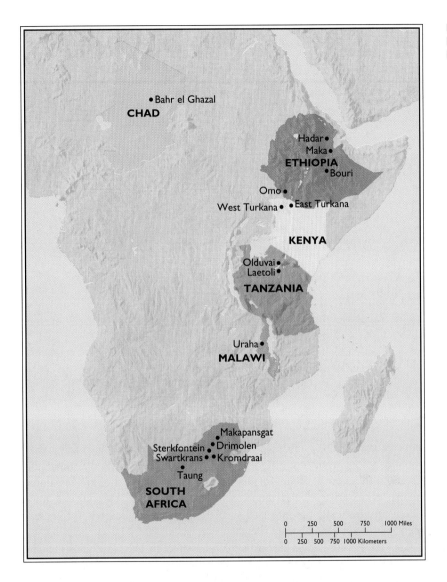

FIGURE 10.9
Map of Major Early Fossil Hominid Sites.

It should be noted that authorities are about evenly divided on the issue of whether *Paranthropus* is a separate genus or is part of *Australopithecus*. I will use the first option here, in part because I think the evidence warrants it and in part because using a different name makes understanding the evolutionary trends of this complex period a little easier.

The earliest-known hominid fossils were first discovered in Ethiopia in 1992 and 1993. The finds consisted of seventeen fossil fragments, including some arm bones, two skull bases, a child's mandible, and some

FIGURE 10.10

Fossil Tooth and a Portion of Jaw from *Ardipithecus ramidus*.

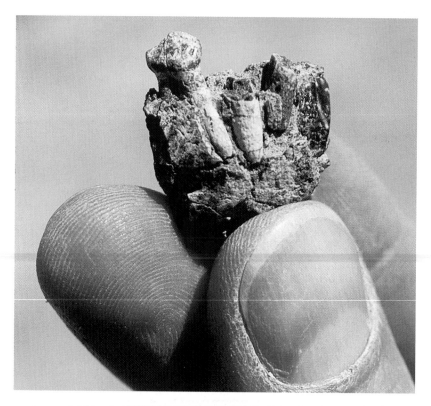

teeth (Figure 10.10). These fossils were different enough from any found previously to warrant creating a fourth hominid genus, called *Ardipithecus ramidus* (the genus name means "ground ape" and the species name means "root" in the Afar language). The fossils are dated at 4.4 mya. These are the fossils, mentioned in the summary in Chapter 9, that had been "ravaged by carnivores."

In 1994, more fossil bones were recovered in Ethiopia, close to the first site. These consisted of ninety fragments representing about 45 percent of a skeleton, including the telltale pelvis, leg, ankle, and foot. These new finds, however, still await published analysis.

Ardipithecus ramidus is considered a hominid because the foramen magnum is more forward than in apes and because of some detailed features of the elbow joint and the teeth. At the same time, it is "the most apelike hominid ancestor known" (White et al. 1994). Among other things, the canine teeth are larger, compared to the other teeth, than in later hominids. It seems, then, that *ramidus* existed very close to the time

FIGURE 10.11
Mandible (*left*) and Maxilla of *Australopithecus anamensis*. The chinless jaw is apelike, but the vertical root of the canine is clearly a hominid trait (the canine roots of apes are angled).

when the hominids and the apes split and so may be, as the name implies, the "root" hominid species. These fossils, however, remain somewhat enigmatic for the moment. Although the evidence from the foramen magnum indicates that they were bipedal, conclusive evidence from the legs, pelvis, and feet must wait until the newest finds can be fully examined and the results published.

In August 1995, the newest well-established hominid species was announced (Leakey and Lewin 1995; C. Ward et al. 1999). Called *Australopithecus anamensis*, it consists, so far, of twenty-one specimens from the Lake Turkana region of Kenya (*anam* means "lake"), including jaws, teeth, a skull fragment, a tibia, and a humerus (Figure 10.11). The specimens are dated at 4.2 to 3.8 mya. Although they exhibit apelike features such as large canine teeth and parallel tooth rows, the root of the canine is vertical as in later hominids rather than angled as in apes, and the tooth enamel is thicker than in apes or in *Ardipithecus ramidus* and more like in later hominids (Figure 10.12). Most notably, the leg bones are clearly those of a biped. There appears to be some consensus that this may represent the ancestor of all later hominids, with *Ard. ramidus* representing a side branch of the hominid family.

The next species is also well established, and its nature is generally agreed upon. The species is *Australopithecus afarensis*, and its first and

Chimpanzee   *Australopithecus afarensis*   Modern human

FIGURE 10.12

Comparison of Upper Jaws and Tooth Rows of Chimpanzee, *Australopithecus afarensis*, and Modern Human. Note the parallel postcanine teeth in the chimp, the slightly divergent tooth row in the early hominid, and the divergent row in the modern human. Note also the large canines and the large gap (*diastema*) in the chimp, the lack of these in the modern human, and the intermediate state in the early hominid. *Australopithecus anamensis* has slightly larger canines than the later *A. afarensis* and tooth rows more like the ape (see Figure 10.11).

FIGURE 10.13

Skeleton of "Lucy," the First Specimen of *A. afarensis*.

most famous specimen is the 3.2-million-year-old skeleton, also from Ethiopia, known as "Lucy" (Figure 10.13), found in 1974 by Donald Johanson and his team. Lucy is remarkable because, as old as she is, nearly 40 percent of her skeleton was preserved, and all parts of her body were well represented except the cranium, the remains of which are fragmentary. We know—based on the kind of osteological analysis described in Chapter 9—that she was a female and that she stood about 3 feet 8 inches and weighed about 65 pounds. Although there is some disagreement about details, there is no doubt that Lucy and her kind were bipeds.

Other fragmentary specimens, including a portion of a skull dated at 3.9 mya, were unearthed in Ethiopia and Tanzania and assigned to this species. Based on this evidence, a reconstruction of the head of *A. afarensis* was attempted, but a single complete fossil skull was not found until 1992. In February of that year, Donald Johanson and his team discovered 200 skull fragments, again in Ethiopia. Once reconstructed, the skull closely resembled the previously discovered fragments, except that it was large and rugged, probably the skull of a male. It was dated at about 3 mya (Figure 10.14).

The evidence, so far—over 300 specimens—indicates that there was a well-established hominid species, *A. afarensis*, that lived from 4 to 3 mya.

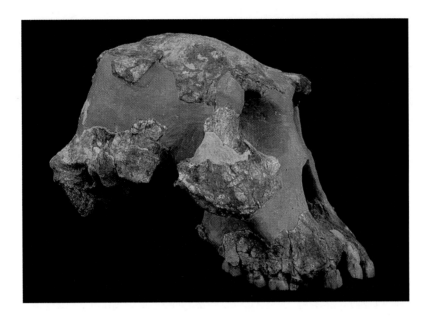

FIGURE 10.14
Side View of Cranium of *Australopithecus afarensis*. Spaces between missing bones have been filled in using information from other specimens and knowledge of related species.

The variation in size of the specimens fits the pattern of sexual dimorphism of apes and other early hominids. We are probably looking at the remains of both males (for example, the skull found in 1992) and females (for example, Lucy) of one species.

However, in 1995 a French team found the remains of a partial hominid jaw in Chad, in north-central Africa, dated at 3.5 to 3 mya. The team announced that this find represents a second species of hominid living during that time (Simons 1996). The species has been named *Australopithecus bahrelghazalia* (after an Arabic name for a nearby riverbed), and it suggests that early hominids were more widely spread on the continent than previously thought. Full acceptance of this classification and the implications of the fossil await further study.

What did Lucy and her kin look like? They might be described as "bipedal apes." Their average brain size was about 440 ml (a can of soda holds 355 ml), close to the average for chimpanzees and with the same maximum size of about 500 ml. *Australopithecus afarensis* had the **prognathism** (projection of the lower face and jaws), the pointy canine teeth, and the gaps in the tooth rows characteristic of apes, though the canine teeth and gaps were not as pronounced as in apes. There was a hint of a **sagittal crest,** a ridge of bone along the top of the skull for the attachment of major chewing muscles. Gorillas have pronounced crests (Figure 10.15). In modern humans, these muscles are attached on the side of the head. (Put your hand on your head, about 2 inches above one ear, and

prognathism: The jutting forward of the lower face and jaw area.

sagittal crest: A ridge of bone, running from front to back along the top of the skull, for the attachment of chewing muscles.

FIGURE 10.15
Skull of a Male Gorilla. Compare the sagittal crest with those in Figures 10.20, 10.22, and 10.23.

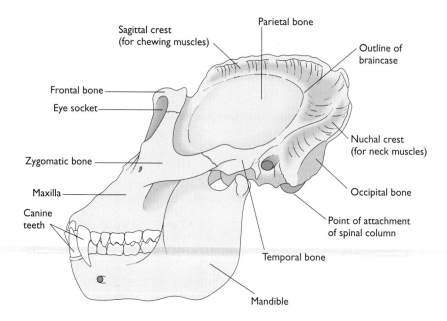

Sagittal crest (for chewing muscles)

Parietal bone

Outline of braincase

Frontal bone

Eye socket

Nuchal crest (for neck muscles)

Zygomatic bone

Occipital bone

Maxilla

Point of attachment of spinal column

Canine teeth

Temporal bone

Mandible

then clench and unclench your teeth. You'll feel the muscle, called the *temporalis*.)

At first, there was some disagreement as to just how bipedal *A. afarensis* was, especially considering the apelike nature of much of the rest of its anatomy. (Disagreements continue; see Stern 2000 for a summary.) All the interpretations, after all, were based on fossilized bones; no one, obviously, had ever actually seen one walk. But in 1976, Mary Leakey recovered the next best thing at a site in Tanzania called Laetoli—a set of footprints made in a fresh layer of volcanic ash that quickly hardened and preserved for us a striking picture of an event that took place 3.7 mya. Two hominids, one large, one small, had walked side-by-side through the ash shortly after an eruption. The hominids' footprints show an anatomy and stride no different from ours today (Figure 10.16).

In October 2000, an even older possible hominid ancestor was proposed by French paleoanthropologists (Balter 2001), based on thirteen fossil fragments from the Tugen Hills in northwestern Kenya. The dating of these fossils—femurs, teeth, portions of a mandible—is agreed upon; they are about 6 million years old. Their identity, however, is a matter of debate. The discoverers claim the fossils represent the real ancestor of modern humans and that the other early hominids, *Australopithecus* and *Paranthropus*, are side branches. They base their claim on their assessment that this hominid—placed by them into a new genus and species,

FIGURE 10.16
The larger photograph shows the Laetoli footprints from Tanzania. The inset shows a reconstruction from the American Museum of Natural History in New York City of male and female *A. afarensis*, who are thought to have made these footprints.

Orrorin tugenensis (*orrorin* means "original man" in the local dialect)—was bipedal and exhibited expressions of certain traits that were more modern than those of other early hominids. Features of the head of the femur and grooves for muscle and ligament attachments are said to point to bipedalism. If true, that would place the origin of bipedalism nearly 2 million years earlier than the earliest existing bipedal fossil forms. Other authorities disagree with this analysis, and some, including Donald Johanson, question whether this form even *is* a hominid. As of this writing, there is too little information to do more than mention this new find. As new data come in, however, a major part of our story could change.

Then, in March 2001, yet another new form of early hominid was announced (Leakey et al. 2001). It is based on a fairly complete, although distorted cranium and a mandible, found in 1998 and 1999 in Kenya and reliably dated at 3.5 mya. The fossils show a combination of features unlike that of any other forms. The brain size, some dental features, and details of the nasal region are like those of members of genus *Australopithecus*. But its face appears flat, it has a tall, vertically oriented cheek area, and shows no depression behind the brow ridges. In these ways, it bears a resemblance to a later hominid form from East Africa (see Figure 10.27). This set of traits, in a fossil contemporaneous with *A. afarensis*, led its discoverers to give it not only a new species name but a new genus name as well—*Kenyanthropus platyops* ("flat-faced hominid from Kenya"). Some authorities have suggested that this new form may be a better common ancestor for *Homo* than *A. afarensis*. More evidence, however, is needed to even establish that these fossils do represent a whole new taxon; more examples with the same set of features will have to be found. In the meantime, then, the well-established *A. afarensis* seems to remain our best candidate for the species that gave rise to subsequent hominids.

Clearly, bipedalism was the first hominid trait to evolve. We know this because it is, essentially, the only hominid trait in an organism that is otherwise an ape. If bipedalism had evolved slowly, one would expect some other traits to have changed as well. Therefore, bipedalism may be seen as the adaptation that began our family of primates.

BIPEDALISM

The Benefits of Bipedalism

What's the benefit of standing upright, an adaptation that involved major realignments of much of the body of a quadrupedal animal? Under what circumstances was it selected for in the earliest members of our lineage?

Not many creatures use this form of locomotion. Kangaroos do and birds do—and many dinosaurs did—but they also use their tails for balance and support and walk with the knees bent and the trunk sloping. Birds' feet are essentially prehensile; they can even sleep perched on a branch. Human bipedalism, although it obviously works quite well, involves a large number of individual physical features and evolutionary changes (see Figure 9.5) and remarkable acts of coordination. When we stand and walk, with our trunk erect and knees straight, we have to balance our bodies vertically on two relatively small points of contact with the ground. We can't run particularly fast, and we aren't very stable on rough or slippery surfaces.

What makes this adaptive change even more puzzling is some recent strong evidence suggesting that, rather than evolving from completely arboreal ancestors who came directly "out of the trees," we evolved from apes with a specialized terrestrial adaptation. This adaptation, called **knuckle walking** (exhibited by modern apes), is a form of locomotion that involves placing the backs of the middle joints of the fingers on the ground (see the gorilla in Figure 9.5). This adaptation allows the individual to hold a small object in its prehensile hand and walk at the same time. The wrist joints (specifically the distal portion, or hand end, of the radius) of the earliest established hominids *Australopithecus anamensis* and *A. afarensis* share a trait with chimps and gorillas that helps keep the arm rigid while walking in this fashion (Begun 2000; Collard and Aiello 2000; Richmond and Strait 2000). It seems reasonable, then, that the common ancestor of the African apes and hominids also had this feature. So if our common ancestor *already* had a specialized adaptation to walking on the ground (on all fours), why did our lineage evolve an even more specialized and complex one (bipedalism)?

Compare the map of early hominid sites (Figure 10.9) with the map of Africa's climatic and vegetation zones (Figure 10.17). Note that the sites are in areas that were savannas or tropical deciduous forests—open grasslands or woodlands more open than the rain forest and with trees that underwent seasonal cycles of growth. Where these zones met, there was a mix of forest and open areas, as one zone graded into another.

To a primate, open areas, particularly the savannas, present a very different set of problems than do dense forests. Primates are basically vegetarian. Although there are plenty of plants on the savannas, there are not as many that can be utilized by the digestive systems of most primates. Most primates cannot digest cellulose as can the *ungulates* (grazing animals such as the African antelopes). Edible plants or plants with edible parts—at least for a hominoid primate—are not as concentrated on the open plains or even open forests. As a result, primates living in such areas have to travel over a wider area to find food. These areas are more affected by sea-

knuckle walking: Walking on the backs of the knuckles of the hand, typical of the African apes.

FIGURE 10.17
General Climatic and Vegetation Zones of Africa Today. Except for the large deserts in the north and south, the zones are much the same as when our evolutionary story began some 5 mya, although specific local conditions may have differed. Moreover, where zones meet, the conditions grade into one another, producing an area of mixed vegetation and other conditions.

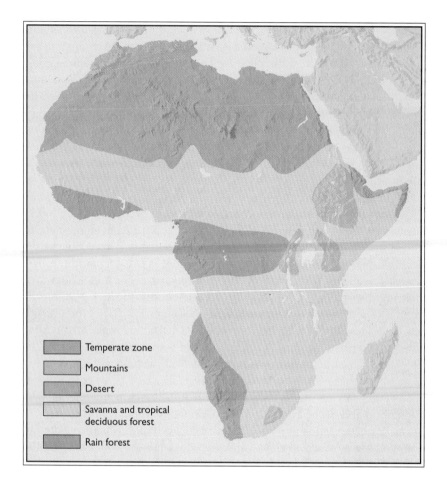

Temperate zone

Mountains

Desert

Savanna and tropical deciduous forest

Rain forest

sonal change than are the rain forests, and so there may be greater variation between the wet and dry seasons. This, too, creates the need for more traveling in search of food. Finally, there is more danger involved in acquiring these widely dispersed foods. Lions, leopards, cheetahs, wild dogs, hyenas, and other predators of the plains and open forests are more than happy to make a meal out of a small primate, as we saw in Chapter 9.

There are, of course, sources of meat, both in the forests and especially on the open savannas with their great herds of herbivores. Chimpanzees are known to hunt, kill, and eat small mammals such as monkeys. They are even known to scavenge kills that leopards have left hanging in trees—although rarely (Byrne and Byrne 1988; Cavallo 1990). While our earliest ancestors may have hunted small animals, it is unlikely they preyed on big game or even animals as large as those hunted by chimps.

They were not as mobile in the trees as the chimps (having legs adapted to bipedalism), and they lacked the powerful musculature and large inter-locking canine teeth of the apes (see Figures 8.4 and 10.15). And, so far at least, there is no physical evidence of big-game hunting on the plains. There is, however, evidence that they scavenged kills, which we will cover later. Nonetheless, although scavenging provided access to meat, it was dangerous. The carcasses had to be taken away and kept away from other predators or scavenged after the predators had finished.

So, we may ask not only how bipedalism could be a benefit for terres-trial walking, but we can structure our inquiry more precisely by asking how it would be adaptive in such a mix of environments.

Explaining the Emergence of Bipedalism

Six different models have been proposed to account for the evolution of bipedalism under the environmental conditions just described.

1. *Carrying model.* Bipedalism could have allowed our early ancestors to accomplish food searching and collecting activities in greater safety and with greater efficiency. Freeing the arms and hands from a role in locomotion would have meant that food could be transported from open areas to safer locations, such as a grove of trees or perhaps at the foot of a steep hill. This would have been especially important if the food were part of an animal carcass, since other meat-eaters would also have found it attractive. Moreover, bipedalism would have al-lowed mothers to carry children in their arms while walking in search of food. Perhaps sticks and rocks were carried and thrown to scare predators and scavengers away from a kill. (Chimps will occasionally hurl rocks and sticks, though not particularly accurately.) Under experimental conditions (Videan and McGrew 2000), it has been shown that having something to carry is a major stimulus for bipedal locomotion in chimpanzees and bonobos (see Figure 8.6). However, Jablonski and Chaplin (2000) claim that if bipedal carrying of any-thing other than small, light objects had been a major selective focus, there would have been other changes as well, such as an enlargement of the lower (lumbar) vertebrae, as seen in modern humans. But this feature had not evolved early on in our evolution, not even in the earliest members of genus *Homo* (about 2.4 mya).

2. *Vigilance model.* It has been proposed that bipedalism, by elevating the head, provides better views of potential sources of food and dan-ger. Observe, for example, how squirrels sit upright to better look

around. Videan and McGrew's (2000) experiment, just noted, showed this to be an important factor in the use of bipedalism, at least in their controlled studies among captive apes. In fact, it was the most frequent context of upright posture. It should be noted here, however, that this model only addresses upright posture, not necessarily upright locomotion.

3. *Heat dissipation model.* The vertical orientation of bipedalism, according to another view, helps cool the body by presenting a smaller target to the intense equatorial rays of the sun and by placing more of the body above the ground to catch any cooling air currents. The savanna can be hot, and the heat built up by hours of walking in search of food needs to be dissipated. (This factor may also explain the adaptive significance of the relatively hairless bodies of modern hominids. Having no hair allows sweat to evaporate more quickly and cool the body more efficiently.) This model, of course, would not apply to the forests, where primates would be sheltered by the shade of trees.

4. *Energy efficiency model.* Data indicate that, although bipedalism is an energy-inefficient way of running compared to quadrupedalism, it is *more* efficient for walking. For example, a 154-pound man uses 140 more joules of energy per meter walking than standing still and 260 more when running than standing still. A 154-pound quadrupedal mammal uses 200 more joules of energy per meter both walking and running (Alexander 1995). Long periods of steady bipedal walking in search of food, then, would seem to require less energy. Remember, however, that the first hominids may not have walked bipedally quite like later members of our family and may not have been any more efficient at walking upright than are chimpanzees. Moreover, it is not certain that what makes our walking more efficient is simply our upright stance. Body mass and other anatomical features may be related as well. So, as Steudel (1996) maintains, efficiency may not have been the initial key factor in selection for bipedal locomotion. It may be that bipedalism had, at first, other advantages and that once it was established, further anatomical changes made it more energy efficient.

5. *Foraging/bipedal harvesting model.* This idea refers to the benefits of standing upright to reach sources of food on bushes and trees, particularly those difficult or impossible to climb. The introduction of raised feeding structures in Videan and McGrew's experiment stimulated bipedal posture in chimps.

6. *Display model.* Jablonski and Chaplin (2000) propose that the important factor was an upright display posture like that seen in chimps

during dominance confrontations and, to a lesser extent, in male bonobos (who sometimes also stand erect, in both senses, as a sexual display). Among these primates, an upright display posture conveys meaning because it makes the individual seem larger; it is also directly related to mating success. Although chimps and bonobos devote relatively little time to this behavior, its adaptive and evolutionary impact among our ancestors, the authors suggest, could still have been great. In their experiment, Videan and McGrew (2000) noted that the introduction of display objects (things the animals could wave around or make noise with) increased rates of bipedalism among chimps, though not among bonobos.

Each of these models has logic and evidence in its support, and each could be argued against as being an important adaptive focus. It seems reasonable, at the moment, to provisionally suppose that *all* these factors, acting together, could have played an adaptive role in the emergence of the hominid lineage and its characteristic mode of locomotion. But do these models—other than the display model—explain why bipedalism would have made some individuals, and eventually some groups, more reproductively successful? Remember that reproductive success is the measure of natural selection. Simple survival and longevity are only part of it.

Once again, we may get a clue from our close relatives, the chimps and bonobos, the former an open-forest species and the latter an inhabitant of dense forests. Although chimps normally have no need to share resources, they do share meat from a hunt, possibly because it is—in some chimp way—considered a luxury item. Bonobos, on the other hand, share even foods that are plentiful. This serves to avoid conflict and to establish and maintain peaceful coexistence within the group. Food sharing is, in a sense, a symbol of group peace and unity. In times of need, of course, food sharing might have practical consequences. Moreover, as you recall from Chapter 8, the bonobos use sex—in various combinations and with a variety of techniques—to strengthen and maintain group unity and to defuse tension. Sex for them is separate from purely reproductive activity. It has social and psychological meaning as well.

Perhaps, then, our earliest ancestors survived by the enhancement of adaptations that promoted peaceful cooperation and group unity, including the sharing of resources. The acquisition of these resources was made easier, safer, and more energy efficient by the ability to walk habitually upright.

Such a set of adaptations would certainly have been one way of aiding survival on the floor of open forests and out on the savannas. But remember that our earliest ancestors also exhibited traits associated with an arboreal adaptation: relatively long arms; heavy shoulder girdles, arm bones, and

FIGURE 10.18
Portion of the Great Rift Valley in Southern Kenya. The Great Rift Valley, formed some 8 mya, stretches 3,500 miles from Mozambique to the Red Sea and is over 2,000 feet deep in some places. Many lakes, such as the Little Magadi in the picture, lie in the valley.

arm muscles; and curved finger and toe bones. Perhaps in the earliest stages of our lineage our ancestors were adapted to both a tree-climbing *and* a terrestrial, open-area way of life. And environmental data bear this out.

Reassessment of the specific local environments of some important early hominid sites has shown them to be more forested than previously thought (see Shreeve 1996 for a summary and C. Ward et al. 1999 for recent descriptions). Our earliest possible ancestor, *Ard. ramidus,* lived in a high-altitude dense woodland. The Lake Turkana site where *Australopithecus anamensis* was found may have been an arid area, but the lake itself was surrounded by forest, and there were woodlands associated with rivers. Lucy, the first specimen of A. *afarensis*, probably lived in a mixed forest and bushland area, and Laetoli was open grassland with scattered trees and forests nearby. A. *bahrelghazalia* from Chad is thought to have inhabited forests with grassy patches. There is, in fact, evidence that East Africa at the time was a "heterogeneous mosaic" of environments, from forests to open plains (Kingston et al. 1994, 958). (The same appears to be true of southern Africa, home to other early hominids to be discussed in the next section.)

Indeed, Richard Potts (1996,1998) gives evidence that the past 6 million years marks a period of increasing environmental fluctuations that produced great oscillations in moisture and vegetation in Africa. Our early ancestors, he says, encountered a variety of environments and underwent selection for the ability to live in both densely wooded and open habitats. Potts calls this "variability selection"—adaptations that result in "flexible, novel responses to surroundings and diversity" that can "buffer" a species against "espisodic change" in its environment (1998, 86). The retention of arboreal features accompanied by the enhancement of bipedal locomotion would seem to be a perfect example of this sort of adaptation, along with, perhaps, other changes that enhanced social cooperation and resource sharing.

Finally, the isolation of our ancestors from the ancestors of the modern African apes may have been reinforced by a geological change—the formation of the Great Rift Valley in East Africa starting about 8 mya (Figure 10.18). Tectonic movements caused some land to sink, forming the valley, with mountains on its western rim. This in turned caused a localized climatic change. As a result, the area west of the valley remained moist and heavily forested, and that east of the valley turned drier to become savanna and more open forest. Today, chimpanzees are found only in the valley or to the west. Early hominid fossils, with the exception of the Chad find, are found only in the valley or to the east.

The details about the early evolution of our hominid family and its characteristic traits are still being debated. Clearly, however, the hominid line had emerged by perhaps 4.4 to 4 mya in a mixed and fluctuating woodland and savanna environment. Clearly, too, the major adaptation of the hominids—the trait that distinguishes them from the other primates—is bipedalism. Accompanying upright locomotion was, perhaps, an emphasis on group unity and survival facilitated by food sharing and perhaps by sexual activity separated from purely reproductive functions and linked to emotional, social, and personal relationships.

Whatever happened, it was successful. At least one hominid species was well ensconced in East Africa by 3 mya. From there our family began to branch out.

THE HOMINIDS EVOLVE

The basic set of early hominid features represented by Lucy and her kin continued for another three-quarters of a million years. Though little changed from *Australopithecus afarensis*, the fossils representing the next period are still called by their original name, A. *africanus* (Dart's "southern ape of Africa"). The remains of this species have been found mostly in South Africa, but there are some fossils from Kenya and Ethiopia as well. They have the same body size and shape and the same brain size as A. *afarensis*. There are a few differences, however (Figure 10.19). Their faces are a bit less prognathous, and they lack a sagittal crest. Their canine teeth are smaller, there are no gaps in the tooth row, and the tooth row is more rounded, as in a human rather than an ape (see Figure 10.12).

The relative sizes and shapes of the teeth of both A. *afarensis* and A. *africanus*, on the whole larger than those of modern humans, indicate a mostly mixed-vegetable diet of fruits and leaves. This is confirmed by analysis of microscopic scratches and wear patterns on the teeth (see Figure 10.20). There is no direct evidence of meat-eating, but a recent study (Sponheimer and Lee-Thorp 1999) of a carbon isotope (^{13}C) in the tooth

FIGURE 10.20
Scanning Electron Microscope Pictures of Teeth Surfaces of Early Hominids. The enamel of the teeth of *Australopithecus africanus* (left) is polished and scratched, while that of *Paranthropus* (right) is pitted and very rough. This is evidence of the hard, tough, gritty foods eaten by the latter.

enamel of a sample of A. *africanus* indicated that members of this species ate either tropical grasses or the flesh of animals that ate tropical grasses or both. (Grasses have more ^{13}C in their tissues than do other types of plants.) Because the dentition examined by these researchers lacked the tooth wear patterns indicative of grass-eating, the carbon may have come from grass-eating animals. While these grass-eating animals may have been plant-eating insects, there is the possibility that the australopithecines either hunted small animals or scavenged the carcasses of larger ones. There is also evidence that early hominids dug up rootstocks (tubers, rhizomes, and bulbs), although prior to the use of fire for cooking, this would have required some other means of deactivating toxins found in some of these food sources, such as crushing, soaking, or drying (Ragir 2000). It is noteworthy in this regard that some early bone tools from South Africa, formerly interpreted as showing signs of tuber digging, are now seen as having wear patterns associated with opening termite mounds (Holden 2001).

The essential similarity of A. *afarensis* and A. *africanus* suggests a plausible, and simple, interpretation. We may consider A. *africanus* as a continuation of A. *afarensis*, more widely distributed in southern and possibly eastern Africa and showing some evolutionary changes. It should be noted that this interpretation is not agreed upon by all investigators and remains hypothetical (Figure 10.21).

Some new evidence lends support to the meat-eating interpretation and to the definition of another new hominid species. The site of Bouri in Ethiopia, dated at 2.5 mya, has revealed (in separate locations) hominid cranial and postcranial bones, as well as the bones of antelopes, horses,

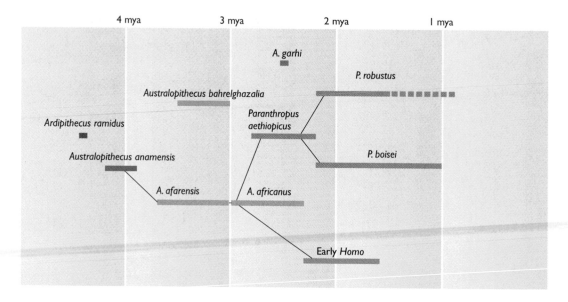

4 mya   3 mya   2 mya   1 mya

A. garhi

P. robustus

Australopithecus bahrelghazalia

Paranthropus aethiopicus

Ardipithecus ramidus

P. boisei

Australopithecus anamensis

A. afarensis   A. africanus

Early Homo

FIGURE 10.21

This diagram illustrates one possible interpretation of the phylogenetic relationships among early hominid species that are well represented in the fossil record and have been well studied. Even here, several different taxonomies and phylogenies have been proposed. The three species that are not connected to others in the diagram are fairly recent finds whose nature and taxonomy are still too uncertain to draw even provisional conclusions.

and other animals that exhibit cut marks made by stone tools (Asfaw et al. 1999; Culotta 1999a; de Heinzelin et al. 1999). The cranial bones indicate a brain size of 450 ml, and the prognathous jaw is similar to that of *A. afarensis*. Several features of the teeth resemble those of early *Homo*, but the molars are unusually large, even larger than those of the southern African robust hominids called *Paranthropus* (to be discussed next). This set of traits led investigators to designate these bones as a new species, *Australopithecus garhi* (*garhi* means "surprise" in a local language). The postcranial remains from Bouri, not clearly from the same species as the cranial specimens, show the relative lengths of the upper arm and upper leg to be humanlike, while the lower arm remains long, as in apes. This may indicate that in the evolution of human limb proportions, the leg elongated first and the arm shortened later. Finally, the stone tool cut marks on the animal bones show that whatever hominid (not necessarily *A. garhi*) made them was butchering animals for meat and smashing bones to get at the fat-rich marrow.

The evolutionary relationship of *A. garhi* to other hominids is still a matter of debate. Its discoverers (Asfaw et al. 1999) feel it is descended from *A. afarensis* and is a direct ancestor of *Homo*. Others disagree (Strait and Grine 1999; and see Culotta 1999b). Clearly, more evidence is needed to interpret these specimens more precisely, but they do show the extent of the variation among hominids during this period.

Two distinctly different types of hominid appear between 3 and 2 mya. One type retains the chimpanzee-sized brains and small bodies of

FIGURE 10.22
The "Black Skull," *Paranthropus aethiopicus,* is a possible ancestor of *P. robustus* and *P. boisei.* It shows a great degree of prognathism and the largest hominid sagittal crest.

Australopithecus but has evolved a notable robusticity in the areas of the skull involved with chewing. This is genus *Paranthropus.* As noted before, some authorities place these fossils in genus *Australopithecus,* but I will use *Paranthropus* both for clarity and because I lean toward that interpretation of current evidence(McCollum 1999).

The fossils representing the beginning of this genus are a single skull from Lake Turkana, Kenya—dubbed the "Black Skull" because of its dark color resulting from minerals in the ground (Figure 10.22)—and some fragmentary fossils from Ethiopia. These fossils are grouped into a separate species, *Paranthropus aethiopicus,* and are dated at between 2.8 and 2.2 mya.

The Black Skull is striking for several reasons. First, at only 410 ml, it has the smallest adult hominid brain ever found. However, it has the largest sagittal crest of any hominid, the most prognathous face, and an extremely large area in the back of the mouth for the molar teeth. Although no teeth were found, its molars appear to have been four or five times the size of a modern human's.

FIGURE 10.23
Paranthropus robustus from Swartkrans, South Africa. Note the remnant of a sagittal crest.

The Black Skull represents the beginning of a second major type of hominid, sometimes referred to as "robust" hominids. Although they were pretty much the same as *Australopithecus* in brain and body size, the members of genus *Paranthropus* were considerably more robust in all those features involved with chewing. The sagittal crest; broad, dished-out face; large cheekbones; huge mandible; and back teeth that are much larger relative to the front teeth—all point to a diet of large amounts of vegetable matter with an emphasis on hard, tough, gritty items like seeds, nuts, hard fruits, and tubers. This is confirmed by microscopic wear pattern analysis (see Figure 10.20).

A little over 2 mya, two more types of robust hominids appear. One species, *Paranthropus robustus*, was found in South Africa and dates between 2.2 and 1.5 mya or even later (Figure 10.23). It retains the body size of *Australopithecus*, but there is a slight increase in average brain capacity to about 520 ml. The jaws are heavy, the back teeth are large, and there is a sagittal crest—all indications of a mixed, tough vegetable diet. The crania, though, are obviously not as robust as in *P. aethiopicus*.

The second robust species continues the extreme ruggedness of *P. aethiopicus*, though it is not quite as pronounced. Found in Tanzania,

FIGURE 10.24
These three views of *Paranthropus boisei* from Lake Turkana, Kenya, reveal a similarity to the first specimen of the species, originally called "Zinjanthropus."

Kenya, and Ethiopia and existing from 2.2 to 1 mya, *Paranthropus boisei* shows features that, along with those of *P. aethiopicus*, are sometimes referred to as "hyperrobust" (Figure 10.24). The specimen that defined the species is the famous "Zinjanthropus," found by Mary and Louis Leakey in 1959. Dubbed "Nutcracker Man," this specimen has extremely large jaws and back teeth and a large sagittal crest. Otherwise *P. boisei* has the body and brain size of the South African robust hominids.

A recent *P. boisei* fossil from Ethiopia (Suwa et al. 1997) consists of the first cranium of this species with an associated mandible. The largest-known skull of the species, it comes from a new site that extends the species' known range in Africa and is clearly associated with a dry grassland environment. It also shows some physical differences from existing *boisei* fossils that indicate a considerable range of phenotypic variation within the species.

The second new hominid genus that appeared about 2.5 mya is the one to which modern humans belong, *Homo*. We will discuss the first species of our genus in the next section. For now, however, we need to account for the overall shape of the early hominid family "bush" (see Figure 10.21). What might have caused the branching that founded the new genera of

FIGURE 10.25
A Sample of Oldowan Tools. The two at the lower right are flake tools. The others are core tools.

Paranthropus and *Homo*? What caused the extinction, around the same time, of genus *Australopithecus*? Finally, what might have caused the extinction of the *Paranthropus* species about 1 mya?

We can't answer these questions with certainty, but recall Richard Potts's evidence for a sharp increase in environmental variability in Africa starting about 6 mya and continuing—and further increasing—through time (1996, 1998). Increased environmental variability resulting in a series of newly emerging, complex, and diverse habitats may have initially promoted different adaptations among hominid populations, as seen in the branching that gave rise to the robust hominids and to *Homo*. But, if the degree of the fluctuations continued to increase, this may have put such pressure on the hominid adaptive responses that those groups less able to cope eventually became extinct. Unable to survive well enough to perpetuate themselves in the face of decreasing resources (this may have been the case for *Paranthropus*, who were specialized vegetarians) these now-extinct hominids were possibly out-competed for space and resources by the better adapted, a phenomenon known as **competitive exclusion.** In this case, only the adaptive response that included an increase in brain size, with its concomitant increase in ability to understand and manipulate the environment, proved successful in the long run.

THE FIRST MEMBERS OF GENUS *HOMO*

When the Leakeys found Zinjanthropus in 1959, they uncovered some simple stone tools at the same level of Olduvai Gorge (Figure 10.25).

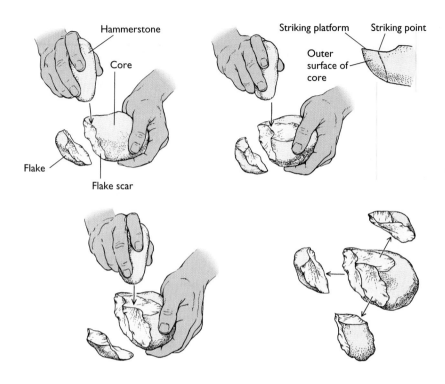

FIGURE 10.26
Process of Removing Flakes from a Stone Core in the Oldowan Tradition. A hard stone was struck in just the right locations to remove sharp, thin flakes.

At first, they thought Zinjanthropus had made the tools, but they began to feel that "Zinj" was too primitive to have made something so sophisticated.

These tools, called **Oldowan** after Olduvai Gorge, seem very simple to us. Also called *pebble tools*, they are nothing more than water-smoothed cobbles, up to 3 or 4 inches across, modified by knocking off a few chips from one or two faces to make a sharp edge. But unlike the termite sticks of the chimpanzees, there is nothing in the raw material—the unmodified stone—that immediately suggests the tools that can be made from it or the method of manufacture. A stone tool requires the maker to be able to imagine within the stone the tool he wants to make and to picture the process needed to make it. Making even a simple Oldowan tool is also a far more complex technological feat than stripping the leaves off a branch to make a stick narrow enough to fit down the hole of a termite mound (Figure 10.26). (I can attest to the difficulty.) This leap of the imagination and increase in technological skill are what make the first evidence of stone toolmaking so important.

competitive exclusion: When one species outcompetes others for the resources of a particular area.

Oldowan: A toolmaking tradition from Africa associated with early *Homo*.

FIGURE 10.27
The Well-Known Skull 1470 from Lake Turkana, Kenya, Front and Side Views. Note the flatter face, smoother contours, lack of a sagittal crest, and more rounded braincase as compared to *Australopithecus* and *Paranthropus*. This fossil was first classified as *Homo habilis* and still is by some authorities. Others consider it a separate species, *Homo rudolfensis*.

Originally, it was thought that the Oldowan tools were all **core tools** and that the flakes were the waste products of their manufacture. Recently, however, it has been shown that though some flaked cores may have been used as tools, the majority were the raw materials for the manufacture of **flake tools** used for a variety of tasks, such as cutting meat and plant material, scraping meat off a bone, and sawing wood or bone (Schick and Toth 1993; Toth 1985). Under microscopic analysis, the edges of these flakes show a polish that is characteristic of these activities.

It also appears that the makers of the Oldowan tools may have traveled some distance to find a source of stone known to be superior for the production of sharp, durable tools. The cores themselves were probably carried around to wherever flakes were needed; it is common to find flakes at a site but not the cores from which they were struck. All this shows a high level of planning (Schick and Toth 1993).

Although there is some evidence for bone tool manufacture among the earlier hominids (Holden 2001), no evidence of stone tool manufacture has been found. One study (Susman 1994) concluded that the thumbs of *Australopithecus* and *Paranthropus* had features that allowed the dexterity required to make stone tools—although this conclusion has been challenged (Gibbons 1997a). Furthermore, some simple stone tools have recently been found in Ethiopia that date to 2.6 mya, 300,000 years earlier than the earliest fossil of *Homo* (Semaw et al. 1997). Still, no hard evidence links any hominid other than *Homo* with the manufacture of stone implements.

It appeared in 1959, and still does, that Zinjanthropus was not a good candidate for having been the maker of the pebble tools. Then, in 1961, the Leakeys found a second hominid from the same time period. Actually, they had found fragmentary fossils of this form in the same year that they found Zinjanthropus, but they had not fully recognized them as something different. They named the new form *Homo habilis*, "handy man" (Figure 10.27).

The reasons for including these fossils in genus *Homo* are twofold. First, there is a notable increase in brain size, from the average of about 480 ml for *Australopithecus* and *Paranthropus* to an average of 680 ml, with a possible maximum of 800 ml, in *H. habilis*. Second, the presence of the stone tools indicated that those larger brains were capable of a complexity of thought not seen in the record of the other two hominid genera. Thus, *H. habilis* seems to mark the beginning of a new trend in hominid evolution—toward bigger brains and greater intelligence. Fossils of *H. habilis* have now been found in Tanzania, Kenya, Ethiopia, and perhaps southern Africa and have been dated at 2.3 to 1.5 mya.

The exact taxonomic affiliations of this group of fossils, however, is far from agreed upon. The specimens from East Turkana, Kenya, are considered different enough by some to be placed in a new species, *Homo rudolfensis*. The specimen pictured in Figure 10.27 is an example. Differences include a larger body and brain size than in *H. habilis* and the lack of a continuous **brow ridge** over the eyes. (See Tattersall 1992 for a review of this argument.) Others (Wood and Collard 1999) feel that the fossils labeled *Homo habilis* and *H. rudolfensis* are in important ways closer to *Australopithecus* than to *Homo* and should thus be lumped into the former genus. This assessment is based on similar body proportions, evidence of continued arboreal ability among "early *Homo*," and similarity of brain size *relative to body size* (rather than absolute differences in brain size). Still others (Sherwood 2000) agree that while *H. habilis* might be lumped into *Australopithecus*, *H. rudolfensis* should remain in *Homo*. For the remainder of this discussion, we will use the term "early *Homo*," in keeping with what is, at the moment, the majority view, and we will also consider all the fossils together. As more fossils that cover a broader span of time are found, the picture of hominid evolution during this period may become clearer. But without methods of genetic comparison, the debate will probably never be fully resolved.

core tools: Tools made by taking flakes off a stone nucleus.

flake tools: Tools made from the flakes removed from a stone core.

brow ridge: A heavy bony ridge over the eyes.

Contemporary Reflections

Where Is the "Missing Link"?

A headline in the December 19, 1912, issue of the *New York Times* proclaimed, "Paleolithic Skull Is a Missing Link." The skull referred to was the now-infamous "Piltdown Man," discovered in England, named *Eoanthropus* (the "dawn man")—and 40 years later shown to be a fraud (see Feder 2001 for details). At the time, however, it was touted as the "missing link" because it possessed traits that were a perfect mix between those of human and ape. Its cranium was the shape and size of a modern human's, and its mandible was decidedly apelike. (In fact, the cranium *was* of a modern human and the jaw *was* of a modern orangutan—modified by the still-unidentified perpetrator to appear ancient.)

For much of the history of evolutionary thought, evolution was conceived of as a ladder or a chain, progressing from primitive to modern, with living forms representing points on that chain. Even when it was generally acknowledged that humans had descended from apes, this evolution was thought of as unilinear—a single line of progress from ape to man. Thus, as we go back into the fossil record, we should eventually find something that is intermediate—half ape and half human. Since modern apes were thought of as the remnants of primitive forms that had never evolved further, the missing link (notice the chain metaphor) was conceived of as a mix of the traits of *modern* humans and *modern* apes. In our hubris, we were sure it was our big brains that separated us from the apes and that had evolved first, so the combination fabricated to concoct the Piltdown skull fit the bill perfectly. It had that big-brain hallmark of humanity, perched on top of an otherwise apelike jaw.

Indeed, even when evolution was recognized as being a branching tree rather than a ladder or chain, the idea of fossil forms that were intermediates between modern species still held. Famed

Finally, on the matter of evolutionary relationships, the arm-to-leg proportions of early *Homo* more closely resemble those of *Australopithecus africanus* (long arms, short legs) than they do A. *afarensis*. Thus, the former species may be the direct ancestor of our genus (Berger 1998), even though later in our evolution the relative limb lengths became reversed (short arms, long legs).

What is it about the stone tools that may have given early *Homo* an edge? Paleoanthropologist Richard Leakey, the son of Louis and Mary, suggests that sharp stone tools allowed these hominids to more quickly cut meat and bones off a carcass, making the addition of meat to the diet through scavenging safer and more efficient. There is evidence for this suggestion.

Ten Olduvai sites from the *Homo habilis* period contain Oldowan tools, flakes, and animal bones. Once thought to be some sort of "home base," these areas are now considered "stone cache" sites (Potts 1984), anatomist Sir Arthur Keith wrote that "to unravel man's pedigree, we have to thread our way, not along the links of a chain, but through the meshes of a complicated network" (1927, 8). Then, on the next page, he accepted the Piltdown find as authentic.

We recognize today that living species are not leftover primitive links on an evolutionary chain but are, themselves, the products of evolution. A missing link in the traditional sense—between modern humans and modern apes—simply does not exist. What *does* exist is a common ancestor of humans and our closest relatives, the chimpanzees and bonobos—and it did not look exactly like any of those modern species. Granted, we have reason to think that the common ancestor resembled a bonobo or chimp more than a modern human, but this is just because evolution happens to have taken place at a more rapid pace in hominids than in the apes. The apes are still modern species.

So what we *can* look for is that common ancestor. It is a "link" not in the sense of a chain, but in the sense of being that point where our two evolutionary lines converge. At the moment, that form is still missing. But as we find older and older fossils, we are closing in on our common ancestor.

What will it look like? It should have characteristics shared by both hominids and pongids, but it will look, on the whole, like neither. Genetic evidence, as well as the fact that we have the very apelike form *Ardipithecus ramidus* from 4.4 mya, suggests that our common ancestor is around 5 million years old. In fact, anthropologists Robert Boyd and Joan B. Silk (1997, 360–61) offer the possibility that *Ard. ramidus* might *be* the common ancestor.

So if you want to get a glimpse of the "missing link" in this modern sense, turn to Figure 10.10. It's probably *not* the common ancestor of modern apes and humans, but—so far—it's the closest we've come.

---

where hominids left supplies of stones and to which they took scavenged animal remains for quick, safe processing and eating. Analysis indicates that these sites were used for short periods but repeatedly, as one would expect of such places.

Archaeologist Lewis Binford (1985) has analyzed the animal bones from these sites and has found that they are mostly the lower leg bones of antelopes. These bones carry little meat and, along with the skull, are about the only parts left after a large carnivore has finished eating. However, such bones are rich in marrow, so a major activity at the sites in question may have been to cut off what little meat remained on these bones and then to break them open for the nutritious marrow inside.

Finally, Pat Shipman has studied the taphonomy of these and other bones with a scanning electron microscope (1984, 1986). She found that marks left by cutting with stone tools were usually on the shafts of the bones as if pieces of meat were cut off, not near the joints as if an entire

FIGURE 10.28
This micrograph of a fossil bone from Olduvai Gorge shows tool marks (the horizontal lines and the diagonal line beginning at the top of the photo) and a carnivore tooth mark (beginning on the right side and angled toward the center). In this case, the tooth mark overlaps the tool mark, indicating that the hominids sliced meat off this part of the bone before a scavenger began eating.

carcass had been butchered. Also, the hominid tool marks sometimes overlapped carnivore tooth marks, showing that the carnivores had gotten there first (Figure 10.28).

We may envision early *Homo* in small cooperative groups, maybe family groups, foraging on the savanna for plant foods and always on the lookout for a carnivore kill, watching for a group of scavengers gathered on the ground or a flock of vultures circling overhead. Their big brains allowed them to better understand their environment and to manipulate it, making imaginative and technologically advanced tools from stone. With these tools they may have cut apart the carcasses they found and taken the pieces back to a safe place, maybe where they had stored more tools. There they cut the remaining meat off the bones and, using large hammerstones, smashed open the bones for marrow. It was no doubt a harsh life, but it was successful. The adaptive themes of bipedalism, large brains, social organization, and tool technology set the stage for the rest of hominid evolution.

Fossils indicate that early *Homo* was around for only about half a million years. Before they disappeared from the fossil record, a new hominid species came on the scene—one that continued and enhanced the trends of big brains and tool technology, adaptations that soon carried this hominid all over the Old World.

▽   ▽   ▽

SUMMARY

The primates are one of the earliest of the existing mammal groups to evolve after the mass extinction of 65 mya. They appear to have evolved first in what are now North America and Europe, but the success of their adaptations allowed them to radiate over the Old World and into the New World.

About 23 mya, the hominoids appear in the form of primitive apes. This successful group has left fossils all over Africa, Europe, and Asia. It is from one of the African apes that our family, Hominidae, branched off some 5 or 6 mya.

The evolution of habitual bipedalism marks the beginnings of our family and was the major distinguishing characteristic of this family for the first half of its time on earth. Bipedalism may have begun as part of one group's adaptation to the forests. We still see this trait—along with food sharing and sexual consciousness—in today's bonobos. However, these adaptations would also prove useful in Africa's increasingly variable environment, and the hominids soon were well established and radiated—perhaps from *Ardipithecus*—into three distinct groups, often classified as separate genera: *Australopithecus*, *Paranthropus*, and *Homo*.

The first two genera, *Australopithecus* and *Paranthropus*, with their chimp-sized brains, remained largely vegetarian and persisted until nearly 1 mya. They eventually lost out to a combination of environmental change and competition from the third hominid genus, *Homo*, with its bigger brain and ability to manipulate its environment both mentally and technologically, including the making of stone tools. These adaptations allowed the earliest members of our genus to more safely and efficiently exploit an abundant and reliable new food source—meat scavenged from natural deaths among the great herds of savanna animals. This adaptive base led, as we will see in the next chapter, to the further radiation of this type of hominid, who eventually became one of the earth's dominant species.

QUESTIONS FOR FURTHER THOUGHT

1. People often ask this logical question: "If humans are descended from apes, then how come there are still apes around?" How would you respond to this?

2. Looking at the fossil record of the hominids, we see that the hominid line that survived after about 1 mya was the one with the big brain. From our perspective, this makes it seem as if our evolution was inevitable. Is this the case? Would the big-brained species have been successful in all circumstances? Once the evolution of hominids got started, were *we* a predictable result?

KEY TERMS

foramen magnum	knuckle walking	core tools
prognathism	competitive exclusion	flake tools
sagittal crest	Oldowan	brow ridge

SUGGESTED READINGS

The primates and their evolution are covered in John G. Fleagle's *Primate Adaptations and Evolution*. The intriguing story of *Gigantopithecus* is told in *Other Origins: The Search for the Giant Ape in Human History*, by Russell Ciochon, John Olsen, and Jamie James. For a more technical account of early primate evolution, see R. D. Martin's article in the May 20, 1993, issue of *Nature*, called "Primate Origins: Plugging the Gaps."

The story of the study of the human fossil record and of some of the major recent discoveries is told in *Lucy: The Beginnings of Humankind*, by Donald Johanson and Maitland Edey, and in a sequel, *Lucy's Child: The Discovery of a Human Ancestor*, by Donald Johanson and James Shreeve. Both of these books are somewhat outdated but still convey the excitement of paleoanthropology. A slightly different perspective on much of the same material is found in Richard Leakey and Roger Lewin's *Origins Reconsidered: In Search of What Makes Us Human*. A beautifully illustrated treatment of the subject, based on an exhibit at the American Museum of Natural History in New York, is Ian Tattersall's *The Human Odyssey: Four Million Years of Evolution*.

A *National Geographic* series, "The Dawn of Humans," covering the 6 million years of our evolution, appears in the following issues: September 1995; January and March 1996; February, May, July, and September 1997; August 1998; and May, July, and December 2000. The photographs and graphics are, as usual, superb.

It would be a good idea to see what a primary report on an important fossil looks like. A good example is the first report on the discovery of *Ardipithecus ramidus* (at the time, lumped into genus *Australopithecus*). It's by White et al. and appears in the September 22, 1994, issue of *Nature*.

For a nice summary of the different views on the possible climate-change influences on human evolution, see "Sunset on the Savanna" by James Shreeve in the July 1996 issue of *Discover*. A nicely illustrated description of the Great Rift Valley explanation is by Yves Coppens in the May 1994 *Scientific American*, titled "East Side Story: The Origin of Humankind."

THE EVOLUTION OF GENUS *HOMO*

The great tragedy of
Science—the slaying of
a beautiful hypothesis
by an ugly fact.
—Thomas Henry
Huxley

William of Ockham (c. 1285–1349), an English philosopher, is credited with the principle popularly known as *Ockham's razor*. The idea actually goes well back into human antiquity. Ockham said in effect that in logic no more things should be presumed to exist than are absolutely necessary. In other words, "keep it simple."

Ockham's idea, also known as the **law of parsimony,** says that if several possible explanations exist to account for something in science or philosophy, *the simplest is the best,* at least as a starting point. It further means that explanations should be based on facts that are already known rather than on facts that *may* exist. Of course, as new facts come to light, explanations will change, and we may find that the simplest explanation is not the best one.

Applied to the interpretation of the human fossil record, Ockham's razor means that we should begin by creating a tree of relationships among fossil species that has the fewest evolutionary lines allowed by the data. It also means that we should not create new taxonomic categories unless the data support them. Moreover, we should not suggest evolutionary relationships that include a species or other taxonomic unit that may *someday* be discovered but for which no evidence exists at present.

Being simple, however, is not always so easy. There is no universal agreement on the dates of all the hominid fossils nor on the interpretation of their phenotypic features or their taxonomic categories. There are, as noted, at least a half-dozen different trees for the early hominids, each—according to whoever proposed it—the most parsimonious. If you understand the tree presented in Chapter 10 (see Figure 10.21), you should then be able to understand all the others if you choose to get deeper into the subject. The "correct" answer, if we can ever find it, awaits more data from the fossil record.

If it is hard for us to agree on the fossils that represent the first 2.5 million years of the hominid record, it gets worse when we address the latest 2 million years. The reason is simple: This is the time during which our genus, *Homo,* evolved. The data from these fossils matter to us because they will tell us just who we are and where we came from.

There are widely different interpretations of the nature, dates, and taxonomic affiliations of the hominid fossils from this period, and there are several divergent schools of thought regarding just what the family tree of our genus looks like. At stake in these discussions is the very identity of the species to which we all belong. In this chapter, we will address the following questions:

How can we best go about describing and organizing the fossil evidence for the evolution of genus *Homo*?

What do we know about the dates, the distribution, and the physical appearance of the various groups of fossils assigned to this genus?

What can we say about their lives, particularly about their cultural behaviors?

LUMPERS AND SPLITTERS: AN ORGANIZING PLAN

Recall from Chapter 10 that there is disagreement over whether the early small-brained hominids all belong to one genus, *Australopithecus*, or to two genera, *Australopithecus* and *Paranthropus*. In this debate, those who support a single genus are "lumpers," and those who advocate two genera are "splitters." Similarly, placing all early *Homo* into species *H. habilis* would be lumping, and separating those fossils into *H. habilis* and *H. rudolfensis* would be splitting.

Splitters tend to focus on differences among fossils and express those differences by assigning the fossils in question to different taxonomic categories—different species if the distinctions are small, different genera if they are more pronounced. Lumpers, emphasizing the extent of the diversity present in living species and genera, consider differences among some fossil groups to reflect a similar degree of diversity. They believe that the most parsimonious course is to lump fossils into the same taxon unless there is clear evidence that they should be split.

Both these approaches are, of course, provisional starting points. All good scientists understand that hypotheses are open to testing and that new data may require new models—sometimes radically new ones. Time and again, someone's "beautiful hypothesis" is slayed by some new "ugly fact." Moreover, no researcher is always a splitter or a lumper. One scientist's approach can vary from group to group. I favor the two-genera classification of the early hominids (*Australopithecus* and *Paranthropus*), but, as you will see, I favor a lumping model with regard to genus *Homo*.

Subsequent to the early *Homo* stage, the lumping and splitting factions are very much at odds regarding the evolution of genus *Homo*. At one extreme is the viewpoint that all members of *Homo* since *habilis/rudolfensis* belong to a single species, *Homo sapiens*. The other extreme claims six species within genus *Homo* over that 2-million-year period. There are also versions of the splitter point of view that recognize two to five *Homo* species. Each model has evidence in its support, and each has opposition based on reasonable counterarguments. The issue is by no means even close to settled. These models are the topic of Chapter 12.

law of parsimony: A principle that relies on using the simplest explanation in formulating a scientific hypothesis. Another name for Ockham's razor.

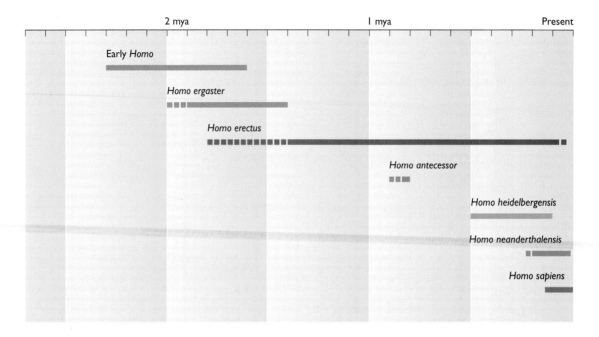

FIGURE 11.1

Timeline of Species within Genus *Homo* According to the Most Extreme Splitting Model. Dashes indicate that some evidence exists for extending the time range of that species as shown. Each species, of course, may be extended in time either way as more fossil evidence is recovered. This model does not necessarily reflect the author's views but is used to clearly sort the fossils into named groups recognized by some authorities as separate species.

How, then, to begin discussing the fossil evidence for the evolution of our genus if authorities cannot even agree on the names? The simplest scheme would, of course, be the one that lumps all the fossils into *Homo sapiens*—that would certainly cut down on the taxonomic categories. But such an approach would make it difficult to describe and discuss differences among groups of fossils that some authorities feel are enough to merit species distinction. And, when these species names are used—regardless of one's point of view on the debate—there is usually no misunderstanding about which fossils are being referred to.

Thus, let's begin with the extreme splitter model—currently, the most complex organization, which divides all later *Homo* into six species (Figure 11.1). We will describe and discuss these species in terms of their phenotypic features, dates, geographic distributions, and behaviors. Then, in Chapter 12, we will discuss the various hypotheses for just how many species these groups represent and, most important, for how they are related evolutionarily. *Understand that I am not necessarily advocating this model.* I just feel that organizing our discussion in this order will allow us to more easily describe the other points of view by lumping species we have already named and defined. I like to think William of Ockham would have approved.

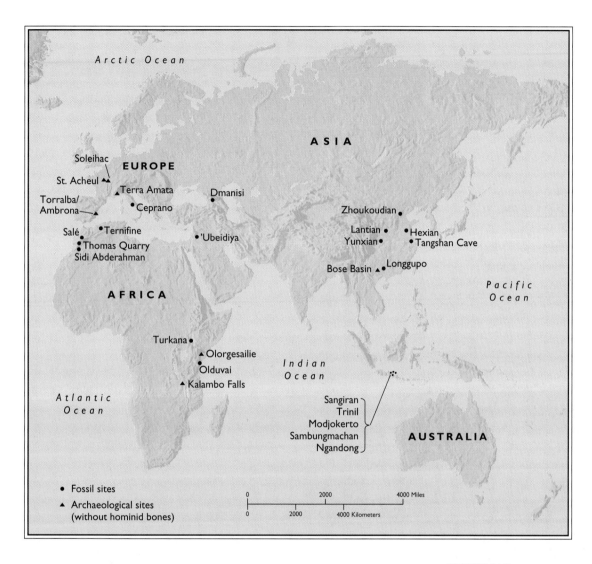

FIGURE 11.2
Map of Major *Homo erectus/
ergaster* Sites.

TO NEW LANDS

Most of the fossils at the beginning of genus *Homo* (subsequent to the still-debated fossils of early *Homo*) are included in species *Homo erectus*. Some authorities split the fossils of this group from Kenya into a second species, *Homo ergaster* (Figure 11.2 and Table 11.1).

TABLE 11.1
Major Fossils of *Homo ergaster* and *Homo erectus*

Country	Locality	Fossils	Crania	Age (million years)	Est. Brain Size (ml)
Homo ergaster					
Kenya	East Turkana	Cranial and postcranial fragments including mandibles and pelvis and long bone fragments	KNM-ER 3733	1.78	850
			KNM-ER 3883	1.57	800
	West Turkana	Nearly complete juvenile individual	KNM-WT 15000	1.6	880
Homo erectus					
Algeria	Ternifine	Three mandibles and a skull	—	0.5–0.7	—
China	Hexian (Lontandong)	Partial skull	"Hexian Man"	0.25–0.5	1000
	Lantian (Gongwangling)	Cranial fragments mandible	"Lantian Man"	>1	800
	Longgupo(?)*	Mandible fragments	—	1.8	—
	Yunxian	Two crania	—	>0.35	—
	Zhoukoudian	Cranial and postcranial remains of 40 individuals	II	<0.46	1030
			III	<0.46	915
			VI	<0.46	850
			X	<0.46	1225
			XI	<0.46	1015
			XII	<0.46	1030
			Locality 13	0.7	—
	Tangshan Cave	Fragments	—	0.58–0.62	—
Georgia	Dmanisi	Mandible fragment, 16 teeth, 2 crania	Subadults	1.8	—
Israel	'Ubeidiya	Fragments	—	<1	—

The first finds ever of *H. erectus* were made in Java by the Dutch physician Eugene Dubois in 1891. Dubois chose Java to look for hominid fossils largely because he was already stationed there with the military. But the choice was also a logical one for the time, since most people thought that humans had first evolved in Asia, despite Darwin's clear suggestion that Africa was the hominid homeland. The idea that our evolutionary line was originally African apparently did not sit well with many Europeans.

When Dubois found a skullcap and a diseased femur at the site of Trinil (Figure 11.3), he thought they represented the "missing link" be-

Country	Locality	Fossils	Crania	Age (million years)	Est. Brain Size (ml)
Homo erectus (continued)					
Italy	Ceprano(?)	Cranium	—	0.8–0.9	—
Java	Modjokerto	Child's cranium	—	1.8(?)	—
	Ngandong	Cranial and postcranial	N-1	<0.1	1170
		fragments from >12	N-6	<0.1	1250
		invidiuals	N-11	<0.1	1230
			N-12	<0.1	1090
	Sambungmachan	Large cranial fragment	Sambungmachan	<0.1	1000
	Sangiran	Cranial and postcranial	S-2	0.7–1.6	800
		fragments from ~40	S-4	0.7–1.6	900
		individuals	S–10	0.7–1.6	850
			S-12	0.7–1.6	1050
			S-17	0.7–1.6	1000
			1993 cranium	1.1–1.4	856
	Trinil	Skullcap, femur	"Java Man"	<1	940
Morocco	Salé	Cranium	Salé	0.4(?)	880
	Sidi Abderrahman	Two mandible fragments	—	—	—
	Thomas Quarry	Mandible and skull fragments	—	0.5	—
Tanzania	Olduvai(?)	Cranial and postcranial fragments, including mandibles and pelvis and long bone fragments	OH9 OH12	1.4 0.6–0.8	1060 700–800
				Mean	984.79

*The (?) indicates that the species identification of that fossil is in question.

tween apes and humans, and he dubbed the specimens "Pithecanthropus erectus" (the "upright ape-man"), popularly known as "Java Man." Since Dubois's work, numerous other fossils have been located in Java (see Table 11.1) and are now recognized as fully hominid and assigned to our genus, *Homo*. The fossils found in Java are similar in phenotype to the African and other Asian specimens, although their average brain size is larger than in some of the earlier fossils, and many are over 1,000 ml.

Perhaps the most famous *Homo erectus* fossils are those from a cave outside of Beijing, China, called Zhoukoudian. Starting in the 1920s, six nearly complete skulls, a couple dozen cranial and mandible fragments,

FIGURE 11.3
Skullcap and Femur of "Java
Man" *Homo erectus*. The
growth toward the top of
the femur is the result of a
pathological condition.

over 100 teeth, and a few postcranial pieces were recovered from the
cave. Stone tools and animal bones, including those of horses and hyenas,
were also recovered. The hominid remains are clearly similar to those of
other specimens of *H. erectus*. Dating indicates that the cave was first occupied about 460,000 ya and was used until about 230,000 ya, although
new evidence (Boaz and Ciochon 2001) suggests that most of the *H. erectus* bones in the cave were the remains of hyenas' meals.

The fame of the Zhoukoudian fossils, called "Peking Man" (from the
old spelling of Beijing), lies mostly in the fact that they are missing.
When Japan invaded China in 1937, U.S. Marines attempting to get the
fossils out of the country were captured by Japanese troops. The fossils
were never seen again. Their whereabouts remain one of the great mysteries in anthropology. Fortunately, extensive measurements had already
been taken on the bones, and accurate casts had been made (Figure 11.4).

Since then, numerous fossils classified as *Homo erectus* have been recovered, and we are filling in—although not without controversy—our
knowledge of this important period in hominid evolution. Among the
oldest fossils of this group are those that some authorities (see, for example, Tattersall 1997) place in a separate species, *H. ergaster* ("work man,"
a reference to stone tools found in association with the fossils). The old-

FIGURE 11.4
Cast of One of the Missing
"Peking Man" Skulls.

est well-established find, from East Turkana in Kenya, is dated at 1.78 mya (Figure 11.5). In some ways it is typical of *H. erectus* crania. It has heavy brow ridges, a prognathous face, a sloping forehead, an elongated profile, a **sagittal keel,** a sharply angled occipital bone with a pronounced **torus,** and a cranial capacity of 850 ml (Figure 11.6). (The sagittal keel should not be confused with the sagittal crest. The crest is a ridge of bone for the attachment of chewing muscles. The keel is an aspect of the shape of the skull.) The average cranial capacity for this hominid group is about 980 ml, just slightly under the modern human minimum of 1,000 ml, but a considerable jump from the 680 ml average for early *Homo*. Some *H. erectus* fossils have cranial capacities within the modern human range (see Table 11.1).

In other ways, however, the Turkana skull differs from others labeled as *H. erectus*. It is thinner and higher in profile, with smaller facial bones. These modern-looking features are what have led to its placement in the species *H. ergaster*. The cranium is thought to have belonged to a female. A similar skull from East Turkana dated at 1.57 mya is more ruggedly constructed. It is thought to have belonged to a male.

From the neck up, then, *H. erectus/ergaster* is quite distinct from early *Homo* in overall size, ruggedness, and especially brain size. The skull, however, still retains primitive features that distinguish it from modern *Homo sapiens*. From the neck down, however, *H. erectus/ergaster* is essentially modern and apparently was so from its beginnings.

We know this because one of the oldest fossils of the group—also included in *H. ergaster*—is also the most complete. It is a nearly whole

sagittal keel: A sloping of the sides of the skull toward the top, as viewed from the front.

torus: A bony ridge at the back of the skull, where the neck muscles attach.

FIGURE 11.5

The *Homo erectus* (or *Homo ergaster*) skull of ER 3733 from Lake Turkana, Kenya, is fairly typical of this group.

skeleton found at West Turkana in Kenya and is dated at 1.6 mya (Figure 11.7). The shape of the pelvis indicates that it was a male. Based on dental eruption and lack of any epiphyseal union, it is estimated that he was 12 years old when he died. "Turkana Boy," as he is commonly known, was about 5½ feet tall, and he might have been 150 pounds and 6 feet tall had he lived to adulthood.

All other fossils from this group—including those from Africa outside Kenya—are assigned to *Homo erectus* (although a few are awaiting confirmation of their species affiliation). For the moment, we will treat them all as potentially *H. erectus*. The implications of the lumping versus splitting points of view for this group will be discussed in Chapter 12.

The *H. erectus* fossils from Africa—except for OH9 from Olduvai Gorge, dated at 1.4 mya—are younger, from 800,000 to 400,000 years old. This means that *Homo erectus* spread throughout the African continent and that populations of the species remained there for about a million years.

However, *H. erectus* did not remain only in Africa. According to recent data, members of the species had reached China and Southeast Asia by at least 1 mya. What prompted the people of this species to leave the savannas to which they were apparently so well adapted?

We can't know the answer for sure, but a good guess is that the spread of *H. erectus* was simply an outcome of their reproductive success.

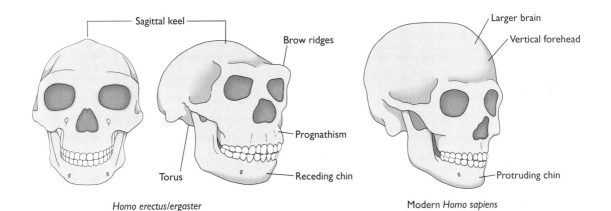

Homo erectus/ergaster   Modern Homo sapiens

FIGURE 11.6
Cranial Features of *Homo erectus/ergaster* (side and front views) Compared with Those of Modern *Homo sapiens.*

Their big brains enabled them to exploit the savannas to a greater extent than had the other hominids to date. They had better and more varied tools (which we'll discuss later), the ability to learn more about their environment and to reason out the problems that their habitat presented, and, no doubt, a more complex social organization. With these adaptations, *H. erectus* would have rapidly increased in population size.

Population increase, however, puts pressure on resources and, perhaps, on social harmony as well. So groups of *H. erectus* probably fissioned and moved outside of familiar areas, in search of less competition over food, space, and two other resources that may have been even more important factors—water and shelter. Water can be scarce on the savannas. There are lakes, rivers, and waterholes, but many of these are seasonal and are dry for months on end. And *H. erectus* may have needed shelter as well. With bodies virtually the same as ours, they were no longer good tree climbers and so had to seek shelter on the ground, in groves of trees or, if they could locate one, in a cave or rock shelter. But, of course, a leopard or other animal may have already taken up residence in the cave and had to be dealt with. They may also have been following migrations of animal herds.

In search of food, water, shelter, and perhaps space and social harmony, *H. erectus* wandered the Old World. Those wanderings eventually carried them as far from their African homeland as what is now Beijing, China, and the Indonesian island of Java, and perhaps to Europe as well. Not only did these journeys take them to new climates, but the travels also brought them into contact with the changeable environments of the Ice Ages, known technically as the **Pleistocene.**

Pleistocene: The geological time period, from 1.6 million to 10,000 years ago, characterized by a series of glacial advances and retreats.

FIGURE 11.7
The "Turkana Boy," *Homo ergaster* fossil KNM-15000, is one of the most complete early hominid fossils ever found. The pelvis is clearly that of a male, and the epiphyses at the top of his left femur are obviously not fused (see Figure 9.3).

Beginning about 1.6 mya and ending 10,000 ya, the Pleistocene was actually a complex series of extremely cold periods separated by warm phases, some warmer than today. There may have been as many as eighteen cold episodes during the Pleistocene, some lasting tens of thousands of years. We still don't know what caused these cold periods. Suggestions range from increased volcanic activity, with dust and ash blocking the sun's rays, to changes in the earth's orbit.

When the average world temperature drops, ice and snow accumulate over the years at the poles and in higher elevations. The pressure of this accumulation forces the movement of great sheets and rivers of ice—**glaciers** (Figure 11.8). During periods of glacial advances, much of North America, Europe, and Asia were covered by ice, sometimes nearly a mile thick (Figure 11.9). Parts of the world not covered by the glaciers were nonetheless affected, having cooler summers and wetter winters. The advance of the glaciers also had the effect of condensing the world's climatic zones into smaller spaces. Several times during the Pleistocene, the temperate oak and pine forests of Connecticut, where I now live, were like the arctic **tundra** of Alaska and northern Canada. Moreover, with so much of the earth's water tied up in the great ice sheets, sea levels dropped as much as 400 feet, exposing large areas of land formerly under water. This allowed humans to migrate to areas previously inaccessible; for instance, modern *Homo sapiens* migrated to North America.

The world of the Pleistocene was the world through which *Homo erectus* was able to migrate and establish themselves, and we find their remains in some of the far corners of the Old World. They undoubtedly also inhabited the areas in between, but we have yet to uncover fossils in these areas.

Redating of early finds from Java has posed interesting questions regarding the spread of *Homo erectus* around the Old World. Using new versions of the potassium/argon dating technique, researchers have redated the Sangiran *erectus* fossils to 1.6 mya and the Modjokerto remains to 1.8 mya—twice as old as previously thought and at least as old as the oldest African *erectus/ergaster* fossil. This could mean that *H. erectus* evolved somewhere other than Africa. But all previous hominid fossils come only from Africa, so it's unlikely that *erectus* evolved anywhere but there.

That leaves two plausible explanations. Perhaps *H. erectus* (or *ergaster*) actually first evolved in Africa earlier than any of the fossils we have—remember how rare fossilization is—and then spread. The other possibility is simply that their expansion began very shortly after they first evolved. Science writer James Shreeve (1994, 86) notes that Java is 10,000 to 15,000 miles from Africa, depending upon the route, and that

glaciers: Massive sheets of ice that expand and move.

tundra: A treeless area with low-growing vegetation and permanently frozen ground.

FIGURE 11.8
A veritable river of ice, the
Moreno Glacier is located in
Patagonia, a region of Ar-
gentina.

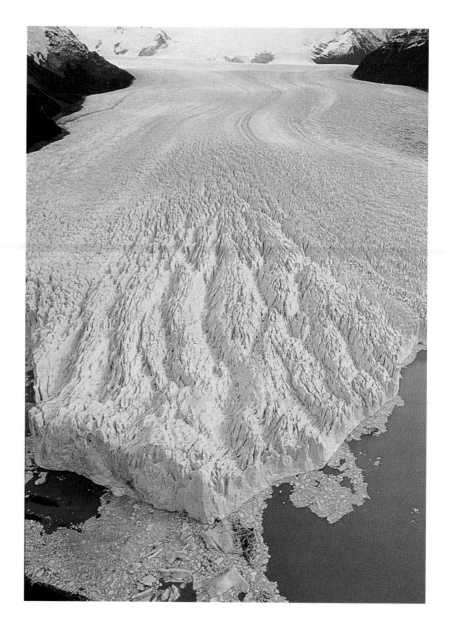

parts of Indonesia were connected to Asia at the time due to lower sea
levels in the Pleistocene. If *erectus* walked just a mile a year, it would only
have taken about 15,000 years to reach Java. That's still pretty fast, considering that they did not necessarily move 1 mile every year *in the right
direction*. I think that if the Java dates are correct, they probably mean

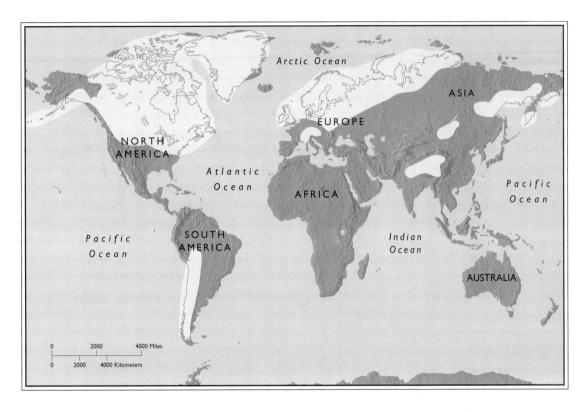

FIGURE 11.9

Maximum Worldwide Glacial Expansion during the Pleistocene. The Antarctic ice cover, not shown here, also expanded during this epoch.

that *H. erectus/ergaster* is older than we now assume based on existing fossils *and* that they began expansion early on.

Another important recent date concerns the Java site of Ngandong. There is evidence that some *erectus* fossils there may be younger than 100,000 years—perhaps as young as 27,000 to 53,000 years old. If so, there were populations of *erectus* still around well after modern *Homo sapiens* had evolved. (We'll discuss the meanings of this in the next chapter.)

It should be noted that, with the exception of the Ceprano find (see Table 11.1), the European evidence of *Homo erectus* comes in the form of cultural artifacts dated at times that have been associated with that species from other locations. At the site of Soleihac in France are tools and animal remains dated at 800,000 ya. Another French site, Terra Amata on the Riviera, has been proposed as a site where *H. erectus* built shelters and established a village around 400,000 ya. This interpretation has recently been called into question, however. Some individuals lived there, but probably not in a village of huts. In Spain, at two adjacent sites

FIGURE 11.10
Bifacially flaked hand axes became one of history's most popular tools and were found in a variety of sizes showing varying degrees of quality. The hand axe on the far right is from the French site of St. Acheul, which lent its name to this tool tradition.

called Torralba and Ambrona, dated at 400,000 ya, are the remains of some large mammals, including elephants, along with some stone tools that suggest a hunting or, more probably, a scavenging site. Until, however, we locate definite fossils of *H. erectus* from Europe—other than the cranium from Ceprano, Italy—we can only conclude that the species was there but was not widespread or, perhaps, that these sites are associated with another hominid species.

What do we know about the lives of *Homo erectus/ergaster*? Like early *Homo*, early *H. ergaster* made stone tools by taking a few flakes off a core, just enough to make the "business end." (They also, of course, used the flakes as tools.) But beginning about 1.4 mya, *H. erectus/ergaster* elaborated on this stone toolmaking technique by flaking the entire stone, controlling the shape of the whole core tool. This toolmaking tradition is called the **Acheulian technique,** after the site in France where it was first identified. The core tool produced by the Acheulian technique is the **hand axe.** It is symmetrical, edged and pointed, and **bifacial** (flaked on both sides; Figure 11.10). It was the all-purpose tool of its time, used for any number of tasks, from butchering to cutting wood. My colleague, archaeologist Ken Feder, calls it the "Swiss Army rock."

In addition to hand axes, *H. erectus/ergaster* also made tools with straight, sharp edges called cleavers. Moreover, making a hand axe or cleaver produces a great many flakes—as many as fifty usable ones by one estimate—and *H. erectus/ergaster* also made flake tools, used either unmodified or further worked to produce a desired shape.

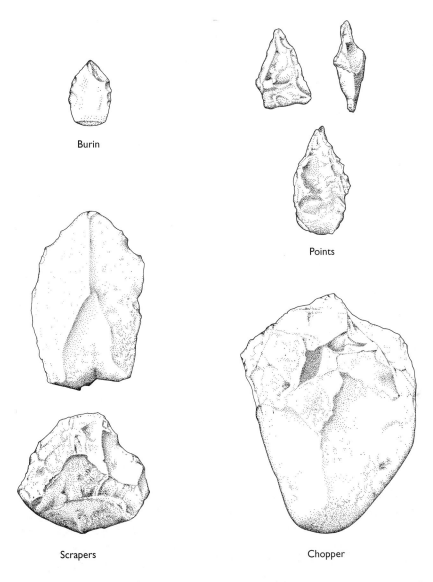

Burin

Points

Scrapers

Chopper

FIGURE 11.11
Flake and Chopper Tools Associated with *Homo erectus* from the Cave at Zhoukoudian. Although the functions of these tools are not known for certain, some are named for inferred use. Burins are thought to have been used to etch out thin slivers of antler or bone, which were then further modified into awls or needles. Points may have served as cutting tools for fine work. Scrapers may have helped remove flesh from animal hides. And choppers chopped wood and perhaps broke open bones to extract marrow.

Acheulian technique: A toolmaking tradition associated with *Homo erectus/ergaster* in Africa and Europe.

hand axe: A bifacial, all-purpose stone tool, shaped somewhat like an axe head.

bifacial: A stone tool that has been worked on both sides.

Hand axes appeared in Africa about 1.4 mya and lasted for over a million years. They spread throughout Africa and into Europe. They are, however, rarely found in Asia. Instead, Asian *erectus* populations, like those at Zhoukoudian, made what are called choppers, with flakes removed from one side, and a few other tools with flakes removed from both sides (Figure 11.11). But these tool types, unlike the Acheulian hand axe, were asymmetrical and not flaked over the whole surface.

On the subject of hand axes, some new evidence from Tanzania (Schuster 2001) includes hand axes dated at 1.5 mya that bear traces of acacia wood on their blades. One interpretation of this is that the toolmakers were using these stone tools for woodworking. No actual wooden artifacts were recovered, however.

Perhaps the most striking behavioral advance associated with *Homo erectus* is the purposeful use of fire. There is some evidence, though it is disputed, for the use of fire in Africa at 1.5 mya and France at 750,000 ya. A rock shelter in Thailand has yielded evidence of fire dated at 700,000 ya. The earliest well-accepted date (although even it is not without its skeptics) is from the cave at Zhoukoudian sometime after 500,000 ya (Binford and Chuan 1985; Binford and Stone 1986).

Fire, of course, provides heat, and so it is not surprising that some of the earliest evidence of fire comes from cold northern areas. Fire also provides protection from animals and can be used for cooking, making meat more easily chewed and digestible. But in the long run, perhaps its most important use is as a source of light. Science writer John Pfeiffer (1969) suggests that fire could extend the hours of activity into the night and provide a social focus for group interaction. Sitting around the campfire at night was when people experimented, created, talked, and socialized. Fire serves these functions in human cultures today. Moreover, the use of fire may well have given people a psychological advantage, a sense of mastery and control over a force of nature, and a source of energy. As Pfeiffer says in the title of his article, "When *Homo erectus* Tamed Fire, He Tamed Himself."

Was *Homo erectus* a hunter of big game, as often portrayed, or did this species continue to scavenge for most of the meat in its diet? At the 400,000-year-old Spanish sites of Torralba and Ambrona, which are located on two hills on either side of a mountain pass, scientists found the remains of fifty elephants and over sixty other game animals (see Figure 9.10). The traditional interpretation is a rather elaborate reconstruction of a cooperative hunt, indeed, of several seasons of cooperative hunting (see, for example, Time-Life Books 1973). In this scenario, the animals were stampeded, possibly with the use of fire, into a bog where they were killed and butchered. The pieces of the carcasses were then taken to a campsite where they were further cut up, cooked, and eaten. There are also some tools at the sites.

Is there evidence for this interpretation? A taphonomic analysis of 3,000 bones from these sites found that 95 percent of them were so damaged that the search for specific evidence of human activity was impossible (Shipman and Rose 1983). Scratches on many of the bones, once thought to be stone tool cut marks, turn out, on examination under a scanning electron microscope, to be merely the results of soil abrasion and root growth. Of the fifty-five bones that could be analyzed, the microscope showed only sixteen cut marks on fourteen bones. The marks are not in a pattern that indicates systematic butchering. There is even little evidence of carnivore tooth marks. Furthermore, the tools found at the site are not associated with the elephants but with the leg bones and mandibles of horses, deer, and wild cattle—the very parts of the animals that would be gathered by scavenging. At best, it appears that *H. erectus* was present at these sites and cut some meat off animal carcasses found there. There is no compelling evidence for cooperative big-game hunting.

Two other alleged kill sites, at Olduvai Gorge and Olorgesailie in Africa, similarly give rise to elaborate interpretations of cooperative big-game hunting, but they too are based on questionable evidence. The bones found at these sites are more indicative of scavenging than of large-scale hunting. (For a good, detailed discussion, see Johanson and Shreeve 1989, chap. 8.)

So, we may probably conclude that *Homo erectus* was a forager, collecting plant foods and scavenging for meat, who also hunted at least smaller animals when the opportunity or necessity presented itself (see Ragir 2000 for a detailed discussion of early hominid diet and food-getting behavior).

Finally, what about the intellectual and linguistic skills of *H. erectus/ergaster*? As noted, their average cranial capacity was just a little short of the modern human minimum, and individual *erectus* remains fall within the modern human range. It's difficult to be certain what this fact means. After all, the modern range of 1,000 to 2,000 ml means that some people have brains twice the volume of others, but there is no solid evidence that within this range brain size has anything to do with intelligence. Was *H. erectus*, then, just a little bit less intelligent than we are?

Anthropologist Ralph Holloway (1980, 1981) has looked at the structure of *H. erectus* brains because the inside of the skull reflects, rather specifically, some of the features of the brain it once held. By making **endocasts** of the inside surfaces of fossil crania, Holloway has produced images of the very brains of our ancestors (Figure 11.12). One intriguing find is that the brains of *H. erectus* were asymmetrical—the right and left halves of the brain weren't the same shape. This is found to some extent in apes but to a greater extent in modern humans, because the halves of our brains perform different functions. Language and the ability to use symbols, for example, are functions of our left hemispheres, while spatial reasoning (like the hand-eye coordination needed to make complex

endocasts: Natural or human-made casts of the inside of a skull.

FIGURE 11.12

Natural Endocasts from South African Australopithecines, Showing the Degree of Detail Possible. Notice the blood vessels, especially in the upper right cast. Such casts may also be made artificially and allow us to compare the brains of our ancestors with those of modern humans.

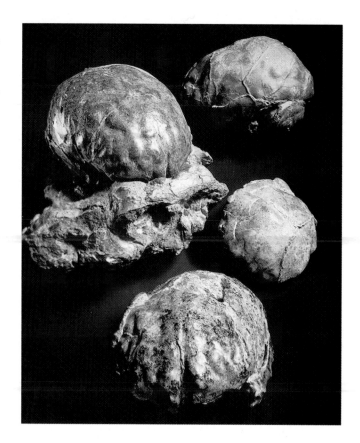

tools) is performed in the right hemisphere. This hints that *H. erectus* also had hemisphere specialization, perhaps even including the ability to communicate through a symbolic language.

Further evidence of language use by *H. erectus* is suggested by the reconstruction of the vocal apparatus based on the anatomy of the cranial base. Even though the vocal apparatus is made up of soft parts, those parts are connected to bone, and so the shape of the bone is correlated with the shape of the larynx, pharynx, and other features (Figure 11.13).

Reconstruction work on australopithecines indicates that their vocal tract was basically like that of apes, with the larynx and pharynx high up in the throat. While this would have allowed them to drink and breathe at the same time (as human infants can do up to 18 months), it would not have allowed for the precise manipulation of air that is required for modern human languages. The early hominids could make sounds, but they would have been more like those of chimpanzees.

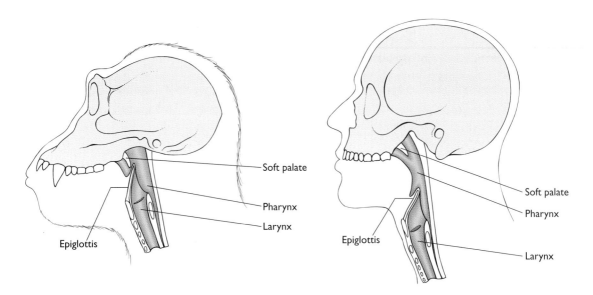

FIGURE 11.13
Vocal Tract of a Chimp Compared to a Modern Human's. The high placement of the chimp's vocal tract makes it impossible for it to produce all of the sounds that are part of modern human languages.

Homo erectus, on the other hand, had vocal tracts more like those of modern humans, positioned lower in the throat and allowing for a greater range and speed of sound production. Thus, *erectus* could have produced vocal communication that involved many sounds with precise differences. Whether or not they did so is another question. But, given their ability to manufacture fairly complex tools, to control fire, and to survive in different and changing environmental circumstances, *erectus* certainly had complex things to talk *about.* It is not out of the question that *erectus* had a communication system that was itself complex, although there are authorities who feel that a communication system with the attributes of modern human language is associated only with the sophisticated behavior of modern *Homo sapiens* (See Holden 1998 for a detailed discussion).

If we can consider it a separate species, *Homo erectus*—although now extinct—was a smashing success by any standards. The species evolved nearly 2 mya in Africa, possibly from an earlier species, *H. ergaster,* and by perhaps 1.8 mya had spread as far as Java. By 500,000 ya, they had reached northern China and Europe. They lasted as an identifiable group in Africa and China until 250,000 ya and may have persisted in Java until less than 100,000 ya. Their adaptations—now focused on learning, technology, and the cultural transmission of information—allowed them to exploit a number of different environments.

There is some debate over just how much *H. erectus* changed during its tenure on earth. There is a small increase in average cranial capacity over this time (about 180 ml), as well as some refinement in hand axe–making technique and in flake tool variety. These changes, however, are small and slow, so the overall impression is one of stability—not a bad thing in evolutionary terms.

Perhaps as early as 800,000 ya, there was another sudden surge in brain size, to an average matching our own. This marks the beginning of perhaps the most complex part of our story.

BIG BRAINS, ARCHAIC SKULLS

The next three hominid species—using the six-species model—are marked by brain sizes within the modern human range that, indeed, match or approximate the modern human average; nonetheless, they have other features, especially of the cranium, that retain primitive characteristics. These hominid groups are sometimes collectively referred to as "archaic." The most recent of these, *Homo neanderthalensis*, will be considered separately in the next section. Here, we will discuss the earlier *Homo heidelbergensis* and the even earlier *Homo antecessor* (Table 11.2 and Figure 11.14).

The newest suggested hominid species, named in mid-1997, is *Homo antecessor* ("advance guard" or "explorer"). Many authorities do not recognize the fossils involved as a separate species, but the discoverers see sufficient distinctions to warrant the new name (Bermúdez de Castro et al. 1997). Fossils have been discovered at the site of Gran Dolina cave in the Atapuerca hills in northern Spain. They consist of more than eighty fragments, including skulls, jaws, teeth, and other portions of the skeleton. There are also associated tools. The site has been dated using paleomagnetism (see Table 9.1) at more than 780,000 ya. If that date is correct, these would be the oldest well-accepted fossil humans found in Europe.

The most striking fossil is the partial face of an 11-year-old boy (Figure 11.15). His features, described by the researchers as "fully modern," include a projecting nose region with a sharp lower margin, hollowed cheek bones (technically, a *canine fossa*), and several details of the dentition. Analysis of specimens indicates a cranial capacity of greater than 1,000 ml.

On the other hand, other fossils from this site show primitive features such as prominent brow ridges and premolars with multiple roots (modern human premolars have a single root). This unique mix of traits, especially the very modern appearance of the face, is what led the investigators to

TABLE 11.2
Major Fossils Classified as *Homo antecessor* and *Homo heidelbergensis*

Country	Locality	Fossils	Age	Est. Brain Size (ml)
Homo antecessor				
Spain	Gran Dolina	More than 80 fragments	>780,000	>1000
Homo heidelbergensis				
China	Dali	Cranium	200,000	1120
	Jinniushan(?)*	Nearly complete skeleton	200,000	1350
	Maba(?)	Cranium	130,000–170,000	—
	Xujiayao(?)	Fragments of 11 individuals	100,000–125,000	—
England	Swanscombe	Occipital and parietals	276,000–426,000	1325
	Boxgrove	Tibia, teeth	362,000–423,000	—
Ethiopia	Bodo	Cranium	600,000(?)	1250
France	Arago	Cranium and fragmentary remains of 7 individuals	250,000	1200
Germany	Bilzingsleben(?)	Cranial fragments and tooth	320,000–412,000	—
	Mauer	Mandible	500,000	—
	Steinheim(?)	Cranium	200,000–240,000	1200
Greece	Petralona	Cranium	160,000–240,000	1200
Hungary	Vértesszölös	Occipital fragment	250,000–475,000	1250
India	Narmada	Cranium	200,000	1300
Spain	Sima de los Huesos	2500 fragments from at least 33 individuals	300,000	— 1390
Tanzania	Ndutu (Olduvai)(?)	Cranium	400,000–700,000	1100
Zambia	Kabwe (Broken Hill)	Cranium and additional cranial and postcranial remains of several individuals	400,000–700,000	1280
			Mean	1247.00

*The (?) indicates that the species identification of that fossil is in question.

FIGURE 11.14

Map of Major *Homo antecessor* and *Homo heidelbergensis* Sites.

assign the new species name—and to further suggest that this species is the direct ancestor both of modern humans and of *Homo heidelbergensis* and *H. neanderthalensis* (see Chapter 12).

A logical objection to the analysis of the Gran Dolina boy is that the modern-looking traits seen so clearly in the boy's face might be juvenile features, not present in adults of his group and, therefore, not of diagnostic value for species assignment. The investigators, however, report that

FIGURE 11.15
Fossil ATD6-69 from Gran Dolina Cave, Atapuerca, Spain. This partial face of an 11-year-old boy who died perhaps more than 780,000 ya is fully modern in many features, including the hollowed cheek bone easily seen here.

some of the other fragmentary facial bones from the site also show these modern traits and that *later* fossils from a nearby site, Sima de los Huesos, do not (Gibbons 1997b).

The fossil bones from Gran Dolina are striking for their antiquity, but some of the 200 tools found at the site are even older, dating back to 1 mya. These early tools resemble pre–hand axe tools from Africa—cores and simple cutting flakes. Later tools found in the same strata as the human remains are more sophisticated. One long flake has a sharp edge on one side and a dulled, flat edge on the other. It was presumably formed to be used as a knife. None of the tools at the site, however, is as complex as some of the Acheulian tools being made by *Homo erectus* and *H. ergaster* at the same time period or earlier.

Finally, there is some intriguing evidence of the diet of the Gran Dolina people. Bison and deer bones, as well as some from other species, have been found that show stone tool cut marks, implying that the people hunted. According to the investigators, there are also cut marks on some of the human bones that were mixed in with animal bones, suggesting cannibalism (Kunzig 1997).

It should also be noted that there is a site in southeastern Spain, called Orce, that some contend is even older than Gran Dolina—900,000 years old or even older. It contains simple stone tools and alleged hominid bones. Other authorities, however, have identified the fragmentary bones as those of wild horses, and the dating is still contested (Bower 1997a). More study is clearly needed at this location.

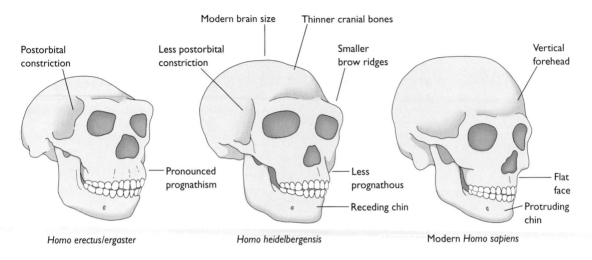

Postorbital
constriction

Less postorbital
constriction

Modern brain size

Thinner cranial bones

Smaller
brow ridges

Vertical
forehead

Pronounced
prognathism

Less
prognathous

Receding chin

Flat
face

Protruding
chin

Homo erectus/ergaster   *Homo heidelbergensis*   Modern *Homo sapiens*

FIGURE 11.16
Cranial Features of *Homo erectus/ergaster, Homo heidelbergensis,* and Modern *Homo sapiens.*

Table 11.2 and Figure 11.14 show that the fossils assigned to *Homo heidelbergensis* are widespread geographically and range over about 600,000 years in time (longer if one includes *H. antecessor*). The species was first named for a mandible found at Mauer, near Heidelberg, Germany, in 1907. Note that the inclusion of several of the fossils is questioned by those who recognize this group as a species.

Members of this group show an average brain size of nearly 1,300 ml, a more than 30 percent increase over the average for *Homo erectus*. The brains are also differently proportioned than those of *H. erectus*, with greater emphasis on the forebrain, reflected by steeper foreheads. This may be important because the frontal lobes of the human brain are the areas thought to be most involved in the control of voluntary movements, speech, attention, social behavior, planning, and reasoning (see Figure 7.7).

The bones of the cranium, compared to those of *H. erectus*, are thinner; the overall size of the face is reduced; the profile is less prognathous; the brow ridges, though still present, are less pronounced; and the **postorbital constriction,** characteristic of *erectus*, is lessened (Figure 11.16). The postcranial skeletons, essentially modern in overall shape, are more rugged and muscular than in modern humans. The 500,000-year-old tibia from Boxgrove in southeast England, for example, is strikingly thicker in cross section than the tibia of a modern person. Figures 11.17 and 11.18 show two of the more complete examples of *H. heidelbergensis* crania.

Given the fragmentary remains of many of these fossils, the fact that some were found early in the history of anthropology or by nonscientists,

FIGURE 11.17
Skull of *Homo heidelbergensis*
from Steinheim, Germany.
Note the more rounded
shape and higher forehead as
compared to *H. erectus*. At
the same time, note the retention of heavy brow ridges.

and the widespread range of the species, fairly little can be specifically said about the lifestyle of these early humans. We do know, however, some things about their tools. For example, we have evidence from Box-grove that the hand axe was in use by 500,000 ya. And about 200,000 ya, people included in *H. heidelbergensis* invented a new and imaginative way to make stone tools. The method appears first in Africa and later in Europe. Called the *prepared core*, or **Levallois technique** (after the suburb of Paris where it was first recognized), it involved the careful preparation of the rough stone core so that a number of flakes of a desired shape (up to four or five) could be taken off. The flakes could then be used for cutting, scraping, or piercing. Figure 11.19 shows the steps involved and a photograph of a replica of such a tool. There is also evidence of other materials used for manufacturing tools, such as some wooden spears from the 400,000-year-old site of Schöningen in Germany. The size and characteristics of these approximately 6-foot-long weapons suggest that they were meant to be thrown at fairly large animals (Thieme 1997).

Finally, an intriguing but still dim glimpse into the lives of the people of this era comes from another site in Atapuerca, near Gran Dolina (Kunzig 1997). Known as Sima de los Huesos ("pit of bones"), it is a shaft inside a cave, dated by electron spin resonance (ESR; see Chapter 9) at

postorbital constriction:
A narrowing of the skull behind the eyes, as viewed from above.

Levallois technique: A Tool technology involving striking uniform flakes from a prepared core.

FIGURE 11.18
The Kabwe (formerly called Broken Hill) specimen is one of the best-known examples of a premodern *Homo sapiens* from Africa. Note the extremely large brow ridges on this skull, which has a cranial capacity of 1,280 ml, quite close to the modern mean.

about 300,000 ya. It contains the bones of animals and the remains of at least thirty-three humans—many so well preserved that even fingertips and small inner ear bones are included. Most of the bones are from teenagers and young adults, both male and female. Although the bones show signs of chewing by a carnivore, it is unlikely that some predator would have selected just that age group, and the nonhuman remains in the pit are not those of prey animals but those of foxes and bears, which may have fallen in and chewed on the human bones before dying. Investigators think the bodies were thrown into the pit after death (one seems to have died from a massive infection), probably not as part of a formal funeral ritual (no artifacts were found) but more likely for simple disposal purposes. Perhaps they all died together in some catastrophe or at least over a short period of time. Many of the bones show signs of childhood malnourishment.

No doubt the peoples labeled *Homo antecessor* and *Homo heidelbergensis* had other mental, cultural, and perhaps physical adaptations to help them deal with the various and changeable environments they encountered as the Pleistocene continued. We certainly know this was true for one famous group of humans from Europe and the Near East. Some crania from Sima de los Huesos are said to show traits that might be ancestral to this next group, the Neandertals.

Side Views   Top Views

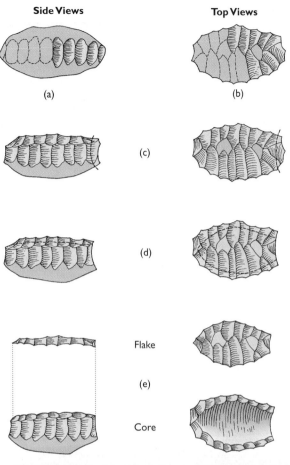

(a)

(b)

(c)

(d)

Flake

(e)

Core

FIGURE 11.19
The illustration shows step-by-step the Levallois technique: (a) produce a margin along the edge of the core, (b) shape the surface of the core, (c, d) prepare the surface to be struck (the "striking platform"), (e) remove the flake, and return to step b for additional flake removal. Shown below is a replica of a Levallois core and tool.

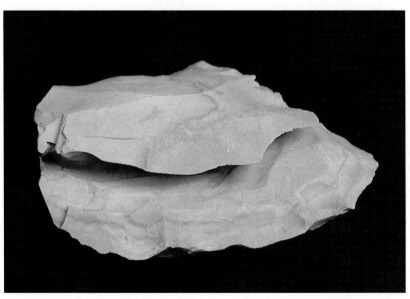

FIGURE 11.20
The Original Neandertal Skullcap from Germany. The cranial vault held a very large brain, but the brow ridges indicate an obvious difference from modern humans.

THE NEANDERTALS

The Neandertals—*Homo neanderthalensis* in the six-species model—were named after one of the first human fossils found and recognized as a human fossil, a skullcap from the Neander Valley in Germany recovered in 1856 (Figure 11.20). This was before Darwin wrote *Origin of Species*. (In German, *thal* means "valley" and is always pronounced *tal*. Recent spelling drops the silent *h*, but some still use it, and it remains in the formal species name because that was the spelling when the name was first applied.) Table 11.3 and Figure 11.21 show the basic data for fossils of this species as well as the locations of these finds.

The Neandertals have had an interesting history in anthropology. At one time they were considered brutish, hunched-over, dim-witted members of a dead-end side branch of human evolution. At other times they have been thought of as just an ancient, slightly different-looking form of modern *Homo sapiens* (Figure 11.22). These are both exaggerations. We now recognize the sophistication of the Neandertals' intellectual and cultural achievements. They were certainly similar to modern humans physically but still different in significant ways. So debate at present centers on whether the similarities place them within our species or whether the differences make them a separate species (see Chapter 12). Figures 11.23 (page 292) and 11.24 (page 293) compare the skulls and skeletons of a Neandertal and a modern *Homo sapiens*.

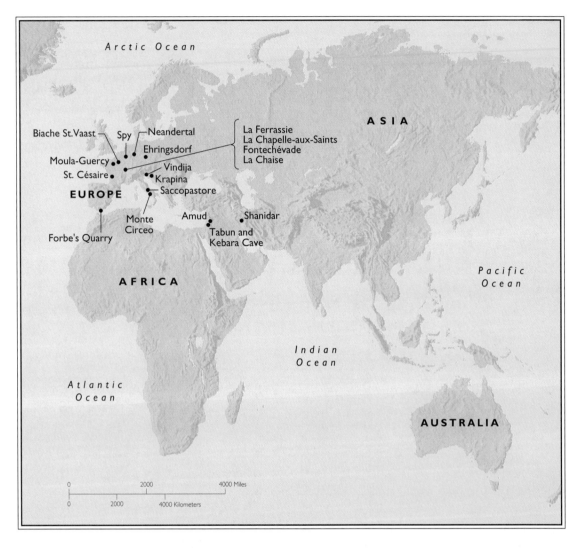

Arctic Ocean

ASIA

Biache St. Vaast
Spy
Neandertal
Ehringsdorf
Moula-Guercy
Vindija
St. Césaire
Krapina
EUROPE
Saccopastore

La Ferrassie
La Chapelle-aux-Saints
Fontechévade
La Chaise

Amud
Shanidar
Monte
Circeo
Tabun and
Forbe's Quarry
Kebara Cave

AFRICA

Pacific
Ocean

Indian
Ocean

Atlantic
Ocean

AUSTRALIA

| 0 | | 2000 | | 4000 Miles |
| 0 | 2000 | | 4000 Kilometers | |

FIGURE 11.21
Map of Major Neandertal Sites.

The crania of the Neandertals are striking in appearance. They had, essentially, more pronounced versions of the cranial features of *H. heidelbergensis*. Their cranial capacities ranged from about 1,300 ml to 1,740 ml, well within the modern range, but their foreheads were still sloped, the backs of their skulls broad, and the sides bulging. The brow ridges were still large, but smaller at the sides than in *Homo erectus*, and they were filled with air spaces (called the *frontal sinuses*), unlike the solid ridges of *Homo erectus*. The brow ridges of the Neandertals were also

TABLE 11.3
Major Fossils of *Homo neanderthalensis*

Country	Locality	Fossils	Age	Est. Brain Size (ml)
Belgium	Spy	2 skeletons	—	—
Croatia	Krapina	Cranial and postcranial fragments of >45 individuals	130,000	1200–1450
	Vindija	52 fossil fragments	28,000–42,000	—
France	Biache St. Vaast	2 crania	150,000–175,000	—
	Fontechévade	Cranial fragments of several individuals	100,000	1500
	La Chaise	Cranium	126,000	—
	La Chapelle-aux-Saints	Skeleton	—	1620
	La Ferrassie	8 skeletons	>38,000	1680
	St. Césaire	Skeleton	36,000	—
Germany	Neandertal	Skullcap	—	>1250
	Ehringsdorf	Cranial fragment	225,000	—
Gibraltar	Forbe's Quarry	Cranium	50,000	—
Iraq	Shanidar	9 partial skeletons	70,000	1600
Israel	Amud	Skeleton	70,000	1740
	Kebara Cave	Postcranial skeleton	60,000	—
	Tabun	Skeleton, mandible, postcranial fragments	100,000	1270
Italy	Monte Circeo	Cranium	—	—
	Saccopastore	Cranium	—	—
			Mean	1478.89

rounded over each eye, rather than forming a straight line, as in earlier archaics. The face was large and prognathous, with a broad nasal opening and widely set eyes. The chin was receding.

From the neck down, there were striking features. The bones of the Neandertals, even the finger bones, were more robust and had heavier muscle markings than their modern counterparts. The Neandertals were stocky, muscular, powerful people. This is seen even in the bones of Neandertal children, so it is assumed to be a result of inheritance, not simply of a hard-working lifestyle.

Although very strong and stocky, the Neandertals were relatively short. Estimates put the average for males at 5 feet 6 inches and for females at 5 feet 3 inches. This short stature was partially a result of relatively short lower legs. The lower arms were short as well. All these physical features hint at adaptations to a strenuous lifestyle and to cold climates. Shorter, heavier bodies with short limbs conserve heat better than narrow, long-limbed bodies (Holliday 1997, and see Chapter 13). As evidence, the limbs of the Neandertals from warmer Southwest Asia are relatively longer than the limbs of those living in Ice-Age Europe, who faced some of the extreme climates of the glacial advances.

FIGURE 11.22

An old reconstruction from the Field Museum in Chicago (*left*) reinforces stereotypes of Neandertals as brutish, hairy, stooped-over distant cousins. In contrast, anthropologist Milford Wolpoff poses with a reconstructed Neandertal in modern dress to attempt to show that the differences between us and them were only minor. Both of these views are exaggerations.

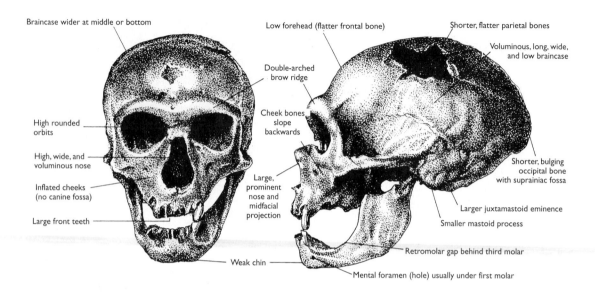

Braincase wider at middle or bottom

Low forehead (flatter frontal bone)

Shorter, flatter parietal bones

Voluminous, long, wide, and low braincase

Double-arched brow ridge

High rounded orbits

Cheek bones slope backwards

High, wide, and voluminous nose

Shorter, bulging occipital bone with suprainiac fossa

Inflated cheeks (no canine fossa)

Large, prominent nose and midfacial projection

Larger juxtamastoid eminence

Large front teeth

Smaller mastoid process

Retromolar gap behind third molar

Weak chin

Mental foramen (hole) usually under first molar

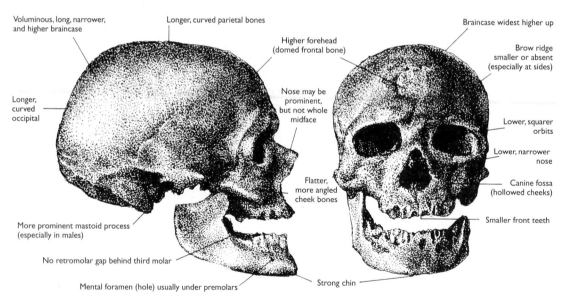

Voluminous, long, narrower, and higher braincase

Longer, curved parietal bones

Higher forehead (domed frontal bone)

Braincase widest higher up

Brow ridge smaller or absent (especially at sides)

Longer, curved occipital

Nose may be prominent, but not whole midface

Lower, squarer orbits

Lower, narrower nose

Canine fossa (hollowed cheeks)

Flatter, more angled cheek bones

Smaller front teeth

More prominent mastoid process (especially in males)

No retromolar gap behind third molar

Strong chin

Mental foramen (hole) usually under premolars

FIGURE 11.23
Cranial Features of the La Chapelle Specimen of Neandertal (*above*)
Compared to Modern *Homo sapiens*.

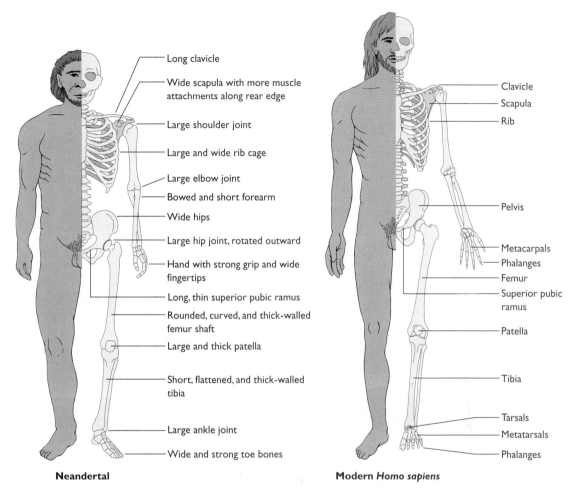

Long clavicle

Wide scapula with more muscle attachments along rear edge

Large shoulder joint

Large and wide rib cage

Large elbow joint

Bowed and short forearm

Wide hips

Large hip joint, rotated outward

Hand with strong grip and wide fingertips

Long, thin superior pubic ramus

Rounded, curved, and thick-walled femur shaft

Large and thick patella

Short, flattened, and thick-walled tibia

Large ankle joint

Wide and strong toe bones

Neandertal

Clavicle

Scapula

Rib

Pelvis

Metacarpals

Phalanges

Femur

Superior pubic ramus

Patella

Tibia

Tarsals

Metatarsals

Phalanges

Modern *Homo sapiens*

FIGURE 11.24
Skeletal Features of Neandertal Compared to Modern *Homo sapiens.*

Another possible adaptation to cold has been suggested by several investigators (see Menon 1997). In eight Neandertal skulls, they found triangular bony projections in the nasal cavity unlike anything seen in modern humans or in any other human ancestors. These projections are thought to have provided increased surface area for the nasal mucous membranes, which would have helped warm and moisten the cold, dry air of Europe during the Pleistocene glaciations. It has also been suggested that the large sinus cavities served a similar function. Moreover, it is thought that the larynx of the Neandertals was higher in the throat than in modern humans (see Figure 11.13), which would have prevented them from gulping in cold, dry air through the mouth.

FIGURE 11.25
Unifacially Retouched Mousterian Flakes from the Original Site, Le Moustier, France.

Neandertal fossils date from 225,000 to as recently as 28,000 ya (see Table 11.3). During this time, it has been proposed, Neandertals were responsible for a number of important cultural achievements. What do we know about their behavior?

Among the well-established accomplishments of the Neandertals is an elaboration on the Levallois stone toolmaking technique. Called the **Mousterian technique,** after the site of Le Moustier in France, it involved the careful retouching of flakes taken off cores. These flakes were sharpened and shaped by precise additional flaking, on one side or both, to make specialized tools (Figure 11.25). One authority has identified no less than sixty-three tool types (Bordes 1972).

Several specific uses of Mousterian tools have been inferred from microscopic wear-pattern analysis on specimens from the Kebara Cave site in Israel. Archaeologist John Shea (1989) notes wear patterns that indicate animal butchering, woodworking, bone and antler carving, and working of animal hides. There are also wear patterns like those produced by the friction of a wooden shaft against a stone spear point. The Neandertals may have been the first to **haft** a stone point.

Though there is still debate about whether the Neandertals were big-game hunters or mostly scavengers, there is no doubt that they were dependent on the animals that abounded during the Pleistocene—animals like reindeer, deer, ibex (wild goats), aurochs (wild oxen), horses, woolly rhinoceroses, bison, bear, and elk. Bones of these creatures have been found in association with Neandertal remains.

Although we now have earlier evidence of intentional human burials (see the next section), the first and most famous evidence comes from the Neandertals. Though many of these "burials" have now been attributed to natural causes, at least thirty-six Neandertal sites show evidence of intentional interment of the dead, and in some graves there were remains of offerings—stone tools, animal bones, and, possibly, flowers (Figure 11.26).

There is some debate, however, over whether or not these Neandertal burials had ritual significance. Did they represent belief in an afterlife or reverence for the physical remains of the deceased, or were the people simply disposing of a corpse, as seems to have been the case much earlier at Sima de los Huesos? The inclusion of animal bones in the graves may have been the result of the bones of both Neandertals and other animals being dragged by predators and scavengers into caves at the same time and subsequently buried by natural processes. The pollen found in a Neandertal grave at Shanidar, Iraq, may not have been from flowers placed in the grave but may have been brought in by burrowing rodents, carried in by water, or blown in by wind at the time of burial. The jury is still out on this issue. But we know the Neandertals did sometimes bury their dead, for whatever reason.

Along the same lines, evidence has traditionally been cited for a Neandertal cave bear "cult" in Europe. The cave bear, now extinct, was a huge, impressive species, about 12 feet tall when standing upright. Caves in Switzerland and France are supposed to contain a number of cave bear skulls placed in special stone chests or in niches in the cave walls. But these interpretations were apparently wishful thinking on the part of early investigators. Reanalysis of the site descriptions indicates that the placement of the skulls was the result of natural processes such as cave-ins. Moreover, none of the bear bones show any signs of cut marks. This intriguing story has fallen to scientific investigation.

It has also been suggested that Neandertals were among the first to care for their elderly, ill, and injured. The famous "Old Man" of La

Mousterian technique: A toolmaking tradition associated with the European Neandertals.

haft: To attach a wooden handle or shaft to a stone or bone point.

FIGURE 11.26
Neandertal Burial from La Ferrassie, France. This body was interred in the flexed position, with the knees drawn up to the chest, perhaps to mimic sleep. (The basket belongs to the excavators.)

Chapelle-aux-Saints in France (Figure 11.27) has been interpreted as aged, lacking most of his teeth, and having a debilitating case of arthritis. That he survived for a time with these infirmities, according to an early interpretation, indicates that he was cared for by his group.

Recent reexamination, though, shows that much of his tooth loss was after death and that his arthritis may not have been quite as debilitating

FIGURE 11.27
The Famous "Old Man" of La
Chapelle-aux-Saints, France.
(See front view and labels in
Figure 11.23.)

as previously thought. Nor was he really old. He died when he was less
than 40, probably rather quickly, as did the vast majority of Neandertals.
Care of the elderly was probably not something they had to contend with
very often.

On the other hand, there is a skeleton of a man from Shanidar, Iraq,
that shows signs of injuries that may have resulted in blindness and loss of
one arm. He lived with this condition for some time and, therefore, was
obviously cared for by his comrades.

But things may not have been completely peaceful among Neandertal populations. There is evidence of cannibalism from the Neandertal
site of Moula-Guercy in France, dated at 120,000 to 100,000 ya (Defleur
et al. 1999). Fragmentary bones from at least six individuals showed stone
tool cut marks in the same anatomical locations as those found on bones
of wild goats and deer at the site. Some of the human long bones also
show signs of having been smashed, in the way that would have allowed
access to the rich bone marrow. Whether the inferred cannibalism was
ritual (ingesting part of, or ashes of, a group member at a funeral cere-
mony) or gustatory (eating the flesh as food) cannot be determined.

Finally, we have the question of the linguistic abilities of the Neandertals. Some investigators have reconstructed the vocal tract of Neandertals based on the structure of the underside of the cranium. They have
concluded that because of the higher larynx noted before, Neandertals

were not capable of making all the vowel sounds of modern humans. However, a recently found hyoid bone—a horseshoe-shaped bone in the throat—from the Neandertal site of Kebara in Israel appears fully modern. This would mean that the vocal tract of the Neandertals *was* like ours and that they *could* make all the sounds of which we are capable. The point, of course, is—as we said for *Homo erectus*—that the Neandertals had sufficiently complex things to talk *about*, and just how they did so is less important than the fact that they did talk.

Archaic members of genus *Homo* were successful in adapting to different environments and, in the case of the Neandertals, harsh and demanding climates. They were clearly intelligent. We will no doubt find more fossils of archaics in new areas in the future. But the archaics differed in their complex of physical features from humans alive today. To begin the story of anatomically modern *Homo sapiens*, we once again return to Africa.

MODERN HUMANS

Beginning perhaps as early as 300,000 ya, fossils with what are considered to be near-modern or modern features appear, earliest in Africa and later in Southwest Asia, Europe, and East Asia. Later still, modern humans migrated to Australia, the islands of the Pacific, and North and South America. Under the six-species model, fossil forms with modern features are the only ones placed in *Homo sapiens*. There is no general agreement among proponents of this model about the exact species affiliation of some transitional forms—fossils with a mix of archaic and modern traits. Table 11.4 and Figure 11.28 give the basic information and locations of some of the more important fossils of early *Homo sapiens* as well as transitional forms.

We call these fossils "anatomically modern" because they lack some features characteristic of earlier hominids and possess features common in humans today. Gone is the prognathous profile. The modern human face is essentially flat. There are no heavy brow ridges. The skull is globular rather than elongated, and the forehead is more nearly vertical. The face is smaller and narrower, and there is a protruding chin. The postcranial skeleton is less robust. Refer back to Figures 11.23 and 11.24, and then look in the mirror.

Note in Table 11.4 that the earliest fossils are all from eastern and southern Africa and that they are considered, at least by some authorities,

TABLE 11.4
Chronological Listing of Some Important Fossils of Early *Homo sapiens*

Country	Location	Age
Kenya	Ileret	270,000–300,000 (trans.)*
South Africa	Florisbad	100,000–200,000 (trans.)
Ethiopia	Omo	130,000 (trans.)
Tanzania	Ngaloba	120,000 (trans.)
Morocco	Jebel Irhoud	100,000 (trans.)
South Africa	Klasies River Mouth Langebaan Lagoon (footprints) Border Cave	84,000–120,000 117,000 62,000–115,000
Israel	Qafzeh Skhul	92,000–120,000 81,000–101,000
Germany	Stetten	36,000
France	Cro-Magnon Abri Pataud	<30,000 >27,000
China	Zhoukoudian	10,000–18,000
Australia	Lake Mungo	30,000
United States	Midland, Texas	11,600

*The abbreviation *trans.* indicates those fossils that are considered transitional between archaic and modern *Homo*.

as transitional between archaic and modern *Homo*. There is also a transitional form from Morocco (Figure 11.29). The implication is that modern humans—whether a new species or just the modern form of an existing species—arose in Africa. Until recently, the earliest dates for the appearance of transitional forms was about 200,000 ya from South Africa, but recent finds from Kenya (Bräuer et al. 1997), dated by several methods that appear to correspond well, have pushed this date back to perhaps 300,000 ya.

By around 120,000 ya, we begin to find fossils that represent humans of fully modern appearance relative to their geographical area. The earliest

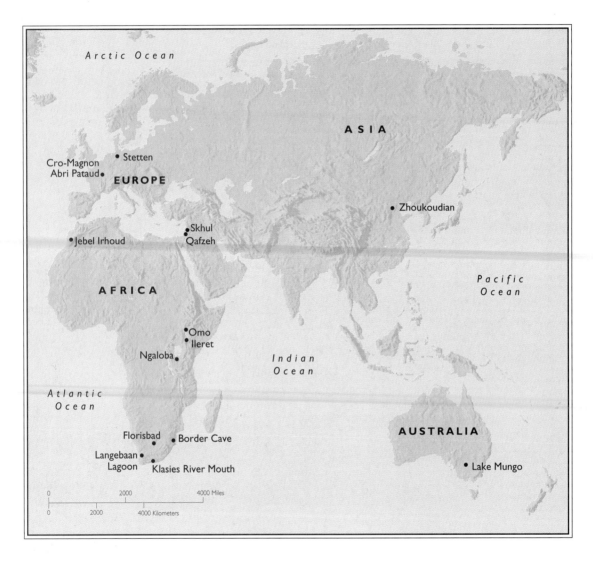

FIGURE 11.28

Map of Major Early *Homo sapiens* sites in Africa, Asia, Australia, and Europe.

of these at present are from South Africa and Israel (Figure 11.30). At the South African site of Langebaan Lagoon, a small human, possibly a female, left her footprints in rock claimed to be dated 117,000 ya—a moment frozen in time reminiscent of the Laetoli footprints from Tanzania (see Chapter 10). As we move farther away from Africa and Southwest Asia, the dates for the early appearance of modern *Homo sapiens* get more recent, a further indication that Africa is the birthplace of modern humans.

FIGURE 11.29
Cranium from Jebel Irhoud, Morocco. This skull, dated at about 100,000 ya, is considered by some to be transitional between archaic and modern *Homo*. The braincase is low, the face is relatively large, and it has distinct brow ridges. Otherwise, its features are modern.

FIGURE 11.30
Examples of Early Modern *Homo sapiens* from (*counterlockwise from top*) Skhul, Israel; Border Cave, South Africa; Qafzeh, Israel. Note the higher foreheads, protruding chins, and flatter faces compared to archaic *Homo*. Despite the rather prominent brow ridges in Skhul, it is still considered fully modern due to its other features.

5 cm

FIGURE 11.31
Blade Tools from Klasies
River Mouth, South Africa.

With modern anatomy came further advances in technology and expressions of modern behavior patterns. Although much of the tool technology of early moderns resembles that of archaics, artifacts from one of the oldest anatomically modern sites do show an important advance. From Klasies River Mouth in South Africa, dated at perhaps 120,000 ya, come long, bifacially worked spear points made from stone blades. These were flaked from cores by the *punch technique* (Figure 11.31). Here, a pointed punch, usually made of an antler, is placed on the core and then struck with a stone hammer. This method directs the force of the blow more precisely so that longer, narrower, thinner flakes of predictable shape may be taken off. The same technique shows up later in Europe.

The Klasies River site also provides evidence that the people there may have hunted adults of such large animals as cape buffalo and eland (a large antelope); both these animals can weigh up to a ton. The site contains a spear point lodged in a buffalo vertebra. Certainly, these people also scavenged and may have hunted only weak or old individuals of

FIGURE 11.32
These bifacially flaked Upper Paleolithic spear points represent some of the finest stonework ever seen.

these dangerous species. But there is good evidence of at least limited big-game hunting. That behavior, it seems, can be associated with the appearance of anatomically modern humans.

Although the Neandertal burials are perhaps the most famous examples of early human symbolic behavior, it is at two of the early *Homo sapiens* sites that we find the earliest established examples. At Qafzeh and Skhul, there are graves, dated at between 120,000 and 80,000 ya, with bodies and grave goods carefully laid out. In one grave at Qafzeh, a child was buried with a deer antler. Another grave at the same site contained the body of a young woman with that of an infant, possibly hers, at her feet. At Skhul, a skeleton was found holding the jawbone of a wild boar.

By the time the Neandertals disappeared, about 30,000 ya, modern *Homo sapiens* had spread all over the Old World, even as far as Australia, and we enter a cultural period called the Upper Paleolithic, known first through finds in Europe. This period is marked by several important cultural innovations. Blades struck off cores become so precisely and beautifully made as to be virtual works of art—in fact, some blades are so thin and delicate we think they may have been just that (Figure 11.32).

Tools in the Upper Paleolithic were also made from bone, antler, and ivory. Some are practical, such as harpoons, spear points, and shaft straighteners. Some have symbolic significance. Even some of the utilitarian items are decorated (Figure 11.33). Indeed, art is seen in the Upper Paleolithic in

FIGURE 11.33
Upper Paleolithic Artifacts. Among the artifacts shown here are a shaft straightener with carved animals (*top*), a harpoon carved from antler (*upper left*), and an example of the famous Venus figurines (*lower right*) that may have served as fertility symbols.

some of its most striking and beautiful forms. Over a hundred cave sites, mostly in France and Spain, have yielded paintings of animals that rival anything produced today (Figure 11.34). There are also carvings in stone, bone, antler, and ivory, among the most famous of which are the so-called Venus figurines, often thought to be fertility symbols (see Figure 11.33, lower right). Some Venus figurines even depict clothing styles such as woven caps (Wong 2000a). There is also an engraved antler from about 32,000 ya that may have been a calendar based on phases of the moon.

There is some evidence of even older art from northern Australia. A hematite "crayon"—used to get red ocher, a pigment—has been dated at almost 60,000 ya at the site of Malakunanja II, and painted ocher figures and carved holes at a rock shelter site called Jinmium may date to between 176,000 and 116,000 ya. Both sites, however, were dated using luminescence dating (see Chapter 9), which is still somewhat experimental. There is other evidence that the Jinmium site may be only about 10,000 years old (Gibbons 1997c).

FIGURE 11.34
One of many beautiful paintings from the cave of Lascaux in southern France, this mural depicts an aurochs (an ancient ox) and several horses. There is an antlered animal, probably a deer, in the lower right. Notice that the left front leg of the red horse is separated from the body, adding a three-dimensional appearance. This photograph is really from Lascaux II, a replica near the actual cave, created because of damage to the original from bacteria and carbon dioxide given off by too many visitors. The walls of the replica cave are reproduced to within 5 mm of the contours of the original cave, and many of the pigments in the paintings are the same as those used by the original artists perhaps 17,000 ya.

As the Upper Paleolithic continued, big-game hunting became a way of life, especially for people living in glacial climates with limited plant resources. People no longer relied on caves or rock shelters for places of habitation but began manufacturing shelters. At Mal'ta, for example, an 18,000-year-old site in south-central Russia, scientists found the remains of a hut built on a wood frame supported by woolly mammoth bones and reindeer antlers and covered with animal hides.

Contemporary Reflections

What Do We Mean by "Human"?

Back in Linnaeus's time, when species were thought to have been separately created, the answer to what was "human" was an easy one. People were human, and everything else wasn't. Then, fossils representing the history of other organisms began to appear and to be recognized as the intermediate evolutionary steps from previous states to present ones. And then Charles Darwin explained how this all happened. As anthropologist Ian Tattersall puts it, when, by the end of the nineteenth century, it had become clear that we too had a fossil record and had evolved like other creatures, the issue of humanness became far more complex (1994).

We use the word *human* all the time in different contexts and with different meanings—and we usually communicate and understand those meanings with little ambiguity. Even in a biological context, it is perfectly clear which present-day species the term refers to. We use *human* as precisely as we use *ape* or *monkey*. But how about a more scientific definition that takes into account what we know about our evolutionary history and, thus, about our place in nature in a broader context? Put another way, although it's clear that *human* refers to us, who *else* might it refer to?

Human could be used as a synonym for *hominid*. In the traditional (and still most common) taxonomic sense of this category, *human*, then, would refer to any habitually bipedal primate and so would include *Australopithecus* and *Paranthropus*, who share few specific traits—other than upright walking—with modern peoples. One cladistic taxonomy (see Chapter 7) includes our sister species—chimpanzees, bonobos, and gorillas—in family Hominidae. Using *human* as a synonym for *hominid* here would be so broad as to be fairly meaningless.

A seemingly more realistic approach is to limit the use of *human* to just *Homo sapiens* (for splitters) or just anatomically modern *Homo sapiens* (for lumpers). No one would deny that

Around 20,000 ya, and possibly earlier, humans moved into North America, coming across a land bridge between Siberia and Alaska that was exposed when the sea level dropped during glacial periods. They soon moved throughout the continent and into South America. Modern *Homo sapiens* had populated every landmass on the planet except Antarctica.

▽   ▽   ▽

SUMMARY

The record of the latest 2 million years of hominid evolution is complex. The fossils from the first 99 percent of this period are scarce, often fragmentary, scattered geographically, physically variable, and, in some cases, modern *H. sapiens* falls into that classification, which could include the criteria of "high intelligence, language, aesthetic sensibilities, and the mastery of complex technologies" (Tattersall 1994, 114)—all those things we know define, delineate, and differentiate our species today. Under this use, the other species of *Homo* (*H. neanderthalensis*, for instance) "possessed [almost nothing] even remotely resembling the restless spirit of innovation and inventiveness that informed the lives of Upper Paleolithic peoples. . . . [I]t is only with the Upper Paleolithic that we find evidence for behaviors that would allow us to characterize their possessors as fully human" (115).

But anthropologist Milford Wolpoff (—in a 1994 rebuttal to the Tattersall piece cited above) argues that this definition is too limited. While older forms of *Homo* may have had less complex cultural behaviors than ours, they nonetheless *had* culture. The makers of the Oldowan tools some 2 mya were the first stone toolmakers and the first hominoids to show a trend toward larger brains. Even with our far more complex cultural expressions, we share with these other members of our genus—and *only* with them—these large brains and the abilities they facilitate. It would seem, then, that to limit the use of *human* to just modern *Homo sapiens* would necessarily require recognizing *degrees* of humanness to account for the behaviors of premodern peoples. Indeed, Tattersall says that despite his limited definition, he finds "great difficulty in denying Neanderthals human status" (1994, 115).

All this may seem rather a matter of philosophical point of view—and on some levels it is. But scientifically, if we link being human to being included in certain taxonomic categories, then just how we classify groups of hominids will make a difference. If, for instance, we limit humanness to members of *Homo sapiens*, then it matters a great deal whether we accept a six-species or a one-species model for the evolution of our genus. This is the real issue of the Tattersall and Wolpoff pieces cited, and it leads directly to the consideration of Chapter 12.

questionably dated. Not surprisingly, the interpretations of these fossils vary as greatly as do the fossils themselves. Our survey uses as a starting point the currently most elaborate model for classifying and naming these fossils—the recognition of six species within genus *Homo* after the early *Homo* stage. I do not necessarily endorse this model but am beginning with it for the purpose of clearly organizing our discussion of a fairly complex topic.

The earliest species, *Homo ergaster*, is found only in Kenya, but a probable branch off this group, *Homo erectus*, spreads through the rest of Africa and into Asia and possibly southern Europe. These two species are characterized by virtually modern postcranial skeletons, brain sizes close to and even overlapping the modern human range, and the invention of more sophisticated stone tools and other cultural innovations, including the use of fire. In Java, *H. erectus* may have persisted until as recently as 27,000 ya.

A geographically and chronologically scattered species, *Homo heidelbergensis*, appears next. The earliest examples of this group, from Spain, are placed by some authorities into a new species, *Homo antecessor*. Located from England to South Africa to China, *H. heidelbergensis* displays brain sizes within the modern human range and at the modern human average, though their crania retain primitive features, giving them the label "archaic." They are known, starting about 200,000 ya, for the invention of the Levallois stone toolmaking technique—a sophisticated way of "mass producing" flake tools. They may have done some hunting as well.

The most famous of the "archaic" humans are the Neandertals, a separate species, *Homo neanderthalensis*, according to many. Living in Europe and Southwest Asia from 200,000 to 28,000 ya, this group exhibits traits that distinguish it from both *H. heidelbergensis* and later *Homo sapiens*. These traits include large, prognathous faces, ruggedly built skulls, and robust, muscular bodies—possibly adaptations to the cold glacial conditions many of their populations encountered. Neandertals are known for their retouched flake tools, which may have been used to carve bone and work wood; perhaps for the first use of hafting stone points on wooden shafts; and for abstract cultural achievements such as burial of the dead and care of the elderly and infirm.

Fossils transitional between archaic and modern *Homo* appear in Africa perhaps as early as 300,000 ya, and the first fully modern *Homo sapiens* are found in Africa and Southwest Asia beginning around 120,000 ya. From there, modern-appearing humans spread throughout the Old World and eventually to the islands of the Pacific and to the Americas. Archaic peoples—or archaic traits—disappear. During this time, big-game hunting develops, tool technology advances, sophisticated shelters are built, and humans create art.

The questions now become: Just how many species of genus *Homo* are we actually dealing with? And, how are all these groups related evolutionarily? These are the questions addressed in the next chapter.

QUESTIONS FOR FURTHER THOUGHT

1. We will discuss the debate over the evolution of genus *Homo* in greater detail in the next chapter. For now, however, does it matter to *you* how many species of our genus have existed? Why or why not? Why do you think it matters so much to professional scientists?

2. The issue of whether groups of organisms are separate species within one genus or are variable populations within a single species has ram-

ifications for living things other than hominids. One related topic is the Endangered Species Act. Why might this issue matter with regard to the implementation of that legislation?

3. As a lead-in to the discussion in the next chapter, consider what the arguments might be in favor of lumping the Neandertals into *Homo sapiens*. What arguments might be made for splitting them into a separate species?

KEY TERMS

law of parsimony	tundra	postorbital constriction
sagittal keel	Acheulian technique	Levallois technique
torus	hand axe	Mousterian technique
Pleistocene	bifacial	haft
glaciers	endocasts	

SUGGESTED READINGS

The *National Geographic* series "The Dawn of Humans," noted in Chapter 10, also covers the topics discussed in this chapter. Refer to the "Suggested Readings" section in Chapter 10 for specific issues.

For summaries of human evolution, see *The Last Neanderthal*, by Ian Tattersall, and *Extinct Humans*, by Ian Tattersall and Jeffrey Schwarz. Be aware that these authors are splitters, who advocate a maximum number of separate species for *Homo* and the other hominid genera. The books, however, are accurate, up-to-date, and beautifully illustrated.

For the fascinating story of Eugene Dubois and the discovery of "Java Man," see Pat Shipman's *The Man Who Found the Missing Link: Eugene Dubois and His Lifelong Quest to Prove Darwin Right*. The story of the missing "Peking Man" fossils is the topic of *The Search for Peking Man*, by C. Janus.

More detailed discussion on the fossil and archaeological records of the genus *Homo* can be found in Kenneth Feder's and my *Human Antiquity: An Introduction to Physical Anthropology and Archaeology*, fourth edition.

Computed tomography (CT) scans have recently been used in paleoanthropology in the reconstruction of fossils of the Neandertals. See www.ifi.unizh.ch/~zolli/Neanderthals.htm.

CHAPTER

12

THE DEBATE
OVER MODERN
HUMAN ORIGINS

We carry within us the
wonders we seek
without us; There is all
Africa and her
prodigies in us.
—Sir Thomas Browne

Many of the current great debates in science involve, not surprisingly, the distant past. Scientists argue about the origin and early history of the universe, about the formation of our solar system and its planets, about the origin of life on earth, and about the causes and effects of mass extinctions seen in the fossil record. There are, of course, also debates about the early evolution of the hominids—the number of early hominid genera, for example, or the exact relationships among the groups of early hominids.

But no point in the history of our evolution is as contentious as the latest chapter—the origin of modern *Homo sapiens*. An astounding number of articles and books advocate one point of view or another, summarize and evaluate the various hypotheses, or analyze and interpret the debate itself. And this debate is far from peaceful. Arguments get heated at times, with some accusing others of poor scholarship or hidden agendas. Comments can get downright nasty.

Moreover, some investigators see, in the choice of hypotheses, implications that are not necessarily directly relevant to the issues being discussed (see the "Contemporary Reflections" box in this chapter.) These connections are picked up by the popular media and passed on to the public, who get the wrong impression of what the debate is really about. None of this helps us sort out, examine, and evaluate an issue that is already complicated enough. There are large amounts of data about the possible origin of modern *Homo sapiens*, much of it interpreted quite differently by various specialists. Even impartial and dispassionate accounts can still be detailed and confusing.

At the risk of adding yet another version, with yet another set of diagrams and names, I will try in this chapter to reduce the competing hypotheses (or models) down to their essential elements in a way that relates them directly to the material we have covered so far, at a level of detail appropriate to this book. I hope that this approach will make sense in terms of the themes and data we have been dealing with and that it will provide you with a basic framework to which you can add further information.

As confusing as the issue might be, it is a good example of science in action—as both a scholarly and a very human endeavor. Even summarizing the debate—with its different interpretations, different theoretical points of view, related agendas, and sometimes rancorous rhetoric—is to catch scientific progress "in the act."

This is a fascinating topic and an understandably important debate, because, as I pointed out in Chapter 11, at stake is our very identity—our specific place in nature, our relationships to the other hominids, and our nature as products of the processes of evolution. We will address the following questions in this chapter:

> **What are the major competing hypotheses regarding the origin of modern *Homo sapiens*?**

> **What evidence has been offered—from the fossil record, from genetics, and from evolutionary theory—for and against each model?**

THE MODELS

It would appear based on current available evidence (see Table 11.4) that fully modern-*looking* people first appeared about 120,000 ya, with transitional forms showing the beginnings of modern traits back as far as 300,000 ya. It also appears that these traits first evolved in Africa. But at issue is the question Do these traits accurately define and distinguish a new species of hominid, *Homo sapiens*, or is the collection of traits we think of as modern just the latest set of variable features in the evolution of a much older species? You should recognize these points of view as another way of stating the lumper-splitter debate (introduced in Chapter 11 between the single-species model of the evolution of genus *Homo* and the five- or six-species model.

In terms of the broad implications of this debate, we can give these models descriptive names. The single-species version is known as the **Multiregional Evolution (MRE) model.** Models that recognize *Homo sapiens* as the most recent of several species of *Homo* are called by a number of names, most commonly the **Out-of-Africa model.** However, the MRE model also recognizes our species as arising in and expanding out of Africa (just a lot earlier), so I prefer to call the second model the **Recent African Origin (RAO) model.** Figure 12.1 has generalized diagrams that depict these models.

The Recent African Origin (RAO) Model

Major proponents of the Recent African Origin model are Christopher Stringer of the Natural History Museum in London (Stringer and McKie 1996) and Ian Tattersall of the American Museum of Natural History in New York (Tattersall 1997; Tattersall and Schwarz 2000). Although

Multiregional Evolution (MRE) model: The hypothesis that *Homo sapiens* is about 2 million years old and that modern traits evolved in geographically diverse locations and then spread through the species.

Out-of-Africa model: Another name for the Recent African Origin model.

Recent African Origin (RAO) model: The hypothesis that *Homo sapiens* evolved recently as a separate species in Africa and then spread to replace more archaic populations.

FIGURE 12.1
Generalized Models for the
Origin of *Homo sapiens.*

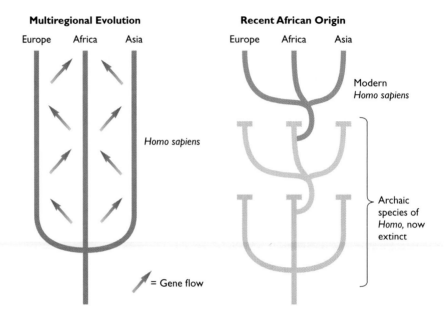

various supporters of this model recognize different numbers of species within genus *Homo,* they all share the view that modern *Homo sapiens* is a separate species that branched from a preexisting archaic *Homo* species in Africa around 200,000 to 150,000 ya. This new species then spread over the Old World, replacing archaic populations when they came in contact, presumably because *H. sapiens* was a better-adapted species. (This model is sometimes called the *Replacement model.*)

If this model is correct, we must be able to find distinctions between our modern species and premodern (or archaic) humans that clearly distinguish us *as separate species.* There must be an anatomical definition of modernity; in other words, there must be traits that all *Homo sapiens* share that are not found in premoderns (that is, all species except *Homo sapiens*), and traits found in premoderns that are lacking in modern humans. We would also expect to find genetic distinctions of a degree that would indicate separate species.

If we can anatomically define and distinguish premodern from modern humans, then we can deduce that fossils transitional between premodern and modern humans should occur only in the single region in which moderns evolved. Elsewhere, there should be evidence of anatomical premoderns and anatomical moderns coexisting in the same regions, once the latter spread out from their initial source area—their "Eden," as opponents of this model somewhat disparagingly characterize it (F. Smith

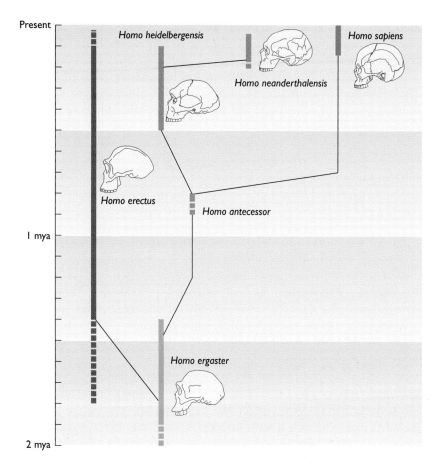

Present

Homo heidelbergensis

Homo sapiens

Homo neanderthalensis

Homo erectus

Homo antecessor

1 mya

Homo ergaster

2 mya

FIGURE 12.2
One Possible Set of Relationships for the Six Proposed Species of *Homo*, According to the RAO model. The data are the same as in Figure 11.1.

et al. 1989; Wolpoff 1989). Eventually, the premodern human forms would have become extinct, unable to compete with their anatomically modern cousins. Figure 12.2 shows one way this model interprets the relationships among the six species of *Homo* described in Chapter 11.

The Multiregional Evolution (MRE) Model

The name most often associated with the Multiregional Evolution model is Milford Wolpoff of the University of Michigan (Wolpoff and Caspari 1997). This model—a bit more complicated than the RAO model—also claims that *Homo sapiens* arose in Africa, but it says that this event occurred as much as 2 mya. Members of this new species (traditionally called *Homo erectus*) spread throughout the Old World, evolving genetic

FIGURE 12.3

Some Representative Fossils Interpreted According to the MRE Model (*facing page*). The vertical arrows indicate regional continuity, the slanted arrows indicate movement of genes through time across geographic locations, and the horizontal arrows indicate exchange of genes between neighboring populations. The arrows do not necessarily mean that these *particular* fossil populations moved or exchanged genes but rather that gene flow and migration across space and time were the prevailing conditions for our species under this model. See Tables 11.1 through 11.4 for details about these finds.

(Adapted from Wolpoff and Caspari 1997, 281.)

and phenotypic regional differences in response to the wide variety of environmental circumstances they encountered and in response to the complex population movements, isolations, mergings, and fissionings that must have taken place. The degree of species mobility resulted in sufficient gene flow to maintain a single species, as no population was isolated long enough or to a great enough degree for speciation to occur. As successful advantageous adaptive features arose, they were dispersed across the species through gene flow. Ideas and technologies spread and were exchanged as well (Wolpoff et al. 2001). Physical features we associate with modern humans appeared everywhere but may have been manifested in different ways in different populations and in different environments. Thus, we are today and have always been a variable species—but a single species.

It is important to understand that this does *not* mean that *every* population within this long-lived and widespread species survived to contribute genes to modern humans. Certainly, individual isolated populations could have become extinct with few or none of their genes passed down. Nor does this deny the distinctive sets of traits that characterize some of the premodern (archaic) populations (like the Neandertals). The MRE model simply says that these populations were not separate species, that *Homo sapiens* did not arise in the recent past, and, thus, that it did not spread and become dominant by replacing other species of *Homo*.

If the MRE model is correct, we should find no clear evidence that modern *Homo sapiens* is a separate species from any of the so-called premodern groups. There should, in other words, be no biologically meaningful definition of modernity—no set of traits that is found among all populations classified as modern that is lacking among all premodern populations. However, populations with transitional sets of traits should be found in many locations. Ideally, there should be some evidence of interbreeding in the form of a mix of traits in fossils from those areas where groups coexisted. Finally, there should be regional continuity of traits—features characteristic of geographical areas that appear not only in modern populations but premodern ones as well.

One conclusion of this model is that if premodern groups are in fact members of our species, then the rules of taxonomy dictate that the earliest name used for any of them must be applied to them all. Thus, if all six species of *Homo* are indeed the same species, they would all be *Homo sapiens*, the name first used by Linnaeus in 1758 (see Chapters 7 and 14). Figure 12.3 shows how this model views the interrelationships among the various regional fossil populations discussed in Chapter 11.

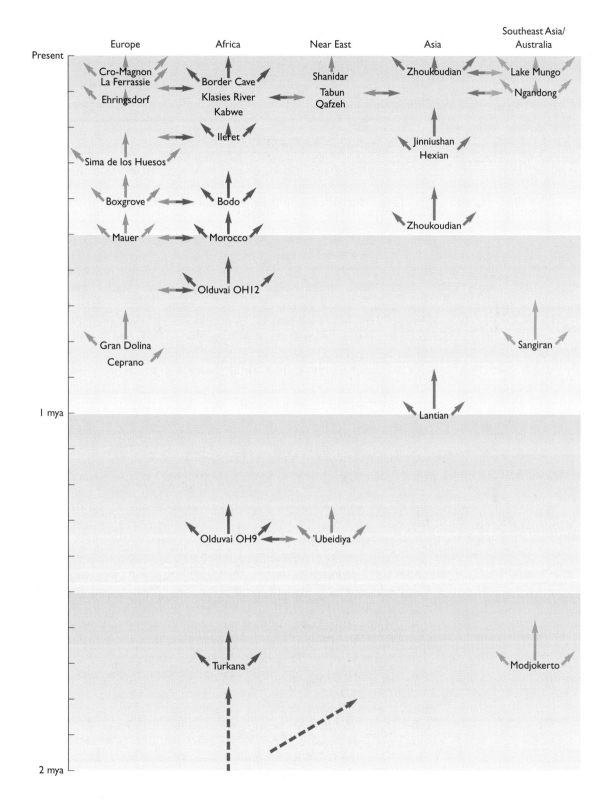

Present

Europe Africa Near East Asia Southeast Asia/ Australia

Cro-Magnon
La Ferrassie
Ehringsdorf
Border Cave
Klasies River
Kabwe
Shanidar
Tabun
Qafzeh
Zhoukoudian
Lake Mungo
Ngandong

Ileret

Jinniushan
Hexian

Sima de los Huesos

Boxgrove
Bodo

Mauer
Morocco

Zhoukoudian

Olduvai OH12

Gran Dolina
Ceprano

Sangiran

1 mya

Lantian

Olduvai OH9
'Ubeidiya

Turkana
Modjokerto

2 mya

317

THE EVIDENCE

Clearly, the evidence for the past 2 million years of our evolution is limited. Fossils exist, but they are often fragmentary, and they are scattered across space and time. The same can be said for archaeological evidence of our ancestors' cultural activities. Genetic data are available but only from fully modern populations alive today—or at least recently. And evolutionary theory is still being debated, both in general terms and more specifically when applied to the history of a specific group.

Thus, in reviewing the extensive literature on modern human origins, we find that different authorities have very different interpretations of the same data. Indeed, the same general data have been convincingly used to support either model, but proponents differ in which specific pieces of data they emphasize. It can become, as anthropologist David Pilbeam once said in another context (1984, 1986), like "peering" too closely at a pointillist painting or trying to look at a newspaper photo with a magnifying glass. The details become a bunch of "meaningless dots." Following, then, is a general summary of the available evidence and interpretations by both "camps."

The Fossil Record

In using the multiple-species model as an organizing format for our previous discussion of genus *Homo,* we have already presented the fossil evidence as interpreted by the Recent African Origin proponents. Look again at the tables and maps in Chapter 11.

As suggested by the RAO model, forms transitional between archaic species (*H. heidelbergensis* and *H. neanderthalensis*) and *Homo sapiens* are found only in Africa. Modern forms appear first in Africa and then show up at increasingly recent dates as one moves away from that continent. And archaics and moderns overlap in time in some areas. Note that the modern fossils from Skhul and Qafzeh in Israel actually predate the Neandertals in the same country and that the two groups shared the area for a time (see Tables 11.3 and 11.4). In Java, if dating is correct, modern humans lived alongside the last remnants of *Homo erectus* until only 27,000 ya. And if the date of 28,000 ya is correct for Vindija in Croatia (see Table 11.3), Neandertals and modern humans, who entered Europe perhaps 36,000 ya, coexisted for 7,000 years in that area. In all these cases, according to the RAO model, modern humans and the archaic populations are unambiguously different at the species level.

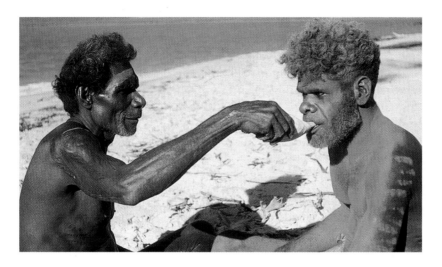

FIGURE 12.4
Two Tiwi from Melville Island, Northern Australia. Note their large, continuous brow ridges—a trait associated with archaic humans yet present here in fully modern *Homo sapiens.* The man on the right is in mourning, which requires that he paint his body and not feed himself, so he is receiving water from a friend.

In stark contrast, Wolpoff and Caspari assert that the variation seen within the fossil record of *Homo* does not warrant division into separate species. They claim, for example, that in broad perspective "just about every way *H. erectus* differs from its australopithecine ancestors also characterizes *H. sapiens:* virtually no features are unique to *H. erectus*" (1997, 256). In other words, *H. sapiens* and *H. erectus* are the same species. They also contend that modern traits did not all arise in one location but in many and that they spread throughout the species through gene flow, to be expressed differently in different geographic locations. Multiregional Evolution advocates support this contention by interpreting important fossils differently than do advocates of the RAO camp. For example, according to Fred Smith, while "clearly still Neandertals . . . it is difficult not to recognize Vindija as a transitional sample between most Neandertals and early modern Europeans" (1994, 232). As required by the MRE model, transitional forms are found in many locations.

Moreover, Wolpoff and Caspari feel that "it has proved impossible to provide an acceptable [physical] definition of modernity" in the first place (1997, 313). Some features proposed to define modern humans *do not* include all recent or living peoples. For example, it has been suggested that Neandertals' large, continuous brow ridges are a major diagnostic feature helping to distinguish them from modern humans. But some living indigenous people of Australia—fully modern biological humans in every sense of the word—also have large, continuous brow ridges (Figure 12.4). There is sufficient variation among modern humans, says Wolpoff, that modernity must be defined regionally, as no general definition includes all clearly modern humans and excludes all other proposed species.

A recent study (Pearson 2000) on postcranial remains and the question of modern human origins notes that defining modernity is also difficult for that area of the skeleton: "Any definition of what constitutes anatomically modern form should take into consideration the fact that some populations of living humans have evolved a body form that is substantially different from that of early modern humans" (241). In other words, through time, populations labeled modern human have undergone notable change, thus making it hard to list the phenotypic criteria for modernity.

Pearson notes too that the Neandertals are frequently used to establish a definition of modern, based on the assumption that they are a "good approximation of generalized archaic human morphology." This assumption, he says, is "partially in error" since the characteristic Neandertal features are very different from those of earlier archaics such as *H. heidelbergensis,* who in fact "more closely approximated modern human morphology" (2000, 231) for many postcranial traits. To use the Neandertals in a comparison with modern populations, then, is sort of "stacking the deck," since they are *more* different from moderns in some ways than are other archaics. Moreover, the Neandertals were a small population, isolated by distance and ecology in an Old World backwater. Even if most of their populations, and thus their phenotypes, became extinct, that does not preclude their being members of our species, nor does it negate the MRE model. A physical definition of modernity thus seems to be in the eye of the beholder, based on one's interpretation and choice of populations and characteristics.

Wolpoff and supporters also see continuity of individual traits in certain areas, especially Asia and Australia, where some modern regional features are said to resemble those from the Sangiran fossils identified as *Homo erectus*. He also says some features show continuity between Neandertal and modern populations in Europe. Especially important are nonadaptive traits, which would not be affected by environmental changes over time but *would* be affected by large-scale population replacement. An example is an opening for a nerve on the inside of the mandible (the mandibular foramen). A form of this opening (of no apparent adaptive significance) found only in European Neandertals is also found in high frequency in early moderns from Europe—and in *no* Asian or African populations—suggesting a direct evolutionary relationship.

In a recent study, Wolpoff and colleagues (2001) compared anatomical features of skulls from both moderns and archaics from different parts of Europe, Africa, and Asia. They used an analytical procedure called *pairwise comparison* (used in many of the DNA studies to be discussed in the following section). They were testing a prediction of the

RAO model that only African archaics gave rise to modern *Homo sapiens*; according to the RAO model, all other archaic populations became extinct. The study and its results are complex, but essentially what these researchers found were a series of similarities and differences that pointed to a mixed ancestry of the modern populations. In some cases, the modern skulls were closer to the archaics from their geographical regions than they were to the African archaics or to those skulls considered to represent the first modern humans out of Africa (such as those from Skhul and Qafzeh in Israel.) In other words, archaic populations, rather than being separate species (as in the RAO model) and becoming extinct, contributed to the ancestry of moderns. This study appears to support the MRE model.

As further potential evidence of the MRE model, we have a 1998 find from Portugal of a 3½- to 5-year-old child who lived 24,500 ya (Duarte et al. 1999). The child's mandible displayed a protruding chin and proportionately small front teeth, diagnostic of moderns. The post-cranial bones, however, were robust, with proportionately short lower arms and legs, diagnostic of Neandertals. The interpretation of the investigators is that the boy represented a hybrid, the result of an interbreeding between a Neandertal and a modern human—making those two groups, by definition, members of the same species. Not unexpectedly, of course, RAO proponents reject this claim. Ian Tattersall suggested that the child was simply a "chunky" anatomically modern human (Holden 1999).

I think that in regard to this debate the fossil record is ambiguous. It can clearly be interpreted to support either point of view, and there is wide disagreement between those points of view. Note that even splitters cannot agree on the exact number of premodern species of *Homo*. They only agree that *Homo sapiens* is a recent, separate species. The fossils that do exist are usually incomplete, not necessarily representative of the populations from which they came, and often of questionable age. Moreover, many of the morphological features being used for these analyses are of unknown heritability; that is, we don't know how much they tell us about actual genetic distinctions (Minugh-Purvis 1995).

Finally, it is hard to translate physical features into species classification. As we saw in Chapters 4 and 5, some separate species look nearly identical, while other species can exhibit an amazing amount of phenotypic variation (see Figure 2.6). The RAO people see the variation in the fossil record as being outside the range of modern human diversity. The MRE people feel that the fossil variation is well within the potential range of our species, just different in specifics at different points in time from modern variation.

Along with fossil evidence, archaeological data have also been cited in support of the two models. Recent African Origin supporters note the appearance of sophisticated toolmaking techniques earlier in Africa than elsewhere (see Figure 11.31 for an example). They also see evidence of the fairly rapid replacement in Europe of tools associated with Neandertals by those associated with modern *Homo sapiens*.

In contradiction, MRE advocates claim that these early African tool forms are not all that different from the tools of Neandertals and that artifacts associated with modern fossils from Skhul and Qafzeh are virtually identical to those associated with nearby Neandertal finds. At Grotte XVI, in the French Dordogne Valley, investigators see a gradual change in cultural behavior over the course of many thousands of years, from Neandertal to moderns, with a great degree of similarity in behavior between these two supposedly different groups. Based on analyses of tools and other archaeological evidence from these populations, researchers conclude that both moderns and Neandertals hunted, fished, and apparently even smoked their catch to preserve it (Wong 2000b). In other words, tool type is not necessarily diagnostic of species, and the variation, scattered nature, and questionable dating of some archaeological data present the same problems as does the paleontological record. (For more detail, see Feder and Park 2001.)

Genetics

We mentioned genetic evidence in Chapter 9 regarding the relationship between humans and the nonhuman primates. Genetic data can also be used to compare living human populations and examine the question of modern human origins. Genetic lines of inquiry have usually been interpreted to support the Recent African Origin model, that is, a recent African source for modern humanity. As we will see, there are other possible interpretations.

In general, living human beings exhibit very little genetic variation—in fact, less than that seen within ape species (Stringer and Andrews 1988, 1264). Indeed, chimpanzee **mitochondrial DNA (mtDNA)** commonly exhibits ten times the amount of variation as does human mtDNA (Wilson and Cann 1992, 71). This suggests a relatively recent, common source for all living humans, which is consistent with the RAO hypothesis. In other words, if there is little genetic diversity, not much time has elapsed since the species first evolved.

On the other hand, the Multiregional Evolution model can also account for this genetic homogeneity. As a mobile species with a network of constant genetic exchange among populations, regional genetic differences (although they do exist in terms of genetic details) would become increasingly lessened as the species increased its population and improved its ability to move around. In such a species, even a very old one, we would also expect relatively little modern genetic variation. Thus, our species' genetic homogeneity does not help us distinguish between the two models.

Although overall genetic variation is low in modern human beings, when some details of our DNA are compared across geographic populations, using the techniques discussed in Chapter 9, some potentially interesting patterns emerge. There are three basic types of DNA that are used in this regard. We may look at the DNA in the nucleus of our cells, the **nuclear DNA.** Some of this DNA codes for proteins that give rise to phenotypic features (see Chapter 3). Most nuclear DNA, however, is noncoding; that is, it does not involve instructions for building proteins. Some of this DNA turns other genes on and off. Other sequences hold chromosomes together. We're not sure what the functions of most of the other sequences are—or even if they have functions. Noncoding DNA is important because it appears to be selectively neutral, so mutations that accumulate in it are neither selected against, resulting in their disappearance, nor selected for, resulting in an increase in their frequency. Thus, this DNA may provide a more accurate record of the genetic history of two or more divergent lineages. Particularly useful for some areas of research (including so-called DNA fingerprinting in criminal cases) are **microsatellites,** long, repetitious strings of noncoding DNA sequences; these long strings make readily distinguishable genetic landmarks.

Of special interest to us is mtDNA. Mitochrondria are the energy factories within the cells of plants and animals. They possess their own distinct DNA, which, in complex interaction with the nuclear DNA, codes for the mitochondria's function of producing the biological fuel that provides energy for the cell. Most human cells contain hundreds or thousands of mitochrondria. At some point in early cellular evolution, the ancestors of mitochrondria were separate organisms. Through what may be the first example of **symbiosis,** they became functional elements within larger cells, maintaining their own genetic code. This code is particularly useful for some genetic studies because mtDNA accumulates mutations at a rate five to ten times faster than nuclear DNA, and there is evidence that the mutation rate is fairly constant. (It was once thought that mtDNA was selectively neutral; that is, that mutations made no difference in the phenotype and therefore in the potential reproductive fitness of the individual. This is not the case. There are now a number of disorders linked to mtDNA mutations. The mtDNA undergoes selection

mitochondrial DNA (mtDNA): The genetic material found in the cell's mitochondria rather than in the cell's nucleus.

nuclear DNA: The genetic material in the nucleus of a cell.

microsatellites: Long, repetitious strings of noncoding DNA. Their length and the fact that they are not influenced by selection make them good genetic landmarks for DNA comparisons.

symbiosis: An adaptive relationship between two different species, often, but not necessarily, of mutual benefit.

just as does coding nuclear DNA.) In addition, the entire mtDNA genome is known; that is, all the base pairs have been identified, and there are large noncoding sequences. Finally, mtDNA is inherited only through the female line; although both human eggs and sperm contain mitochondria, the 50 to 100 mitochondria from the sperm disappear from the egg shortly after fertilization. Thus, one's mtDNA is not a combination of the mtDNA from two parents, as is nuclear DNA. (Recently, this last idea has been called into question [Awadalla et al. 1999], with some evidence appearing of mixing between paternal and maternal mtDNA in humans and chimpanzees. Further study is awaited, but if true, this would have important ramifications for all research using mtDNA.)

The third type of DNA used is that on the Y chromosome. Analogously to mtDNA, Y-chromosome DNA is inherited only from one's father and is passed on only by males. Moreover, since the X and Y chromosomes are not paired, they don't exchange sections like the other paired chromosomes, a process called *recombination* (see Chapter 3), except at their tips. Thus Y-chromosome analysis allows us to trace inheritance through one parental line with little or no influence from the other.

How are data from these types of DNA used to study the question at hand? The basic idea is that with our ability to sequence DNA, we can specifically compare species and populations within a species at the most basic genetic level. Since at that level evolution is the accumulation of genetic variation through mutation, the genetic differences among populations tell us how many mutations have taken place since they were a single population. We get a measure of relative evolutionary relationships, which allows us to construct "family trees."

Moreover, if we can estimate the mutation rate for a given type of DNA, we can turn these data into a "molecular clock." We ask how long it would take for a certain degree of difference to accumulate between two groups. This, we assume, is how long they have been evolving separately (if two species) or relatively separately (if populations within a species). Then, we may add dates to the family tee.

So what have these studies, based on this reasoning, told us about the question of modern human origins? Two conclusions from many of these studies are that (1) the world's peoples tend to cluster into two genetic groups, those from sub-Saharan Africa and those from everywhere else, and (2) Africa is more genetically diverse than the rest of the world put together (Figure 12.5). This evidence seems to support the RAO model and a recent African origin of modern humanity. If people have been evolving in Africa longer than elsewhere and only recently spread to the rest of the world, then the African population should be distinct from those of Europe and Asia and should show greater genetic diversity.

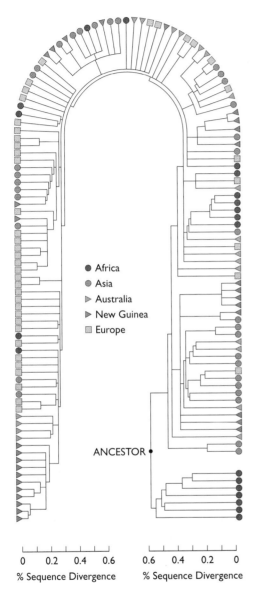

FIGURE 12.5
This computer-generated tree shows the lines of descent of 147 women sampled in one of the first important studies of this kind (Cann et al. 1987). The diagram is drawn as a horseshoe simply to fit on the page; mentally straighten it out, and you have a more familiar-looking family tree. The higher the percentage figure at the point of divergence (measured against the scale at the bottom of each end), the more different were the women's mtDNA and so the longer ago the divergence took place. Note the cluster of African women at the lower right. They are distinct from other African women and all others (0.6 percent on the scale). They also show greater diversity in their mtDNA, as seen by the fact that their lines of descent converge closer to the center of the diagram, that is, in the more distant past.

- Africa
- Asia
- Australia
- New Guinea
- Europe

ANCESTOR

```
0    0.2   0.4   0.6      0.6   0.4   0.2   0
% Sequence Divergence    % Sequence Divergence
```

The first study to conduct this analysis, and some subsequent ones, initially concluded that we can all trace our ancestry back to a single African female. Naturally, she was dubbed "Eve" and this model the "Eve Theory." This concept has been radically altered because of some of the new information about genetic systems to be discussed shortly.

The data from the preceding studies could, however, also result if the species were an old, single evolving lineage. Since most of hominid evolution occurred strictly in Africa, that continent has had the largest population for most of human history. A large population on a large and environmentally diverse continent would be expected to have a great deal of genetic diversity and thus be genetically different from all the rest of humanity, which (whether 2 million or 200,000 years old) is more recent (Relethford and Harpending 1995). Moreover, it might be the case that, given the geography of the continents, there was more gene flow within Africa and within populations in the rest of the world than *between* Africa and the rest of the world. This would also contribute to a genetic distinction.

In a rather alternative interpretation, biologist Alan Templeton (1993, 1996, 1997) concludes, based upon complex statistical analyses, that the mtDNA as well as the nuclear DNA of modern humans shows "no evidence that supports the hypothesis of an African–non-African population split" (1996, 1363). Rather, the data show "recurrent gene flow" within a "single evolutionary lineage," with restrictions in that flow giving rise to limited regional genetic differentiation. Templeton indicates that this interpretation can support either the MRE model or the RAO model; which model is correct can only be discerned through the fossil data. In general, then, neither our species' genetic homogeneity nor the large-scale differences between continents (if they exist) help us distinguish between the two models.

All the studies mentioned so far have used DNA from living populations. What about DNA from ancient remains? DNA is not a very stable molecule, and scientists at one time doubted that it could be recovered from old bones. But this has proved possible. In 2000, mtDNA was extracted from ten skeletons in Australia dated at 60,000 to 2,000 ya (Holden 2001a). The oldest skeleton had an mtDNA sequence that differed both from that of similarly dated fossils from other regions and from modern peoples as well. This sequence is, in fact, now extinct in modern mtDNA. This means that an anatomically modern individual with very old, very different DNA lived thousands of miles away from where modern humans are supposed to have originated, supporting the idea that moderns are the result of a multiregional ancestry.

Perhaps the most famous ancient DNA samples have come from four Neandertal specimens. The first, from the original Neandertal (see Figure 11.20) consisted of a short sequence of 379 base pairs of mtDNA (out of a total of about 16,500 for human mtDNA). When compared to the same sequence in modern humans there were more than three times the number of differences between the Neandertal and the moderns than between any two groups of moderns (Krings et al. 1997). Moreover the sample showed no special similarity to modern Europeans, being equally distinct from all modern populations. The investigators concluded from this that the Neandertals made no contribution to modern human mtDNA and that our two lines diverged 690,000 to 550,000 ya. A follow-up study from the same sample on another section of mtDNA, this time with about 600 base pairs, came to a similar conclusion (Krings et al. 1999). Another mtDNA sample, from a Russian Neandertal fossil, showed a similar result (Ovchinnikov et al. 2000), although there is a question about whether this fossil is actually a Neandertal in the first place (Hawks and Wolpoff 2001).

The third and fourth samples, this time nuclear DNA, came from a German and a Croatian fossil (Scholz et al. 2000). Here, the researchers also compared the Neandertal DNA to that of an ancient but modern-looking fossil from Stetten, Germany. The Stetten DNA was more similar to moderns than to that of its Neandertal contemporary—yet more seeming support for a species distinction.

As you might imagine, MRE proponents have questioned these conclusions. The DNA sequences are short, they note. And, says geneticist Simon Easteal, the fact that chimpanzees have much more mtDNA diversity than do humans shows that "the amount of diversity between Neanderthals and living humans is not exceptional" (Wong 1998). Moreover, one would expect there to be more genetic diversity in the human species in the past, before the larger populations, less isolation, and extensive gene flow of more recent times increased our genetic homogeneity. Clearly, more and larger ancient DNA samples will have to be obtained and studied.

Another conclusion from the early mtDNA studies is that the origin of all modern mtDNA can be traced—based on the degree of diversity and the estimated mutation rate—back to somewhere around 150,000 ya. This has been supported by a recent study (Ingman et al. 2000) that used, for the first time, the entire mtDNA sequence of approximately 16,500 base pairs in a comparison of fifty-three individuals of diverse geographic origins. The study shows a tree rooted in Africa with the most recent common ancestor of all modern humans dated at 171,500 $\pm$ (plus or minus) 50,000 ya. This general age has also been supported by some studies on Y-chromosome DNA (Gibbons 1997d). One of these studies also found two important variants on the Y-chromosome that are shared by other primates and in humans are found today only among Africans—mostly among Khoisan peoples. These, then, could be considered the oldest versions of the genes and those populations the closest, genetically, to the first modern humans (Figure 12.6). This seems strong support for the RAO model.

FIGURE 12.6
Recent studies have indicated that the oldest versions of certain genes on the male-inherited Y chromosome are found among Khoisan men, like this !Kung San hunter from the Kalahari Desert in southern Africa (the "!" indicates a click sound). These data are taken to mean that Khoisan may be the closest living populations, genetically, to the earliest modern humans.

Similarly, geneticist David Goldstein and his team (Bower 1995b) compared segments of nuclear DNA microsatellites from 148 individuals representing 14 indigenous populations from around the world. Based on similarities and differences at the microsatellite sites and on rates of change at those genetic locations, the researchers suggest that all modern humans originated in Africa and then spread from there at about 150,000 ya.

A team coordinated by Ken Kidd at Yale University (Tishkoff et al. 1996) compared more than 1,600 people from forty-two populations for two segments of DNA on chromosome 12. Sub-Saharan Africans showed a relatively great variety of genetic patterns for these segments, northeast Africans showed fewer varieties, and the populations from the rest of the world all shared a similar pattern. The suggestion is, again, an African origin for all modern humans. The team's calculations of the variation of one of the DNA segments points to a date of origin of around 100,000 ya.

These dates, however, have been called into question. Other studies, particularly those of Y-chromosome genes, have given widely divergent dates, some as old as 500,000 ya and some as recent as 135,000 ya (Donnelly et al. 1996; Fu and Li 1996; Rogers et al. 1996; and Weiss and von Heasler 1996).

A more general problem is the fact that the history of mtDNA or any other gene "does *not* reflect population history" (Wolpoff and Caspari 1997, 302). Rather, it reflects the history of a specific genetic system, in the same way the history of "a single Scottish name might be different from the history of the Scottish people" (304). The evolutionary history of a population involves the histories of many genes. If there was a recent origin of a separate modern human species, then all genetic systems should have similar histories, which does not seem to be the case. Wolpoff suggests that there were genetic bottlenecks in the past—different periods when in regional populations genetic diversity was greatly limited because of some event that decreased the population size or limited lines of descent. These bottlenecks, then, would have differentially affected the present diversity in genetic systems, limiting the diversity of some more than others. Thus, the great homogeneity of modern mtDNA (as well as the genes of the Y chromosome) might reflect a severe bottleneck in the past that had the effect of making the last common ancestor of mtDNA lines a recent one, while our actual common ancestor could be much older.

Templeton (1997, 353) also suggests that because mtDNA is inherited only through females, it may show a more recent time of origin for all existing mtDNA than does nuclear DNA. Calculations based on certain features of the two forms of DNA suggest, says Templeton, that if all our current mtDNA can be traced to 200,000 ya, it is likely that all our

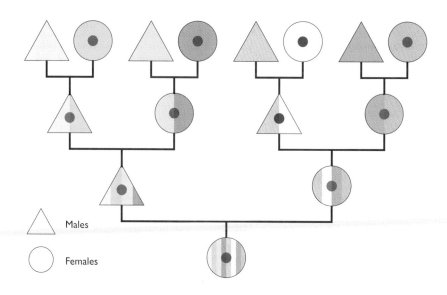

FIGURE 12.7

The Different Inheritance Patterns of Mitochondrial DNA and Nuclear DNA. The four couples at the top each have one child. These children pair off, and each pair has a child. These children then mate and produce the individual at the bottom. The colored dot in the center of each figure represents the mtDNA. The other colors represent nuclear DNA. Notice that the person at the bottom has inherited her mtDNA through only one line. The other mtDNA lines have become extinct because the other matings eventually produced a male who could not pass on his mtDNA. The nuclear DNA of the individual at the bottom, however, is a combination of the genes of *all* her ancestors. Her nuclear DNA, therefore, is much older than is her mtDNA. Similarly, all modern humans could have inherited their mtDNA from a recent common ancestor while tracing their nuclear DNA to a common ancestor back much further in time.

(Drawn using the concept in a diagram from Hammer and Zegura 1996, 122; after Jobling and Tyler-Smith 1995.)

nuclear genes—which we inherit from both parents—have their point of origin at more than 1 or 2 mya—coincident with the MRE model (Figure 12.7). It is this concept that undermined the oversimplified Eve Theory. While we might be able to trace all our *mtDNA* back to a single female in the recent past, our actual biological progenitor could be much older.

Here's an analogy: The earliest occurrence of my last name does not indicate my earliest ancestor, nor does the history of my last name tell my whole family history. There are lots of different last names and, thus, family lines involved in my genealogy, each with its own history. My last name is *Park* because it is my father's last name and because in our society last names are inherited through males. My mother's last name did not get passed on to me, so her contribution to my family history would not be noted if I just looked at the history of *Park*. Similarly, mtDNA, and Y-chromosome DNA, for the same reason, are specific genetic systems, passed down through only one sex, whose histories may be quite different from the history of an entire genome.

Finally, the variety of the histories of different genetic systems is being demonstrated by ongoing studies of new systems, especially within nuclear DNA. Rosalind Harding of Oxford University, for example (Wong 1998), found a lineage for the betaglobin gene (the gene for the beta chain of hemoglobin, a mutation of which causes sickle cell anemia), which has been dated to 200,000 ya. It is found in high frequency in Asia but is rare in Africa, suggesting that premodern populations in Asia contributed to the modern gene pool.

As with fossils and artifacts, the genetic evidence is ambiguous. While most of the analyses appear to support an RAO model, there are serious questions due to the fact that we have so far been able to look at just portions of specific genetic systems. Now, however, with our new and ever-increasing knowledge of the entirety of the human genome, we should see more extensive research and, eventually, better results. Still, with such a huge amount of data, analytical techniques will have to be refined. For example, even for the data shown in the tree in Figure 12.5, there are millions of different versions, with significantly different results, depending on just how those data are analyzed (Barinaga 1992; Hedges et al. 1992). Genetics may hold the key to resolving this debate, but not yet.

Evolutionary Theory

From the preceding discussion, it is clear that much of the haggling over these two major hypotheses focuses on details of the data. What about some of the broader considerations of evolutionary theory? What happens when we step back and look at the bigger picture? A major issue from this perspective is the plausibility of the gene flow required by the Multiregional Evolution model. Could gene flow have taken place, and, if so, how?

Christopher Stringer (Stringer and McKie 1996, 142) thinks that such gene flow is unlikely at best, for three reasons. First, he says, until recent times, hominid populations were too thinly spread across the three continents of the Old World to be so connected by gene flow. The gaps between groups were too large for genes to move around as much as MRE requires.

Second, there were—again, until recently—too many geographical barriers. There were mountain, desert, and water barriers, and over the past million years or so, large portions of the world were in the grip of the Pleistocene Ice Ages, which caused extreme climatic disruptions and fluctuations. The flow of genes would have been severely limited by these geographical obstacles.

Third, even supposing that different human groups were potentially interfertile, would they have *wanted* to share their genes? Science writer James Shreeve (1995) offers the possibility that Neandertals and moderns in Southwest Asia never interbred because they looked so different that they didn't even recognize members of the other group as potential mates. Quoting geneticist L. L. Cavalli-Sforza (Cavalli-Sforza et al. 1994), Stringer suggests that cultural and social barriers to fertility may have been very powerful, and interbreeding might have been considered "taboo."

There are—as you must suspect by now—responses to these issues from the MRE point of view. On the issue of population density, one estimate that Stringer quotes (Stringer and McKie 1996, 144) uses mtDNA variation to calculate the number of females our species possessed in its early evolution. The figure derived is 7,000 females, too few to have allowed much gene flow. But the use of mtDNA assumes the conclusion from other studies of that genetic system—that our species arose very recently from a localized group. The reasoning seems circular.

In addition, the apparently thin spread of early human populations across the Old World may be in part attributable to the nature of the fossil record. Remember that most individual hominids who ever lived did not leave fossilized remains, nor have we found but a fraction of all the fossil hominid remains that *were* left. The actual distribution of early populations may have been quite different from the distribution of the fossils recovered.

Moreover, there are two processes involved in gene flow. One is the kind of genetic exchange Stringer cites, where "populations essentially sat still while genes passed through them" (144), that is, exchanged between neighboring groups. But genes also flow as a result of migration. Hominids for the past 2 million years have been a migratory genus. In a short period of time, members of *Homo erectus* got all the way from Africa to Java. There is no reason why humans, having once arrived in these far-flung areas, would necessarily all stay put. They moved because they were following needed resources or looking for better conditions—and the Pleistocene climatic changes may have required a great deal of moving. As Templeton puts it, "all that is needed is to have humans distributed throughout the Old World and able to disperse a little bit in any direction every generation" (1997, 357).

In response to the second issue, geographical barriers to human habitation and movement certainly existed and still do. They did not, however, prevent the spread of human populations. Even if there were six different species of *Homo*, the fossil record shows that most managed to move around a bit (see the tables and maps in Chapter 11). And the climatic disruptions of the Pleistocene fluctuated. Barriers changed in severity and location. Sea levels rose and isolated some land areas but then dropped again. Dry periods followed wet periods. Glaciers covered huge masses of land but then retreated. Spread over a 2-million-year period, such temporary and changeable barriers might not have presented severe limitations to gene flow.

Regarding the third issue, what can we say about behavioral barriers to interbreeding? Without a time machine, we obviously cannot conduct the only conclusive test. We do know, however, that different physical appearances have not been absolute barriers to interbreeding in modern humans. For example, despite claims by slave owners in this country that Africans were, at best, less civilized and, at worst, virtually a different species, genetic exchange (usually forced by the slave owners) still took place. Even cultural barriers that enforce **endogamy** (marriage within one's group) are temporary over long periods of time as rules and group definitions change, and such rules are not always adhered to anyway.

We even have evidence for interbreeding between nonhuman populations that we classify as different species. Different species of Darwin's finches on the Galápagos hybridize when climatic disruptions bring them into contact. Some species (or subspecies) within the baboon genus *Papio*—groups that are usually easily identified and distinguished, both by us and, presumably, by them—hybridize in zones where their ranges meet. So *our* assessment of physical differences among ancient human groups and *our* assumptions about their behavioral taboos can't really tell us much about how they were really behaving.

Furthermore, we must consider the evidence of possible hybridization between archaics and moderns. We've already discussed the young child from Portugal with both modern and Neandertal features. While some supporters of the Recent African Origin model insist the child must be one species or the other, Christopher Stringer, a major RAO proponent, has said that even if this child was a hybrid, hybridization between moderns and Neandertals was a rare occurrence with little impact

endogamy: Restricting marriage to members of the same culturally defined group.

Contemporary Reflections

Is There a Connection between Modern Human Origins and Race?

"The Out-of-Africa model makes mincemeat of racial difference" reads a quote on the back of Christopher Stringer and Robin McKie's *African Exodus: The Origins of Modern Humanity* (1996). The title of Milford Wolpoff and Rachel Caspari's (1997) book is *Race and Human Evolution: A Fatal Attraction*. What is the connection between race and the models we have been examining?

We will cover the topic of human biodiversity and the issue of race in detail in Chapter 14. For the moment, let me give away the punch line of that chapter and state that, in the view of modern biological anthropology, the human species *is not* and *cannot* be divided into *any* number of clearly defined biological subgroups that warrant the title *race*. To be sure, we display phenotypic variation—in everything from skin color to relative frequencies of blood types—and this variation sometimes has geographic correlations. We can often accurately identify people's regional backgrounds from their visible physical features. But those correlations are merely the results of different frequencies of alleles that have accumulated in different areas in response to some combination of environmental circumstances and population dynamics (in other words, in response to the operations of natural selection, gene flow, and genetic drift). Genetically, the whole species is remarkably homogeneous, and the genetic variation is relatively evenly spread. Nonetheless, it is these outward physical similarities and differences that cultures use to divide humans into races. Race is a cultural construct.

The biological unity of our species is now a well-documented fact, and it leads to certain socially relevant ideas and ideals—namely, that, although individual humans vary in many ways, there exist no profound inherent differences *among human groups* that would warrant differential treatment in social and cultural environments. Skin color, for example, is no predictor of intellectual capabilities.

A majority of anthropologists have leaned toward the Recent African Origin model not only because many believe the data support it but also because it neatly explains our species' current homogeneity. If our species is very young—only a few hundred thousand years at most—and if it arose from one localized population, then it could not possibly display deep and profound variations among its populations. There simply hasn't been enough time. If the RAO model is correct, human races could not exist. This makes the RAO model attractive indeed.

on evolution (Bower 1999). Elsewhere, Stringer (1994) has claimed that interbreeding may have taken place between archaics and moderns in Eurasia but that it was limited and left no genetic or physical results in modern populations. In a later article, Stringer and G. Bräuer (1997) indicate they think interbreeding did occur, and O. M. Pearson (2000), writing on postcranial remains, admits the possibility of some admixture between moderns and Neandertals.

Moreover, it has been stated by some RAO supporters that one fatal problem with the Multiregional Evolution model is that it does "suggest, at face value, that modern humanity's constituent races are divided by fundamental and deep-rooted differences" (Stringer and McKie 1996, 60). If, such arguments go, local populations show continuity of features into the distant past, that implies that modern racial groups are themselves very ancient and profoundly different. Such a suggestion goes against current social ideals, not to mention the scientific facts regarding our relative homogeneity.

There were, to be sure, earlier models of a multiregional perspective that did make such suggestions. In his 1962 book, *The Origin of Races*, anthropologist Carleton Coon proposed that five subspecies, or races, of *Homo erectus* independently evolved into five major races of *Homo sapiens*, crossing "a critical threshold from a more brutal to a more *sapient* state" (1962, 658). To make matters worse, he claimed that the different races crossed the "sapiens threshold" at different times and that this accounted for some of the differences we see today in levels of cultural complexity. "If all races had a recent common origin," he asked, "why were the Tasmanians and many of the Australian aborigines still living during the nineteenth century in a manner comparable to that of Europeans of over 100,000 years ago?" (1962, 4). It is clear who Coon thought crossed the threshold first and last. Such ideas may well have sensitized anthropologists against any model of our evolution that included great time depth for the species and regional continuity of traits.

The modern MRE model, however, is quite different from Coon's and other early ideas. The MRE model does not claim that *populations* show continuity but that some regional *traits* do, especially traits that are found in fairly isolated areas, such as Australia and other places on the margins of the human geographical range. So-called racial groups are not now, nor were they ever, completely isolated. Rather, the species has displayed continual gene flow, enough to maintain species identity and spread physical features and their genes all over the world. Say Wolpoff and Caspari, "a past race has descendants in all living races, just as a living race has ancestors in all past ones" (1997, 208).

But this is all really a nonissue. Even if the extreme single-species MRE model proves correct, today's human species is *still* genetically and physically homogeneous. We know this because of well-established, scientific studies of genetics and morphology. How we got to be this way doesn't change how we are, and either major model under debate could account for our current nature. As anthropologist Matt Cartmill puts it, "We are what we are, not what our ancestors were. . . . The truth of racial egalitarianism hinges on the facts about living people. Their genealogies are irrelevant" (1997, 62).

The problem here is that if there was any interbreeding between Neandertals and moderns that led to hybrid individuals, then, by definition, they were members of the same species. This is true even if few or no Neandertal genes or morphological features are still present in modern humans (a debatable point itself). Gene flow between archaics and moderns, no matter how limited, refutes the RAO model and is, rather, basic to the MRE model (Wolpoff et al. 2001, 296, n. 3)

Another relevant aspect of evolutionary theory involves the process of speciation (see Chapter 5). New species evolve when a portion of an existing species is completely isolated from the parent species for a long enough period of time that subsequent genetic and phenotypic change eventually creates an absolute barrier to reproduction. Humans are and have been a mobile species, and our big brains have allowed our genus to experience increasing control over our environments and adaptations to those environments. It would seem to be a rare event for any individual group of such a genus to be isolated long enough to evolve sufficient differences in reproductive behavior or biology to become a technically separate species. The most extreme RAO model (Tattersall and Schwarz 2000) recognizes as many as *eight* species of *Homo* (including *H. habilis* and *H. rudolfensis*). In terms of how new species evolve, and the nature of genus *Homo*, this appears highly unlikely indeed. As Kenneth Weiss and Anne Buchanan point out, humans and chimpanzees, after 5 million years of separation, are 98 to 99 percent genetically identical. Modern humans are about one tenth as diverse (99.9 percent identical). "Even under the most melodramatic Big Replacement [RAO] scenario, how different could the winners and losers have been?" (2000, 198).

Perhaps we have been misled because we have examined every available minute genetic and phenotypic variation in living humans and our fossil ancestors through a microscope—literally and figuratively. A single species, as it responds to the processes of evolution through time, may change, of course, and it certainly may show regional variation. But over the long haul, the temporal changes and regional variation within a species occur around some central adaptive theme that defines that species. Our central adaptive theme is our big brains and the resultant behaviors, especially culture, that those brains make possible. Evidence of this theme is found in all accepted members of genus *Homo*—and is absent in all other hominids.

Where does the debate stand, then? It is still one of the hottest topics in biological anthropology, with many articles in professional and popular journals and lectures and symposia at professional meetings. For my part, considering the ambiguity of the evidence from the fossil and archaeological records and from genetics, I find most compelling the arguments from evolutionary theory. Thus, I am in the MRE camp. The fascinating thing about science, however, is that the discovery of a new fossil, the announcement of some new high-tech genetic evidence, or a well-argued new interpretation could change my mind overnight. That's why this debate is so exciting.

▽　　　▽　　　▽

SUMMARY

The "hottest" current debate in bioanthropology is over the origin of modern *Homo sapiens*. Authorities at present support either of two major models. One, the Recent African Origin (RAO) model, proposes that modern humans evolved as a separate species 200,000 to 150,000 ya in Africa, having a set of characteristics that made them distinctly different from their ancestor, and other contemporary, species. They then spread throughout the Old World, replacing populations of archaic humans because of their better-adapted traits.

The other model, the Multiregional Evolution (MRE) model, claims that our species is as much as 2 million years old and incorporates other previously recognized species of genus *Homo* possibly back through *H. erectus*. After first evolving in Africa, the species spread around the Old World, developing regional differences but always maintaining species identity through gene flow. As new and successful adaptations arose in different areas, they were shared across the species. Thus, "modern" humans are those of us—all 6 billion living today—who share a collection of traits that is the latest set of physical features in a very ancient species.

The data from paleontology, archaeology, and genetics are ambiguous on this issue. Either model may be supported by the same basic facts. The arguments from evolutionary theory, however, I believe more strongly support the MRE model. Deductive testing and data collection continue, and it would seem that this debate will be ongoing for some time to come.

QUESTIONS FOR FURTHER THOUGHT

1. Having read about the debate over the evolution of genus *Homo*, think back to Question 1 from Chapter 11. Now what are your thoughts on the issue? Is this debate interesting and important to you? Why or why not?

2. Aside from the alleged race implications, why do you think professionals are so emotional about this debate? Do you see any issues other than purely scientific ones—philosophical ones, perhaps—that could be involved?

3. Some claim that the Multiregional Evolution model is potentially "racist." (Someone said it to me.) How would you respond to such an accusation?

KEY TERMS

Multiregional Evolution (MRE) model	Recent African Origin (RAO) model	nuclear DNA microsatellites symbiosis endogamy
Out-of-Africa model	mitochondrial DNA (mtDNA)	

SUGGESTED READINGS

There is extensive literature about this debate. I would especially recommend the two books by the major proponents of each point of view: *Race and Human Evolution: A Fatal Attraction*, by Milford Wolpoff and Rachel Caspari, in support of the MRE model, and *African Exodus*, by Christopher Stringer and Robin McKie, in support of the RAO model. The Wolpoff and Caspari book includes a good historical review of the issue. See also Ian Tattersall's article in the January 2000 *Scientific American*, "Once We Were Not Alone."

On the fascinating topic of mitochondria, see "Symbionts and Assassins," by Guy C. Brown, in the July/August 2000 issue of *National History*.

A fairly technical but accessible article by Michael Hammer and Stephen Zegura, "The Role of the Y Chromosome in Human Evolutionary Studies," not only discusses data about that chromosome but also gives a nice description of many of the other aspects of the debate.

A good description of some of the genetic research and the analogy to human family names can be found in "After You, Eve," by Carl Zimmer, in the March 2001 *Natural History*.

On the topic of the race connection, see Matt Cartmill's "The Third Man" in the September 1997 issue of *Discover*, and have a look at Carleton Coon's *The Origin of Races* to see why that book caused such a furor.

For an overall discussion similar to the one in this chapter, but more detailed, see Feder and Park, *Human Antiquity*, fourth edition.

For a collection of twenty-nine articles on all aspects of the debate, see *Conceptual Issues in Modern Human Origins Research*, edited by G. A. Clark and C. M. Willermet.

For the most recent discussion, as of this writing, see "The Riddle of Co-existence," by Ann Gibbons, and "Anthropologists Duel over Modern Human Orgins," by Michael Balter, both in the March 2001 issue of *Science*.

CHAPTER

13

THE STUDY OF LIVING PEOPLES

From distant climes,
o'er widespread seas
we come . . .
—George Barrington

We have followed the evolutionary history of the hominids up to *Homo sapiens* in its anatomically modern biological state. But the story of hominid evolution doesn't end just because we finally arrive at modern humans. The processes of evolution within a species, including our own, are continuous. A species undergoes change over time, even as it remains a single species. Remember the Darwin's finches from Chapter 4.

Ever since the basic nature of our species was established, all the processes of evolution have continued to operate, acting on the human "theme" and changing us over time and across geographic space. As we divided ourselves into groups based on ethnic identity, nationality, language, and religion, we provided those evolutionary processes with new and varying breeding populations, or demes. Because evolution takes place within populations, the nature of those cultural groups also affected the further evolution of our species as a whole. So did the behaviors—the cultural systems—of the people in those populations. In other words, our biology and our culture are interrelated and affect one another.

As biological anthropologists, then, we are interested not only in how we evolved but also in what we evolved into, how we continued to evolve over the recent past, and how we are evolving even today. In this chapter, we will look at some of the ways bioanthropologists study living peoples in terms of genetic change, evolution within populations, the nature of our populations, the adaptive differences among populations, the influence of disease, and, finally, our individual life histories. We will address these questions:

How do we recognize genetic changes in populations and identify and study their causes?

What basic data do we gather in order to describe human populations?

What sorts of trends can we see in populations within our species?

In what ways have we humans adapted to the varying environments in which we live?

How have diseases influenced human populations?

What are the results of our species' evolution on the life histories—the "personal evolution"—of the human individual?

GENES IN POPULATIONS

In Chapter 4, I introduced the concept of allele frequency. The genetic definition of evolution is *change in allele frequency over time*. A process of evolution is, therefore, any process that alters the frequencies with which alleles of genes appear in a population. We can use the concept of allele frequency more specifically by applying actual allele frequency numbers in our study of human evolution.

The example of evolution we focused on in Chapter 4 was sickle cell anemia. Let's continue with that example. Suppose we can test a population for the sickle cell genotypes at two points in time. Our first test gives the following numbers (based on an example in Relethford 2001):

AA (normal hemoglobin)	50 people
AS (sickle cell trait)	100 people
SS (sickle cell anemia)	50 people
Total	200 people

(A and S are *alleles of a single gene*, the *Hb* gene for hemoglobin.)

Now, when we return to test the population at some point in the future, we find the following numbers:

AA	35 people
AS	100 people
SS	10 people
Total	145 people

Obviously, some change has taken place in the frequency of the genotypes and in the total population size. Have allele frequencies changed as well? In other words, has evolution, by the genetic definition, taken place? To calculate the allele frequencies, we add up the total number of each allele and divide by the number of alleles in the population, which would be twice the number of people since each person has two alleles at each locus. Thus, for the first test, the number of A alleles is:

$(50 \times 2) + 100 = 200$ (since each AA person has two A alleles and each AS heterozygote has one)

The frequency of A alleles in the population is thus:

200/400 (since each of the 200 people has two alleles) = .50 (50%)

Using the same reasoning, the frequency of the S allele is also .50 (50%).

Now, let's calculate the allele frequencies in the second test, after the obvious changes in genotype frequency and number of people have taken place. Using the same procedure:

frequency of A = ([35 × 2] + 100) / (145 × 2) = .59 (59%)
frequency of S = ([10 × 2] + 100) / (145 × 2) = .41 (41%)

(The results are rounded for simplicity.) Thus, the frequency of the A allele has increased and that of the S allele has decreased. Evolution, by technical definition, is taking place.

The reason for this change is obvious, because we understand sickle cell anemia. Those individuals with the SS genotype have a fatal disease, so only 20 percent (10 out of 50) of them survived between the two tests. Those with the AA genotype don't have sickle cell, but some may have succumbed to malaria; here there was a 70 percent survival rate (35 out of 50) for the AA genotype. All of the heterozygotes survived since they have nonfatal symptoms of sickle cell and also possess an immunity to malaria.

If, however, we did not already understand the situation, the calculation of these figures would show that *something* was happening and would indicate in which direction the change was taking place. It would be clear in this case that one allele is increasing in frequency because both homozygote genotypes are decreasing in number, but to different degrees. As a result of *this*, the heterozygote genotype is becoming more common. We would then try to figure out why.

Suppose, however, we could only examine the population once, as is often the case. How could we possibly see evidence for change over time? There is a formula, known as the **Hardy-Weinberg equilibrium**, that provides us with a tool. The formula is an example of a *null hypothesis*, a condition where nothing occurs. If you can state the conditions of *no* change, you can then compare them to a real situation and see whether change is taking place and, if it is, state the nature and direction of that change. The Hardy-Weinberg formula assumes that the genotype frequencies in a population will remain the same under certain conditions: (1) if mating is random (that is, everyone stands an equal chance of mating with anyone else of the opposite sex), and (2) if there is no gene flow, no drift, no mutation, and no natural selection for any allele over another. In other words, none of the processes of evolution is taking place.

For example, using our two alleles for hemoglobin, A and S, we designate the frequency of A as p and the frequency of S as q. (These letters, although they may make it a bit confusing at first, are used because of a mathematical convention.) So, for our population in the second test above:

$p = .59$ and $q = .41$

Now, we calculate the probability (the chance) of creating each of the three possible genotypes *based solely on the percentages of the two alleles*. The probability is the product (the result of multiplication) of the frequencies of the alleles that make up each genotype. How often a genotype is produced depends on how often the alleles of that genotype appear in the first place. Thus, the following applies:

GENOTYPE	PRODUCT OF FREQUENCIES
AA	$p \times p = p^2$
AS	$p \times q = pq$
SA	$q \times p = qp$ $\Big\} = 2\,pq$
SS	$q \times q = q^2$

The heterozygote is counted twice because there are two ways of producing it, depending on which allele comes from which parent. Because all genotypes are now accounted for,

$$p^2 + 2pq + q^2 = 1 \text{ (or 100\%)}$$

This is the Hardy-Weinberg formula for a two-allele gene.

We can now return to our population and see what its genotype frequencies would be if they were based only on the frequencies of the alleles, that is, if there were no evolutionary processes taking place and the percentages of the genotypes were strictly a matter of chance. For the AA genotype, for example, we calculate p^2 as $.59 \times .59 = .3481$. Next, we multiply this by the population size, 145, to show how many people would be *expected* to have this genotype if no evolution were taking place: $145 \times .3481 = 50$. Looking back, however, we observed that only 35 people actually possessed this genotype. We can do the rest of the calculations, producing the following results:

GENOTYPE	EXPECTED FREQUENCY	EXPECTED NUMBER	OBSERVED NUMBER
AA	$p^2 = .59^2 = .3481$	$.3481 \times 145 = 50$	35
AS	$2pq = 2 \times .59 \times .41$ $= .4838$	$.4838 \times 145 = 70$	100
SS	$q^2 = .41^2 = .1681$	$.1681 \times 145 = 24$	10

(The numbers in the expected and observed columns should both add up to 145 but don't exactly because of rounding.)

The observed numbers of people possessing each genotype are not the same as those expected if chance alone were determining them. In evolutionary terms, then, our sample population is not in Hardy-Weinberg

Hardy-Weinberg equilibrium: The formula that shows genotype frequencies in a population under hypothetical conditions of no evolutionary change.

equilibrium. Something else is going on; namely, some evolutionary processes are in action.

In real life, we would still have to run certain statistical tests on our results, because even if the expected and observed numbers do not match, that could still be the result of chance. For the record, I ran a chi-square test and found that the above results are not a matter of chance. They are, therefore, in mathematical terms, statistically significant.

At any rate, we can note the direction of the differences. Again, comparing expected with observed frequencies, we see that there are large drops in the numbers of people with the AA and SS genotypes and a large increase in those with the AS genotype. This hints that the heterozygote is being selected for and that the two homozygotes are being selected against. We know, of course, that this is the case with sickle cell anemia in malarial areas.

The other processes of evolution may also be quantified and studied in a similar fashion, by observing changes in allele frequencies over time or by calculating deviations from Hardy-Weinberg equilibrium, and then by noting the direction of change and determining probable causes of that change. Some references to more extensive coverage of mathematical population genetics are given in the "Suggested Readings" section at the end of the chapter with an exercise in the Appendix.

EVOLUTION WITHIN POPULATIONS

Using the techniques of population genetics just discussed, we may study the processes of evolution taking place within living populations at the phenotypic level. Today, of course, we are able to characterize populations and study their evolution at the genetic level, including the most basic level of the individual letters (the four bases) of the genetic code (see Chapter 3). A variation in these letters is known as a **single nucleotide polymorphism** (known as a **SNP,** pronounced *snip*). It is estimated that in comparing any two human DNA sequences, there will be one SNP every 1,000 to 2,000 nucleotides, meaning that any two humans will differ in 1.6 to 3.2 million of their 3 billion nucleotides (Stoneking 2001). Imagine the total number of variations within the whole species. Although most SNPs are in noncoding regions, most human phenotypic variation influenced by genes can be traced to SNPs. These differences in letters of the code are what distinguish alleles of a gene. Thus, we have the basis for eventually understanding our biological diversity (the topic of the next chapter). In addition, because SNPs reflect past mutations, we

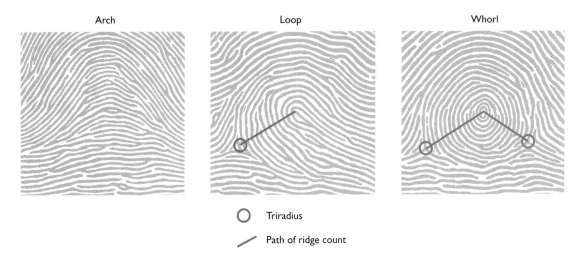

Arch   Loop   Whorl

○ Triradius

╱ Path of ridge count

FIGURE 13.1
Fingerprint Features Used as Anthropological Data. Arches have no triradius and, therefore, no ridge count. Loops have one ridge count. Whorls have two ridge counts; the largest is used as data. The ridge count of the loop is 13 and that of the whorl is 14.

can use them to estimate evolutionary relationships among individuals and populations (as we discussed in Chapters 9 and 12).

This exciting new technology makes one aspect of my study of the Hutterites (see Chapter 1) rather obsolete. If I were conducting my research today, I'd collect genetic instead of phenotypic data. But the research model would remain the same, and so I'll use my old study as an example of how we might examine evolution within a population, regardless of the data used.

When I conducted my study of evolutionary processes among the Hutterites, I used **dermatoglyphics**, the study of the parallel ridges on the skin of the fingers, palms, toes, and soles of the feet. I focused on those of the fingers—in a word, fingerprints. I was not collecting data about the small features that make each individual's fingerprints absolutely unique from everyone else's. Rather, I was looking for the frequencies of various types of fingerprint patterns and for data about the size, or *ridge count*, of the patterns. The ridge count is measured by counting the number of ridges between a reference point, the *triradius*, and the center of the pattern (Figure 13.1).

We know that one's fingerprints are under some genetic control since certain features, especially the ridge count, are similar among members of a family line. Moreover, certain unusual dermatoglyphic traits or characteristic frequencies of some traits have been correlated with abnormalities of known or suspected genetic origin. We also know, however, that other fingerprint traits are affected by prenatal environmental factors or simply by chance. Not knowing what genes were involved in my study, I obviously

single nucleotide polymorphism (SNP): A single base pair of the genetic code that displays variable expressions among individuals.

dermatoglyphics: The study of the parallel ridges and furrows on the fingers, palms, toes, and soles of the feet.

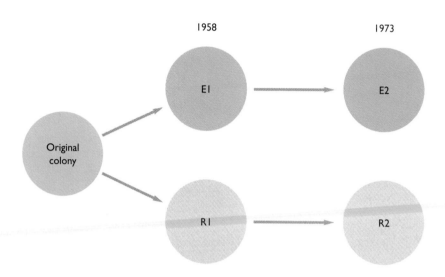

FIGURE 13.2
Hutterite Colonies in the Study Described. E and R are code letters I used to identify each colony to maintain my subjects' anonymity. The original colony, in Alberta, Canada, split in 1958. Half of the families stayed in the Alberta colony (R1), and half founded a new colony in Saskatchewan (E1). By 1973, when I conducted my study of the two colonies (R2 and E2), a second generation had been born.

couldn't calculate allele frequencies and run Hardy-Weinberg tests, so how did I use these features?

In 1973, I collected fingerprint data from two Hutterite colonies that were the result of the splitting of an original colony in 1958 (Figure 13.2). As you recall from Chapter 1, I was interested in examining the effects of gene flow and genetic drift. I examined 133 sets of fingerprints for pattern type, pattern size, and a few other variables (about 1,330 individual prints—although many of the men in this farming society had fewer than ten fingers). I then statistically compared the fingerprint data of various subgroups to get a numerical *approximation* of the genetic distances among them. I used different methods of analysis to see if some dermatoglyphic data were better than others for estimating genetic distance.

First, I was specifically interested in seeing how much genetic change was brought about by splitting (fissioning) the population. This would measure the form of genetic drift known as the founder effect (see Chapter 4). Second, I wondered how much change had occurred between generations and how much of that change was the result of the fact that about half of the mothers of the second generation had moved into the two colonies after marriage (gene flow). Natural selection was ruled out as a cause of change since there is no evidence that it makes any difference in reproductive success what ridge patterns you have and how big they are. Nor do people choose mates based on their fingerprints.

I felt I could apply what I found to a broader perspective on human evolution. The Hutterites nicely mirror the nature of many human populations throughout much of our history—small groups of interrelated fam-

Comparisons for genetic distance ⟷
① Founder effect
② Difference between generations
③ Difference after one generation

FIGURE 13.3
Diagram of Tests Run.
(1) Founded colonies were compared. These were reconstructed by using only those individuals still alive in 1973 who were involved in the split. (Most were still living.) (2) The members of the founded colonies (those present in 1958) were compared with all the offspring born since 1958. (3) All members of the 1973 colonies were compared.

ilies that split and merged in various ways as they moved about in search of resources.

I proposed and tested two hypotheses (Figure 13.3). First, I guessed that there would be a founder effect after the original population split in 1958 to create two new populations. That is, I hypothesized that the new populations would be genetically different from one another as a result of being founded by nonrepresentative samples of the original. I did not think the effect would be particularly extensive, however, since splitting a sample into two nearly equal halves lessens the chance of a major difference between them. In addition, all the families involved were descended from seven brothers, so there would not be a whole lot of genetic variation to begin with.

As a second hypothesis, I expected some effect from genetic drift and a significant effect from gene flow, making the next generations after the split (E2 and R2 in Figures 13.2 and 13.3) different from their parental generations (E1 and R1). I expected the second generations of the two colonies to be even more different from one another than were the two founded colonies. As noted in Chapter 4, nearly three-quarters of the mothers of the second generation "flowed" into the colonies of their husbands at marriage, and families with one of these women accounted for about half the children of the second generation. A lot of new genes were brought into each colony, and all of the women carrying those genes became parents. By reasoning, then, the parents should have been distinctly genetically different from the nonparents.

What did I find? For the first hypothesis, the data showed evidence of a founder effect, but there was more difference between the two founded populations than I expected. You obviously can't base a whole conclusion on one limited study, but my results did suggest that fission and the founder effect could be important processes not only within the Hutterites but in the small, interrelated human populations that they represent.

My second hypothesis was not supported by the evidence. The two second-generation populations were *more* similar to one another than were the founder populations. This was surprising at first, but then the reason became clear.

The colonies from which the flow-group women came belonged to the same subgroup of Hutterites. The Hutterites are divided into three subgroups. Since World War I, these groups have been endogamous—members only marry within their group. Thus, the women were more closely related than if they had come from the Hutterite population in general.

Moreover, since the two colonies I studied were geographically close, the colonies from which the women came were also geographically close. Hutterites often find their mates in colonies they regularly visit. This increased the chances that the flow-group women were themselves closely related to each other. The genes flowing into the two colonies were similar, so the differences between the colonies were lessened over time, even over a single generation. Differences among populations, then, can increase and decrease, back and forth, depending upon how the memberships of those populations are organized and exactly who marries whom. Culture, in other words, influences biology.

Finally, I observed which statistical tests most closely matched the predicted results (once I had figured out that gene flow *decreased* the genetic distance). I was able to suggest that ridge count (the size of the fingerprint patterns) was the best dermatoglyphic feature to use in such a study.

This dermatoglyphic research on the Hutterites is just one of many examples of a population genetic study—and a somewhat outdated one in terms of the data used. It does, however, show the ways in which we can make genetic comparisons among various populations and then analyze the evolutionary processes behind the differences we find.

This example also points out the importance of collecting and organizing data about the populations we study. How do we do this, and what can we learn from such data about the nature of the human species as a whole and of the groups into which we have divided ourselves?

DESCRIBING POPULATIONS

The statistical study of the size and makeup of human populations, and of changes in those measures, is called **demography.** Normally examined in detail by those who study human or cultural geography, demographic data are also of importance to biological anthropologists. Populations are, after all, the units of evolutionary change, and so the nature of the groups we study cannot be separated from the evolutionary processes that affect those groups. The Hutterite example clearly shows this.

The most obvious thing we need to know about a population is its size—how many people there are. Since we're interested in change over time, we also want to know to what extent and in what direction the size of a population has changed during a given period. For example, we know that the population of Europe dropped from about 70 million in 1347 to 45 million by 1352—a 35 percent decrease over a mere 5 years. It then took 118 years (until 1470) for Europe to once again achieve a population of 70 million. By contrast, the number of Hutterites in North America has increased from about 300 in 1875 to about 35,000 at present. This is more than a hundredfold increase over 126 years.

In bioanthropology, we are interested in the causes of population changes, in these and other cases. Clearly, there are three variables involved: births, deaths, and migration into or out of the population. When the birth rate exceeds the death rate, the population size increases. It decreases when the death rate is greater. Only in rare cases is migration a major factor, though it certainly may play a significant role.

In the case of fourteenth-century Europe, we know that the drop in population was the result of plague, mostly bubonic plague, a fatal bacterial disease carried by fleas, which are in turn transported by rats. A major outbreak began in Italy in 1347 and spread rapidly across Europe over the next 5 years, killing 25 million people, including William of Ockham (see Chapter 11). The period came to be known as the Black Death (Figure 13.4). No birth rate could have made up for this rate of death. The fact that it took longer to replace the 25 million than to kill them off results from two facts. First, there were further, though smaller, outbreaks of plague over the next century that kept the death rates high. Second, a phenomenal growth rate of around 100 persons per thousand would have been required each year to restore the population in only 5 years. (*Growth rate* is birth rate minus death rate.) By comparison, the U.S. growth rate for 1970 was only about 9 persons per thousand.

Bubonic plague appeared earlier than the fourteenth century and is still around today. It spread so quickly in Europe during those years

demography: The study of the size and makeup of populations.

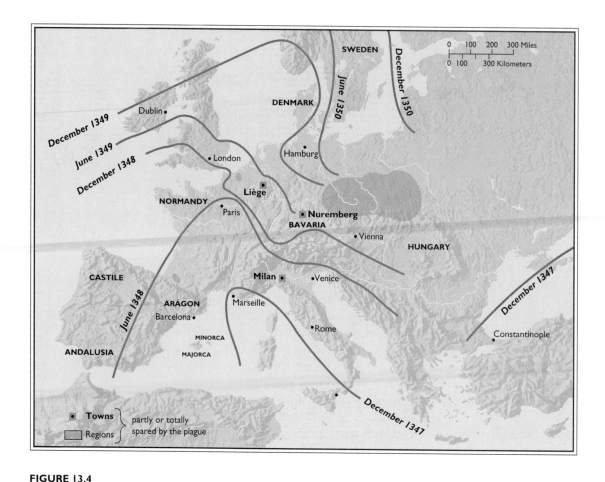

FIGURE 13.4

This map shows the progression of the Black Death across Europe in the fourteenth century, an event that killed over one-third of Europe's people in only 5 years.

because of the dense populations of many of Europe's cities and because of the extensive trade networks that linked those cities. Rats that carried the fleas moved easily from place to place, and the bacteria easily moved from person to person. Culture affected a biological event—and vice versa. Many aspects of European culture were affected by the Black Death—everything from economy to art to religious dissent and reform movements.

The increase in the Hutterite population in North America can be attributed to the high birth rate among this group. They have, on average, 10.4 children per family, one of the highest recorded rates for any population. This results in a birth rate of about 46 per thousand. The death rate is about 4 per thousand, yielding a growth rate of 42 per thousand. This high growth rate is the result of Hutterite religious beliefs—

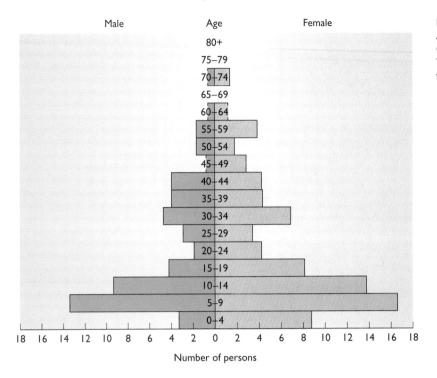

FIGURE 13.5
Age-Sex Graph of Hutterite Colonies Used in My Study. This is typical of such graphs for the Hutterites in general.

their firm adherence to the biblical injunction to "be fruitful and multiply"—and, most likely, because of the healthy lifestyle they lead, which includes hard work in nonurban areas and excludes drugs and all but occasional alcohol.

Biological anthropologists are also interested in the composition of populations. How many people are there of each sex, in each age group, and in various other ethnic, occupational, economic, and religious groups? We can display these data with a pyramid diagram. Figure 13.5 shows the age-sex structure of the Hutterite colonies I studied, but the data are typical for all Hutterites.

As you might expect for a group with such a high birth rate, the graph is wider on the bottom, showing that there are more children than adults. The fact that there are many more children between ages 5 and 9 than between 0 and 4 may indicate that the growth rate is slowing, at least in these colonies.

That females outnumber males (79 to 54) may indicate any number of factors that would have to be examined more closely. Perhaps male death rates are higher—they are in the general population. It could also be that despite what I was told and what I calculated, I *did not* get to see

FIGURE 13.6
Age-Sex Graph for a Typical
Developing Nation Showing
Large Numbers of Children.

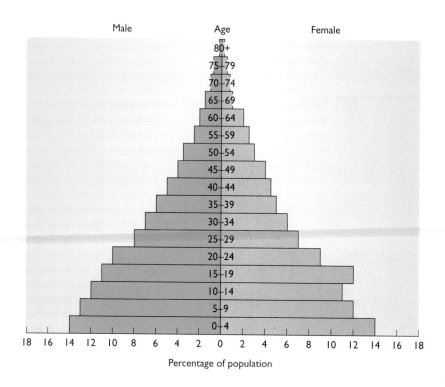

everyone in the colonies. Maybe some of the men did not want to participate, and I never knew they existed.

Now, compare the graph for the Hutterites with one representing developing nations—nations like Mexico, where industrialization is fairly
recent (Figure 13.6). This age-sex graph also shows larger numbers of
children, but, unlike the Hutterite graph, the numbers of adults rapidly
decrease with age. This second graph reflects higher death rates, especially in the higher age ranges.

For adults, the Hutterite graph more closely resembles a graph for developed nations, like the United States, that have been industrialized for
some time (Figure 13.7). Here the numbers of adults do not decrease as
quickly with age, indicating that people in developed countries live
longer in general. Regarding children, however, the developed nations
differ from the Hutterites in having lower birth rates.

What are the cultural connections here? As we noted, the Hutterites
are responding to their religious beliefs by having many children. Their
communal, self-sufficient lifestyle can accommodate large families, and
their practice of splitting colonies prevents local overpopulation.

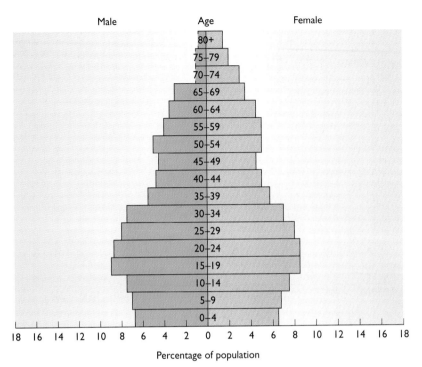

Male   Age   Female

Percentage of population

FIGURE 13.7

Age-Sex Graph for Typical Developed Nations Showing Fewer Children and Longer Life Expectancy.

Developing nations have high mortality rates. This provides one incentive to produce as many children as possible—simply to try to offset the deaths. In addition, birth control technology is not always available, and there may be cultural rules against it. But although the bottom of the pyramid diagram is wide for such populations, it narrows quickly. Because of poor medical care and poor nutrition and sanitation, people have a decreasing chance of living into the next age group. Recent data have shown, however, that family size is decreasing in many developing countries. This may eventually narrow the bottom of the graph for such countries (see Figure 13.6) and might lead to better living conditions that would, in turn, widen the top of the graph, as people's chances of longevity increase.

In developed countries, there is increasing motivation to limit population, and there is greater access to the means of birth control than in developing nations. Moreover, the quality of medical care and diet in general allow people to live longer—thus, the nearly vertical shape of the diagram.

FIGURE 13.8
World Population Curve.

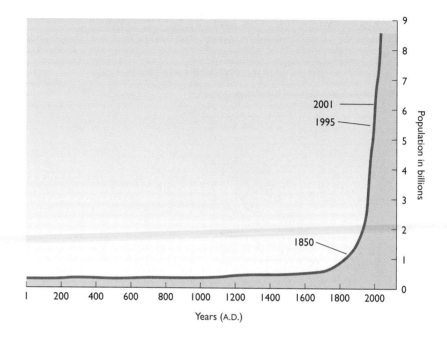

Finally, what can we say from demographic statistics about the human species in general? One thing is certain—our total population is going to increase. Since the beginning of farming and animal domestication some 12,000 years ago, the rate of increase of the human population has accelerated, jumping sharply with the Industrial Revolution of the eighteenth century (Figure 13.8). As of March 1, 2001, at 10:57 A.M., the U.S. Census Bureau estimated the world population at 6,131,717,841. Based on current growth rates, the world population is expected to reach 9.3 billion by the middle of this century.

In addition to a growing population, the structure of the population over this century will change. As birth rates and death rates continue to drop in developed nations and, perhaps, as other nations become increasingly developed, the age-sex pyramids will become top-heavy. There will be more older people than younger people. This will radically change the social and economic nature of such cultures.

Both of these changes carry implications that are beyond the scope of this book. Clearly, though, they will require responses and actions that will put a very different face on the world of the next generation and that will profoundly affect *Homo sapiens* of the twenty-first century (see the "Contemporary Reflections" box in this chapter).

Ventilation hole

Entrance chamber faces east or south

Ice window

Curved wall to keep out snow and wind

Snow block to reflect light from window for illumination

Sleeping platform   Floor   Removable door

FIGURE 13.9
Cultural Adaptation. The famous igloo of the Inuit has many ingenious features that make it remarkably adapted to life in a harsh climate.

HUMAN ADAPTATIONS

Living human populations inhabit every continent except Antarctica (though there are small, temporary groups of people who live there, mostly doing scientific research). We have to deal with nearly every imaginable set of environmental circumstances the earth presents, and we have been doing this for just about as long as modern *Homo sapiens* has existed. Indeed, even back in *Homo erectus* times, humans successfully moved into a wide range of environments.

One would expect, therefore, that different populations of our species would be differently adapted to those various environments. Obviously, most of our adaptations are cultural. We build shelters, manufacture clothing, make tools, and invent various technological devices that are specifically geared to the environmental conditions with which we have to contend (Figure 13.9).

Human populations also differ in their physical appearance and in features of their physiology. Our species displays variations in phenotypic traits that are the results of genetic variation. Most of this genetic variation can be explained by the single nucleotide polymorphisms, discussed earlier, that produce different alleles of a gene, but other **polymorphisms**—any variations in the genetic code—contribute as well. Are some of these variable traits adaptive responses to different environments?

polymorphisms: Variations in genetic code within a species.

Species Adaptations

As members of the same species, all humans certainly share many adaptations to variable conditions (see Beall and Steegmann 2000 for a detailed discussion). One important environmental variable is temperature. All humans sweat as a means of dissipating heat from the body. In addition, there is a widening of surface blood vessels. As noted in Chapter 10, our relative hairlessness may be an adaptation to promote the quick evaporation of sweat. Alternatively, when it becomes too cold, we shiver, our metabolic rate increases, and our blood vessels alternately widen and narrow to increase or decrease the flow of blood, and therefore warmth, to various body parts as needed.

Similarly, we are all exposed to ultraviolet radiation from the sun. An excess of UV radiation can damage skin cells, alter the cells' DNA (thereby causing skin cancer), and adversely affect the body's immune system. Excess UV radiation can also break down folate, a chemical necessary for embryo development. To protect tissues from UV damage, specialized skin cells called **melanocytes** produce the pigment **melanin** and deliver it to the upper layer of skin, where it absorbs UV radiation. Melanocytes respond to increased UV levels by increasing their melanin production and darkening the skin. This, of course, is tanning. Even dark-skinned individuals can exhibit a tanning response.

Another example of a variable condition is the low oxygen level at high altitudes, which can have damaging, even deadly effects on the human body. All humans, however, have some ability to respond biologically to this condition. After a time at higher-than-normal altitudes, a person's respiratory and heart rates will increase, as will one's red blood cell count. Hemoglobin concentration may go up as well. All this helps the body better acquire and use what oxygen is available.

Humans, however, live in such a variety of conditions—including those related to temperature, UV radiation, and high altitudes—that these species-wide responses may not be sufficient to adapt all populations to their environments.

Variation in Adaptations

melanocytes: Specialized skin cells that produce the pigment melanin.

melanin: The pigment largely responsible for human skin color.

Humans have settled in places from the hottest deserts and rain forests to the coldest reaches above the Arctic Circle. No matter how much we may sweat, shiver, increase our metabolic rate, and change the shape of our blood vessels, it may not be enough to deal with some environmental extremes. For example, there is no difference in the number of sweat

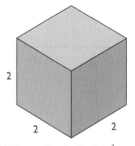

Volume = 2 × 2 × 2 = 8 in.³
Surface area = (2 × 2)(6 sides)
= 24 in.²
(Numbers in inches)

Volume = 1 × 2 × 4 = 8 in.³
Surface area = (1 × 2) (2)
+ (1 × 4) (2)
+ (2 × 4) (2)
= 28 in.²

FIGURE 13.10

The body build of the Inuit (*left*) is adapted to heat retention, while that of the Masai cattle herder from Kenya (*right*) is built to promote heat loss. The relationship between surface area and shape for two solids of equal volume (*above*) explains the adaptations of the two men pictured.

glands among human populations, regardless of regional temperature. There are, however, other adaptations to temperature that do vary with location.

Populations that inhabit hot climates tend to be linear in build, and those in cold areas tend to be stockier (Figure 13.10). This is because the linear individual has a greater surface area and so loses heat more rapidly, whereas the stockier person has a smaller surface area and so retains heat better. There is also a tendency for people in cold climates simply to be bigger in general than those in hot climates since, obviously, the larger person would have more body mass away from the surface and so retain heat more efficiently.

Ultraviolet radiation varies with latitude. Sunlight strikes the earth more directly at the equator; it strikes at an increasingly greater angle the farther one gets from the equator. The greater the angle, the more atmosphere the solar radiation must travel through. Thus, more UV radiation is absorbed by the ozone in northern latitudes. Not only do humans have the ability to tan in response to increased UV levels, but, as is obvious to

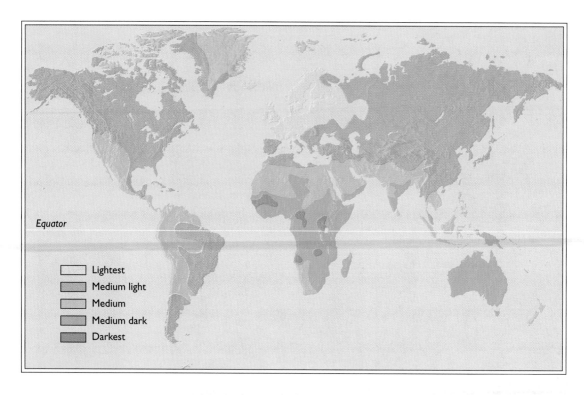

FIGURE 13.11

Skin Color Distribution (using five arbitrary categories). Darker skin is concentrated in equatorial regions.

us all, populations are genetically programmed for differences in skin color, and these differences also vary by latitude. In general, peoples closer to the equator have darker skin. Skin color gradually gets lighter in populations away from the equator (Figure 13.11). It is generally agreed that the relationship between dark skin and high levels of UV radiation is an example of an adaptive response (Beall and Steegmann 2000; Jablonski and Chaplin 2000b). Because of the damaging effects of UV radiation, peoples at or near the equator have undergone selection for permanently higher levels of melanin production. Darker-skinned people do not have more melanocytes than lighter-skinned ones, just more melanin production. An implication of this, of course, is that dark skin was the original human skin color, since—at least according to all the evidence—our species first evolved in equatorial Africa. Moreover, the African great apes, our closest relatives, have darkly pigmented skin, so it could be a shared trait inherited from a common ancestor. The adaptation would have become even more important when hominids lost their protective covering of hair (as noted before, an adaptation to promote more efficient heat loss.)

The question then becomes Why did populations who moved away from the equator evolve lower melanin production and therefore lighter skin? It is easiest to say that since dark skin was no longer needed, it became light. Evolution, however, doesn't really work this way. More likely, there was an adaptive reason why lighter skin was actively selected *for*.

A common answer has to do with vitamin D production. Vitamin D can be synthesized by the body in the lower layers of skin when a precursor of the vitamin is activated by UV radiation. This vitamin is important in regulating the absorption of calcium and its inclusion in the manufacture of bone. This is especially important during pregnancy and lactation, possibly accounting for the fact that, in all populations, females tend to be more lightly pigmented than males (Jablonski and Chaplin 2000b). Deficiency in vitamin D can lead to a condition of skeletal deformity in children known as rickets. (There is an adult version of the abnormality as well.) Bones with rickets are also more prone to breakage, and the disease can cause a deformity of the pelvis that can make childbirth difficult.

It has been thought that, as populations moved away from the equator, those with darker skin could not manufacture sufficient vitamin D for normal bone growth and maintenance. Those with lighter skin, therefore, were at an adaptive and, thus, a reproductive advantage. Over time, lighter skin became the normal, inherited condition in these groups. Skin color was thus seen as a balancing act—dark enough to protect from the damaging effects of UV radiation and light enough to allow the beneficial effects.

The vitamin D explanation has been questioned, however (Robins 1991). Rickets is associated with recent urban populations (in narrow city streets, children get little direct sunlight) and is seldom found in rural areas. There is little evidence for it in the fossil record. Moreover, although dark skin does slow down the production of vitamin D, it can still allow for sufficient synthesis to maintain healthy levels. Vitamin D synthesis, therefore, may not have been a selective factor for our ancestors.

Now, of course, we can also obtain vitamin D through vitamin supplements and by drinking vitamin D–fortified milk. It is also found in fish liver oils and egg yolks. A correlation between dark-skinned urban populations and rickets—once proposed as evidence for the adaptive connection—may be based more on socioeconomic matters resulting in poor diet than on skin color differences (see Beall and Steegmann 2000 for a detailed discussion of this debate).

Another possibility for an active selective factor for light skin concerns injury to the skin from cold. Data from the military suggest that darker skin is more prone to damage from frostbite than is lighter skin (Post et al. 1975; Robins 1991). Selection for light skin may not be related to UV radiation but to temperature, while selection for darker skin remains related to UV radiation. Beall and Steegmann (2000) discredit this hypothesis, however. The evolution of light skin pigmentation, it would seem, remains a matter of some debate.

As these examples of body build and skin color demonstrate, our species, despite its ability to adapt through culture to a wide array of environments, has still undergone natural selection for and against certain features in response to those environments. The adaptation of sickle cell anemia in malarial areas is another example. Although we might like to think we have buffered ourselves against this process of evolution, natural selection has occurred in modern *Homo sapiens*, and it continues to affect populations of our species.

Are All Polymorphisms Adaptively Important?

We can see in the distribution of body build and skin color some obvious correlations with environmental factors that lead us rather directly to our conclusions about the adaptive significance of these polymorphic traits. Other variable traits, on the other hand, seem distributed among our populations in such a way that there is no obvious relationship to environmental circumstances.

The distribution of blood types in the ABO system (see Chapter 3) is a perfect example of a polymorphism with no obvious relationship to the environment (Figure 13.12). There seems to be no rhyme or reason to how the various frequencies of the phenotypes are dispersed around the world. Type A, for example, is totally absent among some native South American groups but is found in frequencies of over 50 percent in parts of Europe and native Australia and among a few native North American groups, where, however, it is generally found among less than a quarter of the population. Type B, although found in moderate to high frequencies in Asia, is nearly absent among Native Americans, who originated from Asian migrants. Type B is also nearly totally absent in Australia but is found in moderate frequencies in New Guinea. Type O, the most common in the species, still ranges from 40 percent in parts of Asia to 100 percent among some native South Americans.

Are the variations of this genetic trait adaptively neutral; that is, do they make no difference in terms of differential reproductive success? We believe this to be the case for some other blood group systems. (There are about thirty different blood group systems besides the ABO system, that is, different chemical phenotypes in the blood that are the results of different genes with multiple alleles.)

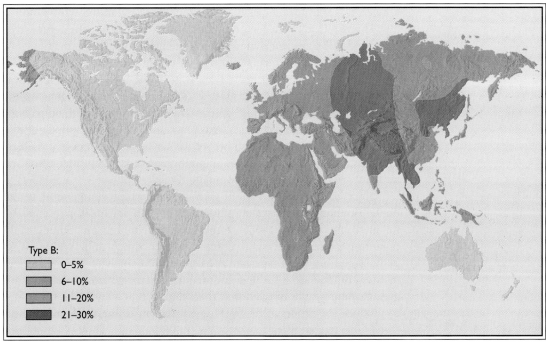

FIGURE 13.12

These maps show the approximate frequency distributions of type A and type B blood, demonstrating the lack of an obvious pattern in the distribution of this polymorphism.

TABLE 13.1
ABO Blood Group Phenotypes and Antibodies

Genotypes	Phenotypes	Antigens	Antibodies
AA AO	A	A	anti-B
BB BO	B	B	anti-A
AB	AB	A, B	none
OO	O	none	anti-A, anti-B

The actual phenotypic trait involved in the ABO system is the presence or absence of certain proteins, called **antigens,** on the surface of the red blood cells. In addition, from shortly after birth, your blood plasma contains other proteins, or **antibodies,** that react against the alternate version of your antigen. For example, the alternate version of antigen A is antigen B. Table 13.1 shows how these are expressed in the ABO system.

The reactions between antigens and antibodies are the reason that blood used for transfusions must match the blood type of the recipient. As a type A person, if I received a transfusion of type B blood, my anti-B antibodies would recognize the B antigen of the transfused blood as foreign to my system. My antibodies would bind with the antigens on the transfused red blood cells and destroy the cells by causing them to burst (*hemolyze*). If extensive enough, this reaction could lead to shock or kidney failure. In emergencies, however (as we all know from TV medical dramas), a person of any blood type may receive type O, since O has no antigens and therefore would stimulate no reaction.

Since antibodies of various sorts are important components of our bodies' immunological system, disease is one obvious factor to examine for an adaptive significance of the ABO polymorphism. Some microorganisms possess antigens that are similar to the A and B antigens, so perhaps certain blood types are predisposed to fight off certain infectious diseases. At the same time, if an infecting microorganism possesses antigens that are similar to your own, then your system may not be stimulated to produce the proper antibodies against the organism, making you more susceptible to that disease.

Some correlations between blood type and susceptibility to diseases have been suggested. Type A has been statistically associated with bronchial pneumonia, smallpox, and typhoid, and type O has shown correlations with bubonic plague. Among the data that support some connections among these factors is the low frequency of type O in India, where there is a long history of frequent plague epidemics.

It should also be noted that there is some evidence that mosquitos are more attracted to type O persons. If so, then diseases carried by mosquitos, such as malaria, would also be influenced, although indirectly, by blood type.

There are correlations as well between blood types and noninfectious gastrointestinal diseases. Type O persons appear to have a greater chance of duodenal and stomach ulcers and type A persons of stomach cancer. Most people have blood group antigens in their body fluids, including their gastric juices, as well as in their blood, and so there may well be some reactions between these antigens and chemicals in the food one eats. The reactions may have a positive or negative effect on the digestive process itself, or they may lead to some irritation of the digestive tract. Thus, certain blood types may have been selected for, and others against, depending upon what foods were typically consumed in certain areas by certain populations.

Along the same lines, there may also be reactions between blood antigens in the digestive tract and some intestinal bacteria. Individuals of certain blood types may be more or less affected by bacterial ailments like infant diarrhea. Such ailments are major factors in infant mortality in many parts of the world. Thus, they are important selective factors, and any polymorphism that influences the severity of these problems could be selected for or against.

What do blood type correlations tell us? Certainly these data indicate that a selective role for the ABO system is possible, especially with diseases that affect people during or before their reproductive years. We must demonstrate, however, that selection is, in fact, taking place. The fact that we have gained control over some of the diseases in question limits our ability to study them in the present, and so we have to rely, as with the plague connection, on historical records.

Moreover, we must establish a cause-and-effect relationship between antigen and disease, and we must also show if, and under what conditions, this would make enough of a difference to affect reproductive success. The ABO system is also found in chimps and gorillas, so the origin of the polymorphism itself may be hidden in our evolutionary past. Some of the more important connections are with diseases of dense urban populations. Thus, selection for certain blood types, and their distribution, may be a fairly recent phenomenon.

As this single example shows, the topic is a complex one. We asked at the beginning of this section, Are all polymorphisms adaptively important? The answer is We don't know for sure. Human polymorphisms need

antigens: Substances, such as proteins, that can trigger an immune response, for example, the production of an antibody.

antibodies: Proteins in the immune system that react to foreign antigens.

to be examined for their selective contributions to populations within the species. We may find, however, that some of our variable traits make no difference at all—or at least make no difference now.

DISEASE AND HUMAN POPULATIONS

We tend to think of diseases as abnormalities—and for individuals suffering from them, they are. But diseases are as much a part of life as any other aspect of our biological world. Since many diseases are caused by other living organisms—viruses, bacteria, and protozoa—and are carried around by other species, they are really perfectly natural. Disease-causing species have adapted to the biology of their hosts, and the hosts at least attempt to adapt to the disease-causing species. Diseases are thus excellent examples of evolutionary processes.

We also tend to think that our species, especially in modern times, has removed itself from many, if not most, such relationships. After all, those of us in developed countries virtually ignore diseases that a generation ago were serious threats. Polio (still a problem during my childhood) has been virtually eliminated from the United States and Europe. Tuberculosis is rare in the United States, as are mumps and measles. In 1980, smallpox was declared eradicated worldwide. In the United States, only two of the twelve most common causes of death (pneumonia/influenza and AIDS) are infectious diseases (Figure 13.13).

But there are still diseases that disable and kill us, and new diseases or new strains of old diseases are even now emerging as the species that cause them continue to undergo the processes of evolution. We have already discussed the examples of sickle cell anemia, malaria, and plague, and there may well be evolutionary relationships between our blood types and certain diseases. These examples all show diseases as important factors of natural selection.

Evolutionary relationships among human and animal viruses (based on some of the same genetic techniques and analyses we've discussed) suggest that some viruses have even played a role in hominid evolution (Van Blerkom, personal communication, 2000, 2001). As major causes of illness and death, viruses can be agents of selection within populations—for example, selecting for resistance factors to specific diseases and maintaining general diversity in the all important human immune system.

Viruses can also be involved in competition between populations. Because some viruses are carried by insects and other animals, affected popu-

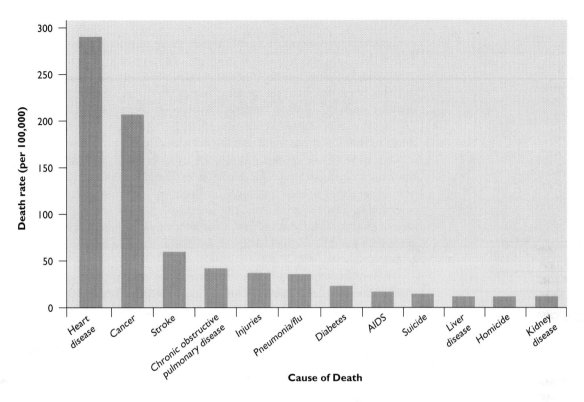

Cause of Death

FIGURE 13.13
The Twelve Leading Causes of Death in the United States in 1994. Note that only two, pneumonia/influenza and AIDS, are infectious diseases.
(From Relethford 2001.)

lations do not even have to be in close contact with one another. The fact that viruses are often more infectious and deadly in a new host could account for the extinction of individual populations within our species. Perhaps early migrants out of Africa—where populations had a long time to develop immunities to certain diseases—carried pathogens to hosts who lacked immunity. An analogous phenomenon occurred, for example, when the Spaniards conquered the Aztecs of Mexico in 1521. European diseases—smallpox, measles, and influenza—to which the Aztecs had no prior exposure and thus no immunity, probably did more to lead to their downfall than did the military actions of the Spanish soldiers.

Finally, since viruses operate by commandeering host cell machinery for their own purposes, some may also have played a more direct role in altering the human genome and thus, perhaps, in accounting for some of the evolutionary changes seen in hominid history (Van Blerkom 2001). Remnants of ancient viruses make up about 1 percent of the human genome. Some of these viral sequences may cause pathological conditions, but others, after millions of years of evolution, may be involved in such normal processes as placental formation and fetal development. An evolutionary tree of certain related virus types mirrors the evolutionary tree of their host species. This is evidence of a long-term coevolution.

Looked at from the evolutionary perspective we have used throughout this book, we may see general trends in the relationship between diseases and the human species. Anthropologist George Armelagos (Armelagos et al. 1996; Armelagos 1998) has outlined these trends and refers to them as three "**epidemiological** transitions."

For most of our species' history, we lived in small, widely dispersed, nomadic foraging groups. Our ancestors certainly experienced diseases of various sorts and would have come into contact with new diseases as they migrated to new environments. But infectious diseases may not have had serious effects on large numbers of people or many different populations since they would have had little chance of being passed on to many other humans.

When some people began to settle down and produce their food through farming and animal domestication—starting about 10,000 years ago—the "first epidemiological transition" occurred. Infectious diseases increased in impact, as larger and denser concentrations of people provided the disease vectors with greater opportunity to be passed from host to host. Animal domestication may have brought people into contact with new diseases previously limited to other species. Working the soil would have exposed farmers to insects and other pathogens. We have already seen how irrigation in some areas provided breeding places for mosquitos, increasing the incidence of malaria. Sanitation problems caused by larger, more sedentary populations would have helped transmit parasitic diseases in human waste, as would the use of animal dung for fertilizer. In addition, agriculture also led to a narrowing of food sources as compared to the varied diets of foragers. This could have resulted in nutritional deficiencies; moreover, the storage of food surpluses attracted new disease carriers like insects and rats. Trade between settled communities, as we saw in the case of the Black Death in Europe, helped spread diseases over large geographic areas. Epidemics, in the sense of diseases that affect a large number of populations at the same time, were essentially nonexistent until the agricultural revolution.

Beginning in the last years of the nineteenth century and continuing into the twentieth, we experienced the "second epidemiological transition." With modern medical science providing immunizations and antibiotics and with better public health measures and improved nutrition, many infectious diseases were brought under control or even, as with smallpox, eliminated. In terms of what ailed and killed us, there was a shift to chronic, degenerative diseases such as cancers, heart and circulatory diseases, and pulmonary disease. The increase in many of these came not only from the fact that fewer people were dying from infectious diseases and were living longer but also from the results of modern lifestyles in developed countries and among the upper classes of developing countries—a more sedentary life leading to less physical activity; more stress; environmental pollution; diets contributing to obesity, clogged arteries, and diabetes; and smoking and alcohol consumption. But at least, we thought, many of these problems were things we could potentially control; all those infectious epidemics were things of the past (or, at least, of developing countries).

But on the heels of the second transition has come the "third epidemiological transition," and we are in it now. New diseases are emerging, and old ones are returning. Both of these phenomena can be understood in terms of evolutionary theory.

The return of old diseases is the result of the fact that microorganisms are evolving species. For example, new and serious antibiotic-resistant strains of tuberculosis have recently appeared. This evolution may have been encouraged by what some authorities consider our overuse of antibiotics, giving microorganisms a greater chance to evolve resistance by exposing them to a constant barrage of selective challenges. Remember, some bacteria reproduce *hourly*, and so the processes of mutation and natural selection are speeded up in these species.

The emerging diseases are also the results of human activity in the modern world, which brings more people into contact with more diseases, some of which were unheard of even a few decades ago. As people and their products become more mobile, and as our populations spread into previously little-inhabited areas, cutting down forests and otherwise altering ecological conditions, we contact other species that may carry diseases to which they are immune but that prove deadly to us. The virus that is the most common cause of AIDS, HIV-1, crossed over to humans from chimpanzees, probably in West Africa as early as 1931 (Hahn et al. 2000; Korber et al. 2000). (Another virus, HIV-2, came from the sooty mangabey monkey.) Hunting, butchering, and the consumption of undercooked contaminated meat probably accounted for the contact that would have initially allowed the virus to be transmitted to humans from the nonhuman primates who had evolved the ability to carry the virus with no adverse effects. Early cases were isolated, so the disease didn't spread, even though the virus easily moves from host to host through the exchange of bodily fluids during sexual activity or as the result of using unsterilized hypodermic needles. AIDS reached epidemic proportions later in the twentieth century (Figure 13.14) as a result of social factors, including but not limited to our increased mobility. In addition, the virus itself has evolved

epidemiological: Pertaining to the study of disease outbreaks and epidemics.

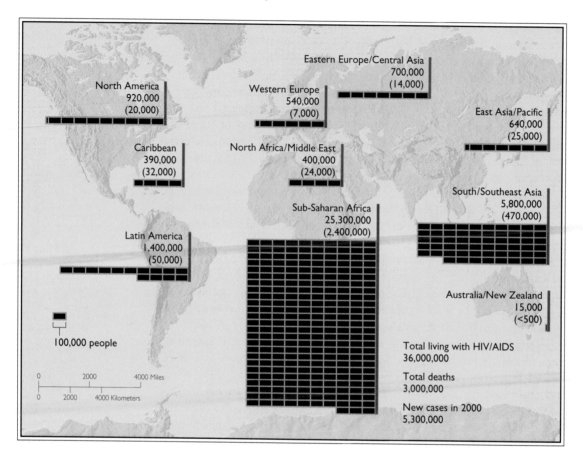

FIGURE 13.14

HIV/AIDS in the Year 2000. This map shows the number of people, by region, living with HIV/AIDS as of December 2000; the numbers of deaths from AIDS in 2000 appear in parentheses. Sub-Saharan Africa alone accounts for 3.8 million new infections; in 1999, 12.1 million children were orphaned there because of the disease. By some estimates there have been 21.8 million cumulative deaths from AIDS since the epidemic first started.

since its transmission to humans, producing strains that might be drug resistant, more virulent, and hard to detect (Hahn et al. 2000).

We have long known of another deadly virus, rabies, that is successful because it can jump from species to species (Mills 1997). Hantavirus from rodents, ebola virus from an as yet unknown source (possibly bats), and *campylobacter*, a bacterium from chickens, are some other examples of pathogens that have recently jumped from other species to ours, with serious consequences.

Finally, and perhaps most frightening, are the *prion* proteins. Not living organisms, prions begin as normal proteins (of as yet unknown function) in the nervous tissue of humans, other animals, and birds; for unknown reasons, however, these prions sometimes rearrange themselves into an abnormal configuration. In this abnormal form the prions trigger the same rearrangement of the normally configured proteins and then build up in brain tissue, which they eventually destroy. The condition is called *spongiform encephalopathy*. "Mad cow" disease in cattle, Creutzfeldt-Jakob disease in humans, and kuru, a disease described among the Fore people of highland New Guinea, are some examples of this condition, as are other manifestations in sheep, goats, minks, and possibly elk and mule deer. Although the trigger for the abnormal shape of the protein may come, not surprisingly, from a genetic mutation (since, as you recall, genes code for the synthesis of proteins), the frightening thing about prions is that they can easily be transmitted across species. Moreover, they are very hard to destroy. Mad cow disease may have been spread because cattle in England were fed meal that contained the remains of other domestic animals. Even though these remains were rendered (cooked and processed into meal), the prions survived and passed to other cows through ingestion (Rhodes 1997). As of December 2000, there were nearly 180,000 reported cases of mad cow disease (bovine spongiform encephalopathy, or BSE) reported from Europe, mostly from the United Kingdom but with some cases from eleven other countries as well (Donnelly 2000). As of the same date, there were 91 confirmed and probable cases of the form of Creutzfeldt-Jakob that is caused by human consumption of contaminated beef, most from Britain and a few from France and Ireland (Aldhous and Abbott 2000).

So, the evolution of our species has been, and is still being, affected by diseases caused by, originating in, and carried by other species that are themselves evolving. An important area for understanding these diseases, then, is evolutionary theory, which explains important factors about their source and transmission. In fact, this approach has been given the name "Darwinian medicine" (Oliwenstein 1995), and I imagine it will become increasingly important in the future.

THE BIOANTHROPOLOGY OF INDIVIDUALS

Individuals don't evolve, at least not in the sense that we are using the term here. And yet bioanthropologists are interested in growth rates, developmental rates, and the timing of important events in the lives of indi-

FIGURE 13.15

Distance Curve for Height and Age.

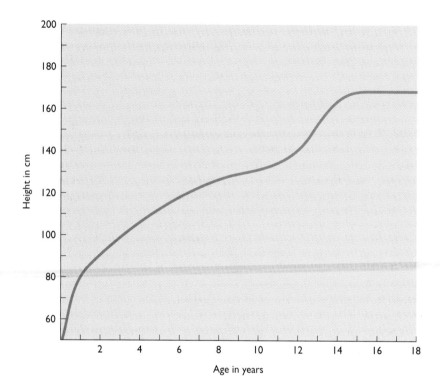

vidual members of our species. Why is this information important to bioanthropology?

First of all, we are interested in these topics simply because they are part of our species' makeup. Studying just the adults of a species does not tell us everything about that species. We need to know such things as how developed an individual is at birth, how fast it reaches certain levels of growth, when it becomes sexually and physically mature, how long its reproductive span lasts, and how long it lives. We also look at rates at which certain components of the body grow and compare them to one another, and we compare all these data for different populations within a species and for different groups within populations—like males and females.

For example, we may plot a curve that shows the height of the members of a human population at certain ages (Figure 13.15). This type of curve is called a **distance curve.** We see from such a curve that change in height as people mature does not occur at a steady rate but alters at different stages. The sudden increase in height in early adolescence is obviously related to puberty and is called, in fact, the *adolescent growth spurt.*

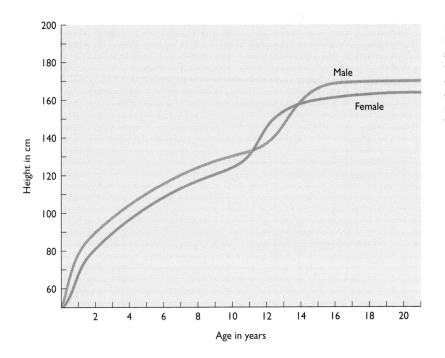

FIGURE 13.16
Distance Curves for Height and Age in Males Compared to Females. Note the difference in timing of the adolescent growth spurt and the resultant differences in relative average stature.

We all remember from our own teen years that the adolescent growth spurt did not occur at the same time for boys and girls. This and other differences in growth rate can be seen by comparing distance curves for males and females (Figure 13.16). These differences will be discussed in the next chapter.

These changes can be seen in another way by plotting the rate of change for different ages. This is called a **velocity curve,** and it measures how *fast* changes are taking place, in this case, how many centimeters per year the plotted individual is growing (Figure 13.17). Note the increase (acceleration) of the growth rate at early adolescence, which follows a basic trend of decreasing growth rate since birth.

Not every part of the body, of course, grows at the same rate. Figure 13.18 compares height with brain size, using the percentage of final adult size as a scale. Note that, unlike the increase in height, the fastest brain growth occurs in the first few years of life.

These and many other analyses show us the patterns of growth of our species in general and of different populations and groups within the species. Observing these patterns leads to other areas of interest.

First, we want to know what factors influence the differences we see between populations of our species and the changes within populations at

distance curve: A graph that compares some variable at different points in time.

velocity curve: A graph that compares the rate of change in some variable at different points in time.

FIGURE 13.17
Velocity Curve for Data in
Figure 13.15.

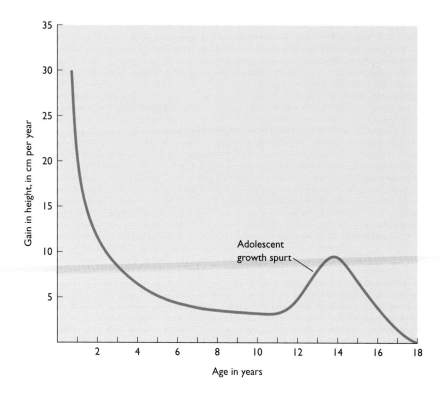

different points in time (see Stinson 2000 for a good, detailed discussion). Different populations, of course, have different average statures and body sizes (see, as an example, Figure 14.1). Some of these differences can be traced to natural selection, for example, with regard to heat loss and retention (see Figure 13.10); these differences may work through such immediate factors as differences in hormone production and utilization.

Environmental factors are also at work. Socioeconomic status (income, education, occupation, possessions), which affects nutrition, disease rate, and access to quality medical care, is an obviously important factor. And there may be feedback in terms of cultural values. Stinson (2000, 430) points out that because tallness is valued in many societies (nearly all U.S. presidents have been taller than average), taller individuals may find it easier to improve their socioeconomic status. Of course, they may have come from privileged backgrounds in the first place.

Differences in environmental factors between urban and rural areas also influence growth. Here, there are other influences such as time period. In the nineteenth century, for example, when urban areas were un-

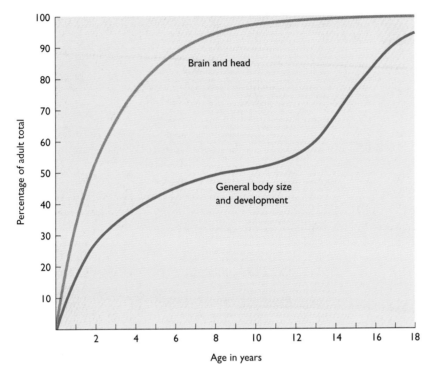

FIGURE 13.18
Distance Curves for Height Compared to Brain Growth.

healthy places, rural children were larger and healthier. As conditions in cities improved, urban children on the whole were larger than their rural counterparts; in the most affluent societies, however (such as the United States), there are no differences between rural and urban areas. Family size (with children in smaller families tending to be larger) and exposure to toxins (such as cigarette smoke) are also factors.

We may also plot changes over time, known as *secular trends*. Over the past century, better nutrition and medical care have made adult height greater and the age of sexual maturity earlier in the United States and other industrialized countries. There are still differences in age of **menarche** between poor women and those of more affluent means within such countries. At the same time, however, age at **menopause** is no different in populations of different nutritional and medical levels. Nor has better food and health expanded the maximum human lifespan, which remains about a hundred years at most (Hill 1993), or the average life expectancy, which is unlikely to rise above 85 years without major scientific and medical advances (Olshansky et al. 2001). Culture can affect some aspects of our stages of life, but not others.

menarche: A woman's first menstrual period.

menopause: The end of a woman's reproductive cycle.

Contemporary Reflections

Where Is the Population Crisis?

A major influence on Darwin's thinking was the English economist Thomas Malthus (1766–1834). In *An Essay on the Principle of Population*, he wrote, "Population, when unchecked, increases in a geometrical ratio. Subsistence increases only in an arithmetical ratio. . . . I can see no way by which man can escape from the weight of this law which pervades all animate nature" (1789, 1). Malthus predicted famine and war if humans continued the population increase that even he in his day perceived. If he only knew.

Since Malthus's time, the human population has increased nearly sixfold (see Figure 13.8). Given the war, famine, and environmental degradation we see around us, we have every reason to believe that Malthus was right and that with our current 1.5-percent-per-year population increase, we will eventually run out of something—food, water, land, clean air, patience with one another—and our species and its world will be in for some very bad times indeed. The human species has even been likened to a cancer—growing uncontrolled, spreading, and eventually destroying its environment (Hern 1993, who even compares photos of malignant brain cancers to diagrams of the spread of London from 1800 to 1955 and to aerial photos of American cities!).

It is tempting to those of us in the developed West to place the blame for rampant growth on the developing countries of Latin America, Africa, and Asia, where some total fertility rates (loosely, the average number of births per woman) have been as high as 8. We tend to see no evidence of a population problem here in the United States and comfortably see the Malthusian predictions as affecting *other* countries. If only *they* would change, the problem could be solved.

In fact, many *are* changing. In some undeveloped and developing nations, frequent birth was traditionally practiced in order to make up for high infant mortality and high mortality rates in general. But many developing countries are experiencing a fairly rapid decline in birth rates (Robey et al. 1993), and this is the result not of becoming more like the West but of having better education about and access to contraceptive technology. People in many of these countries realized the prob-

The second reason we are interested in life course data is that it may help explain how we evolved. An approach called **life history** collects such data and compares it within and between groups of organisms to try to draw some general rules about the life histories of living things and therefore explain their evolution. For example, humans have a shorter infancy (the period of dependency on the mother for survival, largely coincident with weaning) but a longer juvenile stage (the period between infancy and adulthood) than other mammals, even the other primates (Bogin and Smith 2000). Among other things, the length of the juvenile period is correlated with the degree of environmental variation (in climate, food, predators, disease, and so on) that a species experiences. A longer developmental period allows for more plasticity, that is, more experience with environmental variation and, thus, more behavioral flexilems inherent in overpopulation but lacked the means to address it. In Thailand, to give just one example, fertility rates dropped by 50 percent from 1975 to 1987 (1993, 61). On the other hand, some countries may find it hard to overcome years of rapid growth. The population has grown so rapidly across Africa that it will continue to increase, more than doubling by the year 2050—this in spite of the predicted millions of future deaths from the AIDS epidemic. (South Africa, which has lowered its fertility rate and has a high frequency of AIDS, is the exception and may experience a decrease in growth; Crossette 2001)

Further, it is rather arrogant to think that *we* are not part of the problem. We do live, as the cliché says, in a global village. All parts of the world are now interrelated in every way imaginable. Global ecological effects are well known. Politics and economics are no different. *Every* new human, no matter where he or she lives, will help use up world food, water, and energy resources and will contribute to the buildup of waste products. *Every* new human adds to the population density of the world and encourages the further spread of people, with its resultant alteration of environments (and also, as we have seen, possible contact with new pathogens).

Moreover, to think that there is no population problem in this country is simply incorrect. The United States is the most fertile of the developed nations, just above the replacement rate of 2.0 (two children to replace two parents), and by 2050 this country will be the only developed nation among the world's top twenty most populated (Crossette 2001). Although we might in theory be able to feed, clothe, and house all the people of the United States, the fact is we don't. Resources here are unevenly distributed, as they are in the rest of the world. Many of the children born in this most affluent of societies are unwanted. One survey concluded that of the 5.4 million pregnancies among American women in 1987, 57 percent were unintended (Cohen 1996).

To be sure, aspects of the population problem are still being debated. There are arguments as to how many people the planet could ideally support, as well as arguments as to how best to (or if it is even possible to) bring about those ideal conditions (see Smail 1999 for a good discussion of these issues). But, that there *is* a population problem is undeniable. And to think that it is not *everyone's* concern is complacent at best.

bility for coping with that variation when an adult. Perhaps this is connected with the need for "variability selection" (see Chapter 10) among the early hominids, a need that might also explain the early hominids' mix of arboreal and bipedal adaptations.

The shortened infancy period means that mothers may give birth more often since they don't nurse as long (lactation interrupts the fertility cycle). The relatively long juvenile stage means that children are not competing as much with adults for food resources. Young children still need food, of course, but it is often provided by members of the group other than the mother. Again, recall the hypothesized importance of social cohesion and cooperation in early hominid evolution. Clearly, recent and future research into life histories promises to shed a great deal of light on human evolution.

life history: The study of the timing of life cycle events such as fertility, growth, and death.

▽   ▽   ▽

SUMMARY

While a major focus of bioanthropology is on the evolutionary history of the hominids, the study of the current product of that evolution—modern *Homo sapiens*—is also important. We study living populations of our species from several different yet interrelated approaches.

If we know the genetic mechanism for a particular phenotypic trait, we can calculate the frequencies of the alleles of the gene involved and then see what changes in allele frequency take place in populations over time. Since evolution is technically defined as change in allele frequency, this allows us to see if evolution is in operation for that phenotype and to try to determine what processes of evolution are involved. The use of the Hardy-Weinberg equilibrium lets us make this analysis even if we cannot examine a population at several different time periods.

Even if we don't know the genetic mechanism of a trait, we may still use that trait to study processes of evolution, provided it is under some genetic control. By statistically comparing populations, or groups within a population, for such a trait, we may estimate their genetic distances. In this way, we can hypothesize what sorts of evolutionary changes are taking place. Now, of course, we may compare individuals and populations at the most specific genetic level, the sequence of base pairs in the DNA. When we analyze such data, we see that the biology of demographic changes is intimately linked to cultural variables of the studied populations.

Since humans live in such a wide range of environmental circumstances, it stands to reason that human groups would have different adaptations to those environments. Most adaptations of our species are cultural, but we still exhibit a number of variable traits based on genetic polymorphisms. There is evidence that our variation in these traits is the result of natural selection at some point in our evolution to climatic and other environmental variables.

Among the environmental factors to which humans respond evolutionarily are diseases. Many diseases are caused by or carried by other species, so evolutionary theory may be applied to our understanding of their epidemiology. Viewed from this perspective, we may see some general trends in the relationship between our species and other disease-causing species, in the past and in the present.

Finally, we understand that we need to study not only adult members of our species but also the growth and development of immature members, who are in the process of becoming adults. The timing of certain changes and the pace at which they occur are part of our species' characteristics. Understanding how these changes and rates of change differ from those of other species is beginning to shed more light on the nature and course of our evolution.

QUESTIONS FOR FURTHER THOUGHT

1. We mentioned in the text that the shape of age-sex pyramids will change over this century, becoming top-heavy as birth rates and death rates continue to drop in developed nations. In this country, for example, members of the "baby boom" generation (those born between 1946 and 1964, a total of 76 million) are now in or reaching middle age and will soon greatly increase the rolls of the elderly. What effects will this have on social and economic factors in the United States? What measures might we take to adjust to this change? Will the effects be different in other nations undergoing similar changes?

2. The AIDS epidemic (with over 21 million deaths so far) could be compared to the Black Death of the fourteenth century (with an estimated 25 million deaths). How do the two epidemics compare? In what ways are they similar? In what ways are they different? Do the effects of the plague of fourteenth-century Europe give us any indication of how the HIV/AIDS epidemic might affect Africa or other regions where its frequency is now on the rise? What sorts of steps should we take to deal with this modern "plague" in this country? in other nations? (To find out what life was like during the Black Death, read Chapter 5 of Barbara W. Tuchman's marvelous book, *A Distant Mirror*.)

3. The population crisis is a controversial topic. Do you think, as do some, that overpopulation is a key problem in the world today, precipitating many other major problems? Or do you think that the world can sustain the current population and the even larger population that will surely inhabit the world in the future? If the latter, how will we deal with such numbers of people in terms of food and water, space, pollution, and intercultural conflict?

KEY TERMS

Hardy-Weinberg
  equilibrium

single nucleotide
  polymorphism
  (SNP)

dermatoglyphics

demography

polymorphisms

melanocytes

melanin

antigens

antibodies

epidemiological

distance curve

velocity curve

menarche

menopause

life history

SUGGESTED READINGS

This chapter merely skimmed the surface of the study of population genetics. For a more detailed treatment, with specific reference to humans, see *Human Variation and Human Microevolution*, by Jane Underwood. For some classic examples of human population studies, try *The Structure of Human Populations*, edited by G. A. Harrison and A. J. Boyce.

If you would like to know more about dermatoglyphics, the standard work is *Finger Prints, Palms, and Soles*, by Harold Cummins and Charles Midlo.

Again, for details on human genome research and its applications, see the February 2001 issues of *Nature* and of *Science*. Particularly relevant to this chapter is the article in *Nature* by Mark Stoneking, "From the Evolutionary Past. . . ."

A very useful and well-done new book is *Human Biology: An Evolutionary and Biocultural Perspective*, edited by Sara Stinson, Barry Bogin, Rebecca Huss-Ashmore, and Dennis O'Rourke. It covers in detail many of the topics of this chapter: genetics, adaptation, disease, nutrition, the life cycle, and demography and population. I highly recommend it.

On the topic of the emerging diseases, see Frank Ryan's *Virus X: Tracking the New Killer Plagues* for a general treatment, Jaap Goudsmit's *Viral Sex: The Nature of AIDS* for a discussion on AIDS, and Richard Rhodes's *Deadly Feasts* for more on prion protein diseases. The perspective of Darwinian medicine is described by Lori Oliwenstein in "Dr. Darwin" in the October 1995 issue of *Discover*.

For information on world population, check out the United States Census Bureau's website, www.census.gov. It has all the latest statistics and some population clocks that show the world population as it increases. Very scary. For more on the nature of the population crisis and some proposals for addressing it, see the roundtable discussion, "World Population Policy," in the September 1997 issue of *Politics and Life Sciences*.

CHAPTER

14

HUMAN
BIOLOGICAL
DIVERSITY

In the previous chapter we discussed some human variable traits. The distribution of some traits, like skin color, points fairly clearly to an explanation involving natural selection to varying environmental conditions. Other traits, like blood type, are distributed in such a way as to make them seem adaptively neutral or at least with an adaptive significance that is complex and not immediately obvious.

If our interest in phenotypic variation among modern humans was limited to describing and explaining the distribution of variable traits, we would still have a challenging task. But our biological variation has further meaning to us. Some of our variable traits—whether they have adaptive significance or not—are distributed with some geographic regularity, enough so that one can very often tell from what part of the world a person comes.

People look European or Asian or African or Native American. But we can often be more specific: People from Japan don't on average look like people from China. Swedes don't look like Italians. Masai from East Africa don't look like the Khoisan from the Kalahari. Inuit don't look like Maya.

Look at Figure 14.1. The photographer in the center and his highland New Guinea subjects—though all are demonstrably members of the same species, *Homo sapiens*—are about as different looking as humans could be. Even if you had not been told where these people were from, even without the cultural cues of clothing and other artifacts, you could still probably venture a good guess as to their geographic origin. We seem to have evidence, in other words, that our species is divided into some number of fairly distinct subgroups. The term usually applied to such groups is *race*. It seems, on the surface, a logical assumption. Indeed, throughout much of its history, anthropology has focused on discovering just how many human races there are and on listing their identifying characteristics.

However—as noted in Chapter 12—races, on a biological level, don't exist within the human species. Races *are* real, but they are *cultural* categories. Every culture responds to and interprets objective reality—in this case human biological and cultural diversity—and creates subjective categories that have meaning to its members. A good example of this process, and a somewhat more clear-cut one, is the way in which different cultures interpret the biological categories of sex into the cultural categories of gender.

These ideas require more detailed examination, and such an examination is, perhaps, one of the more important contributions of biological anthropology. Let's look at the following questions:

How are the two human sexes interpreted differently by different cultures, and how can we use this as a model for examining "racial" variation?

FIGURE 14.1
A European American photographer who is 6 feet 2 inches tall stands among a group of Yali people from the highlands of Irian Jaya (the western half of New Guinea). There is little doubt as to who is who—or that members of our species can display a striking degree of phenotypic variation. The major question then becomes Does this degree of variation mean that there are distinguishable human races?

Is race a valid biological concept?

What is the scientific evidence for our statement that there are no biological human races?

What, then, *are* human races?

How can bioanthropology contribute to understanding some of the problems that the idea of race has presented?

SEX AND GENDER

Most human beings are unambiguously either biologically male or female. As noted in Chapter 9, with regard to skeletal features, we exhibit sexual dimorphism—varying phenotypic traits that distinguish the two sexes. In living humans there are more clearly dimorphic traits—hair distribution, for example. Other differences exist as well.

Human males, on average, are larger and more heavily muscled than females. They have relatively larger hearts and lungs, a faster recovery time from muscle fatigue, higher blood pressure, and greater oxygen-carrying capacity. Males are more susceptible than females to disease and death at all stages of life. During the first year of life, one-third more males die, mostly from infectious disease. Males are also more likely to have speech disorders, vision and hearing problems, ulcers, and skin disorders.

Females have a greater proportion of body fat than do males. They mature faster at almost all stages of life, most notably exhibiting earlier puberty and the adolescent growth spurt. They are less likely than males to be thrown off their normal growth curve (see Figure 13.16) by disease or other factors and, if they are, will recover more quickly than males. Although females appear to have a greater tendency than males to become obese, males suffer more from the effects of too much weight—strokes, for example. Females seem to be more sensitive to touch and pain and perhaps to higher sound frequencies, and they are said to be better at locating the sources of sounds. Smell sensitivity is about the same in both sexes, but females seem better at identifying smells. (For more detail, see Barfield 1976.)

These dimorphic features are not completely understood, and there is a good deal of overlap in the range of variation of these traits—for example, there are some females who are more heavily muscled than some males. But the preceding tendencies do suggest an adaptive explanation. Many of the characteristics of the human male are aimed at sustained, stressful physical action at the expense, however, of overall health. Females' overall better health, earlier maturity, and greater sensitivity to stimulation of the senses might be geared toward their reproductive and child-rearing roles. Perhaps some basic themes of primate dimorphism (we find these size and strength differences in apes as well) were retained and some others selected for in our early ancestors as their small, cooperative bands (described in Chapter 10) confronted the challenges of life in the changing environments of Africa.

Although there is some individual and regional variation in the degree and nature of our sexually dimorphic traits, in general we rarely have any difficulty telling the **sex** of another human being. Male and female are two biological categories that are objectively real and are common to all human groups.

The biological differences between male and female begin at the genetic level. Two of the human chromosomes are sex chromosomes, X and

FIGURE 14.2
The evolved sexual identities and roles common to all members of the human species are translated by individual cultural systems into gender identities and roles.

Y. Females have two X chromosomes; males have an X and a Y. Although the Y chromosome is smaller than the X and carries far fewer genes (several dozen compared to the X's 2,000 to 3,000), it carries a single gene that determines maleness. This gene codes for a protein that triggers the formation of the testes by activating genes on other chromosomes. Products of the testes, including testosterone, then make the developing embryo a male. Some interesting recent research indicates that the X and Y chromosomes were once a pair—like the other 22 pairs of human chromosomes (see Figure 3.6)—that diverged an estimated 300 million years ago through various processes of mutation to take on different versions of their original biological roles (see Jegalian and Lahn 2001 for more detail about the evolution of and relationship between these chromosomes).

As these two real categories of sex—male and female—are incorporated into various cultural systems, however, differences arise. The identity, place, and role of males and females under different cultural systems vary depending upon the nature of those systems—their economies, politics, family organizations, and abstract beliefs. Thus, *males* and *females* of the human species become the *men* and *women* of a particular society practicing a particular culture. We refer to the cultural interpretation of biological sex categories as **gender** (Figure 14.2).

From cultural anthropology we acquire data about the incredible range of variation in gender identity and gender roles among the world's cultures. The variable factors include the roles of genders in economic activities, differences in political and other decision-making power and influence, and expected norms of behavior. All these may change over time within a single culture.

For example, in the United States only a century ago, men were educated because they were seen as the gender that properly had political,

sex: The biological categories and characteristics of males and females.

gender: The cultural categories and characteristics of men and women.

economic, and social power. Women were far less likely to receive a college education, seldom held any sort of management position (if they did any work outside the home at all), and until 1920 were not even allowed to vote. Women were sometimes thought of as "the weaker sex." Obviously, things are different now, at least to a degree. As our culture has changed over the past hundred years, our gender roles and identities have changed to fit our evolving cultural system.

We refer to culturally defined categories as **folk taxonomies,** or cultural classifications. A society of people orders its world in ways that reflect objective reality, as its people see and understand that reality, and that also meet its particular cultural needs and fit the totality of its cultural system.

To take an example from a different area, our society has a scientific viewpoint about the causes of disease. We understand that diseases are the results of natural processes, and one way we classify them is by the nature of their cause. Diseases are genetic, bacterial, viral, parasitic, environmental (drugs, radiation, pollutants), nutritional, congenital (where the development of the embryo is disrupted), emotional, and so on. The Fore, a farming people of Papua New Guinea (Lindenbaum 1979), also classify disease by cause, but the causes are very different. The Fore believe that all disease is the result of the malicious intent of either sorcerers or spirits. Life-threatening diseases are thought to be caused by sorcery—the malevolent action of one person against another. This reflects the political and economic tensions, rivalries, and jealousies that have become prevalent parts of Fore lives. Less severe diseases are caused by nature spirits inhabiting important places or by the ghosts of the recently deceased. These diseases are punishments for violating important norms with regard to nature or the dead. Minor illnesses are attributed to a person's having violated some social rule among the living. The Fore folk taxonomy for disease, though it differs a great deal from our own, makes perfect sense within the context of the Fore cultural system.

Similarly, folk taxonomies for gender differ to a great degree among the cultures of the world, even though we are all dealing basically with two sexes and two gender categories. We need to note, however, that biological sex is not always unambiguous. There are people born with underdeveloped sexual characteristics, sometimes as a result of having too many or too few of the sex chromosomes. For example, about 1 in every 3,000 female births has a missing or defective X chromosome, and 1 in 500 male births has one or more extra X chromosomes. An estimated 2 percent of humans are *intersexes*, born with characteristics (including genitalia) of both sexes (Fausto-Sterling 2000.)

folk taxonomies: Cultural categories for important items and ideas.

In addition, there are those who are ambivalent toward their own sexual identity. As a result, some cultures recognize more than two genders. A striking example is the *hijras* of India (Nanda 1990). The word means "not men," and, indeed, *hijras* are men who have been voluntarily surgically emasculated. They make up a third gender, and they have very specific identities and roles within the culture of Hindu India. Although often mocked and ridiculed because of their exaggerated feminine expressions and gestures, they are also in demand as performers at important rituals such as marriages and births (Figure 14.3).

A less extreme example comes from a number of traditional Native American cultures in which some men dressed as women and assumed the occupations and behaviors of women. Such men have been referred to by the term *berdache* (a French term with derogatory implications but still in common use). In some cases, they engaged in sexual relations with other men, and certain rituals could be performed only by them. Within their respective cultures, *berdaches* were not considered abnormal but were thought of as another gender.

It appears, then, that various societies acknowledge that some of their members are, or think of themselves as, ambiguous with regard to the two standard sex categories. These societies have evolved third or even fourth gender classifications to accommodate them, and these classifications have developed defined places, identities, and roles within these societies' cultures. Sex is biological. Gender is a folk taxonomy; so, as we will see, is race in humans.

RACE AS A BIOLOGICAL CONCEPT

The processes of evolution ensure that each species of living thing possesses genetic variation and displays some degree of phenotypic variation. Some species are more variable than others, depending upon the nature of the species' geographic distribution and the variety of specific environments to which its members are adapted.

As noted in Chapter 5, some species are said to be *specialized*. They inhabit a relatively small geographic area or are adapted to a highly specific set of ecological circumstances—a narrow niche. Such species, of course, tend to be relatively homogeneous genetically and phenotypically. Natural selection has selected for essentially the same characteristics in all members of specialized species. A classic example is the koala, which lives only in Australia and eats primarily the leaves of the eucalyp-

FIGURE 14.3
Hijras, emasculated men who dress and behave like women, make up a third gender category in India. These *hijras* are blessing a child, one of the important ritual functions they perform.

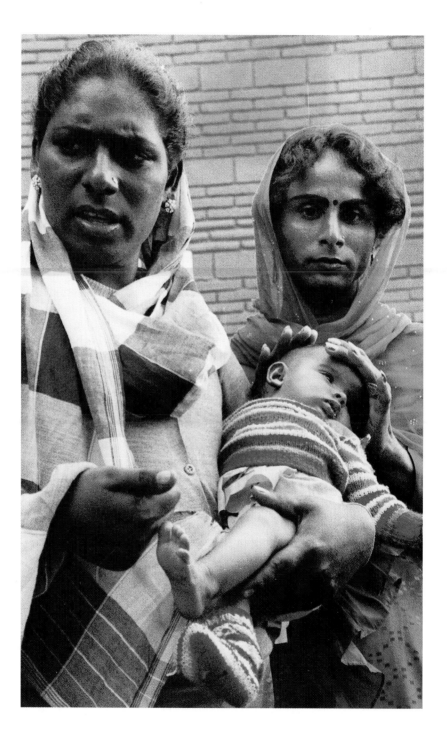

tus tree. We would not expect koalas to show a whole lot of variation, and, relatively speaking, they don't.

A species that inhabits a wide geographic range and is adapted to many niches is said to be *generalized*. Selection will promote variations in the species' basic traits in response to the environments found in different parts of its range. Such species tend to be more variable.

To remain a single species, of course, all males and females of the group must be potentially capable of interbreeding. Furthermore, there must be sufficient gene flow to prevent one or more groups from becoming completely isolated. Gene flow, however, is not always even. Members of a species may be clustered into breeding populations, or demes (see Chapter 4). More genes are exchanged within demes than between different demes, often because some geographic barrier prevents extensive gene flow or because the environments to which the species are adapted come in clusters themselves with gaps between them that limit steady genetic exchange (see Figure 4.5).

Demes may be thought of as an important stage in many cases of speciation. If a deme becomes so isolated that virtually no genes are exchanged with another deme, if its environment is different enough to cause selection for a distinct set of traits, and if enough time elapses, the deme may eventually become a separate species, unable to interbreed with what were formerly other demes of the same species.

If, however, isolation is not complete or the preceding conditions have not been in operation for a long enough time, the demes may represent phenotypically distinguishable regional populations within the same species. Such a species is said to be **polytypic** ("many types"), and such demes may be referred to as **subspecies** or **races.**

For example, the reindeer of Europe and Asia and the caribou of North America are classified as a single species, *Rangifer tarandus* (Figure 14.4). Now isolated from one another in separate hemispheres, the reindeer and caribou were no doubt able to interbreed when Alaska and Siberia were joined during the Pleistocene, connecting the Old and New Worlds. Reindeer and caribou, then, have been separated for only 10,000 years, generally not enough time for speciation to have occurred in a large mammal. Enough time has elapsed, however, for the two populations to become physically distinguishable. They might legitimately be considered subspecies or races of a single species.

The North American population of this species has been further classified into at least four subspecies, the result of their distribution in different environments of Alaska, Canada, and Greenland. These subspecies, some woodland and some tundra dwellers, are distinguishable by such

polytypic: A species with physically distinguishable regional populations.

subspecies: Physically distinguishable populations within a species.

races: In biology, the same as subspecies. In culture, cultural categories to classify and account for human physical diversity.

FIGURE 14.4

The Caribou, *Rangifer tarandus*. This woodland caribou of Alaska and Canada is sometimes classified as subspecies *Rangifer tarandus caribou*. Well adapted to a wide range of environments, the caribou has such traits as hollow outer guard hairs that give it extra bouyancy for swimming and extra insulation for warmth. This feature makes caribou hides a favorite material among the Inuit for making parkas.

features as size, antler shape, and coat color (Figure 14.5). There are, then, five named subspecies or races of *Rangifer tarandus*, at least one in the Old World and four in the New World.

The utility of the race/subspecies concept, however, has been questioned. The identification and naming of subspecific groups is rather arbitrary. Zoologists Paul Ehrlich and Richard Holm (in Montagu 1964) have noted two problems with the idea. First, we need to decide *what* phenotypic traits we should choose in defining racial groups within a species. Are all traits equally useful, or are some more useful than others? If so, which ones?

Second, we need to decide *how much* difference in phenotypic characteristics should be recognized as amounting to subspecific difference.

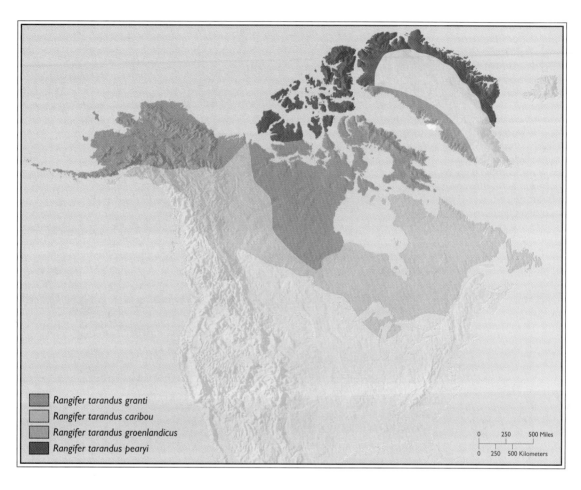

Rangifer tarandus granti
Rangifer tarandus caribou
Rangifer tarandus groenlandicus
Rangifer tarandus pearyi

0   250   500 Miles

0   250   500 Kilometers

FIGURE 14.5

North American populations of caribou are considered by some to represent subspecies or races.

Should there be a certain number of traits? a particular degree of difference in the measurements of certain traits?

One might well be justified in calling the caribou and reindeer subspecies, but their complete isolation in separate hemispheres for the past 10,000 years might mean they are on the way to becoming separate species. This state is better acknowledged with the use of the term **semispecies**—populations at an intermediate state between being a single interbreeding group and being different species (Mettler et al. 1988). They still *can* interbreed (it has been done artificially), but they *don't*.

The four North American subspecies pose a different problem. Since all the populations are members of a single species that maintains its species identity through the flow of genes among those populations, these subspecies distinctions are rather artificial. In reality, the dividing lines

semispecies: Populations of a species that are completely isolated from one another but have not yet become truly different species.

FIGURE 14.6
Distribution of Size Variation in Male House Sparrows, (determined by sixteen skeletal measurements). The larger the number, the larger the sparrow. The classes, however, are arbitrary. If a line is drawn from Atlanta to St. Paul or from St. Paul to San Francisco, the size variation in the sparrows is distributed as a cline. (Notice also that the birds tend to be larger in the north, another example of a trait adaptation to the cold; see Chapter 13.)

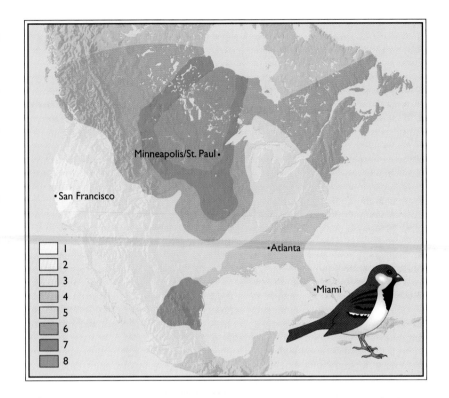

on the map in Figure 14.5 don't exist. The caribou at the extremes of the ranges may look quite different, but one doesn't step over one of these geographic lines and find the caribou suddenly looking completely different. Rather, their variable traits grade into one another over geographic space. This gradual variation is known as a **cline**, a continuum of change from one area to another, as opposed to a sudden and distinct change (Figure 14.6)

Recent books on evolutionary biology, in fact, indicate that the concept of race or subspecies is generally falling into disfavor. In Mark Ridley's *Evolution* (1996), for example, neither term appears in the index or glossary, nor is either used formally in the discussions of species variation or formation. In *Population Genetics and Evolution*, by Lawrence Mettler and colleagues (1988), the term *race* is said to be "a subjective convenience," and the authors favor, as just noted, the recognition of only semispecies as important and definable groups within species. Now, with this general biological background in mind, we can address the question of human races.

WHY ARE THERE NO BIOLOGICAL RACES WITHIN THE HUMAN SPECIES?

It is all too easy to agree that there are no human biological races because we don't *want* them to exist. The nonexistence of definable racial groups coincides with and reinforces our ethical ideas of human equality. But wishful thinking cannot take the place of scientific rigor. We must be able to say *why* there are no races. It's not enough to be sure it's the case or to assume it is because it makes us feel good. We need to present sound scientific evidence for it.

This evidence comes from three intersecting, interrelated areas. As we discuss them, we need to be as objective as possible, to try not to argue toward a predetermined conclusion. In the end, this will make our affirmation of the nonexistence of races all the more meaningful.

Human Phenotypic Variation

Given the perceived wide range of human phenotypic variation (see again Figure 14.1), could it be that, like the caribou and reindeer, at least some of our populations were isolated enough and have become distinct enough to warrant semispecies status? What do our variable traits indicate?

To address this question, we need to go back to Figures 13.11 and 13.12. Although skin color varies by latitude and ranges from very dark to very light, in no way does this variation assort itself into distinct geographical groups. My categories (*lightest, medium light*, and so on) are arbitrary, as are my geographical dividing lines. I could have demonstrated the relationship between skin color and latitude with any number of different schemes, with actual numbers for color (we can measure skin color quantitatively) and more categories, which would have required more geographical boundaries. Human skin color variation, like size variation in the sparrow (see Figure 14.6), is distributed as a cline—gradually going from dark to light or light to dark across geographical space—and is not limited to any one traditional racial population. Dark skin, for example, usually conceptually associated with Africa, is an equatorial trait that is also found almost halfway around the world in New Guinea. Clearly, skin color is of no use in defining subgroups within the human species that have any biological meaning.

Skin color, of course, doesn't come in nice, neat categories. It is said to be a continuous trait. So how about traits that do come in discrete,

cline: A geographic continuum in the variation of a particular trait.

FIGURE 14.7
Diagram of Discordant Variation. Each layer represents the geographic variation in one variable trait. Each "core," or cylinder, represents a sample of individuals from a particular area. Notice that each core is different and that any other four cores are very likely to be different as well. The expression of one trait does not predict a particular expression of another. There are no natural racial divisions based on specific combinations of traits.

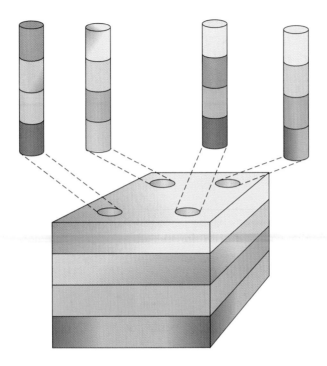

either/or categories? Maybe these would better describe discrete biological populations. Blood type is a good example, since, as discussed in Chapter 13, everyone on earth falls into one of four groups for the ABO system. There are no intermediates.

But look at Figure 13.12. Again, the percentage categories on the maps are arbitrary. I could have divided them into more groups or fewer. Each category is a range and, thus, a generalization. For instance, across Africa, type A is shown to appear in 1 to 20 percent of the population in some areas and 21 to 49 percent of the population in other areas. With more detail, in fact, we would see the distribution of blood group frequencies as clinal, just as we did with skin color. And notice that the distribution of type A is very different from that of type B. In other words, blood group frequencies are of no more use than is skin color in pointing out and defining discrete subspecific human groups.

No matter what phenotypic trait one uses, the human species simply cannot be divided into distinct subgroups based on biological differences. Nor will such a division show up if we use combinations of traits, because the distributions of traits are discordant—that is, a particular expression of one trait does not necessarily predict a particular expression of another (Figure 14.7). The nature and distribution of human variable traits, then, is like that of other species—varying as clines with no clear-cut boundaries. Clearly defined biological groups below the species level are not scientifically supported for *Homo sapiens* by these data.

Genetic Variation

Phenotypic features, as we pointed out in Chapter 4, can be deceptive, influenced as they are by multiple genes, environmental factors, and natural selection (see Figure 2.6). For the past several decades, we have had the ability to look at aspects of the genetic code itself. Some have thought that perhaps this type of research could provide better data for determining the identity of subspecific groups of *Homo sapiens*.

From the beginning, however, it was clear that, if anything, genetic data did more to refute the concept of biological race than did phenotypic data. When scientists genetically compared samples from traditional racial groups, they determined that the groupings accounted for only a small percentage of genetic diversity; in other words, there was actually little genetic difference among the groups (see Brown and Armelagos 2001 for a review of these studies.) Most diversity in genes (80 percent or more in most studies, depending on the genetic system used) was found between individuals, even individuals of the same "racial" affiliation.

This means that diversity on the genetic level is not clustered into any definable subspecies divisions but is, rather, fairly evenly distributed. As an expression of this conclusion, population geneticist Richard Lewontin (1982, 123) calculated that if some great cataclysm left only Africans alive, the remaining members of the human species would still retain 93 percent of the variable genes of the former species, although, of course, some of the variations would be found in different frequencies from the previous average (a higher frequency for alleles that increase melanin production, for example).

As previously mentioned, new technologies allow us access to the most specific genetic data (the sequence of base pairs in the human genome), and we are quickly gathering data about the extent of diversity at that level—the single nucleotide polymorphisms (SNPs), which account for most human genetic variation and some of which account for our phenotypic differences. What do these tell us? When comparing any two humans, it looks as if only, at most, about 3 million of our 3 billion nucleotides are SNPs (Stoneking 2001). In other words, any two humans differ genetically by less than one-tenth of one percent (0.1 percent). Moreover, most of those SNPs are in noncoding regions. Only an estimated 60,000 are in actual coding genes (International SNP Map

Working Group 2001). All the phenotypic variation that we try to assort into race is the result of a virtual handful of alleles.

Finally, the nature of the genetic variation that influences phenotype is such that variation may well show a geographic pattern due to the processes of evolution. We see this in skin color, blood type, and other physical features that are characteristic of certain areas. But these patterns are no indication of the distribution of variation in other parts of the genome. Thus, two people from the same part of the world who look alike superficially may actually be less genetically similar than either is to people from different parts of the world who look distinctly different (Pääbo 2001.) The genetic data also indicate that no discrete biological subspecific groups exist within modern humans.

This does not mean, however, that we cannot learn about the history of our species from our genetic diversity. We have already discussed the application of genetic studies to the question of modern human origins (see Chapter 12). Similarly, we can find patterns of differences at the most detailed genetic levels that may help us trace the relationships and genetic histories of human populations (Figure 14.8). As more SNPs and other variations are identified, these studies should become more precise. These studies can also be combined with archaeological and linguistic research to try to trace the migrations of groups across geographical space. The settling of the islands of the Pacific, for example, is now the subject of research that focuses on similarities and differences in artifacts (like pottery), features of languages, and the distribution of genetic markers—unique features characteristic of certain populations (Gibbons 2001b).

Evolutionary Theory

Let's look at the question from a more general perspective. Given the nature of our species and what we know of the workings of evolution, we could ask whether groups distinct enough to be semispecies (the only group below the species level that has scientific support) *could* exist within *Homo sapiens*. After all, semispecies have developed over 10,000 years in *Rangifer tarandus* (reindeer and caribou), and even by the most conservative estimates, our species is ten times as old. Moreover, we are a populous species; we live in a vast variety of environmental conditions, sometimes in fairly isolated regions; and we further isolate our populations through cultural boundaries. These characteristics would seem to be the perfect circumstances for creating definable groups.

However, one noteworthy feature of our species for its entire biological history has been mobility. We evolved first in Africa—whether that

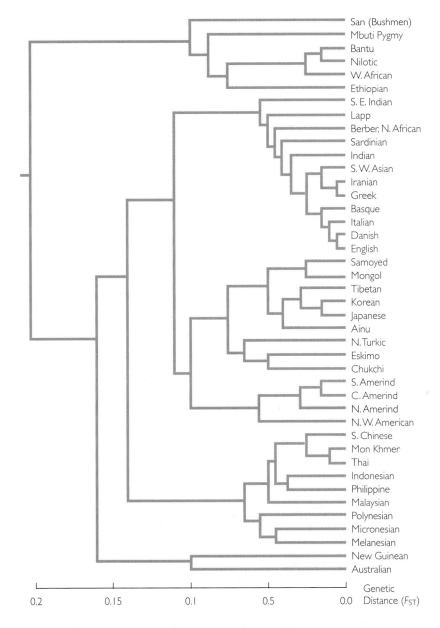

FIGURE 14.8

Genetic Family Tree for Forty-Two Populations. This tree is based on a statistical comparison of variation within forty-two genetic systems with a total of 120 alleles (Cavalli-Sforza et al. 1994, 78). This is clearly a rough approximation, as it is based on a limited genetic sample; eventually, studies using SNPs and other unique genetic variants should prove more detailed and accurate.

was 2 million or 200,000 years ago (see Chapter 12)—and then spread with amazing speed all over the Old World, despite mountains, water, and other barriers. And when we reached the far corners of Africa and Eurasia, we did not stay put. We continued to move around in search of resources and space. As we evolved, we acquired increasing ability to move around (with the domestication of the horse and with inventions like boats and navigation instruments), and we found increasing motivation for doing so. Such mobility leads to extensive gene flow, and it's fair to say we tend to exchange genes at nearly every opportunity.

But what about our cultural rules of endogamy? Don't they genetically isolate populations at certain times? To answer these questions, recall the Hutterites, who have been largely endogamous for 470 years. The Hutterites' nearly half a millennium history is not all that long in evolutionary terms; not much genetic variation can arise over such a short period, especially in a species such as our own with a long generation time. Moreover, cultural rules change, and the political, ethnic, and religious populations they define change over time. Also, rules of endogamy are not always fully upheld. As such, biological isolation through the cultural institution of endogamy is a temporary condition.

Gene flow, then, is the norm for our species, and as widespread as we are, we still manage to exchange enough genes—through intermediary populations—to prevent any group of humans from being isolated long enough to evolve the differences sufficient for semispecies status.

Finally, what about all the different environments our species inhabits? Couldn't natural selection have led to differentiation of some populations? Certainly, the variation and distribution of some of our traits—skin color, for example—can be attributed to natural selection. But our major adaptive mechanism is culture, with its values, social systems, and, especially, its technologies that, to a great extent, have increasingly buffered us against the constant editing of natural selection. Adaptively, we change less biologically than we do culturally. Culture and the big brains that make culture possible are species characteristics, shared by all humans. They are the basis of our modern identity. Culture, in a sense, *is* our environment, and we may say that, for some time, our species has experienced little of the kind of environmental variation that would lead to the development of distinct, isolated subpopulations. As anthropologist C. Loring Brace puts it, we all have undergone the "same selective pressures" leading to essentially the "same lifeway," (personal communication).

If this reasoning sounds familiar, that's because it is much the same argument proposed by supporters of the Multiregional Evolution model for why genus *Homo* did not branch into multiple species. If an organism with our characteristic network of genetic (and cultural) exchange has not divided into definable *subspecific* groups, how likely is it to have split into different related *species*? Thus, aside from what we *want* to think about human biological diversity, sound scientific evidence and reasoning make it clear that there is no basis for the recognition of biologically meaningful groups within the species *Homo sapiens*. Human *variation* exists, to be sure, and some of it shows patterns of geographic distribution. But human *races*—in a biological sense—do not exist.

WHAT, THEN, *ARE* HUMAN RACES?

Like gender categories, human races are folk taxonomies. Several years ago I gave one of my classes a weekend assignment to pose two questions to ten people, preferably from different backgrounds and of different ages and both sexes: How many races are there? What are they?

Nearly all the responses were versions of a familiar set of categories: "white," "black," and "yellow"; or "Caucasian," "Negro," and "Oriental"; or some other terms that varied by individual. The similarity of most responses is an indication that some basic taxonomy is shared among members of our culture.

However, there was some interesting variation in the responses as well. One respondent said there were three races: "black," "white," and "Polish." Jews were considered a race by some, as were Hispanics. A few people added Native Americans and native Australians to the usual three. This showed that, despite the similarities, there was no universally agreed-upon classification, as there would be for some scientific fact like the speed of light. Specific responses, though variations on a theme, were as different as the individual backgrounds of the respondents.

Cultures classify other people relative to themselves. Isolated societies with some knowledge that others exist will have a very simple racial classification: us and them. Among more mobile or cosmopolitan groups, as the relations among people become more varied, the classifications become more complex. These classifications reflect a knowledge about other groups' cultural practices, their relations with our group, and their physical appearance. Thus, a racial taxonomy also carries implications about a society's attitude toward others. In short, race—which differs from society to society—is a folk taxonomy used by a particular society at a particular time for particular culturally based reasons.

The categories of race that we in North America recognize are no exception. The categories' origins can be traced to European knowledge and attitudes first acquired during the Age of Exploration. European explorers, using mostly water transportation, could observe only a limited range and distribution of human variation. They sampled points along the continuum of human variation. Because points along a continuum can differ greatly from one another, depending upon how far apart they are, it appeared to

FIGURE 14.9

Columbus's First Contact with Natives of the New World. To the Europeans, the Indians were so strikingly different in physical and cultural features that it was natural to consider them as a distinct category of human. Notice the men planting the cross to claim the land as theirs.

(From a seventeenth-century Spanish version of a 1594 engraving by de Bry. The Granger Collection.)

these explorers that human variation fell into a number of relatively discrete categories (Figure 14.9, and see again Figure 14.1).

In addition, the peoples contacted were not seen as simply different human beings; instead, they were compared to and ranked against European peoples, usually unfavorably. They had, after all, a different appearance, different cultures, often less complex technologies, and—this was important to the Europeans—non-Judeo-Christian beliefs. Furthermore, the motivation for the explorers' voyages was less to acquire knowledge than to find new territories, sources of labor, spices, and gold. An attitude of dominance was built in to the Europeans' relationships with these new peoples. Witness the way Europeans would claim new lands "in the name of the crown," entirely ignoring the fact that there were already people to whom the lands belonged. Obviously, it was thought, the indigenous people were too primitive to really have laws of ownership.

The racial folk taxonomy that resulted from these cultural events was formalized, and thus made more real, by Linnaeus. In the final edition of his taxonomy in 1758, he included *Homo sapiens* and divided the species into "varieties," or races. Actually, he recognized a second species, *Homo monstrosus*, to accommodate explorers' yarns of wild "half-men" covered with hair and sporting tails, and a variety of *Homo sapiens* he called *ferus* ("wild man") for the probably retarded and abandoned children who were sometimes found wandering in the woods and were said to have been raised by wolves and other animals. His main races were American, European, Asiatic, and African, and his descriptions of these races were a blend of biological generalizations and, as Stephen Molnar says "personality profiles" based on European perspectives (1992, 10). Here is Linnaeus's taxonomy for humans (based on translations in Gould 1996b and Kennedy 1976)

Class: Mammalia
  Order: Primates
    Genus: *Homo*

Species: *monstrosus*	Varying by climate or art
sapiens	Diurnal; varying by education and situation
Varieties:	
ferus	Four-footed, mute, hairy
americanus	Red, choleric [angry], upright. Hair black, straight, thick; nostrils wide; face harsh; beard scanty; obstinate, content free. Paints himself with fine red lines. Ruled by habit.
europeaus	White, sanguine [cheerful], muscular. Hair yellow, brown flowing; eyes blue; gentle, acute, inventive. Covered with cloth vestments. Ruled by custom [or law].
asiaticus	Pale-yellow, melancholy, stiff. Hair black; eyes dark; severe, haughty, covetous. Covered with loose garments. Ruled by belief [or opinions].
afer	Black, phlegmatic [sluggish], relaxed. Hair black, frizzled; skin silky; nose flat; lips tumid [swollen]; crafty, indolent, negligent. Anoints himself with grease. Ruled by caprice [impulse].

Because the history of the United States has been so influenced by European cultures, it makes sense that these basic categories and attitudes would be carried over to this country and altered by its subsequent history. For example, the reason we distinguish Hispanics from other European Americans is, in part, because of the conflicts between Spain and other European countries over territory in the New World and later between Mexico, a former Spanish colony, and the United States. Notice, too, that in some lists of race, Puerto Rican has been separated from Hispanic. It's not that some new group of people has arisen, but rather that, for certain purposes, we choose to distinguish people from that U.S. territory—people who previously and still in other lists are categorized as Hispanic.

Our racial categories are real. They may not reflect universal biological reality on the species level, but they do have meaning within our cultural system, for better or for worse.

RACE, BIOANTHROPOLOGY, AND SOCIAL ISSUES

The issue of race in the human species is not just a matter of whether to apply the biological concept of subspecies or semispecies. Would that it were. Rather, the idea of race can be, and is, used to make prejudgments about people and to determine their place in society, often without regard to their individual characteristics. This is **racism.** The moral dimension of this problem should be important to everyone, but it is not something we can or should deal with in a brief book about bioanthropology. We may, however, show how bioanthropology, through the use of science, can examine some claimed connections between racial categories and biological traits. In so doing, we can help make ourselves more informed about just what race is and what it is not.

Let's briefly look at one topic. If a group of people were interested in limiting the social position and power of another group, they could argue that the other group possessed some unalterable biological difference that inherently limited their abilities and therefore justified their lower social status. The practice of slavery in the United States was often justified by the claim that the African slaves were biologically less intelligent than the whites and therefore could never hope to attain the dominant race's social, political, and intellectual level. Claims like this have been quite common, even during the past century (Gould 1996b).

Such broad statements about race and intelligence, or even race and evolutionary level, are so clearly motivated by social and economic aims as to be at least questionable, if not obviously false. Perhaps more danger-ous, however, are the more subtle correlations whose propositions are based on scientific investigation. Ideas that sound scientific are often treated more seriously, especially because, even today, many people feel that science is something so complex and obscure that only a handful can really understand it. Many people take the position that if something sounds scientific and they don't get it, it must be valid.

Such is the case for the claimed connection between the American black and white races and IQ (intelligence quotient). The most famous (or infamous) example is educational psychologist Arthur Jensen's 1969 article in the *Harvard Educational Review* titled "How Much Can We Boost IQ and Scholastic Achievement?" The article is 123 pages long and quite scientific in its wording, logic, and methodology, and it in-cludes a lengthy mathematical formula or two. As a result, many people, both supporters and critics of Jensen's work, have never bothered to ac-tually read it. A more recent and perhaps better-known work, *The Bell Curve* by Richard Herrnstein and Charles Murray (1994), repeats and greatly expands the same essential argument (see Gould 1996b for a de-tailed critique).

A focus of Jensen's article was the documented fact that American black children score, on average, fifteen points lower on IQ tests than American white children. Jensen wondered why programs aimed at the obvious solution of culturally enriching children's lives had basically failed; some studies showed that the fifteen-point IQ difference remained. Hence, the title of his article (emphasis mine for the right intonation): "How Much *Can* We Boost IQ and Scholastic Achievement?"

Jensen embarked on a scientific investigation. His first conclusion was that IQ tests measure something called *g*, or general intelligence—a biological, inherited entity. This entity, *g*, has a **heritability** of .80 (80 percent). This means that 80 percent of the variation in intelligence within a population is explained by genetic differences. Only 20 percent is the result of environment—that is, having been brought up under dif-ferent cultural conditions. (It bears restating that heritability measures the amount of variation *within a group* that is due to genetic differences. It does not measure the amount of genetic control of a trait in an indi-vidual. It does not say that 80 percent of my intelligence is genetically determined.)

The obvious conclusion, then, is that the difference in intelligence between these two racial groups must be largely the result of some genetic difference, and, thus, all the cultural enrichment programs in the world can have only a limited effect. The answer to the question in Jensen's title is "Not much." He stated, "No one has yet produced any evidence

racism: Judging an indi-vidual based solely on his or her racial affiliation.

heritability: The amount of variation of a particular trait within a population that is caused by genetic differences.

based on a properly controlled study to show that representative samples of Negro and white children can be equalized in intellectual ability through statistical control of environment and education" (1969, 82–83).

Jensen went further, however. He compared scores from different parts of IQ tests and concluded that the different IQs of blacks and whites are the result of their having different kinds of intellectual abilities: Whites are better at problem solving and abstract reasoning, while the abilities of blacks are focused on memorization, rote learning, and trial-and-error experience. His ultimate conclusion was that education should be as individualized as possible, taking into account not only individual differences in ability and skill but these racially based differences as well.

As you can imagine, Jensen's article caused a great deal of controversy. He was labeled a racist, and, certainly, those with racist leanings embraced his work enthusiastically. I don't know what Jensen's social attitudes were, but we can look at his article from a scientific point of view, drawing especially on what we have learned from anthropology.

First, the idea that IQ tests measure some innate mental ability is fraught with problems. It has been said that IQ tests measure the ability to take IQ tests. This is not, as it sounds, just a sarcastic remark. IQ tests, in fact, measure particular knowledge and abilities that are largely learned through one's culture. IQ tests can be a valuable tool, however. They may, for example, point out some learning disability that could be biologically based. Moreover, because they measure the kinds of skills required by education in our culture as well as by many occupations, they do have predictive value as to one's success within those aspects of our cultural system.

But we don't even really know what intelligence is. How, then, can we apply a single number to such a complex and multifaceted concept through a test given in a cultural language, in a cultural setting, with cultural problems? When we do this, we commit the logical error called **reification**. With IQ scores we have reified intelligence—translated a complex idea into a single entity, in this case, a number, which we then use to classify people into groups such as different learning tracks in schools.

Let's put this another way. As anthropologist Jonathan Marks suggests, there is a difference between *ability* and *performance* (1995, 240 ff.). One's score on an IQ test is a score of one's performance. Certainly some internal factor—one's innate intellectual abilities, whatever those are—plays a part in one's performance on an IQ test. But that performance is also affected by all sorts of external factors. In test taking, for example, your cultural background, quality of education, personality, home life, even your mood on the day of the test can all affect your performance.

We cannot, therefore, infer innate abilities from the test score, any more than we can, say, infer a person's athletic abilities from their performance in one game. We cannot do so, in part, because there *are* so many external influences; and we have no way of accounting for them, controlling them, or even knowing what they are. More importantly, though, to make such an inference from IQ is to reify intelligence—to take the measurement of performance on a test and assume that it is also a measurement of an innate ability. As Marks puts it, "We can't measure ability; we can only measure performance" (1995, 241).

But what about the claimed heritability of IQ? This is a complicated issue (see Gould 1996b for the best discussion), but there is one major problem we can point out here. Heritability studies—estimating the genetic and environmental components of the phenotypic variation in a population—are done regularly, but these studies are done on organisms like fruit flies, whose genetic mechanisms for phenotypic traits are well known (and can even be manipulated) and whose environmental variables can be controlled in detail. Numbers may be placed on these genetic and environmental variables that may then be plugged into the heritability formula. This is the formula that Jensen reproduces in his article.

To apply the heritability formula to humans, however, is virtually impossible. What numbers can we place on the external environmental variables that affect us? How, in other words, can we reify culture? What number is applied to having a culturally enriched childhood? to being a member of a minority group? to having a poor early education?

Heritability has been *estimated* for humans based on twin studies. Because identical twins have no genetic variation between them, any phenotypic difference, including intelligence, must be the result of environmental differences. IQ scores of identical twins are generally very similar, even in twins raised separately, and this seems to indicate that environment has little effect on intelligence. We must remember, however, that IQ does not measure intelligence but rather one's performance on an exam. Therefore, IQ is measuring, to a great extent, the results of environmental influences in the first place and not just the results of genetic endowment. Even in twins raised apart, it may well be that their environments are similar enough to result in similar IQ scores. On those rare occasions when identical twins are separated shortly after birth, it is likely that they are raised in homes of similar socioeconomic level and so receive educations of similar quality. It cannot be denied that identical twins are probably similar in whatever those innate abilities are that we call intelligence, but studies based on the IQ scores of such twins reflect a whole lot more than those innate abilities.

reification: Translating a complex set of phenomena into a single entity such as a number.

Contemporary Reflections

Are There Racial Differences in Athletic Ability?

Nearly 80 percent of players in the National Basketball Association are African American. The figure is 70 percent for professional women's basketball. The National Football League is 65 percent black. In track and field, nearly every men's world record belongs to an African or someone of African descent. These statistics pose an obvious question, which we may address by focusing on a recent and controversial book by journalist and TV producer Jon Entine called *Taboo: Why Black Athletes Dominate Sports and Why We're Afraid to Talk About It*. This complex book nicely covers many aspects of the topic of sports and race. Entine wrote it, he says, because "sport remains a haven for some of our most virulent stereotypes" and because he believes "that open debate beats backroom scuttlebutt"(8). And open debate it does.

Our immediate explanation for the disproportionate representation of athletes of African descent in some sports is what might be called "social selection." This is the idea that, in this country and others, sports—particularly those not requiring specialized and often expensive equipment—became an outlet for members of minority groups, an achievable goal when access to numerous opportunities such as higher education and careers were limited by social prejudices, poor primary and secondary education, and lower socioeconomic status.

Entine points out that this, in fact, was the case with Jews and basketball in the first half of the twentieth century; basketball (as well as boxing) was a way out of the ghetto and ethnic prejudice. So stereotyped did the association between Jews and basketball become that one 1930s sportswriter made a semibiological connection, claiming that Jews were better at the game because of their "alert, scheming mind" and "flashy trickiness" (quoted in Entine 2000, 203).

But Entine also claims that there are biological explanations and that these are, in some cases, more influential. Specifically, he documents evidence that three regions of Africa—the west coast, North Africa, and East Africa—have populations with physical attributes more common to them than to other populations that make them innately better at sports involving endurance, sprinting, and jumping. These traits include such things as a lower percentage of body fat, a higher proportion of certain muscle fibers, and physiological features related to the efficiency of oxygen use. He says that the reason these traits—of obvious adaptive utility—are more common in Africa is that "while people of African descent have spent most of their evolutionary history near to where they originated, the rest of the world's populations have had to modify their African adaptations after migrating to far different regions and climates" (18).

The arguments in Entine's book and in reviews of it (Bogin 2001; DiPietro 2000; Malik 2000, for example) are complex and should be discussed and further examined, but for our purposes here we can address two issues. First, is it possible that there are variable human phenotypic traits, even

To further claim that two races have different kinds of intellectual abilities is to ignore the very nature of the modern human species. This claim says that there is a major degree of difference in the very abilities—to solve problems or to formulate abstractions and generalizations—that ones that might show patterns of geographic distribution, that might relate to athletic ability? Of course it is. How many heavyweight boxers could hail from the highlands of New Guinea (see Figure 14.1), where indigenous people are, on average, much smaller than the average European or African? Could the average Inuit compete successfully in a 400-meter sprint against someone built like the Masai in Figure 13.10? And there's no reason that physiological differences—for example, in muscle fiber or oxygen use—could not exist and also have an impact on athleticism. These are legitimate areas of research.

Second, a serious problem with Entine's overall argument—one that relates to a major theme of this chapter—is that he uses exceptional individuals to make generalizations not only about particular populations (many record-holding runners come from one region of Kenya, for instance) but about whole racial groups. He starts with the assumption that these groups exist and have some degree of time depth, definition, and internal homogeneity. He says, for example, that "although there is considerable disagreement, the *three major racial groupings—Caucasian, Mongoloid, Negroid*—split from 100,000 years ago to as recently as the beginning of the last ice age [emphasis mine]" (113); he even espouses a minority view that "different races [may not be] modifications of *Homo sapiens*, they were in existence before the emergence of *Homo sapiens*" (116). In other words, he assumes that the populations he is examining *are* races in the traditional, biological sense of that word. This, then, is the basis on which he attempts to explain the dominance of African Americans in some sports, namely as a result of their African heritage. According to Entine, Africans are on average innately better athletes for some skills and so a great number of African Americans have inherited these innate skills.

These are logical leaps with little if any validity. We understand that variation exists and some is geographically patterned. But clear-cut racial groups do not exist. While a small Kenyan population just might have some features that make them better runners (and this still needs, I think, to be seriously studied), that in no way means that those features are necessarily more common on the African continent, because this assumes that Africa is synonymous with a racial group. And it certainly doesn't explain the sports phenomenon in the United States. Among other problems with Entine's conclusions is the fact that the average African American can trace a fair percentage of his or her genes to Europe. This should mean that African Americans would be expected to be worse athletes than West Africans, but this is not the case (Malik 2000).

This is a complex issue. Obviously, *both* biological and sociocultural components contribute in different degrees to various aspects of sports. We should not be afraid to examine this issue. But doing so in terms of the demonstrably nonexistent biological races only serves to detract from an accurate understanding of the topic and might further reinforce those "virulent stereotypes" that Entine justly seeks to refute.

are a hallmark of our species' evolution. Certainly, we express individual variation in some of these abilities, and some of this variation may well be based on some sort of biological difference. I have no doubt that Beethoven and Einstein had some fundamental innate processes going on in their brains that I don't. But to think that natural selection would promote, in two different groups, profoundly different expressions of the major adaptive mechanism of a species makes little sense in light of what we know about the workings of adaptive evolution.

Finally, if you are looking to make biological comparisons between two groups, the groups need to be biologically defined. American whites and American blacks are decidedly not biological groups. We have already established that race is not a biological concept for the human species (or, perhaps, for any other species) in the first place. What variation does exist is distributed in such a way as to make distinct, discrete groups of *Homo sapiens* nonexistent. We perceive differences in these two groups—average skin color, major geographic area of origin, frequency of diseases like hypertension, and even frequency of some genes such as that for sickle cell anemia—but the groups themselves are cultural. There's simply not much genetic difference, certainly not on the level of genes for different intellectual abilities. Indeed, it has been estimated that about 15 percent of all genes in African Americans have come from European Americans because of gene flow between the two populations over the past several hundred years (Lewontin 1982).

So, the difference in performance on IQ tests can be seen as heavily influenced by the socioeconomic limitations imposed on African Americans over the past several centuries, limitations that have resulted in separate and often poor-quality education, limited access to various forms of cultural enrichment, and even the psychological effects of being identified as members of a minority group. These are all intangible factors that are impossible to fully control or even identify. Scores on IQ tests certainly involve some aspect of a person's innate intellectual abilities, but, again, because of all these external factors, we cannot infer those abilities from the results of test performances. And we certainly cannot make a biological generalization about a culturally defined group of people based on those performance results.

Our folk taxonomies are powerful and influential. We respond to them often without realizing that they are *our* culture's way of ordering *our* world and are not necessarily scientific universals. The influence of the American folk taxonomy for race can easily be seen in Jensen's work. By understanding what race is, and what it's not, and by applying what we know about the workings of genetics and evolution, we may see the fallacies of this and similar pieces of research. This perspective is an important one for helping us deal with the other issues of race that confront us almost daily.

▽   ▽   ▽

SUMMARY

Human societies need to find order in, and to make sense of, the environments in which they live. Cultural systems, therefore, translate objective reality into categories that have meaning to them. We call these categories folk taxonomies.

So important are the relationships between the sexes and the relative places in society of males and females that different cultural systems have evolved very different folk taxonomies for sex. These are gender roles and identities and, in some societies, they may even comprise more than two genders if those societies formally classify persons of ambiguous sex or sexuality.

That humans in general display variable traits is obvious, on some level, to all societies, and so all cultural systems also include folk taxonomies for race. On a biological level, however, races or subspecies do not exist for our species. Indeed, the concept of race is falling from use in biology in general. But even if we attempt to apply the race concept to humans, we find that the biological nature of our species does not lend itself to division into clear-cut, discrete units.

So powerful is the folk taxonomy for race that our categories take on a reality beyond that which is warranted, and we find that we use them as cues to tell us how to think about other groups of people and how to treat them. We can all too easily confuse culture and biology, and this effect can even be seen in scientific investigations, such as those that look for some biological racial difference in the cultural measure of intelligence called IQ.

QUESTIONS FOR FURTHER THOUGHT

1. Expand upon the brief discussion in the text, considering the identities and roles of the two genders in this culture. How would you characterize them? How have they changed during your lifetime? Do you see a need for further change? Why? How would it come about?

2. Still looking at your own culture, think about gender categories. Are there just two? Should there be more in light of what we know about the frequency of intersexes? Are more categories possible within this culture? Where does homosexuality fit into this discussion?

3. Discuss further the North American categories of race. What specific historical events or sequences may have influenced our commonly understood racial groups? If you are familiar with the racial taxonomy of another culture, similarly analyze it.

4. Apply the race and athleticism argument to a specific sterotype: "White men can't jump." Watching an NBA game, it sure can appear to be true. What *is* true about it? Why does it appear so?

5. On a practical level: Suppose it was shown that some populations in Kenya have a disproportionate number of members who possess physical and physiological features that make them better runners. How should we accommodate this in organized sporting competitions such as the Olympics?

KEY TERMS

sex	subspecies	racism
gender	races	heritability
folk taxonomies	semispecies	reification
polytypic	cline	

SUGGESTED READINGS

A good book on sex and gender from an anthropological perspective is *Female of the Species*, by M. Kay Martin and Barbara Voorhies. Despite the title, it is really about both sexes and all the gender categories found in various cultural systems. The fascinating case of India's *hijras* is documented in *Neither Man Nor Woman: The Hijras of India*, by Serena Nanda. I cover the topic of sex and gender in more detail, with more on the cultural dimension, in my *Introducing Anthropology: An Integrated Approach*.

On race, I highly recommend Stephen Molnar's *Human Variation: Races, Types, and Ethnic Groups* for a text covering the entire issue as a part of anthropology. It includes detailed sections on our variable traits. Another treatment of the same subject, but from a biologist, is Richard Lewontin's *Human Diversity*. A recent book on the subject, and one that includes an extended discussion of race and athletic ability, is Jonathan Marks's *Human Biodiversity: Genes, Race, and History*.

For a collection of articles on the nonexistence of human biological races, see *The Concept of Race*, edited by Ashley Montagu, and for a nice treatment of the history of race studies, try Kenneth A. R. Kennedy's *Human Variation in Space and Time*.

The analysis of human genetic differences and what they tell us about the history of human groups is nicely covered by Luigi Luca Cavalli-Sforza and Francesco Cavalli-Sforza in *The Great Human Diasporas: The History of Diversity and Evolution*.

The best book on racism, emphasizing an examination of scientific attempts to find correlations between race (and sex) and intelligence is Stephen Jay Gould's *The Mismeasure of Man*.

I do recommend Jon Entine's *Taboo*. Even though I disagree with major aspects of his analysis, his thought-provoking book succeeds very well in its goal of stimulating "open debate" on the subject.

BIOLOGICAL ANTHROPOLOGY AND TODAY'S WORLD

We too are part of
history's seamless web.
—Reinhold Niebuhr

A s I am writing this (late winter 2001), it is only a few months away from the scheduled execution of the man who was convicted of blowing up a federal building in Oklahoma City on April 19, 1995. The death toll from the bombing was 168. Many of the bodies were difficult to identify because they were literally blown apart by the blast, which left only fragments.

One of the people involved in the grim task of identifying the dead was forensic anthropologist Clyde Snow, himself an Oklahoman. Though certainly not to everyone's taste, such work is one of the ways that biological anthropology makes a tangible contribution to our lives. It is, of course, unfortunate that such services are needed. But they are, and the work of identifying human remains and, sometimes, of identifying the cause of death, is an important one, bringing some comfort to the survivors and justice to the slain.

Although the work of all biological anthropologists is useful in its contribution to knowledge, there are some practical ways in which our field can be applied and some lessons all people can learn from biological anthropologists' unique perspective on our species. In this last chapter, we will address the simple question:

What are some of the applications and lessons of biological anthropology?

FORENSIC ANTHROPOLOGY: READING THE BONES

The term *forensic* means "relating to courts of law or public discussion or the application of science to legal matters." The skills anthropologists use to retrieve information from ancient skeletons (see Chapter 9) have also proved useful in retrieving information from more modern ones—the victims of violent crimes and accidents. Forensic anthropology is increasingly called upon to examine skeletal remains and the conditions under which they were found to determine identity, time and cause of death, and any other information that may prove helpful to law enforcement agencies. In turn, some of the methods developed by forensic anthropologists have been applied to older remains that are of strictly scientific, rather than legal, interest.

Perhaps the best-known case of the latter is the well-publicized "Ice Man," or "Ötzi." He was found by hikers in September 1991, at over 10,000 feet in the Ötztaler Alps, just on the Italian side of the border with Austria. He had been naturally mummified by the dehydrating action of the cold and the wind and was in a remarkable state of preserva-

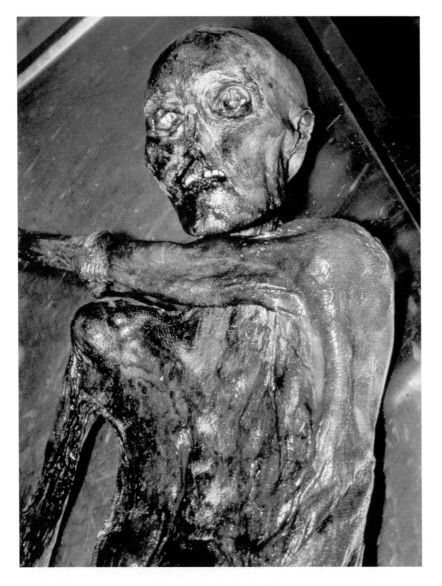

FIGURE 15.1
The Ice Man's body, preserved for over 5,000 years in the Italian Alps, was naturally mummified by cold and wind. Pressure from the ice disfigured his nose and lip and pushed his left arm into this odd position. We are still learning about his life and death from his preserved body, which includes his brain and internal organs.

tion. The find became all the more remarkable when carbon-14 dating of the body itself, and of grass with which he had stuffed his boots, provided a date of 3300 B.C. The body was over 5,000 years old.

The Ice Man was found with a fascinating array of artifacts, including much of his clothing and some tools. Details on these may be found in the readings listed at the end of the chapter. Here, we'll concentrate on the body itself (Figure 15.1).

Investigators X-rayed the body and, using techniques we discussed in Chapter 9, determined that it was that of a male about 5 feet 2 inches tall. Initially, he was thought to have been in his late 20s or early 30s when he died, but more recent analysis has indicated he was around 50 or slightly younger. Oddly, he had only eleven pairs of ribs, instead of the usual twelve, and eight ribs had been broken at one time or another but were healed, or were healing, at the time of his death. He had arthritis of the neck, lower back, and right hip, and the joints of his knees and ankles were worn. There is some evidence of hardening of the arteries, and his lungs were blackened, probably by smoke from open fires.

There are odd sets of parallel lines resulting from needle marks on the Ice Man's lower back, left thigh, and right ankle that resemble tattoos. One hypothesis is that these are related to the arthritic and joint pain he probably suffered in those areas. Interestingly, some of the needle marks are near acupuncture points, hinting to some that his culture may have known about this therapy 2,000 years before it was described by the Chinese (Stone 2000).

The Ice Man's teeth show considerable wear, some of which can be clearly seen on his upper incisors. This probably indicates that he used his teeth as tools, perhaps for leather working, and that he ate a tough diet including dried meat and the products of flour from grains that had been mixed with sand to aid in grinding. Both practices are known from the archaeological record.

His diet, however, may not have been particularly good. Patterns on a fingernail recovered later (the others had fallen off) suggest periods of reduced nail growth from disease or malnutrition. And eggs found in his stomach show that the Ice Man suffered from an intestinal parasite called a whipworm. The parasite causes diarrhea and acute stomach pains.

How did the Ice Man die? We may never know for sure, but we can make a good guess. There was no evidence that insects had laid any eggs on his body, and some sloe berries were found along with him. These facts point to his death in late summer or early fall, when insect reproductive activity has ceased and when the berries are available. It is a time when the weather in that area can turn suddenly and unexpectedly bad. Given his ill health and possible poor diet, he may simply have been caught in foul weather and froze to death.

Finally, in part to put to rest the inevitable questions about possible fraud, mitochondrial DNA analysis was performed. It indicated that the Ice Man was a European and that he was related to living populations from the northern Alps. Techniques of reconstruction have even given us an idea of what he looked like (Figure 15.2). In the fall of 2000, Ötzi was thawed for 4 hours to allow scientists to take better tissue samples, so we will probably learn even more about him in the future.

All the preceding information and more can be gleaned about a mummified corpse over fifty centuries old. When the Ice Man died, writing was just being invented in Mesopotamia, the great pyramids of Egypt had yet to be built, and the lives of Julius Caesar and Jesus were over 3,000 years in the future.

As famous as the Ice Man is, we do not, of course, know his name. Forensic studies, however, have provided us with new information about some famous people whose names we do know. For example, the late forensic anthropologist William Maples (Maples and Browning 1994) helped identify the skeletal remains of the assassinated Russian tsar Nicholas II and his family. (The bones did not, by the way, include those of Anastasia, the tsar's daughter, said to have survived and escaped to the West.) Maples also examined the remains of U.S. president Zachary Taylor to prove that he was not murdered by arsenic poisoning. He also helped identify the true remains of Spanish conquistador Francisco Pizarro and proved that a mummy reported to be Pizarro's was actually someone else's.

Clyde Snow, another well-known forensic anthropologist, identified a skeleton found in Brazil as that of Nazi war criminal Josef Mengele. The standard information about the skeleton fit what was known about Mengele, but Snow clinched it by superimposing images of the skull over photographs of the man known as the "Angel of Death." They matched, and the identification was verified shortly after, when Mengele's dental records were discovered. Snow has also been involved in a review of the assassination of John F. Kennedy and has, as mentioned in Chapter 1, searched in Bolivia for the remains of the famous outlaws Butch Cassidy and the Sundance Kid, so far without success.

More important, however, than these cases of the rich and famous are those involving the remains of common, everyday people who, for one reason or another, need to be identified and who, perhaps, require justice. Clyde Snow has, for example, examined and tried to identify the remains of some of the more than 10,000 people who "disappeared" during the military rule in Argentina from 1976 to 1983. His evidence has been used to help prosecute some of those responsible. He has done similar work in the Philippines and in Southwest Asia, and he has helped identify the victims of airline crashes, including one that took place in Chicago in 1979 that killed 273 people.

Investigating smaller tragedies, however, is not outside the activities of the forensic anthropologist. For a typical example, we can look at one of Clyde Snow's cases, a case that, coincidentally, began around Oklahoma City (Snow and Luke 1970). In the summer of 1967, two young girls, ages 5 and 6, disappeared in the Oklahoma City area within a few weeks of one another. In November of that year, two hunters found some bones, including a human cranium, in a rural area outside the city. The bones were scattered on the surface of the ground. Further investigation, however, revealed a crude grave that contained more bones and children's clothing. An extensive excavation was conducted. Among the several hundred bones eventually recovered—most of which belonged to various nonhumans—were those of a young child. Snow investigated further to see if the bones could reveal a specific identity and perhaps a cause of death. There was a good chance that these were the bones of one of the missing girls, and perhaps even both.

Snow determined that the bones had been buried fairly recently. They still had the greasy texture of fresh bone, and there were no signs of weathering that would indicate they had been there over winter. Although the bones had been damaged by scavengers, there were no rodent gnaw marks on them (rodents gnaw well-weathered bones for minerals and protein). The bones were recent, but how recent?

FIGURE 15.2

Artist John Gurche reconstructed the face of the Ice Man. He began with measurements, computer images, X rays, and CAT scans and produced a model of the Ice Man's skull. Next, he added clay to resemble the mummified face and then, like a plastic surgeon, rebuilt the face, reconstructing the nose and adding fatty tissue and muscles (represented by the red pegs) using anatomical data and his own interpretation from anthropological training.

They were completely skeletonized, but this could certainly have happened during the previous summer. It was shown that in Oklahoma's climate, a child's body would be reduced to bone within 2 to 6 weeks. There were spider webs and other signs of insect activity in the skull, so it was determined that the bones had been completely exposed before cold weather set in and those creatures became inactive. Burial had occurred in early September at the latest.

Soon, the possibility that more than one human was represented was ruled out. The cause of death was a problem, though. Much of the skeleton was missing, and the bones that remained were found scattered about. Some bones were damaged, and some teeth were missing. None of this, however, could be clearly attributed to trauma before death or purposeful dismemberment afterward. More likely, it was the result of decomposition and the work of carnivorous scavengers that dug up the grave, scattered the bones, and carried off those with fleshy parts.

Determining the sex of the skeleton was difficult. No pelvis was found, nor was there enough of the remainder of the skeleton to make a good assessment for a preadolescent. The clothing found was that of a little girl, however.

Both the missing girls were white, and the presence of a Carabelli's cusp on one of the remaining teeth pointed to that population. Carabelli's cusp is a small dental feature found in about 50 percent of U.S. whites, 34 percent of blacks, and only 5 to 20 percent of Native Americans. The incisors were not shovel-shaped, a form found in over 80 percent of Native Americans. It was important to rule out Native Americans since Oklahoma has a high Native American population. Some remaining hair verified the assessment, as its color and shape were those common to white populations.

Age was determined through cranial sutures, epiphyseal union, and dental eruption and development (see Chapter 9). In addition to the four separate bones of the cranial vault, each bone itself grows in separate pieces. The occipital, at birth, is in four pieces, which fuse together at 4 or 5 years of age. The occipital found was completely fused with no trace of sutures.

The epiphyses at the proximal (closest to the torso) femur and radius and the distal (farthest from the torso) humerus were all open. These close at 17, 14, and 14 years respectively. Taken with the evidence from the occipital, an age range of 4 to about 15 was determined. This was narrowed to 5 to 12 years by looking at further sites of bone union in the vertebral column.

Both first permanent molars were fully erupted. The central incisors were missing, but the size and form of the sockets indicated that they too had erupted. Taking into account the range of variation at which eruption occurs among individuals, these data provided an age range of about 5½ to 8 years. In addition, X rays of unerupted teeth below the gum line further narrowed the age range to about 6 to 8 years. The evidence, then, favored the skeleton being that of the older missing girl. Finally, stature was estimated using formulas that compare the length of various long bones to total height. The skeleton was estimated to have belonged to someone about 50 inches tall. The older missing girl was about that height, while the younger was 8 inches shorter.

Snow concluded that the remains probably belonged to one of the two missing girls. There had been no other unsolved cases of missing girls of that age from the area in several years. The bones most likely were those of the 6-year-old. Sadly, the remains of the other girl have not been found, and no suspect has been identified. But Snow's forensic work helped strengthen the identification, which would have been little more than a good guess without the precise information he was able to extract by reading the bones.

LESSONS FROM THE PAST

Besides applying the skills of the biological anthropologist to legal matters, we may also apply the perspective of our discipline to areas of modern life. Our evolutionary perspective tells us that we are not a species that suddenly appeared a few million years ago, nor are we, as modern humans, what evolution was somehow directed toward all along.

Rather, humans evolved from previous primate species. We are variations on the primate theme. We retain many of the major primate characteristics, and our unique features are still based on them. Moreover, in no way can we say that the modern manifestation of our species is the culmination or the best-adapted form of our evolutionary line. We have manipulated our environment, our very biology, and our behavior through culture, so our present environment may not be the one to which our species was biologically adapted. We may well learn a few valuable lessons by taking a closer look at what we were like in the past, before culture played so great a part in our lives.

For instance, anthropologists Marcia Thompson and David Harsha (1984) have looked at the daily routines of people in modern industrial societies and compared them with those of people in nonindustrial cultures and nonhumans living in the tropics. They conclude that in the common structure of our workdays, we are violating a pattern that evolved in our tropical ancestors and cousins that programs us for a two-peaked rhythm of daily activity, one peak in the late morning and another in the late afternoon, with a lull in between. That period of tiredness we often feel after lunch may have nothing to do with eating.

Tropical animals and people in many human societies take an afternoon break. Originally, this break may have been a response to the heat of the midafternoon sun, but as we are coming to understand it, this behavior may reflect a real biological decrease in human activity level. After all, other bodily functions—more than 100 physiological and performance variables—fluctuate in predictable cycles during the 24 hours of our day. Thus, the afternoon nap is a natural phenomenon. (I knew it!)

Thompson and Harsha suggest that the best way to respond to this fluctuation—given that most of us can't nap, at least during weekdays—would be to move lunch back a few hours to correspond to the afternoon lull. As it is, we often take lunch during one of our peak activity periods. By taking into account a possible biological pattern, we might make ourselves more productive in our modern cultural environment.

Another anthropologist, James McKenna (in Small 1992), has looked at the sleep behavior of other primate groups and of people in other cultures in which it is common for young babies to sleep with their parents. In the West, we have long been advised that babies should sleep by themselves, probably as a response to our emphasis on independence and the idea that the parents' lives, perhaps especially in bed, are separate from those of their children.

McKenna suggests that, in fact, infant nonhuman primates and human babies seem better off psychologically and physically if they sleep with their parents. In humans, this may even extend to learning to breathe properly. For humans, speech is so important that we have two kinds of breathing—automatic and controlled—and we need to learn to switch between kinds. In addition, remember that the vocal tract of human infants is different from that of adult humans and is like that of chimpanzees in being higher in the throat at first. As the vocal tract begins to drop early in life, the baby goes through a great physical change.

These two facts—the development of the two kinds of breathing and the physical change in the vocal tract—may explain Sudden Infant Death Syndrome (SIDS), where babies inexplicably die in their sleep. It is thought that, perhaps because of miscues in regulating breathing, these babies stop breathing and fail to wake themselves up so they can start breathing again. Sleeping with a parent, McKenna argues, may help prevent SIDS, because the parent's movement causes the baby to wake up periodically, and so the infant learns better how to jump between kinds of breathing. McKenna notes that SIDS is twice as common in the United States as in Japan, where infants normally sleep with parents. A more recent study (Mosko et al. 1997) has also suggested that close proximity to the mother while sleeping, especially sleeping face-to-face, may also provide the infant with increased levels of CO_2 from the mother's respiration, which might help stimulate its breathing.

From bioanthropology we may also learn more about disease. For example, the evolutionary perspective that sheds light on the nature of sickle cell anemia may also be applied to other diseases, especially those associated with particular populations. Biologist Jared Diamond (1991) offers an intriguing evolutionary explanation for the high frequency of Tay-Sachs disease among Eastern European (Ashkenazic) Jews and their descendants. Tay-Sachs is a lethal disease caused by a recessive gene. In homozygotes, it results in the body's inability to produce an enzyme that breaks down a particular fatty substance. This substance accumulates in nerve cells and literally destroys the victim's nervous system. Most sufferers die by age 4. The disease is incurable and cannot be prevented.

Tay-Sachs has a frequency of about 1 in 400,000 worldwide but is found in 1 of every 3,600 Ashkenazim. In other Jewish populations, Tay-Sachs is no more common than in the general population. The usual explanation for this incredibly high frequency among the Ashkenazim is the founder effect. The founders of the Ashkenazic populations happened to have a high frequency of the gene, which then persisted through genetic drift, aided by the fact that it was usually hidden from natural selection as a recessive. Some of the other ten diseases that are overrepresented among Ashkenazim have been explained in this way (Glausiusz 1995), as has the high frequency of Tay-Sachs in a Pennsylvania Dutch population (see Chapter 4).

But Diamond contends that the founders of the Ashkenazim were large populations and that their communities in Eastern Europe were widespread. The founder effect has significant results only in small populations. In the numerous and widespread communities, drift would have increased the frequency of the gene in some but decreased it in others. In addition, since these communities were first founded almost a thousand years ago, one would expect natural selection to have had sufficient time to decrease the frequency of this lethal gene to that found in the general population.

Moreover, it seems as if there are several different mutations along the same segment of DNA that can cause Tay-Sachs and that two of them are overrepresented among the Ashkenazim. It is unlikely that the same random evolutionary events could have happened twice. In addition, two of the other diseases that are more common in Eastern European Jews than in the general population also result from the excess accumulation of fatty substances.

Diamond suggests that, as with sickle cell, the heterozygous condition for Tay-Sachs must confer some selective advantage. He notes that Ashkenazic Jews were confined to towns for much of the past 2,000 years. They were forbidden to own land and so lived as businessmen in confined, urban areas known as ghettos (this is the origin of the term *ghetto*). A common ailment in such towns was TB (tuberculosis). In the early twentieth century, for example, TB caused up to 20 percent of all deaths in Eastern Europe. One study, however, indicates that relatively few Jews died from TB (1 in 306 people for whom data were available, a far cry from 20 percent). Thus, a reasonable hypothesis is that heterozygotes for Tay-Sachs, who do not exhibit symptoms of the disease, nevertheless have slightly elevated levels of the fatty substance, and this—for reasons that are still unknown—may provide some immunity to TB. Though the cause-and-effect relationship has not been established, this hypothesis provides a basis for further investigation and is an example of how our knowledge of evolutionary processes can provide a possible answer to a question involving modern human populations.

Finally, S. Boyd Eaton and Melvin Konner propose that the major chronic illnesses that we in the industrialized West suffer from are caused by a "mismatch between our genetic constitution" and various factors in our modern lifestyles, including diet, exercise, and exposure to such things as alcohol and tobacco. Our genes, they suggest, "must now function in a foreign and, in many ways, hostile Atomic Age [environment]" (1985, 1).

They note that some studies indicate that our ancestors who lived before the advent of farming, about 12,000 years ago, were taller and more heavily muscled than we are. Their teeth also showed a much smaller percentage of dental caries (tooth decay). The authors suggest that by looking at the lives of recent hunter-gatherer groups, we may have a "window" into the world of our Stone Age ancestors (Figure 15.3). (They are careful, of course, to caution that recent hunter-gatherer groups are fully modern humans with technologies, such as the bow and arrow, that were not available until about 15,000 years ago.) One thing we note right away is that such people have a lower incidence of coronary disease, emphysema, hypertension (high blood pressure), and cancer of the breast, prostate, colon, and lung.

When the diets of fifty hunter-gatherer groups were analyzed, it was seen that, on average, they ate more red meat than we do now. This doesn't sound like a healthy eating habit at first, until we understand that wild game has much less saturated fat than do domestic animals and that most

FIGURE 15.3
The Ju/'hoansi, a population of Khoisan peoples from the Kalahari Desert in Namibia, Botswana, and South Africa, are, of course, fully modern humans. Yet their way of life, until recently that of hunters and gatherers, can give us a window into the lives of our ancestors before the invention of farming and animal domestication. Here, members of a Ju/'hoansi family are on the move, carrying with them their children, tools, weapons, and other possessions. The lives of the Ju/'hoansi, and of all Khoisan, have been changed forever by political and military events in southern Africa since this photo was taken nearly 40 years ago (See also Figure 12.6.)

of that is "structural" fat (rather than "storage" fat), which is largely polyunsaturated—not the harmful kind, in other words. Thus, our ancestors ate about three times the protein we do but only about half the fat.

Because most of the plant foods eaten were wild and unprocessed, they had a higher nutritional value, fewer calories, more complex carbohydrates (rather than simple ones that turn to fat), more fiber, and less salt (a contributor to hypertension). Furthermore, our ancestors drank mostly water and seldom were exposed to alcohol and tobacco.

Additionally, rather than concentrating on one sort of exercise, our ancestors were more like "decathlon athletes," responding to the harsh physical demands of their lives with a varied "exercise program" that changed daily and seasonally.

As an example of this, a recent study (Cooper et al. 1999) compared rates of hypertension in subjects from Nigeria (7 percent), Jamaica (26 percent), and Chicago (33 percent; all of the subjects from Chicago were African American). The subjects sampled shared, on average, 75 percent of their genes (probably more; this study was done before the genome was sequenced), so major genetic differences were ruled out. Rather, differences in lifestyle, diet, and exercise were suggested as accounting for 40 to

---

Contemporary Reflections

What Can One Do with a Degree in Bioanthropology?

It's safe to say that most people who work as professional biological anthropologists (or, for that matter, any sort of professional anthropologist) have at least a master's degree and, more likely, a Ph.D. The majority of these do what I do—teach in a college or university while researching and writing. Although acquiring a Ph.D. requires, on average, 4 additional years of university classwork and a variable number of years after that to complete a doctoral dissertation (I took 6 years), it is a career I can highly recommend. Essentially, you get paid to learn about and think about the subject you're most interested in and then to impart that knowledge to your students. There's a good deal of (often inconsequential) committee work and other related activities required, but all in all it's a very rewarding life.

Unfortunately, at the moment, there are more Ph.D.s and near Ph.D.s in anthropology than there are university faculty jobs. The job market, however, has improved and worsened several times in the nearly 30 years I've worked at my university, and the situation could improve again. You shouldn't let current conditions dissuade you if a Ph.D. and a university position are your goal.

Some bioanthropology Ph.D.s work in other departments of universities. It is not uncommon to find them in medical, dental, and nursing programs, or in biology, genetics, psychology, public health, or physical therapy departments. Others work outside academia. I glanced through the list of current members of the American Association of Physical Anthropologists and found people who work for museums, medical research and forensics institutes, the armed forces, and government agencies such as the Bureau of Land Management. As I mentioned, the Connecticut State Archaeologist is a former student of mine who has his Ph.D. in bioanthropology.

---

50 percent of the increased risk for hypertension characteristic of African Americans over Nigerians. Specifically, by comparison, African Americans were more prone to being overweight, getting little exercise, and having a poor diet that included a high salt intake.

The lessons from this research are obvious and are, indeed, suggestions we hear all the time. We know we're supposed to eat low-fat foods, cut down on salt, get plenty of fiber, and exercise regularly. Evolution, though, provides an explanation and rationale for following those suggestions.

BIOANTHROPOLOGY AND GLOBAL ISSUES

Global issues are global in two senses: in their impact on a wide geographic range and large number of people and in the sense that they in-

Most of you reading this book, however—if you are working toward a degree in anthropology—will get a B.A. It has been said that one bachelor's degree is as good as another in terms of finding jobs that require a college education. On a practical level, that may well be true. What a 4-year degree means is that you have shown mastery of a certain core curriculum at a certain level with a focus on a particular discipline and that you have the skills, dedication, and persistence to achieve that degree. In terms of specific skills needed for a certain job, the college degree essentially tells an employer that you will have the ability to learn and use those skills.

But *what* degree you get may have deeper meaning, and—although I'm clearly biased—I think a degree in biological anthropology is a good choice. The breadth of knowledge inherent in the field is wide. There is the focus on scientific methodology but with the need—because it *is* anthropology—to understand other areas of knowledge and other cultures. The central theme of evolution necessarily involves a deep understanding of biology in general and of the biology of other species in particular. Genetics, anatomy, physiology, behavior, ecology, chemistry and physics (for dating techniques), geology, paleontology, and medical topics are all integral parts of the field. The number of careers to which such topics, such a breadth of knowledge, and such a perspective could be applied is huge—limited only by your imagination.

The only barrier might be the fact that many people have little understanding of what bioanthropology is and so might not at first think such a degree would be appropriate for certain jobs. I tell my students that in such instances they must be prepared to make their case, to explain to potential employers what bioanthropology is and why that background would be ideal for their job.

For some sound practical advice, read *Careers in Anthropology*, by John T. Omohundro (2001). In the meantime, the answer to the question about what you can do with a degree in bioanthropology is: Just about anything you want.

volve many different aspects in a complex set of interrelationships. Biological anthropology can neither address in detail all those aspects nor hope to solve any of these problems alone. But the perspective of bioanthropology—its evolutionary and holistic point of view—can help us gain insight into some of these issues and can certainly make a contribution as we seek responses and possible solutions.

In Chapter 13 we examined in some detail two global issues: overpopulation and emerging diseases. Each of these encompasses other problems and leads to still others. Another major issue on the same level of concern is global warming. Although there is still some debate on the existence of this phenomenon, most dissent is economically or politically motivated. People, corporations, and governments don't *want* global warming to be acknowledged because having to deal with it will adversely affect them. Few scientists today, however, doubt that global warming is a real trend (Epstein 2000).

Even in these areas of practical concern, however, anthropology in general can play a role. We humans will have to make adjustments if we are to slow, much less reverse, the warming trend. Changes in energy use, consumption of resources, waste disposal, and transportation habits will affect everyone—from the individual consumer to the largest multinational corporation. And even changes brought about initially by one nation will have effects on other nations, because we truly live in a global economy and a global environment. Anthropology can help predict what ramifications such changes will have on individual cultural systems and on the relationships among different cultural systems.

Some of the potential results of global warming relate directly to the subjects we've covered in this book. Climatic change is a major category. Genus *Homo* certainly has dealt with climatic change since first appearing on the planet, but global warming threatens to produce changes at a much more rapid rate than usual. Furthermore, it must be understood that the modern world we know has come about in just the past few hundred years; during this time we have not seen climatic change of the scale predicted. In other words, modern cultures have adapted to a relatively unchanging set of environments and could be severely disrupted by the more sudden changes that computer models of global warming project.

For example, if warming continues, ocean temperatures will increase, and polar ice caps and glaciers will melt. This will cause sea levels to rise and thus flood coastal areas, where populations tend to be concentrated. As a result, large numbers of people will have to move. The influx of salt water will destroy crops and natural plants and render land unusable for agriculture. There will be severe heat waves, which will produce droughts, heat-related deaths, and an increase in smog production. Global warming will also have an impact on disease. As climates warm, disease-causing and disease-carrying organisms will expand their ranges. Already we have had cases of West Nile virus in New York City and malaria in Toronto, as the associated mosquito species move into regions formerly inhospitable to them. Rodent-borne disease will also increase as those highly adaptable mammals expand their ranges, aided by decreases in predator populations as climates change. Dryness will cause major fires, which will add to pollution-caused ailments.

The risks are many and multifaceted. The perspective of biological anthropology—looking for connections, seeing our species as a biological/cultural system adapted to environmental systems—is a valuable one for understanding the causes and ramifications of global warming and for suggesting and implementing ways of dealing with them.

While the theoretical issues covered in this book are interesting in and of themselves, I believe they also make anthropology uniquely qualified to play a role in these and other global concerns. Indeed, I think we as anthropologists are obligated to do so.

▽   ▽   ▽

SUMMARY

Biological anthropology studies the human species, past and present, from the perspective of evolutionary processes, change, and adaptation. To understand how these affected our ancestors, we have developed skills that allow us to squeeze an amazing amount of information out of the meager skeletal remains that those ancestors left us. These skills are now being increasingly recognized and used by law enforcement agencies in the identification and analysis of skeletal remains of missing persons and accident and murder victims. Forensic anthropology is a fast-growing specialty within our field.

Our evolutionary perspective can also be useful in more abstract ways. By understanding the nature of our adaptations as a species, we may evaluate some of our behaviors and practices in light of the recent cultural environment we have made for ourselves. We find that some of our cultural adaptations may be out of step with our biological ones. Using the evolutionary viewpoint to look at daily biological rhythms, sleep patterns, the nature of our breathing, diseases that affect us, our diet, and our exercise habits—among other aspects of our lives—may enable us to adopt behaviors that are more in line with how our species is actually adapted and, in so doing, improve our lives.

Biological anthropology may also be applied to modern global issues such as overpopulation and emerging diseases (see Chapter 13.) Even something as seemingly removed from anthropology as global warming can be examined from anthropology's holistic and evolutionary perspectives.

In the end, however, it must be noted that, to be useful and important, knowledge need not have a practical, concrete application. There is nothing wrong with the idea of knowledge for its own sake, and, certainly, learning about our species—where we came from, what processes brought about our evolution, who we are and where we fit in the natural world—should be important to us as individuals and as members of our own society and the society of all the world's peoples.

QUESTIONS FOR FURTHER THOUGHT

1. What other issues of personal health and lifestyle do you think bioanthropology could address? How might the perspective of this discipline add something that other fields might have missed?

2. Within or resulting from the major issues of population, emerging diseases, and global warming are other matters of concern: pollution, deforestation and other examples of environmental destruction, and warfare between nations, religions, and ethnic groups. How might anthropology, especially biological anthropology, shed some light on these issues? What avenues of research would be opened up by applying bioanthropology in these cases?

3. In Chapter 14, we concluded that biological races do not exist for the human species. But on page 422 of this chapter, I describe the use of racial categories and biological traits in the identification of the two missing girls from Oklahoma. Is this contradictory? If not, why not?

4. Finally, a real challenge. As noted back in Chapter 1, science and belief systems are two very different areas of inquiry and knowledge. And yet, the nature of the real world certainly influences religious, philosophical, and ethical ideas. Consider some current ethical debates—abortion, euthanasia, stem cell research, for example—and ask whether the perspective of bioanthropology and the facts about the real world that our science has discerned might contribute to the direction and possible resolution of these debates.

SUGGESTED READINGS

The Ice Man story is summarized by Konrad Spindler in *The Man in the Ice*. Paul Bahn's review of that book, which adds some additional information, is in the May/June 1995 issue of *Archaeology* magazine. The June 1993 issue of *National Geographic* includes an article, "The Ice Man," by David Roberts that covers the Ice Man as well as some of the related archaeology of his time and place. For a more technical article, see "The Stone Age Iceman from the Alps," by Torstein Sjøvold in *Evolutionary Anthropology*.

Two recent finds of mummified bodies have been reported from western China and from Peru. See "The Silk Road's Lost World," by Thomas B. Allen, in the March 1996 *National Geographic* and three articles by

Johan Reinhard in the June 1996, January 1997, and November 1999 issues of the same magazine.

More on the reconstruction of ancient faces can be found in John Prag and Richard Neave's *Making Faces*.

On forensic anthropology, see *Dead Men Do Tell Tales*, by William R. Maples and Michael Browning; *Bones: A Forensic Detective's Casebook*, by Douglas Ubelaker and Henry Scammell, *Flesh and Bone*, by Myriam Nafte; and *Bone Voyage*, by Stanley Rhine. See also two articles in the August issue of *Science*: "A New Breed of High-Tech Detectives," by Andrew Watson, and "Where Dead Men Really Do Tell Tales," by Robert Service.

The Clyde Snow case covered in this chapter is recounted in detail in "The Oklahoma City Child Disappearances," by Snow and James Luke, in Aaron Podolefsky and Peter Brown's, *Applying Anthropology*. A profile of Snow appears in the December 1988 issue of *Discover* in a piece by Patrick Huyghe called "No Bone Unturned."

The global warming situation is nicely discussed in "Is Global Warming Harmful to Health?" by Paul R. Epstein in the August 2000 *Scientific American*.

Appendix

Exercises in Biological Anthropology

Some of the ideas covered in this text can be better understood when applied to specific situations. Here are four brief exercises that might be helpful in increasing your grasp of four important areas of bioanthropology. These can be done individually but would also be useful as a focus for study groups. A discussion of the answers follows.

Exercise I   MENDELIAN GENETICS

Understanding the basic features of genetic inheritance described by Mendel is important for grasping larger-scale processes of evolution. Answer the following questions using the Punnett Square (as shown in Figure 3.8) to help visualize your reasoning.

1. Suppose two people who are both heterozygous for the taster trait produce offspring. What are the possible genotypes and phenotypes of their offspring? In what proportions will they be produced; that is, what are the chances (ratios or percentages) of producing each genotype and each phenotype?

2. For this example, we will add a second simple (Mendelian) trait. We'll use earlobes. These are either free (where the lobe extends downward from its point of connection to the side of the head) or attached (where the lobe slopes upward from the point of connection). Free is the dominant condition (F); attached is the recessive (f). The gene for earlobes and that for the taster trait are on different chromosomes, so they assort independently. Now, if two nontasters with attached earlobes produce offspring, what can you predict about the phenotypes of their offspring? Why?

3. If two people who are both heterozygous for the taste and earlobe traits produce offspring, what possible genotypes and phenotypes can they produce? In what proportions? (Remember, these traits assort independently.)

434

4. Blood type for the ABO system (see Table 13.1) is determined by a single gene with three alleles: A, B, and O. A and B are codominant, and both are dominant over O. Suppose a type B woman has given birth to a type O child and has identified a type A man of being the father. Could he possibly be the father? Why or why not?

Exercise 2   TAXONOMY

The difference between phenetic and cladistic taxonomies (Chapter 7) can be further appreciated by applying the two methods to categorize some nonbiological items. Consider these seven items: laser pointer, portable CD player, portable tape recorder, digital watch, self-winding analog watch, electric analog watch, and cell phone.

1. Categorize the items phenetically, that is, by phenotypic features and adaptive functions. Your scheme should consist of sets of nested categories. Now, construct a family tree based on your classification (see Table 7.1 and Figure 7.2).
2. Using shared derived characteristics, construct a cladistic diagram of the items (see Figure 7.3). You may have a hard time sorting out the relative importance of the shared derived characteristics and thus the "branching order" of the cladogram. There may be several equally reasonable trees. This exercise illustrates one of the difficulties inherent in the cladistic method.

Exercise 3   POPULATION GENETICS

Following are some examples that will ask you to apply the basic population genetics concepts discussed in Chapter 13. First, we need some numbers: Suppose in a class of eight students we have five tasters and three nontasters. (If you have access to PTC [phenylthiocarbamide] paper—which is either extremely bitter or tasteless, depending on a person's phenotype for the taster trait—you could test the members of your class and use those data.)

1. For the taster trait, calculate the *phenotype* frequencies for the class. (A frequency is a percentage: Divide the number of people with each expression by the total number in the class.)
2. Now, calculate the *genotype* and *allele* frequencies for the class for the taster trait. You should immediately see a problem: Unlike the

case with sickle cell anemia, where we could distinguish the three genotypes (see page 169), here we can't distinguish homozygous tasters from heterozygotes (because of the complete dominance of the taster allele). There is, however, one piece of information we *do* know and can use to estimate the frequencies. (*Hint:* Assume the class is in Hardy-Weinberg equilibrium for these traits.)

3. Let's say we could distinguish the three genotypes for the taster trait. A population of 208 people presents us with the following data: There are 119 homozygous tasters, 76 heterozygote tasters, and 13 nontasters. Is this population in Hardy-Weinberg equilibrium for the taster trait?

Exercise 4   SKELETAL IDENTIFICATION

Practice analyzing skeletal remains with the following examples. Refer to Figures 9.1, 9.2, and 9.3. (You may want to consult additional sources, such as those listed in Chapter 9, for more information.)

1. A human mandible was recovered from a burned building. Muscle markings were not pronounced, the chin was rounded, and the gonial angle (the angle at the back of the jaw) was about 110°. All the teeth were permanent. The first molar, the central and lateral incisors, and the first premolar (bicuspid) were all fully erupted. The canine and second premolar were just starting to break through the gum line.

    Sex: _____   Age at death: _____

2. A set of postcranial bones was uncovered at a construction site. All epiphyses were fused except for the medial clavicle (the end of the clavicle nearest the middle of the body). The pelvis was badly damaged, but the subpubic angle appeared to be about 90°.

    Sex: _____   Age at death: _____

3. After all other victims of an airline accident had been positively identified, all that remained were one skull and one pelvis. There was little question that they came from the same person, yet initial analysis seemed contradictory. The skull showed slight muscle markings, the gonial angle was large, and the forehead was fairly vertical with no brow ridges. The pelvis, however, had a narrow sciatic notch and small subpubic angle, with vertical ilia. What do you think is the sex of this individual? How were you able to resolve the seeming contradiction?

Discussion and Answers

Exercise I   MENDELIAN GENETICS

1. A heterozygote produces gametes with the dominant allele (*T*) and the recessive allele (*t*) in equal numbers. The Punnett Square for a mating between two heterozygotes is like that in Figure 3.8.

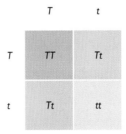

The chances of producing the two phenotypes are 75 percent for the taster trait and 25 percent for the nontaster trait. Genotype frequencies are 25 percent *TT*, 50 percent *Tt*, and 25 percent *tt*.

2. Since nontasters are homozygous recessive, they produce only gametes with the recessive allele. Similarly, those with attached earlobes only pass on the recessive allele. Thus, all the offspring from a mating between two nontasters with attached earlobes will also be nontasters with attached earlobes.

(To fill in this Punnett Square with two traits, simply combine the individual gamete alleles of each gene into genotypic pairs. Thus, the taster alleles, *t* for both gametes, combine to make a *tt* genotype And the same holds true for the earlobe alleles, which combine to form the *ff* genotype.)

3. Since these traits assort independently, each double heterozygote person can produce four different types of gametes with regard to these alleles: *TF, Tf, tF,* and *tf.* Thus, all genotypic and phenotypic combinations are possible.

	TF	Tf	tF	tf
TF	TT FF	TT Ff	Tt FF	Tt Ff
Tf	TT Ff	TT ff	Tt Ff	Tt ff
tF	Tt Ff	Tt Ff	tt FF	tt Ff
tf	Tt Ff	Tt ff	tt Ff	tt ff

(This Punnett Square works the same way as the one in the preceding question, only there are more boxes since there are more possible gametes. Again, simply combine the individual gametic alleles from the vertical and horizontal margins and fill each genotype pair in the corresponding intersecting box. *Note:* For computing purposes, begin each allele combination with the dominant trait, where applicable— for example *Ff,* not *fF.*)

Phenotypically, there are nine tasters with free earlobes, three tasters with attached earlobes, three nontasters with free earlobes, and one nontaster with attached earlobes.

Genotypically, the numbers are as follows:

TTFF	1
TTFf	2
TTff	1
TtFF	2
TtFf	4
Ttff	2
ttFF	1
ttFf	2
ttff	1

4. If both the man and woman were heterozygotes (*AO* and *BO*), then there's a one-quarter chance the child could be type O (*OO*).

Exercise 2   TAXONOMY

1. As with classifications of living organisms, there are probably several taxonomies that could be imposed on these items, all with different-looking family trees. The following tree is based on function. All the watches, of course, serve to tell time. The digital and electric analog watches both use batteries and so are more closely related, like "species" of watches. The tape recorder and CD player play sound, but the tape recorder can also record it. Thus, I have chosen to separate these two items at the same level as the two general types of watches (requiring batteries or not). The cell phone and laser pointer each serve a separate function.

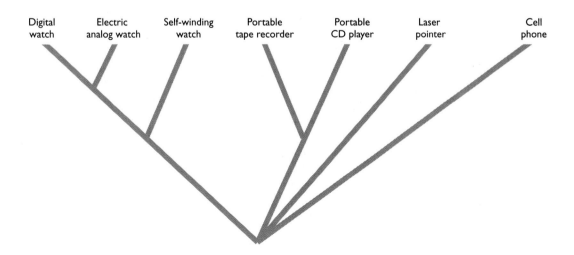

2. Following is a taxonomy based on shared derived characteristics: All of the items but the self-winding watch use electricity. The electric analog watch and the tape recorder are fairly simple mechanisms, but all the others require a microchip. The laser pointer and the CD player share the use of laser beam technology.

   As an example of another approach to this taxonomy, notice that the cell phone, digital watch, and CD player all feature LCDs (liquid crystal displays) or LEDs (light-emitting diode displays). Using this as a shared derived characteristic would result in a different-looking tree. Can you think of any other schemes?

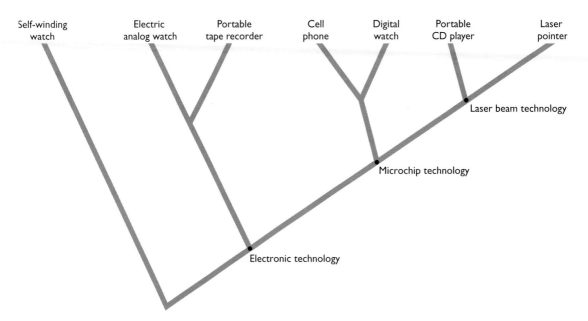

Self-winding watch · Electric analog watch · Portable tape recorder · Cell phone · Digital watch · Portable CD player · Laser pointer

Laser beam technology

Microchip technology

Electronic technology

Exercise 3   POPULATION GENETICS

1. Of the eight students in the class, five are tasters. To arrive at the phenotype frequency for tasters, we divide by eight to get 62.5 percent, or, stated as a decimal (which is easier to work with), .625. The frequency of nontasters is everyone else: 1.00 (100 percent) − .625 = .375.

2. We don't know how many tasters are homozygous dominant and how many are heterozygotes. But we do know that all three nontasters must be homozygous recessives. Here's where the Hardy-Weinberg equilibrium comes in (refer to pages 342–344 in Chapter 13). Remember that it states that

$$p^2 + 2pq + q^2 = 1 \text{ (or 100 percent)}$$

where each factor to the left of the equation is the frequency of each genotype ($p = T$, $pq = Tt$, and $q = t$).

As calculated in the preceding example, we know that q^2, the frequency of the homozygous recessive genotype (tt), is .375. Thus, q (the frequency of the t allele) is the square root of .375, or .612.

Now, to find the value of p (the frequency of the T allele), we subtract .612 from 1.00 to get .388.

We can now calculate the other genotype frequencies:

p^2 (the frequency of TT) is $.388^2 = .150$

$2pq$ (the frequency of the heterozygote Tt) is $2(.388)(.612) = .475$

Summarizing, the frequency of

$$TT = .150$$
$$Tt = .475$$
$$tt = .375$$

Added together, these equal 1.00 (100 percent).

3. As discussed in Chapter 13, the Hardy-Weinberg equilibrium compares actual numbers with expected numbers. First, we calculate allele frequencies assuming Hardy-Weinberg equilibrium. We know that q^2, the frequency of nontasters (tt), is 13 divided by 208, or .062. Thus, q (the frequency of the t allele) is the square root of that, or .25. Then p (the frequency of the T allele) must be .75. Thus, we have expected genotype frequencies as follows:

TT $(p^2) = .75^2 = .563$
Tt $(2pq) = 2(.75)(.25) = .375$
tt $(q^2) = .062$

Now we multiply the expected frequencies by the total population (208) to get the expected numbers for each genotype:

TT $.563 \times 208 = 117$
Tt $.375 \times 208 = 78$
tt $.062 \times 208 = 13$

These numbers, however, don't match exactly the actual numbers of 119, 76, and 13, given earlier in the appendix. Thus, based on a comparison of the actual and expected numbers, this population is not in Hardy-Weinberg equilibrium. Some processes of evolution are occurring. (Actually, we would have to run a statistical test such as a chi-square test to see if the deviation from Hardy-Weinberg expectations is statistically significant and, thus, meaningful. In this case, it is not. This example, however, illustrates how the process works.)

Exercise 4   SKELETAL IDENTIFICATION

1. All indications suggest the skull of a female. Keeping in mind that all the teeth were permanent, or adult teeth, we note that if the first premolar had erupted, the person would have to be older than 10 years. The canine and second premolar erupt at 11 years. Since they had not yet erupted in this individual, we can set the age of death at between 10 and 11 years.

2. The subpubic angle of 90° indicates a male. Because all epiphyses except the medial clavicle were fused, we know that the lateral clavicle (the end of the clavicle at the shoulder) was fused. This epiphysis fuses at 20 years. The medial clavicle (not yet fused in this individual) fuses at 28 years. Thus, this man died at between 20 and 28 years of age.

3. The features of this skull were characteristically female, yet the pelvis had male features. If these came from the same person, it is likely the person was a male. While the features of the skull, even these related to sex, can show some degree of variation, those of the pelvis are less ambiguous because of their relationship to childbearing. Everything about the female pelvis is wider than in the male pelvis.

Glossary of Human and Nonhuman Primates

Adapidae (*ah-da'-pih-day*) A group of early primates from the previously connected landmass of North America and Europe, dating to more than 50 mya and thought to be ancestral to prosimians such as lemurs and lorises.

Aegyptopithecus (*ee-gyp'-tow-pith'-ah-cuss*) An extinct monkey genus with several apelike traits. Discovered in Egypt and dating to more than 25 mya, it may represent a form of primate ancestral to Old World monkeys and apes.

Ankarapithecus (*ahn-ka-ra-pith'-ah-cuss*) A fossil ape genus from Turkey dated at 9.8 mya, which shows similarities to *Sivapithecus*.

Anthropoidea (*an-throw-poy'-dee-ah*) According to the traditional taxonomic system, one of the two suborders of order Primates (the other is Prosimii). Means "humanlike" and includes monkeys, apes, and humans.

Ardipithecus ramidus (*ar-di-pith'-ah-cuss rah'-mi-dus*) A recently identified hominid genus from Ethiopia and dated at about 4.4 mya, based on skeletal fragments and teeth. Not yet fully documented or accepted, it is thought by its discoverers to represent the earliest species in the hominid line. Thus, the species name, which means "root" in the local language.

Australopithecus afarensis (*os-trail-oh-pith'-ah-cuss ah-far-en'-sis*) A fossil species from East Africa, the oldest well-established species in the hominid line. Dated from 4 to 3 mya, *afarensis* had a small, chimp-sized brain but walked fully upright.

Australopithecus africanus (*os-trail-oh-pith'-ah-cuss ah-frih-cane'-us*) A fossil hominid species from South Africa dated from about 3 to 2.3 mya. It is similar to *A. afarensis* and may well be a direct evolutionary descendant of the earlier species. It retained the chimp-sized brain and was fully bipedal.

Australopithecus anamensis (*os-trail-oh-pith'-ah-cuss ana-men'-sis*) The earliest well-documented fully bipedal hominid, found in Kenya and dating from 4.2 to 3.8 mya.

Australopithecus bahrelghazalia (*os-trail-oh-pith'-ah-cuss bar-el-gah-zahl'-ya*) A new species of this genus, based on a jaw and several teeth found in Chad and dated at 3.5 to 3 mya. The species name is based on an Arab name for a nearby riverbed. It is noteworthy as the only early hominid found outside of East Africa or southern Africa.

Australopithecus garhi (*os-trail-oh-pith'-ah-cuss gar'-hee*) Recently discovered fossils from Ethiopia, dated to 2.5 mya, that display resemblances to both *Australopithecus afarensis* and early *Homo*, leading some authorities to consider them a new species and a direct ancestor of *Homo*.

Catarrhini (*cat-ah-rhine'-eye*) One of two infraorders of suborder Anthropoidea (the other is infraorder Platyrrhini, the New World monkeys). Catarrhini is the infraorder of the Old World monkeys, apes, and hominids. Along with the geographical distinction, catarrhines can be distinguished from platyrrhines by their narrow nose shape, fewer premolar teeth, and lack of a prehensile tail.

Cercopithecoidea (*sir-co-pith-ah-coy'-dee-ah*) The superfamily of all monkeys of Europe, Africa, and Asia.

Eosimiidae (*ee-oh-sim-ee'-ih-day*) A group of early primates from Asia, dated at around 45 mya, that may represent direct ancestors of monkeys, apes, and hominids.

Equatorius (*ee-kwa-tor'-ee-us*) A fossil genus from East Africa dated at 15 mya and showing similarities in arm and ankle structure to the modern chimpanzee. Lumped by some authorities into *Kenyapithecus*.

Gigantopithecus (*ji-gan-tow-pith'-ah-cuss*) A genus of fossil apes, dated at 12 to perhaps 1 mya, found in China, India, and Vietnam. It may have reached a height of 12 feet when standing erect and may have weighed 1,200 pounds, making it the largest primate known.

Gorilla gorilla (*go-rill'-a go-rill'-a*) The gorilla (well, duh!), one of the three great ape species from Africa and the largest living primate.

Haplorhini (*hap-low-rhine'-eye*) According to the cladistic taxonomic system, one of two suborders of order Primates (the other is Strepsirhini). Haplorhini are primates lacking a moist nose and other primitive features. Includes the tarsier and all primates traditionally included in suborder Anthropoidea.

Hominidae (*ho-mih'-nih-day*) In a traditional taxonomy, the family of modern and extinct human species, defined as the primates that are habitually bipedal. Members of this group are called hominids.

Hominoidea (*ho-min-oy'-dee-ah*) The superfamily that includes the large, tailless primates: apes and hominids, living and extinct.

Homo antecessor (*ho'-mow an-tee-sess'-or*) A recently proposed species from Spain and dated at 780,000 ya or more. The fossils show a mix of primitive and modern human features and are interpreted by their discoverers as possibly ancestral to *H. heidelbergensis* and *H. neanderthalensis*. This species is not widely recognized at present.

Homo erectus (*ho'-mow ee-wreck'-tuss*) A fossil hominid species dating from at least 1.8 mya to 100,000 ya or so. First appearing in Africa, *H. erectus* was the first hominid species to expand beyond that continent. Fossils are found throughout Africa and Asia, and there is possible evidence from Europe. Members of this species had a brain size average about two-thirds that of modern humans, made advances in stone tool technology, and were able to control fire late in their existence.

Homo ergaster (*ho'-mow er-gas'-ter*) The earliest *H. erectus* fossils from Kenya, said by some researchers to be sufficiently different that they represent a separate species that was ancestral to both *H. erectus* and, later, *H. sapiens*.

Homo habilis (*ho'-mow ha'-bill-us*) Fossil hominid species dating from about 2.2 to 1.5 mya and found in East Africa. Fully bipedal and with an average brain size of 680 ml, *H. habilis* was the first confirmed hominid stone toolmaker. Because this was the first hominid with a brain larger than that of a chimpanzee, and because of the association with stone tools, *H. habilis* is thought to be the earliest member of our genus, *Homo*.

Homo heidelbergensis (*how'-mow high-del-berg-en'-sis*) A proposed species from Africa, Asia, and Europe, dated at between 475,000 and 200,000 ya. They had a modern human brain size but retained primitive features such as brow ridges, prognathism, and postorbital constriction.

Homo neanderthalensis (*ho'-mow knee-an-dir-tall-en'-sis*) A proposed species from Europe and Southwest Asia, dated at between 225,000 and 36,000 ya. They had more pronounced versions of some of the cranial features of *H. heidelbergensis*, such as brow ridges and prognathism. The postcranial skeletons were robust and heavy, with short arms and legs, possibly adaptations to cold climates.

Homo rudolfensis (*ho'-mow rue-dolf-en'-sis*) Thought by some authorities to be a separate species made up of the East Turkana, Kenya, specimens traditionally placed in *H. habilis*.

Homo sapiens (*ho'-mow say'-pee-ens*) The taxonomic name for modern humans. There is debate as to whether or not this name covers certain other species, including *H. erectus, ergaster, antecessor, heidelbergensis,* and *neanderthalensis*.

Hylobatidae (*high-low-bat'-ah-day*) The family that includes the gibbons and siamangs, the arboreal, so-called lesser apes of Southeast Asia. They are highly efficient brachiators.

Kenyanthropus platyops (*ken-yan'-throw-pus plat'-ee-ops*) A new fossil genus from Kenya, dated at 3.5 mya and suggested by some authorities, because of its flat face and other features, to represent a better human ancestor than *Australopithecus afarensis*. Thus far, it is based on only two specimens.

Kenyapithecus (*ken-ya-pith'-ah-cuss*) A fossil genus from East Africa dated at 14 mya. A possible candidate for the first hominoid.

Morotopithecus (*more-row-tow-pith'-ah-cuss*) A fossil genus from Uganda dated at 20 mya. A possible candidate for the first hominoid, it may have been capable of occasional upright walking.

Omomyidae (*oh-mow-me'-ah-day*) A group of early primates that lived in the previously connected landmass of North America and Europe. Dating to more than 50 mya, they are thought to be ancestral to tarsiers and may have been ancestral to Anthropoidea as well.

Orrorin tugenensis (*oar-oar'-in two-gen-en'-sis*) A new fossil genus from Kenya, based on thirteen specimens and dated at 6 mya. Its purported bipedal features have led some to suggest it represents the ancestor of all later hominids. The identity and features of this form are still a matter of much debate.

Ouranopithecus (*oo-ran-oh-pith'-ah-cuss*) An ape from Greece dated at 9 or 10 mya. Based on some hominidlike features, it is thought by some to be a member of the ape line that led to the hominids.

Pan paniscus (*pan pan-iss'-cuss*) The bonobo, sometimes called the pygmy chimpanzee. One of the three great ape species from Africa.

Pan troglodytes (*pan trog-low-dye'-tees*) The chimpanzee. One of the three great ape species from Africa.

Papio (*pah'-pee-oh*) A genus within superfamily Cercopithecoidea (the Old World monkeys) other comprises several species of baboons, large monkeys living in social groups on the African savannas.

Paranthropus aethiopicus (*par-an'-throw-pus ee-thee-oh'-pih-cuss*) A species from East Africa dating from 2.8 to 2.2 mya. They were the first members of the so-called robust early hominids, having large, rugged features associated with chewing, although their other features, including brain size, were very similar to those of members of genus *Australopithecus*. Many authorities still include it in that genus. It is thought they were adapted to tough, gritty, hard vegetable foods. The most famous, and first, specimen of this species was the "Black Skull."

Paranthropus boisei (*par-an'-throw-pus boys'-ee-eye*) The East African robust hominid, dated from 2.2 to 1 mya. It had large features associated with chewing, although less pronounced than in *P. aethiopicus*. The first specimen was "Zinjanthropus." Sometimes included in genus *Australopithecus*.

Paranthropus robustus (*par-an'-throw-pus row-bus'-tus*) The southern African robust hominid, dated from 2.2 to 1.5 mya. It was marked by robust chewing features, although they were less robust than in either *P. aethiopicus* or *P. boisei*. The postcranial skeleton and the brain size remained similar to those of *Australopithecus*. It is sometimes included in that genus.

Platyrrhini (*plat-ee-rhine'-eye*) One of two infraorders of suborder Anthropoidea (the other is infraorder Catarrhini, the Old World monkeys, apes, and hominids). Platyrrhines comprise the New World monkeys. Members of this group can be told apart from the catarrhines by their broad nose shape, greater number of premolar teeth, and the fact that several species have prehensile tails.

Pongidae (*pon'-jih-day*) The family of the so-called great apes, the orangutans of Southeast Asia and the gorillas, chimpanzees, and bonobos of Africa.

Pongo pygmaeus (*pon'-go pig-may'-us*) The orangutan. The only great ape from Southeast Asia.

Primates (*pry-mate'-ees*) An order within class Mammalia. Large-brained arboreal mammals with stereoscopic color vision and grasping hands (and sometimes feet). Includes prosimians, monkeys, apes, and hominids.

Prosimii (*pro-sim'-ee-eye*)   According to the traditional taxonomic system, one of two suborders of order Primates (the other suborder is Anthropoidea). Prosimians are the more primitive of the two suborders in that they retain features of some of the oldest primate fossils. Many lack color vision, are nocturnal, and have limited opposability of the thumb.

Sivapithecus (*she-vah-pith'-ah-cuss*)   Genus of fossil ape from India and Pakistan, dated from 15 to 12 mya. Thought to be ancestral to the orangutan.

Strepsirhini (*strep-sir-rhine'-eye*)   According to the cladistic taxonomic system, one of two suborders of order Primates (the other is Haplorhini). Primates with a moist nose and other primitive features. Includes all primates traditionally in suborder Prosimii except the tarsier.

Glossary of Terms

absolute dating technique Dating method that gives a specific age, year, or range of years for an object or site. Compare with **relative dating technique.**

Acheulian technique A toolmaking tradition associated with *Homo erectus/ergaster* in Africa and Europe. Includes hand axes, cleavers, and flake tools.

adaptation The state in which an organism is adjusted to and can survive in its environment through its physical traits and behaviors. Also, the process by which an organism develops this state through natural processes.

adaptive radiation The evolution and spreading out of related species into new niches.

allele frequency The percentage of times a particular allele appears in a population. Another name, and the preferred term, for gene frequency.

alleles Variants of a gene. Most genes possess more than one possible allele, the different alleles conveying different instructions for the development of a certain phenotype (for example, different blood types).

altruistic Benefiting others without regard for one's own needs or safety.

amino acids The chief components of proteins. Each "word" in the genetic code stands for a specific amino acid.

analogies Traits shared by two or more species that are similar in function but unrelated evolutionarily, for example, the wings of a bird and of an insect. Compare with **homologies.**

anthropology The holistic study of the human species. Anthropology includes the study of human biology, human physical evolution, human cultural evolution, and human adaptation.

antibodies Proteins in the immune system that react to foreign antigens.

antigens Substances, such as proteins, that can trigger an immune response, for example, the production of an antibody. The antigens of the ABO blood group system are examples.

applied anthropology Anthropology used to address current practical problems and concerns.

arboreal Organisms that are adapted to life in the trees.

archaeology A subfield of anthropology that studies the human cultural past and the reconstruction of past cultural systems.

argon/argon dating A radiometric dating technique that uses the decay of radioactive argon into stable argon gas. Can be used to date smaller samples and volcanic rock with greater accuracy than does potassium/argon dating.

asexually Reproducing without sex, by fissioning or budding. Compare with **sexually.**

belief systems Ideas that are taken on faith and cannot be scientifically tested. Examples are religions, philosophies, and ethical and moral beliefs. Compare with **scientific method.**

bifacial A stone tool that has been worked on both sides.

bioanthropology Another name for biological anthropology.

biological anthropology A subfield of anthropology that studies humans as a biological species.

biostratigraphy The study of fossils in their stratigraphic context. Used as a relative dating technique.

bipedal Walking on two legs.

bottleneck A severe reduction in the size of a population such that only certain genes survive and come to characterize the descendant population.

brachiation   Locomotion by swinging arm-over-arm.

breeding populations   Populations within a species that are genetically isolated to some degree from other populations. See also **demes.**

brow ridges   Heavy, bony ridges over the eyes.

carnivore   An organism adapted to a diet of mostly meat. See also **omnivore.**

catastrophists   Those who believe the history of the earth is explained by a series of global catastrophes, either natural or divine in origin. See also **uniformitarianism.**

chromosomal mutations   Mutations of a whole chromosome or a large portion of a chromosome. Compare with **point mutations.**

chromosomes   Strands of DNA in the nucleus of a cell.

chronometric techniques   Another name for absolute dating techniques.

cladistics   A classification system based on order of evolutionary branching rather than on present similarities and differences. Compare with **phenetic taxonomy.**

cline   A geographic continuum in the variation of a particular trait.

codominant   When both alleles of a pair are expressed in the phenotype.

codon   The three-base sequence that codes for a specific amino acid. Technically, the sequence on the mRNA.

comparative anatomy   Comparing the anatomical features of various species. Used to reconstruct a fossil species from fragmentary remains.

competitive exclusion   When one species outcompetes others for the resources of a particular area.

core tools   Tools made by taking flakes off a stone nucleus. See also **flake tools.**

crossing over   When sections of chromosomes switch between chromosome pairs during meiosis. See also **recombination.**

cultural anthropology   A subfield of anthropology that focuses on human cultural behavior and cultural systems and the variation in cultural expression among human groups.

culture   Ideas and behaviors that are learned and transmitted. Also, the system made up of the sum total of these ideas and behaviors that is unique to a particular society of people. Nonbiological means of adaptation.

Darwinian gradualism   The view, held by Darwin, that evolution is slow and steady with cumulative change. Compare with **punctuated equilibrium.**

deduction   Suggesting specific data that will be found if a hypothesis is true, a step in the scientific method involving the testing of hypotheses. See also **induction.**

demes   Populations within a species that are genetically isolated to some degree from other populations. Another name for breeding population, but sometimes implies physical distinctions.

demography   The study of the size and makeup of populations.

deoxyribonucleic acid (DNA)   The molecule that carries the genetic code.

dermatoglyphics   The study of the parallel ridges and furrows on the fingertips, palms, toes, and soles of the feet, commonly referred to as fingerprints, palm prints, and so on.

distance curve   A graph that compares some variable at different points in time, for example, height and age. Compare with **velocity curve.**

diurnal   Active during the day. Compare with **nocturnal.**

DNA   See **deoxyribonucleic acid.**

dominance hierarchy   A social pattern among animal species where there are recognized individual differences in power, influence, and access to resources and mating. Found in many primate species.

dominant   In a heterozygous pair of alleles, the one that is expressed in the phenotype. Compare with **recessive.**

electron spin resonance dating (ESR)   An absolute dating technique that measures the number of electrons excited to higher energy levels by natural radiation and trapped at those levels. Can be used to date tooth enamel, shells, corals, mineral cave deposits, and volcanic rock, but does not work well on bone.

endocasts Natural or human-made casts of the inside of a skull. The cast reflects the surface of the brain and allows us to study the brains of even extinct species.

endogamy Restricting marriage to members of the same culturally defined group.

environmental Any nongenetic influence on the phenotype. Also refers to the conditions under which an organism exists, such as climate, altitude, other species, food sources, and so on.

enzymes Proteins that control chemical processes.

epidemiological Pertaining to the study of disease outbreaks and epidemics.

estrus The period of fertility. The signals indicating this condition.

ethology The study of the natural behavior of animals under natural conditions.

evolution Change through time, usually with reference to biological species, but may also refer to changes within cultural systems.

fission A process of evolution that involves the splitting up of a population to form new populations.

fitness The relative adaptiveness of an individual organism, measured ultimately by reproductive success.

flake tools Tools made from the flakes removed from a stone core. See also **core tools.**

folk taxonomies Cultural categories for important items and ideas. Gender and race are examples of folk taxonomies.

foramen magnum The hole in the base of the skull through which the spinal cord emerges and around the outside of which the top vertebra articulates.

forensic anthropologist One who applies anthropology to legal matters. Usually used with reference to the identification of skeletal remains and the assessment of time and cause of death.

fossils Remains of life forms of the past.

founder effect A process of evolution. Genetic differences between populations produced by the fact that genetically different individuals established (founded) those populations.

gamete sampling A process of evolution. The genetic change caused when genes are passed to new generations in frequencies unrepresentative of those of the parental generation. An example of sampling error.

gametes The cells of sexual reproduction, commonly sperm and egg, which contain only half the chromosomes of a normal cell.

gender The cultural categories and characteristics of men and women. The translation of sex into a folk taxonomy. Compare with **sex.**

gene flow A process of evolution that involves the exchange of genes among populations through interbreeding.

gene frequency See **allele frequency.**

gene pool All the alleles in a population.

generalized Species that are adapted to a wide range of environmental niches. Such species tend to be genetically and physically variable. Compare with **specialized.**

genes Those portions of the DNA molecule that code for specific proteins.

genome The total genetic endowment of an organism.

genotypes The alleles possessed by an organism. See also **phenotypes.**

glaciers Massive sheets of ice that expand and move. Found on the polar ice caps and in mountains.

grooming Cleaning the fur of another animal, which promotes social cohesion. Common among primate groups.

haft To attach a wooden handle or shaft to a stone or bone point.

half-life The time needed for one-half of a given amount of a radioactive substance to decay.

hand axe A bifacial, all-purpose stone tool, shaped somewhat like an axe head. First invented by *Homo erectus* and usually associated with that species.

Hardy-Weinberg equilibrium The formula that shows genotype frequencies in a population under hypothetical conditions of no evolutionary change.

heritability The amount of variation of a particular trait within a population that is caused by genetic, as opposed to environmental, differences.

heterozygous Having two different alleles in a gene pair. Compare with **homozygous.**

holistic   Assuming an interrelationship among the parts of a subject. Anthropology is a holistic discipline.

hominids   Modern human beings and our ancestors, generally defined as the primates who habitually walk erect. Technically, the members of family Hominidae.

homologies   Traits shared by two or more species through inheritance from a common ancestor. An example would be the arms of a human and the wings of a bat. We assume that many similar behaviors among humans and chimpanzees are also homologies. Compare with **analogies.**

homozygous   Having two of the same allele in a gene pair. Compare with **heterozygous.**

human ecology   A specialty of anthropology that studies the relationships between humans and their environments.

hunter-gatherers   Societies that rely upon naturally occurring sources of food. They have no domestic plants or animals except, perhaps, dogs.

hypotheses   Educated guesses to explain natural phenomena. In the scientific method, hypotheses must be testable. See also **theory.**

inclusive fitness   The idea that fitness is measured by the success of one's genes, whether possessed by the individual or by that individual's relatives.

independent assortment   When genes on different chromosomes segregate to gametes independently of one another.

induction   Developing a general explanation from specific observations. The step in the scientific method that generates hypotheses. See also **deduction.**

inheritance of acquired characteristics   The incorrect idea, associated with Lamarck, that adaptive traits acquired during an organism's lifetime can be passed on to its offspring.

inorganic   A molecule not containing carbon. Compare with **organic.**

intelligence   The relative ability of the brain to acquire, store, retrieve, and process information.

knuckle walking   Walking on the backs of the knuckles of the hand, typical of the African apes.

law of parsimony   A principle that relies on using the simplest explanation in formulating a scientific hypothesis. Another name for *Ockham's razor.*

Levallois technique   A tool technology involving striking uniform flakes from a prepared core. See **core tools** and **flake tools.**

life history   The study that examines the timing of life cycle events such as fertility, growth, and death.

linkage   When genes occur on the same chromosome and are inherited together.

luminescence dating   An absolute dating technique that measures trapped electrons by releasing their energy in the form of light. Can be used to date fired clay, pottery, brick, and burned stones. It may have some application in soil dating.

macromutations   Mutations with extensive and important physical results. The mutations for sickle cell anemia and Down syndrome are examples.

meiosis   The process of cell division in which gametes are produced, each gamete having one-half the normal complement of chromosomes and, therefore, only one allele of each original pair. See also **mitosis.**

melanin   The pigment largely responsible for human skin color.

melanocytes   Specialized skin cells that produce the pigment melanin.

menarche   A woman's first menstrual period.

Mendelian genetics   The basic laws of inheritance, discovered by Gregor Mendel in the nineteenth century.

menopause   The end of a woman's reproductive cycle.

messenger ribonucleic acid (mRNA)   The molecule that carries the genetic code out of the nucleus for translation into proteins. See also **transfer RNA.**

microsatellites   Long repetitious strings of noncoding DNA. Their length and the fact that they are not influenced by selection make them good genetic landmarks for DNA comparisons.

mitochondrial DNA (mtDNA)   The genetic material found in the cell's mitochondria, rather than in the cell's nucleus. The mtDNA does not play a role in inheritance and thus may give a more accurate measure of the genetic differences among populations.

mitosis The process of cell division that results in two exact copies of the original cell. See also **meiosis.**

monogenic A trait coded for by a single gene. The ABO blood group system is a monogenic trait. Compare with **polygenic.**

Mousterian technique A toolmaking tradition associated with the European Neandertals.

Multiregional Evolution (MRE) model The hypothesis that *Homo sapiens* is about 2 million years old and that modern human traits evolved in geographically diverse locations and then spread through the species. Compare with **Recent African Origin model.**

mutation Any mistake in an organism's genetic code.

natural selection Evolutionary change based on the differential reproductive success of individuals within a species.

niche The environment of an organism and its adaptive response to that environment.

nocturnal Active at night. Compare with **diurnal.**

notochord A stiff cartilaginous rod that supports the body and protects the dorsal nerve. The evolutionary precursor of the vertebral column.

nuclear DNA The genetic material in the nucleus of a cell.

nucleotide The basic building block of DNA and RNA, made up of a sugar, a phosphate, and one of four bases.

Oldowan A toolmaking tradition from Africa associated with early *Homo.*

omnivore An organism with a mixed diet of animal and vegetable foods. Compare with **carnivore.**

opposability The ability to touch (oppose) the thumb to the tips of the other fingers on the same hand.

organic Molecules that are part of living organisms. They are based on the chemistry of carbon and contain mostly hydrogen, oxygen, carbon, and nitrogen. Even carbon-based molecules that are not found in living things are sometimes referred to as organic. Compare with **inorganic.**

oscillating selection Adaptive variation around a norm, rather than in one direction, in response to environmental variation in a species' habitat.

osteology The study of the structure, function, and evolution of the skeleton.

Out-of-Africa model Another name for the Recent African Origin model.

paleoanthropology A specialty that studies the human fossil record.

paleopathology The study of disease and nutritional deficiency in prehistoric populations, usually with reference to the use of skeletal material.

Pangea The supercontinent that included parts of all present-day landmasses. It formed around 280 mya and began breaking up around 200 mya.

particulate The idea that biological traits are controlled by individual factors rather than by a single all-encompassing hereditary agent.

petrified A fossil that has turned to stone. As the organic material decays, it is slowly replaced by minerals, leaving a cast in stone of the organism or some of its parts.

phenetic taxonomy A classification system based on existing phenotypic features and adaptive traits.

phenotype The chemical or physical results of the genetic code. See also **genotypes.**

photosynthesis The process by which plants manufacture their own nutrients from carbon dioxide and water, using chlorophyll as a catalyst and sunlight as an energy source.

physical anthropology The traditional name for biological anthropology.

plate tectonics The movement of the plates of the earth's crust caused by their interaction with the molten rock of the earth's interior. The cause of continental drift.

Pleistocene The geological time period, from 1.6 mya to 10,000 ya, characterized by a series of glacial advances and retreats. See **glaciers.**

point mutations Mutations of single codons. The mutation that causes sickle cell anemia is an example. Compare with **chromosomal mutations.**

polygenic   A trait coded for by more than one gene. Skin color is a polygenic trait. Compare with **monogenic.**

polymorphisms   Variations in the genetic code within a species.

polytypic   A species with physically distinguishable regional populations.

postnatal dependency   The period after birth during which offspring require the care of adults to survive.

postorbital constriction   A narrowing of the skull behind the eyes, as viewed from above.

potassium/argon (K/Ar) dating   A radiometric dating technique using the rate at which radioactive potassium, found in volcanic rock, decays into stable argon gas. See also **argon/argon dating.**

prehensile   Having the ability to grasp.

primates   Large-brained, mostly tree-dwelling mammals with three-dimensional color vision and grasping hands. Humans are primates.

primatology   A specialty of anthropology that studies nonhuman primates.

prognathism   The jutting forward of the lower face and jaw area.

progressive   In evolution, the now-discounted idea that all change is toward increasing complexity.

prosimian   A primate with primitive features, most closely resembling the ancient primates.

protein synthesis   The process by which the genetic code puts together proteins in the cell.

proteins   Molecules that make cells and carry out cellular functions. Proteins are made of amino acids.

provenience   The precise location where a fossil or artifact was found.

pseudoscience   Scientifically testable ideas that are taken on faith, even if tested and shown to be false. Scientific creationism is a pseudoscience.

punctuated equilibrium   The view that species tend to remain stable and that evolutionary changes occur fairly suddenly. Compare with **Darwinian gradualism.**

quadrupedal   Walking on all four limbs.

races   In biology, the same as subspecies. In culture, cultural categories to classify and account for human diversity. See **folk taxonomy.**

racism   Judging an individual based solely on his or her racial affiliation.

radiocarbon dating   A radiometric dating technique using the decay rate of a radioactive form of carbon found in organic remains.

radiometric   Referring to the decay rate of a radioactive substance. See **argon/argon dating; carbon dating;** and **potassium/argon dating.**

Recent African Origin (RAO) model   The hypothesis that *Homo sapiens* recently evolved as a separate species in Africa and then spread to replace more archaic populations. Compare with **Multiregional Evolution model.**

recessive   The allele of a heterozygous pair that is not expressed. For a recessive allele to be expressed it must be homozygous. Compare with **dominant.**

recombination   The exchange of genetic material between pairs of chromosomes during meiosis. An important source of genetic variation. See also **crossing over.**

reification   Translating a complex set of phenomena into a single entity such as a number. IQ test scores are an example.

relative dating technique   A dating method that indicates the age of one item in comparison to another. Stratigraphy provides relative dates by indicating that one layer is older or younger than another. Compare with **absolute dating technique.**

replication   The copying of the genetic code during cell division.

reproductive isolating mechanism   Any difference that prevents the production of fertile offspring between members of two populations. Necessary for the production of separate species.

reproductive strategies   Behaviors that evolve to maximize an individual's reproductive success.

RNA   See **messenger RNA** and **transfer RNA.**

sagittal crest   A ridge of bone, running from front to back along the top of the skull, for the attachment of chewing muscles.

sagittal keel   A sloping of the sides of the skull toward the top, as viewed from the front.

sampling error   When a sample chosen for study does not accurately represent the population from which the sample was taken. See **gamete sampling.**

savanna The open grasslands of the tropics. The savannas of Africa are important in early hominid evolution.

science The method of inquiry that requires the generation, testing, and acceptance or rejection of hypotheses.

scientific creationism The belief in a literal biblical interpretation regarding the creation of the universe, with the connected belief that this view is supported by scientific evidence. An example of a pseudoscience.

scientific method The process of conducting scientific inquiry. See **science.**

segregation In genetics, the breaking up of allele pairs in the production of gametes.

semispecies Populations of a species that are completely isolated from one another but have not yet become truly different species.

sex The biological categories and characteristics of males and females. Compare with **gender.**

sexual dimorphism Physical differences between the sexes of a species not related to reproductive features. See **sex.**

sexually Reproducing by combining genetic material from two individuals. Compare with **asexually.**

shared derived characteristics Phenotypic features shared by two or more taxonomic groups that are derived from a common ancestor and that are not found in other groups.

single nucleotide polymorphism (SNP) A single base pair of the genetic code that displays variable expressions among individuals.

sites Locations that contain fossil or archaeological evidence of human presence.

sociobiology The scientific study that examines evolutionary explanations for social behaviors within species.

specialized Species that are adapted to a narrow range of environmental niches. Compare with **generalized.**

speciation The evolution of new species.

species A group of organisms that can produce fertile offspring among themselves but not with

members of other groups. A closed genetic population, usually physically distinguishable from other populations.

stereoscopic vision Three-dimensional vision; depth perception.

strata Layers; here, the layers of rock and soil under the surface of the earth. Singular, *stratum.*

stratigraphy The study of the earth's strata.

subspecies Physically distinguishable populations within a species. See **races.**

superposition The principle of stratigraphy that, barring disturbances, more recent layers are superimposed over older ones.

symbiosis An adaptive relationship between two different species, often, but not necessarily, of mutual benefit.

symbolic A communication system that uses arbitrary but agreed-upon sounds and signs for meaning.

systematists Another name for taxonomists.

taphonomy The study of how organisms become part of the paleontological record—how fossils form and what processes affect them through time.

taxa Categories within a taxonomic classification; singular, *taxon.* See **taxonomy.**

taxonomists Those who classify and name living organisms.

taxonomy A classification based on similarities and differences. In biology, the science of categorizing organisms and of naming them so as to reflect their relationships. Compare with **cladistics** and see **phenetic taxonomy.**

theory A hypothesis that has been well supported by evidence and testing. In science, theory is a positive term.

torus A bony ridge at the back of the skull, where the neck muscles attach.

transfer ribonucleic acid (tRNA) RNA that lines up amino acids along mRNA to make proteins. See also **messenger RNA.**

trephination Cutting a hole in the skull, presumably to treat some illness, a practice within some societies with prescientific knowledge.

tundra A treeless area with low-growing vegetation and permanently frozen ground. Located in the Arctic today, tundra conditions were found during the Pleistocene in the vicinity of glaciers far to the south.

uniformitarianism   The idea that present-day geological and biological processes can also explain the history of the earth and its life. See also **catastrophists.**

velocity curve   A graph that compares rate of change in some variable at different points in time, for example, rate of growth at different ages. Compare with **distance curve.**

vertebrates   Organisms with backbones.

zygote   The fertilized egg before cell division begins.

Bibliography

Aiello, L., and C. Dean. 1990. *An Introduction to Human Evolutionary Anatomy*. London: Academic Press.

Aiello, L. C. 1993. The fossil evidence for modern human origins in Africa: A revised view. *American Anthropologist* 95 (1): 73–96.

Aldhous, P., and A. Abbot. 2000. Battling the killer proteins. *Nature* 408:902–3.

Alexander, R. McN. 1995. Standing, walking and running. In *Gray's Anatomy*. 38th ed. New York: Churchill Livingston.

Allen, T. B. 1996. The silk road's lost world. *National Geographic* 189 (3): 44–51.

Appleman, P. 1979. *Darwin: A Norton Critical Edition*. 2nd ed. New York: Norton.

Armelagos, G. 1998. The viral superhighway. *The Sciences* 38 (1): 24–29.

Armelagos, G., K. C. Barnes, and J. Lin. 1996. Disease in human evolution: The re-emergence of infectious disease in the third epidemiological transition. *AnthroNotes* 18 (3): 1–7.

Asfaw, B., T. White, O. Lovejoy, B. Latimer, S. Simpson, and G. Suwa. 1999. *Australopithecus garhi*: A new species of early hominid from Ethiopia. *Science* 284:629–35.

Attenborough, D. 1979. *Life on Earth*. Boston: Little, Brown.

Awadalla, P., A. Eyre-Walker, and J. M. Smith. 1999. Linkage disequilibrium and recombination in hominid mitochondrial DNA. *Science* 286:2524–25.

Bahn, P. G. 1995. Last days of the iceman. *Archaeology*, May/June, 66–70.

Balter, M. 2001a. Scientists spar over claims of earliest human ancestor. *Science* 291:1460–61.

———. 2001b. Anthropologists duel over modern human origins. *Science* 291:1728–29.

Barfield, A. 1976. Biological influences on sex differences in behavior. In *Sex Differences*, edited by M. S. Teitelbaum. Garden City, NY: Anchor Press/Doubleday.

Barinaga, M. 1992. "African Eve" backers beat a retreat. *Science* 255:686–87.

Bass, W. 1971. *Human Osteology: A Laboratory and Field Manual of the Human Skeleton*. Columbia: Missouri Archaeological Society.

Beall, C. M., and A. T. Steegmann, Jr. 2000. Human adaptation to climate: Temperature, ultraviolet radiation, and altitude. In *Human Biology: An Evolutionary and Biocultural Perspective*, edited by S. Stinson et al., 163–224. New York: Wiley-Liss.

Begun, D. R. 2000. Knuckle-walking and the origin of human bipedalism. Paper delivered at the 69th Annual Meeting of the American Association of Physical Anthropologists, San Antonio, TX.

Berger, L. 1998. Redrawing our family tree? *National Geographic* 194 (2): 90–99.

Bermúdez de Castro, J. M., J. L. Arsuaga, E. Carbonell, A. Rosas, I. Martinez, and M. Mosquera. 1997. A hominid from the Lower Pleistocene of Atapuerca, Spain: Possible ancestor to Neandertals and modern humans. *Science* 276 (30 May): 1392–95.

Binford, L. 1985. Ancestral life ways: The faunal record. *Anthroquest* 32 (1): 15–20.

Binford, L. R. 1987. *Bones: Ancient Men and Modern Myths*. Orlando, FL: Academic Press.

Binford, L., and K. Chuan. 1985. Taphonomy at a distance: Zhoukoudian, "The Cave Home of Beijing Man." *Current Anthropology* 26:413–43.

Binford, L., and N. M. Stone. 1986. Zhoukoudian: A closer look. *Current Anthropology* 27:435–76.

Boaz, N. T., and R. L. Ciochon. 2001. The scavenging of "Peking Man." *Natural History* 110 (2): 46–51.

Boesch, C. 1999. A theory that's hard to digest. *Nature* 399 (17 June): 653.

Boesch, C., and H. Boesch-Achermann. 1991. Dim forest, bright chimps. *Natural History*, September, 50–57.

Bogin, B. 2001. Book review. *Evolutionary Anthropology* 114 (2): 172–74.

Bogin, B., and B. H. Smith. 2000. Evolution of the human life cycle. In *Human Biology: An Evolutionary and Biocultural Perspective*, edited by S. Stinson et al. New York: Wiley-Liss.

Bordes, F. 1972. *A Tale of Two Caves.* New York: Harper & Row.

Bower, B. 1997a. Ancient roads to Europe. *Science News* 151 (4 January): 12–13.

———. 1997b. Ancient ape shuffles to prominence. *Science News* 152 (18 October): 244.

———. 1999. Fossil may expose humanity's hybrid roots. *Science News* 155:295.

Bowlby, J. 1990. *Charles Darwin: A New Life.* New York: Norton.

Boyd, R., and J. B. Silk. 1997. *How Humans Evolved.* New York: Norton.

Bramblett, C. A. 1994. *Patterns of Primate Behavior.* 2nd ed. Prospect Heights, IL: Waveland Press.

Bräuer, G., and C. Stringer. 1997. Models, polarization, and perspectives on modern human origins. In *Conceptual Issues in Modern Human Origins Research*, edited by G. A. Clark and C. M. Willermet. New York: Aldine de Gruyter.

Bräuer, G., Y. Yokoyama, C. Falguères, and E. Mbua. 1997. Modern human origins backdated. *Nature* 386 (27 March): 337.

Brown, G. C. 2000. Symbionts and assassins. *Natural History* 109 (6): 66–71.

Brown, R. A., and G. J. Armelagos. 2001. Apportionment of racial diversity: A review. *Evolutionary Anthropology* 10 (1): 34–40.

Byrne, R. W., and J. M. Byrne. 1988. Leopard kills of Mahale. *Natural History* 97 (3): 22–26.

Cann, R. L., M. Stoneking, and A. C. Wilson. 1987. Mitochondrial DNA and human evolution. *Nature* 325:31–36.

Cartmill, M. 1992. New views on primate origins. *Evolutionary Anthropology* 1 (3): 105–11.

———. 1997. The third man. *Discover*, September, 56–62.

Cavalieri, P., and P. Singer. 1993. *The Great Ape Project: Equality Beyond Humanity.* New York: St. Martin's.

Cavalli-Sforza, L. L. 1991. Genes, peoples, and languages. *Scientific American* 265:104–10.

Cavalli-Sforza, L. L., and F. Cavalli-Sforza. 1995. *The Great Human Diasporas: The History of Diversity and Evolution.* Reading, MA: Addison-Wesley.

Cavalli-Sforza, L. L., P. Menozzi, and A. Piazza. 1994. *The History and Geography of Human Genes.* Princeton, NJ: Princeton University Press.

Cavallo, J. A. 1990. Cat in the human cradle. *Natural History* 99 (2): 53–60.

Ciochon, R., J. Olsen, and J. James. 1990. *Other Origins: The Search for the Giant Ape in Human Prehistory.* New York: Bantam Books.

Ciochon, R. L., and J. G. Fleagle, eds. 1993. *The Human Evolution Source Book.* Englewood Cliffs, NJ: Prentice Hall.

Clark, G. A., and C. M. Willermet, eds. 1997. *Conceptual Issues in Modern Human Origins Research.* New York: Aldine de Gruyter.

Cohen, J. E. 1996. Ten myths of population. *Discover*, April, 42–47.

Collard, M., and L. C. Aiello. 2000. From forelimbs to two legs. *Nature* 404:339–40.

Conroy, G. C. 1997. *Reconstructing Human Origins: A Modern Synthesis.* New York: Norton.

Conway Morris, S. 1998. *The Crucible of Creation: The Burgess Shale and the Rise of Animals.* New York: Oxford.

Conway Morris, S., and S. J. Gould. 1998/1999. Showdown on the Burgess Shale. *Natural History* 107 (10): 48–55.

Coon, C. 1962. *The Origin of Races.* New York: Knopf.

Cooper, R. S., C. N. Rotimi, and R. Ward. 1999. The puzzle of hypertension in African-Americans. *Scientific American*, February, 56–63.

Coppens, Y. 1994. East side story: The origin of humankind. *Scientific American* 270:88–95.

Cowen, R. 1995. *History of Life.* 2nd ed. Boston: Blackwell Scientific Publications.

Crossette, B. 2001. Against a trend, U.S. population will bloom, U.N. says. *New York Times*, 28 February, A6.

Culotta, E. 1999a. Anthropologists probe bones, stones, and molecules. *Science* 284:1109–11.

———. 1999b. A new human ancestor? *Science* 284:572–73.

Cummins, H., and C. Midlo. 1961. *Finger Prints, Palms, and Soles: An Introduction to Dermatoglyphics*. New York: Dover.

Darwin, C. R. 1898. *On the Origin of Species by Means of Natural Selection*. 1872. 6th ed. New York: Appleton.

De Bonis, L., and G. D. Koufos. 1994. Our ancestor's ancestor: *Ouranopithecus* is a Greek link in human ancestry. *Evolutionary Anthropology* 3 (3): 75–83.

Defleur, A., T. White, P. Valensi, L. Slimak, and E. Crégut-Bonnoure. 1999. Neanderthal cannibalism at Moula-Guercy, Ardèch, France. *Science* 286:128–31.

de Heinzelin, J. J., D. Clark, T. White, W. Hart, P. Renne, G. Wolde-Gabriel, Y. Beyene, and E. Vrba. 1999. Environment and behavior of 2.5-million-year-old Bouri hominids. *Science* 284: 624–29.

de Waal, F., and F. Lanting (photographer). 1997. *Bonobo: The Forgotten Ape*. Berkeley: University of California Press.

de Waal, F. B. M. 1995. Bonobo sex and society. *Scientific American*, March, 82–88.

Diamond, J. 1991. Curse and blessing of the ghetto. *Discover*, March, 60–65.

DiPietro, L. 2000. Tackling race and sports. *Scientific American*, May, 73–76.

Dobzhansky, T. 1970. *Genetics of the Evolutionary Process*. New York: Columbia University Press.

Dolhinow, P., and A. Fuentes, 1999. *The Nonhuman Primates*. Mountain View, CA: Mayfield.

Donnelly, C. A. 2000. Likely size of the French BSE epidemic. *Nature* 408: 787–88.

Donnelly, P., S. Tavaré, D. J. Balding, and R. C. Griffiths. 1996. Technical comments: Estimating the age of the common ancestor of men from the ZFY intron. *Science* 272:1357–58.

Dorit, R. L., H. Akashi, and W. Gilbert. 1995. Absence of polymorphism at the ZFY locus on the human Y chromosome. *Science* 268:1183–85.

Duarte, C., J. Mauricio, P. B. Pettiee, P. Souto, E. Trinkhaus, H. Van der Plicht, and J. Zilhão. 1999. The early Upper Paleolithic human skeleton from the Abrigo od Lagar Velho (Portugal) and modern human emergence in Iberia. *Proceedings of the National Academy of Sciences* 96:7604–9.

Dunham, I., N. Shimizu, B. A. Roe, S. Chissoe, et al. 1999. The DNA sequence of human chromosome 22. *Nature* 402:489–95.

Eaton, S. B., and M. Konner. 1985. Diet: Paleolithic genes and twentieth-century health. *Anthroquest*, The L. S. B. Leakey Foundation, 1985.

Eldredge, N. 1991. *The Miner's Canary: Unraveling the Mysteries of Extinction*. New York: Prentice Hall.

———. 1995. *Dominion*. New York: Henry Holt.

Entine, J. 2000. *Taboo: Why Black Athletes Dominate Sports and Why We're Afraid to Talk About It*. New York: PublicAffairs.

Epstein, P. R. 2000. Is global warming harmful to health? *Scientific American*, August, 50–57.

Fagan, B. 1994. *In the Beginning: An Introduction to Archaeology*. 8th ed. New York: Harper Collins.

Fagan, B. M. 1990. *The Journey from Eden: The Peopling of Our World*. London: Thames and Hudson.

Fausto-Sterling, A. 1993. The five sexes. *Sciences*, March/April, 20–24.

Feder, K. L. 1996. *The Past in Perspective: An Introduction to Human Prehistory*. Mountain View, CA: Mayfield.

———. 1997. Indians and archaeologists: The conflicting views of myth and science. *Skeptic* 5 (3): 74–80.

———. 1999. *Lessons from the Past: An Introductory Reader in Archaeology*. Mountain View, CA: Mayfield.

———. 2001. *Frauds, Myths, and Mysteries: Science and Pseudoscience in Archaeology*. 4th ed. Mountain View, CA: Mayfield.

Feder, K. L., and M. A. Park. 2001. *Human Antiquity: An Introduction to Physical Anthropology and Archaeology.* 4th ed. Mountain View, CA: Mayfield.

Fedigan, L. M., and L. Fedigan. 1988. *Gender and the study of Primates: Curricular Module for the Project on Gender and Curriculum.* Washington, DC: American Anthropological Association.

Ferris, Timothy. 1988. *Coming of Age in the Milky Way.* New York: William Morrow.

Fleagle, J. G. 1988. *Primate Adaptation and Evolution.* San Diego: Academic Press.

Fortey, R. 1998. *Life: A Natural History of the First Four Billion Years of Life on Earth.* New York: Knopf.

Fossey, D. 1983. *Gorillas in the Mist.* Boston: Houghton Mifflin.

Fouts, R., with S. T. Mills. 1997. *Next of Kin: What Chimpanzees Have Taught Me About Who We Are.* New York: William Morrow.

Fouts, R. S., and D. H. Fouts. 1999. Chimpanzee sign language research. In *The Nonhuman Primates*, edited by P. Dolhinow and A. Fuentes. Mountain View, CA: Mayfield.

Francione, G. L. 1996. *Rain Without Thunder: The Ideology of the Animal Rights Movement.* Philadelphia: Temple University Press.

Frayer, D. W., M. H. Wolpoff, A. G. Thorne, F. H. Smith, and G. G. Pope. 1993. Theories of modern human origins: The paleontological test. *American Anthropologist* 95 (1): 14–50.

———. 1994. Getting it straight. *American Anthropologist* 96:424–38.

Fu, Y-X, and W-H Li. 1996. Estimating the age of the common ancestor of men from the ZFY intron. *Science* 272:1356–57.

Gaffney, E. S., L. Dingus, and M. K. Smith. 1995. Why cladistics? *Natural History* 104 (6): 33–35.

Galdikas, B. 1995. *Reflections of Eden: My Years with the Orangutans of Borneo.* Boston: Little, Brown.

Gebo, D. L., M. Dagosto, K. C. Beard, T. Qi, and J. Wang. 2000. The oldest known anthropoid postcranial fossil and the early evolution of the higher primates. *Nature* 404:276–78.

Gebo, D. L., L. MacLatchy, R. Kityo, A. Deino, J. Kingston, and D. Pilbeam. 1997. A hominoid genus from the early Miocene of Uganda. *Science* 276 (18 April): 401–4.

Gibbons, A. 1997a. Tracing the identity of the first toolmakers. *Science* 276 (4 April): 32.

———. 1997b. A new face for human ancestors. *Science* 276 (30 May): 1331–33.

———. 1997c. Doubts over spectacular dates. *Science* 278 (10 October): 220–22.

———. 1997d. Y chromosome shows that Adam was an African. *Science* 278 (31 October): 804–5.

———. 1998a. Genes put mammals in age of dinosaurs. *Science* 289:675–76.

———. 1998b. Which of our genes makes us human? *Science* 281:1432–34.

———. 2001a. The riddle of coexistence. *Science* 291:1725–29.

———. 2001b. The peopling of the Pacific. *Science* 291:1735–37.

Gish, Duane T. 1979. *Evolution: The Fossils Say No!* San Diego: Creation-Life Publishers.

Glausiusz, J. 1995. Unfortunate drift. *Discover*, June, 34–35.

Goodall, J. 1971. *In the Shadow of Man.* Boston: Houghton Mifflin.

———. 1986. *The Chimpanzees of Gombe: Patterns of Behavior.* Cambridge, MA: Belknap Press.

———. 1990. *Through a Window: My Thirty Years with the Chimpanzees of Gombe.* Boston: Houghton Mifflin.

Gore, R. 1989. Extinctions. *National Geographic* 175 (6): 662–99.

———. 1993. The Cambrian period: Explosion of life. *National Geographic* 184 (4): 120–36.

———. 1997a. Expanding worlds. *National Geographic* 191 (5): 84–109.

———. 1997b. The first Europeans. *National Geographic* 192 (1): 96–113.

Goudsmit, J. 1997. *Viral Sex: The Nature of AIDS.* New York: Oxford University Press.

Gould, S. J. 1977. *Ever Since Darwin.* New York: Norton.

———. 1980. *The Panda's Thumb.* New York: Norton.

———. 1983. *Hen's Teeth and Horse's Toes.* New York: Norton.

———. 1985. *The Flamingo's Smile.* New York: Norton.

———. 1989. *Wonderful Life: The Burgess Shale and the Nature of History*. New York: Norton.

———. 1991. *Bully for Brontosaurus*. New York: Norton.

———. 1992. What is a species? *Discover*, December, 40–45.

———. 1993a. *Eight Little Piggies*. New York: Norton.

———., ed. 1993b. *The Book of Life*. New York: Norton.

———. 1994a. In the mind of the beholder. *Natural History* 103 (2): 14–23.

———. 1994b. The evolution of life on the earth. *Scientific American* 271 (4): 84–91.

———. 1995a. *Dinosaur in a Haystack: Reflections in Natural History*. New York: Harmony.

———. 1995b. Of tongue worms, velvet worms, and water bears. *Natural History* 104 (1): 6–15.

———. 1995c. Evolution by walking. *Natural History* 104 (3): 10–15.

———. 1996a. *Full House: The Spread of Excellence from Plato to Darwin*. New York: Harmony.

———. 1996b. *The Mismeasure of Man*. 2nd ed. New York: Norton.

———. 1997/1998. The paradox of the visibly irrelevant. *Natural History* 106 (11): 12–18, 60–66.

———. 1998. *Leonardo's Mountain of Clams and the Diet of Worms: Essays on Natural History*. New York: Harmony.

———. 1999. *Rocks of Ages: Science and Religion in the Fullness of Life*. New York: Ballantine.

———. 2000. *The Lying Stones of Marrakech: Penultimate Reflections in Natural History*. New York: Harmony.

Grant, P., and R. Grant. 2000. Non-random fitness variation in two populations of Darwin's finches. *Proceedings of the Royal Society of London* 267 (1439): 131–38.

Greene, J. C. 1959. *The Death of Adam*. New York: Mentor.

Groves, C. P. 1997. Thinking about evolutionary change: The polarity of our ancestors. In *Conceptual Issues in Modern Human Origins Research*, edited by G. A. Clark and C. M. Willermet, 319–26. New York: Aldine de Gruyter.

Guth, A. H. 2000. Genesis: The sequel. *Natural History* 109 (1): 77–79.

Hahn, B. H., G. M. Shaw, K. M. De Cock, and P. M. Sharp. 2000. AIDS as a zoonosis: Scientific and public health implications. *Science* 287:607–14.

Hammer, M. F., and S. L. Zegura. 1996. The role of the Y chromosome in human evolutionary studies. *Evolutionary Anthropology* 5 (4): 116–34.

Hansen, J. P., J. Meldgaard, and J. Nordqvist. 1985. The mummies of Qilakitsoq. *National Geographic* 167 (2): 191–207.

Harpending, H., and J. Relethford. 1997. Population perspectives on human origins research. In *Conceptual Issues in Modern Human Origins Research*, edited by G. A. Clark and C. M. Willermet. New York: Aldine de Gruyter.

Harris, C. L. 1981. *Evolution: Genesis and Revelations*. Albany: State University of New York Press.

Harrison, G. A., and A. J. Boyce, eds. 1972. *The Structure of Human Populations*. Oxford: Clarendon.

Harrison, G. A., J. S. Weiner, J. M. Tanner, and N. A. Barnicot. 1977. *Human Biology: An Introduction to Human Evolution, Variation, Growth, and Ecology*. 2nd ed. Oxford: Oxford University Press.

Hawks, J., and M. H. Wolpoff. 2001. Brief communication: Paleoanthropology and the population genetics of ancient genes. *American Journal of Physical Anthropology* 114:269–72.

Hedges, S. B., S. Kumar, K. Tamura, and M. Stoneking. 1992. Technical comments. *Science* 255:737–39.

Hern, W. M. 1993. Is human culture carcinogenic for uncontrolled population growth and ecological destruction? *BioScience* 43 (11): 768–73.

Herrnstein, R. J., and C. Murray. 1994. *The Bell Curve: The Reshaping of American Life by Difference in Intelligence*. New York: Free Press.

Hill, K. 1993. Life history theory and evolutionary anthropology. *Evolutionary Anthropology* 2 (3):78–88.

Holden, C. 1998. No last word on language origins. *Science* 282:1455–58.

———. 1999. Patrimony debate gets ugly. *Science* 285:195.

———. 2001a. Oldest human DNA reveals Aussie oddity. *Science* 291:230–31.

———. 2001b. Dinner in a mound. *Science* 291:587.

Holliday, T. W. 1997. Postcranial evidence of cold adaptation in European Neandertals. *American Journal of Physical Anthropology* 104:245–58.

Holloway, R. 1980. Indonesian "Solo" (Ngandong) endocranial reconstructions: Preliminary observations and comparisons with Neandertal and *Homo erectus* groups. *American Journal of Physical Anthropology* 53:285–95.

———. 1981. The Indonesian *Homo erectus* brain endocasts revisited. *American Journal of Physical Anthropology* 55:503–21.

Hostetler, J. A. 1974. *Hutterite Society*. Baltimore: Johns Hopkins University Press.

Ingman, M., H. Kaessmann, S. Pääbo, and U. Gyllensten. 2000. Mitochondrial genome variation and the origin of modern humans. *Nature* 408:708–13.

Ingmanson, E. 1996. Tool-using behavior in wild *Pan paniscus*: Social and ecological considerations. In *Reaching into Thought: The Minds of the Great Apes*, edited by A. Russon, K. Bard, and S. Taylor. Cambridge: Cambridge University Press.

Ingmanson, E., and H. Ihobe. 1992. Predation and meat eating by *Pan paniscus* at Wamba, Zaire. Paper delivered at the 61st Annual Meeting of the American Association of Physical Anthropologists, Las Vegas, NV.

Ingmanson, E., and T. Kano. 1993. Waging peace. *International Wildlife*, November/December, 30–37.

International SNP Map Working Group. 2001. A map of human genome sequence variation contains 1.42 million single nucleotide polymorphisms. *Nature* 409:928–33.

Jablonski, N. G., and G. Chaplin. 2000a. Do theories of bipedalization stand up to anatomical scrutiny? Paper delivered at the 69th Annual Meeting of the American Association of Physical Anthropologists, San Antonio, TX.

———. 2000b. The evolution of human skin coloration. *Journal of Human Evolution* 39 (1): 57–106.

Jaeger, J.-J., et al. 1999. A new primate from the Middle Eocene of Myanmar and the Asian early origin on anthropoids. *Science* 286:528–30.

Janus, C. 1975. *The Search for Peking Man*. New York: Macmillan.

Jegalian, K., and B. T. Lahn. 2001. Why the Y is so weird. *Scientific American*, February, 56–61.

Jensen, A. R. 1969. How much can we boost IQ and scholastic achievement? *Harvard Educational Review* 39 (1, Winter): 1–123.

Jobling, M. A., and C. Tyler-Smith. 1995. Fathers and sons: The Y chromosome and human evolution. *Trends in Genetics* 11:449–56.

Johanson, D., and J. Shreeve. 1989. *Lucy's Child: The Discovery of a Human Ancestor*. New York: William Morrow.

Johanson, D. C., and M. A. Edey. 1981. *Lucy: The Beginnings of Humankind*. New York: Simon & Schuster.

Johnson, T. C., C. A. Scholz, M. R. Talbot, K. Kelts, R. D. Ricketts, G. Ngobi, K. Beuning, I. Ssemmanda, and J. W. McGill. 1996. Late Pleistocene dessication of Lake Victoria and rapid evolution of cichlid fishes. *Science* 273 (23 August): 1091–93.

Jolly, A. 1985. *The Evolution of Primate Behavior*. New York: Macmillan.

———. 1988. Madagascar's lemurs: On the edge of survival. *National Geographic* 174 (2): 132–61.

Kano, T. 1990. The bonobos' peaceable kingdom. *Natural History*, November, 62–71.

Kay, R. F., C. Ross, and B. A. Williams. 1997. Anthropoid origins. *Science* 275 (7 February): 797–804.

Keith, A. 1927. *Concerning Man's Origin*. London: Watts.

Kennedy, K. A. R. 1976. *Human Variation in Space and Time*. Dubuque, IA: William C. Brown.

Kingston, J. D., B. D. Marino, and A. Hill. 1994. Isotopic evidence for neocene hominid paleoenvironments in the Kenya rift valley. *Science* 264:955–59.

Kirkpatrick, M. 2000. Fish found in *flagrante delicto*. *Nature* 408:298–99.

Korber, B., M. Muldoon, J. Theiler, F. Gao, R. Gupta, A. Lapedes, B. H. Hahn, S. Wolinsky, and T. Bhattacharya. 2000. Timing the ancestor of the HIV-1 pandemic strains. *Science* 288: 1789–96.

Krings, M., H. Geisert, R. W. Schmitz, H. Krainitzki, and S. Pääbo. 1999. DNA sequence of the mitochondrial hypervariable region II from the Neandertal type specimen. *Proceedings of the National Academy of Sciences* 96 (10): 5581–85.

Krings, M., A. Stone, R. W. Schmitz, H. Krainitzki, M. Stoneking, and S. Pääbo. 1997. Neandertal DNA sequences and the origin of modern humans. *Cell* 90 (1): 19–30.

Kunzig, R. 1997. The face of an ancestral child. *Discover* 18 (12): 88–101.

Lack, D. 1947. *Darwin's Finches: An Essay on the General Biological Theory of Evolution.* Cambridge: Cambridge University Press.

Leakey, M. G., C. S. Feibel, I. McDougall, and A. Walker. 1995. New four-million-year-old hominid species from Kanapoi and Allia Bay, Kenya. *Nature* 376:565–71.

Leakey, M. G., F. Spoor, F. H. Brown, P. N. Gathogo, C. Kiarie, L. N. Leakey, and I. McDougall. 2001. New hominid genus from eastern Africa shows diverse middle Pliocene lineages. *Nature* 410:433–40.

Leakey, R., and R. Lewin. 1992. *Origins Reconsidered: In Search of What Makes Us Human.* New York: Doubleday.

———. 1995. *The Sixth Extinction: Patterns of Life and the Future of Humankind.* New York: Doubleday.

Lemonick, M. D. 1994. One less missing link. *Time,* 3 October, 68–69.

Lewin, R. 1991. The biochemical route to human origins. *Mosaic* 22 (3): 46–55.

Lewontin, R. 1982. *Human Diversity.* New York: Scientific American Books.

Lindenbaum, S. 1979. *Kuru Sorcery: Disease and Danger in the New Guinea Highlands.* Mountain View, CA: Mayfield.

Lyell, C. 1873. *The Geological Evidences of the Antiquity of Man.* London: Murray.

Madigan, M. T., and B. L. Marrs. 1997. Extremophiles. *Scientific American,* April, 82–87.

Malik, K. 2000. Sporting colours. *Nature* 407:131–32.

Malthus, T. R. 1789. *An Essay on the Principles of Population as It Affects the Future Improvement of Society with Remarks on the Speculations of Mr. Godwin, M. Condorcet and Other Writers* (facsimile of the first edition, 1926), London: Macmillan.

Maples, W. R., and M. Browning. 1994. *Dead Men Do Tell Tales.* New York: Doubleday.

Marks, J. 1994. Book reviews. *Human Biology* 66: 1113–17.

———. 1995. *Human Biodiversity: Genes, Race, and History.* New York: Aldine de Gruyter.

Marks, J., and R. B. Lyles. 1994. Rethinking genes. *Evolutionary Anthropology* 3 (4): 139–46.

Martin, M. K., and B. Voorhies. 1975. *Female of the Species.* New York: Columbia University Press.

McCollum, M. A. 1999. The robust australopithecine face: A morphogenic perspective. *Science* 284:301–4.

McCrossin, M. L. 1997. New postcranial remains of *Kenyapithecus* and their implications for understanding the origins of hominoid terrestriality. Paper delivered at the 66th Annual Meeting of the American Association of Physical Anthropologists, St. Louis, MO.

McGrew, W. C. 1998. Culture in nonhuman primates? *Annual Review of Anthropology* 27:301–28.

Menon, S. 1997. Neanderthal noses. *Discover,* March, 30.

Mettler, L. E., T. G. Gregg, and H. E. Schaffer. 1988. *Population Genetics and Evolution.* Englewood Cliffs, NJ: Prentice Hall.

Miller, K. R. 1999. *Finding Darwin's God.* New York: HarperCollins.

Mills, C. 1997. The deadliest virus. *Sciences,* January/February, 34–38.

Minugh-Purvis, N. 1995. The modern human origins controversy: 1984–1994. *Evolutionary Anthropology* 4 (4): 140–47.

Molnar, S. 1992. *Human Variation: Races, Types, and Ethnic Groups,* 3rd ed. Englewood Cliffs, NJ: Prentice Hall.

Montagu, A., ed. 1964. *The Concept of Race.* New York: Collier Books.

Morris, H. M. 1974. *The Troubled Waters of Evolution.* San Diego, CA: Creation-Life Publishers.

Mosko, S., C. Richard, J. McKenna, S. Drummond, and D. Mukai. 1997. Maternal proximity and infant CO_2 environment during bedsharing and possible implications for SIDS research. *American Journal of Physical Anthropology* 103 (3): 315–28.

Mowat, F. 1987. *Woman in the Mists.* New York: Warner Books.

Muchmore, E. A., S. Diaz, and A. Varki. 1998. A structural difference between the cell surfaces of humans and great apes. *American Journal of Physical Anthropology* 107:187–98.

Nafte, M. 2000. *Flesh and Bone.* Durham, NC: Carolina Academic Press.

Nanda, S. 1990. *Neither Man nor Woman: The Hijras of India.* Belmont, CA: Wadsworth.

Napier, J. R., and P. H. Napier. 1985. *The Natural History of the Primates.* Cambridge, MA: M.I.T. Press.

Nichols, M., J. Goodall, G. B. Schaller, and M. G. Smith. 1993. *The Great Apes: Between Two Worlds.* Washington, DC: National Geographic Society.

O'Brien, S. J., and R. Stanyon. 1999. Ancestral primate revealed. *Nature* 402 (25 November): 356–66.

Oliwenstein, L. 1995. Dr. Darwin. *Discover,* October, 111–17.

Olshansky, S. J., B. A. Carnes, and A. Désesquelles. 2001. Prospects for human longevity. *Science* 291:1491–92.

Omohundro, J. T. 2001. *Careers in Anthropology.* 2nd ed. Mountain View, CA: Mayfield.

Orgel, L. E. 1994. The origin of life on the earth. *Scientific American* 271 (4): 76–83.

Ovchinnikov, I., A. Götherström, G. Romanova, V. Kharitonov, K. Lindén, and W. Goodman. 2000. Molecular analysis of Neandertal DNA from the northern Caucasus. *Nature* 404:490–92.

Pääbo, S. 2001. The human genome and our view of ourselves. *Science* 291:1219–20.

Park, M. A. 1979. Dermatoglyphics as a tool for population studies: An example. Ph.D. dissertation, Department of Anthropology, Indiana University, Bloomington.

———. 1982/1983. Palmistry: Science or hand-jive? *The Skeptical Inquirer* 7 (2): 21–32.

———. 1999. The homegoing. In *Lessons from the Past,* edited by K. L. Feder, 80–83. Mountain View, CA: Mayfield.

———. 2000a. *Biological Anthropology: An Introductory Reader.* 2nd ed. Mountain View, CA: Mayfield.

———. 2000b. *Introducing Anthropology: An Integrated Approach.* Mountain View, CA: Mayfield.

Passingham, R. 1982. *The Human Primate.* New York: W. H. Freeman.

Pearson, O. M. 2000. Postcranial remains and the origin of modern humans. *Evolutionary Anthropology* 9 (6): 229–47.

Perry, W., and M. Blakey. 1999. Archaeology as community service: The African Burial Ground Project in New York City. In *Lessons from the Past,* edited by K. L. Feder, 45–51. Mountain View, CA: Mayfield.

Pfeiffer, J. 1969. *The Emergence of Man.* New York: Harper & Row.

Pilbeam, D. 1984. The descent of the hominoids and hominids. *Scientific American* 250 (3): 84–96.

———. 1986. Human origins. *David Skomp Distinguished Lecture in Anthropology.* Bloomington: Indiana University.

Podolefsky, A., and P. J. Brown, eds. 1994. *Applying Anthropology: An Introductory Reader.* Mountain View, CA: Mayfield.

Podos, J. 2001. Correlated evolution of morphology and vocal signal structure in Darwin's finches. *Nature* 409:185–87.

Post, P. W., F. Daniels, Jr., and R. T. Binford. 1975. Cold injury and the evolution of "white" skin. *Human Biology* 47:65–80.

Potts, R. 1984. Home bases and early hominids. *American Scientist* 72:338–47.

———. 1996. Evolution and climate variability. *Science* 273 (16 August): 922–23.

———. 1998. Variability selection in hominid evolution. *Evolutionary Anthropology* 7:81–96.

Power, M. 1991. *The Egalitarians—Human and Chimpanzee: An Anthropological View of Social Organization.* Cambridge: Cambridge University Press.

Prag, J., and R. Neave. 1997. *Making Faces: Using Forensic and Archaeological Evidence.* College Station: Texas A&M University Press.

Prusiner, S. B. 1997. Prion diseases and the BSE crisis. *Science* 278 (10 October): 245–51.

Raby, P. 1996. *Bright Paradise: Victorian Scientific Travelers.* Princeton: Princeton University Press.

Ragir, S. 2000. Diet and food preparation: Rethinking early hominid behavior. *Evolutionary Anthropology* 9 (4): 153–55.

Reinhard, J. 1996. Peru's ice maidens. *National Geographic* 189 (6): 62–81.

———. 1997. Mummies of Peru. *National Geographic* 191 (1): 36–43.

———. 1999. Frozen in time. *National Geographic* 196 (5): 36–55.

Relethford, J. H. 2001. *The Human Species: An Introduction to Biological Anthropology*. 4th ed. Mountain View, CA: Mayfield.

Relethford, J. H., and H. C. Harpending. 1995. Ancient differences in population size can mimic a recent African origin of modern humans. *Current Anthropology* 36 (4): 667–74.

Rhine, S. 1998. *Bone Voyage: A Journey in Forensic Anthropology*. Albuquerque: University of New Mexico Press.

Rhodes, R. 1997. *Deadly Feasts: Tracking the Secrets of a Terrifying New Plague*. New York: Simon & Schuster.

Richmond, B. G., and D. S. Strait. 2000. Evidence that humans evolved from a knuckle-walking ancestor. *Nature* 404:382–85.

Ridley, Mark. 1996. *Evolution*. 2nd ed. Boston: Blackwell Scientific.

Ridley, Matt. 1999. *Genome: The Autobiography of a Species in 23 Chapters*. New York: HarperCollins.

Rischer, C. E., and T. A. Easton. 1992. *Focus on Human Biology*. New York: HarperCollins.

Roberts, D. 1993. The ice man. *National Geographic* 183 (6): 36–67.

Robey, B., S. O. Rutstein, and L. Morris. 1993. The fertility decline in developing countries. *Scientific American,* December, 60–67.

Robins, A. 1991. *Biological Perspectives on Human Pigmentation*. Cambridge: Cambridge University Press.

Rogers, J., P. B. Samollow, and A. G. Comuzzie. 1996. Estimating the age of the common ancestor of men from the ZFY intron. *Science* 272: 1360–61.

Rowe, N. 1996. *The Pictorial Guide to the Living Primates*. East Hampton, NY: Pogonius Press.

Rowen, L., G. Mahairas, and L. Hood. 1997. Sequencing the human genome. *Science* 278 (24 October): 605–7.

Ryan, F. 1997. *Virus X: Tracking the New Killer Plagues out of the Present and into the Future*. Boston: Little, Brown.

Sagan, C. 1977. *The Dragons of Eden: Speculations on the Evolution of Human Intelligence*. New York: Random House.

———. 1996. *The Demon-Haunted World: Science as a Candle in the Dark*. New York: Random House.

Savage-Rumbaugh, E. S., S. Shanker, T. J. Taylor, and S. Savage-Rumbaugh. 1998. *Apes, Language, and the Human Mind*. Oxford: Oxford University Press.

Savage-Rumbaugh, S., and R. Lewin. 1994. Ape at the brink. *Discover,* September, 91–98.

Schadewald, R. 1981/1982. Scientific creationism, geocentricity and the flat earth. *Skeptical Inquirer* 6 (2): 41–48.

———. 1986. Creationist pseudoscience. In *Science Confronts the Paranormal*, edited by Kendrick Frazier. Buffalo, NY: Prometheus Books.

Schick, K. D. and N. Toth. 1993. *Making Silent Stones Speak: Human Evolution and the Dawn of Technology*. New York: Morrow.

Schoeninger, M. J. 1995. Stable iostope studies in human evolution. *Evolutionary Anthropology* 4 (3): 83–98.

Scholz, M., L. Bachmann, G. J. Nicholson, J. Bachmann, I. Giddings, B. Rüschoff-Thale, A. Czarnetzki, and C. M. Pusch. 2000. Genomic differentiation of Neanderthals and anatomically modern man allows a fossil DNA-based classification of morphologically indistinguishable hominid bones. *American Journal of Human Genetics* 66:1927–32.

Schultz, E., and R. Lavenda. 1998. *Anthropology: A Perspective on the Human Condition*. 2nd ed. Mountain View, CA: Mayfield.

Schwartz, J. H. 1995. *Skeleton Keys: An Introduction to Human Skeletal Morphology, Development, and Analysis*. New York: Oxford University Press.

Semaw, S., P. Renne, J. W. K. Harris, C. S. Feibel, R. L. Bernor, N. Fesseha, and K. Mowbray. 1997. 2.5-million-year-old stone tools from

Gona, Ethiopia. *Nature* 385 (23 January): 333–36.

Service, R. F. 2000. Where dead men really do tell tales. *Science* 289:855–57.

Sewa, G., B. Asfaw, Y. Beyene, T. D. White, S. Katoh, S. Nagaoka, H. Nakaya, K. Uzawa, P. Renne, and G. WoldeGabriel. 1997. The first skull of *Australopithecus boisei*. *Nature* 389 (2 October): 489–92.

Sharer, R. J., and W. Ashmore. 1993. *Archaeology: Discovering Our Past*. 2nd ed. Mountain View, CA: Mayfield.

Shea, J. 1989. A functional study of the lithic industries associated with hominid fossils in Kebara and Qafzeh Caves, Israel. In *The Human Revolution: Behavioural and Biological Perspectives in the Origins of Modern Humans*, edited by P. Mellars and C. Stringer, 611–25. Princeton, NJ: Princeton University Press.

Sherwood, R. J. 2000. The status of early *Homo*. Paper delivered at the 69th Annual Meeting of the American Association of Physical Anthropologists, San Antonio, TX.

Shipman, P. 1981. *Life History of a Fossil: An Introduction to Taphonomy and Paleoecology*. Cambridge, MA: Harvard University Press.

———. 1984. Scavenger hunt. *Natural History* 93 (4): 20–27.

———. 1986. Scavenging or hunting in early hominids: Theoretical frameworks and tests. *American Anthropologist* 88:27–43.

———. 2001. *The Man Who Found the Missing Link: Eugene Dubois and His Lifelong Quest to Prove Darwin Right*. New York: Simon & Schuster.

Shipman, P., and J. Rose. 1983. Evidence of butchery and hominid activities at Torralba and Ambrona: An evaluation using microscopic techniques. *Journal of Archaeological Science* 10:465–74.

Shreeve, J. 1994. *Erectus* rising. *Discover*, September, 80–89.

———. 1995. The Neanderthal peace. *Discover*, September, 70–81.

———. 1996. Sunset on the savanna. *Discover* 17 (7): 116–25.

———. 1999. Secrets of the gene. *National Geographic* 196 (4): 42–75.

Shuster, A. M. H. 2001. World's earliest woodworking? *Archaeology Online News*. www.archaeology.org/online/news. January 31.

Simons, E. L., and T. Rasmussen. 1994. A whole new world of ancestors: Eocene anthropoideans from Africa. *Evolutionary Anthropology* 3 (4): 128–39.

Simons, M. 1996. New species of early human reported found in Africa. *New York Times*, 23 May, A8.

Sjøvold, T. 1992. The stone age iceman from the Alps: The find and current status of investigation. *Evolutionary Anthropology* 1 (4): 117–24.

Smail, J. K. 1999. Beyond population stabilization: The case for dramatically reducing global human numbers. *Politics and Life Sciences* 16 (2):183–92.

Small, M. F. 1992. A reasonable sleep. *Discover*, April, 83–88.

Smith, B. H. 1993. Life history and the evolution of human maturation. *Evolutionary Anthropology* 1 (4): 134–42.

Smith, F. H. 1994. Samples, species, and speculations in the study of modern human origins. In *Origins of Anatomically Modern Humans*, edited by M. Nitecki and D. Nitecki, 227–52. New York: Plenum.

Smith, F. H., A. B. Falsetti, and S. M. Donnelly. 1989. Modern human origins. *Yearbook of Physical Anthropology* 32:35–68.

Smith, J. M. 1984. Science and myth. *Natural History* 93 (11): 10–24.

Smith, S. L., and F. B. Harrold. 1997. A paradigm's worth of difference? Understanding the impasse over modern human origins. *Yearbook of Physical Anthropology* 40: 113–38.

Smuts, B. 1985. *Sex and Friendship in Baboons*. Hawthorne, NY: Aldine de Gruyter.

———. 1995. Apes of wrath. *Discover*, August, 35–37.

Snow, C. C., and J. L. Luke. 1970. The Oklahoma City child disappearances: Forensic anthropology in the identification of skeletal remains. In *Applying Anthropology*, edited by A. Podolefsky and P. J. Brown. Mountain View, CA: Mayfield.

Specter, M. 1999. Decoding Iceland. *New Yorker*, 18 January, 40–51.

Spindler, K. 1995. *The Man in the Ice*. New York: Harmony.

Sponheimer, M., and J. A. Lee-Thorp. 1999. Isotopic evidence for the diet of an early hominid, *Australopithecus africanus*. *Science* 283:368–69.

Stanford, C. 1999. *The Hunting Apes: Meat Eating and the Origins of Human Behavior*. Princeton: Princeton University Press.

Stanford, C. B. 1995. To catch a colobus. *Natural History* 104 (1): 48–55.

Stern, J. T. Jr. 2000. Climbing to the top: A personal memoir of *Australopithecus afarensis*. *Evolutionary Anthropology* 9 (3): 113–33.

Steudel, K. 1996. Limb morphology, bipedal gait, and the energetics of hominid locomotion. *American Journal of Physical Anthropology* 99 (2): 345–56.

Stinson, S. 2000. Growth variation: Biological and cultural factors. In *Human Biology: An Evolutionary and Biocultural Perspective*, edited by S. Stinson et al. New York: Wiley-Liss.

Stinson, S., B. Bogin, R. Huss-Ashmore, and D. O'Rourke, eds. 2000. *Human Biology: An Evolutionary and Biocultural Perspective*. New York: Wiley-Liss.

Stone, R. 2000. Ice man warms up for European scientists. *Science* 289:2253–54.

Stoneking, M. 1993. DNA and recent human evolution. *Evolutionary Anthropology* 2 (2): 60–73.

———. 2001. From the evolutionary past . . . *Nature* 409:821–22.

Strait, D. S., and F. E. Grine. 1999. Cladistics and early hominid phylogeny. *Science* 285:1210.

Stringer, C. 1994. Out of Africa: A personal history. In *Origins of Anatomically Modern Humans*, edited by M. H. Nitecki and D. V. Nitecki, 149–72. New York: Plenum.

Stringer, C., and P. Andrews. 1988. Genetic and fossil evidence for the origin of modern humans. *Science* 239:1263–68.

Stringer, C., and C. Gamble. 1993. *In Search of the Neanderthals: Solving the Puzzle of Human Origins*. London: Thames & Hudson.

Stringer, C., and R. McKie. 1996. *African Exodus: The Origins of Modern Humanity*. New York: Henry Holt.

Strum, S. 1987. *Almost Human*. New York: Random House.

Susman, R. L. 1994. Fossil evidence for early hominid tool use. *Science* 265 (9 September): 1570–73.

Sussman, R. W. 1997. Exploring our basic human nature: Are humans inherently violent? *Anthro Notes* 19 (3).

Takai, M., F. Anaya, N. Shigehara, and T. Setoguchi. 2000. New fossil materials of the earliest New World monkey, *Branisella boliviana*, and the problem of platyrrhine origins. *American Journal of Physical Anthropology* 111:263–81.

Tattersall, I. 1992. The many faces of *Homo habilis*. *Evolutionary Anthropology* 1 (1): 33–37.

———. 1994. What do we mean by human—and why does it matter? *Evolutionary Anthropology* 3 (4): 114–16.

———. 1995. *The Last Neanderthal: The Rise, Success, and Mysterious Extinction of Our Closest Human Relatives*. New York: Macmillan.

———. 2000. Once we were not alone. *Scientific American*, January, 56–62.

Tattersall, I., and J. Schwarz. 2000. *Extinct Humans*. Boulder, CO: Westview.

Teitelbaum, M. S., ed. 1976. *Sex Differences*. Garden City, NY: Anchor Press/Doubleday.

Templeton, A. R. 1993. The "Eve" hypothesis: A genetic critique and reanalysis. *American Anthropologists* 95:51–72.

———. 1996. Gene lineages and human evolution. *Science* 272:1363.

———. 1997. Testing the Out of Africa replacement hypothesis with mitochondrial DNA data. In *Conceptual Issues in Modern Human Origins Research*, edited by G. A. Clark and C. M. Willermet. New York: Aldine de Gruyter.

Thieme, H. 1997. Lower Paleolithic hunting spears from Germany. *Nature* 385:807–10.

Thompson, M. J., and D. W. Harsha. 1984. Our rhythms still follow the African sun. *Psychology Today*, January, 50–54.

Time-Life Books, eds. 1973. *The First Men*. New York: Time-Life Books.

Tishkoff, S. A., E. Dietzsch, W. Speed, A. J. Pakstis, J. R. Kidd, K. Cheung, B. Bonné-Tamir, A. S. Santachiara-Benerecetti, P. Moral, M. Krings,

S. Pääbo, E. Watson, N. Risch, T. Jenkins, and K. K. Kidd. 1996. Global patterns of linkage disequilibrium at the CD4 locus and modern human origins. *Science* 271:1380–87.

Todd, T. W. 1920. Age changes in the pubic bone. *American Journal of Physical Anthropology* 3:285–384.

Toth, N. 1985. The Oldowan reassessed: A close look at early stone tools. *Journal of Archaeological Science* 2:101–20.

Tuchman, B. W. 1978. *A Distant Mirror: The Calamitous Fourteenth Century.* New York: Knopf.

Tullar, R. M. 1977. *The Human Species: Its Nature, Evolution, and Ecology.* New York: McGraw-Hill.

Ubelaker, D., and H. Scammell. 1992. *Bones: A Forensic Detective's Casebook.* New York: Harper Collins.

Underwood, J. H. 1979. *Human Variation and Human Microevolution.* Englewood Cliffs, NJ: Prentice Hall.

Van Blerkom, L. M. 2000. Traces of ancient viruses. Poster presented at the Human Origins and Disease Meeting, Cold Spring Harbor, NY.

———. 2001. Evidence of ancient viruses and their role in hominid evolution. Paper delivered at the 70th Annual Meeting of the American Association of Physical Anthropologists, Kansas City.

Venter, J. C., et al. 2001. The sequence of the human genome. *Science* 291:1304–51.

Videan, E. N., and W. C. McGrew. 2000. Bipedality in chimpanzees and bonobos: Testing hypothesized selection pressures. Paper delivered at the 69th Annual Meeting of the American Association of Physical Anthropologists, San Antonio, TX.

Wade, N. 1998. Human or chimp? 50 genes are the key. *New York Times*, 20 October F1, 4.

Ward, C., M. Leakey, and A. Walker. 1999. The new hominid species *Australopithecus anamensis*. *Evolutionary Anthropology* 7 (6): 197–205.

Ward, S., B. Brown, A. Hill, J. Kelley, and W. Downs. 1999. *Equatorius*. A new hominoid genus from the Middle Miocene of Kenya. *Science* 285:1382–86.

Watson, A. 2000. A new breed of high-tech detectives. *Science* 289:850–54.

Weaver, K. F. 1985. The search for our ancestors. *National Geographic* 168:560–623.

Weaver, R. F. 1984. Changing life's genetic blueprint. *National Geographic*, December, 818–47.

Weiss, G., and A. von Haeseler. 1996. Estimating the age of the common ancestor of men from the ZFY intron. *Science* 272:1359–60.

Weiss, K. M., and A. V. Buchanan. 2000. Rediscovering Darwin after a Darwinian century. *Evolutionary Anthropology* 9 (5): 187–200.

White, F. J. 1996. *Pan paniscus* 1973 to 1996: Twenty-three years of field research. *Evolutionary Anthropology* 5 (1): 11–17.

White, T. D., and P. A. Folkens. 1991. *Human Osteology.* San Diego: Academic Press.

White, T. D., G. Suwa, and B. Asfaw. 1994. *Australopithecus ramidus*, a new species of early hominid from Aramis, Ethiopia. *Nature* 371 (22 September): 306–12.

Whiten, A., and C. Boesch. 2001. The cultures of chimpanzees. *Scientific American*, January, 60–67.

Whiten, A., J. Goodall, W. C. McGrew, T. Nishida, V. Reynolds, Y. Sugiyama, C. E. G. Tutin, R. W. Wrangham, and C. Boesch. 1999. Cultures in chimpanzees. *Nature* 399 (17 June): 682–85.

Wilford, J. N. 1994. Fog thickens on climate and origin of humans. *New York Times*, 17 May,: C1, 8.

Wilmut, I., A. E. Schnieke, J. McWhir, A. J. Kind, and K. H. S. Campbell. 1997. Viable offspring derived from fetal and adult mammalian cells. *Nature* 385 (27 February): 810–13.

Wilson, A. C., and R. L. Cann. 1992. The recent African genesis of humans. *Scientific American* 266 (4): 68–73.

Wilson, E. O. 1992. *The Diversity of Life* (College edition with study materials). New York: Norton.

———. 1998. *Consilience: The Unity of Knowledge.* New York: Knopf.

Wolpoff, M. 1989. Multiregional evolution: The fossil alternative to Eden. In *The Human Revolution: Behavioural and Biological Perspectives in the Origins of Modern Humans*, edited by P. Mellars and C. Stringer, 62–108. Princeton, NJ: Princeton University Press.

————. 1994. What do we mean by human—and why does it matter? *Evolutionary Anthropology* 3 (4): 116–17.

Wolpoff, M., and R. Caspari. 1997. *Race and Human Evolution*. New York: Simon & Schuster.

Wolpoff, M. H., J. Hawks, D. W. Frayer, and K. Hunley. 2001. Modern human ancestry at the peripheries: A test of the replacement theory. *Science* 291:293–97.

Wong, K. 1998. Ancestral quandary. *Scientific American* 278 (1): 30–32.

————. 2000a. The caveman's new clothes. *Scientific American*, November, 32–34.

————. 2000b. Paleolithic pit stop. *Scientific American*, December, 18–20.

Wood, B., and M. Collard. 1999. The human genus. *Science* 284:65–71.

Woodruff, D. S., and P. A. Morin. 1995. Geneticists out on a limb. *Natural History* 104 (1): 54.

Yoon, C. K. 1996a. Lake Victoria's lightning-fast origin of species. *New York Times*, 27 August, C1, 4.

————. 1996b. Parallel plots in classic evolution. *New York Times*, 12 November, C1, 7.

————. 1998. Iguanas sail from Guadeloupe to Anguilla and into history. *New York Times* 8 October.

Zimmer, C. 1995. Tooling through the trees. *Discover*, November, 46–47.

————. 2001. After you, Eve. *Natural History* 110 (2): 32–35.

Photo Credits

Chapter 1 CO1, Courtesy of the author; 1.1, From John Hostetler. *Hutterite Society*. page 156, © 1974, 1997. Reprinted by permission of the Johns Hopkins University Press; 1.2, © Momatiuk/Eastman/Woodfin Camp & Associates; 1.3, Courtesy of the author; 1.4, Courtesy of the author; 1.5, © William F. Keegan; 1.6, Photography by Michael Kodas/The Hartford Courant, 7/25/93

Chapter 2 CO2, Courtesy K. L. Feder; 2.1, © Julia Margaret Cameron/National Portrait Gallery, London; 2.2, From J. Best Publishing Co.; 2.4, Courtesy K. L. Feder; 2.4, Courtesy NASA; 2.6, © Robert F. Sisson/NGS Image Collection

Chapter 3 CO3, © David Robert Austen; 3.4, © David Robert Austen; 3.6, © CNRI/SPL/Science Source/Photo Researchers, Inc.

Chapter 4 CO4, © G. Merlen/OSF/Animals Animals; 4.1a, Courtesy J. M. Beatty; 4.1b, Courtesy K. L. Feder; 4.2, © March of Dimes; 4.3, © G. Merlen/OSF/Animals Animals; 4.9, © Meckes/Ottawa/Photo Researchers, Inc.

Chapter 5 CO5, © Stephen Dalton/Animals Animals; 5.2a, © Stephen Dalton/Animals Animals; 5.2b, © Robert Lubeck/Animals Animals; 5.2c, © Zigmund Leszczynski/Animals Animals; 5.4, © Tom and Theresa Stack/Tom Stack & Associates; 5.6, Courtesy J. M. Beatty

Chapter 6 CO6, © Reg Morrison; 6.2a, © Fred Bavendam/Peter Arnold, Inc.; 6.2b, © Reg Morrison; 6.5, © Marvin Mattelson/NGS Image Collection; 6.7, *The Age of Reptiles*, a mural by Rudolph F. Zallinger. © 1966, 1975, 1985, 1989, Peabody Museum of Natural History, Yale University, New Haven, Connecticut.; 6.8, Courtesy of the author

Chapter 7 CO7, © Frans Lanting/Minden Pictures; 7.1, From Barnes et al., *The Invertebrates: A New Synthesis*, © 1988. Reprinted by permission of Blackwell Science, Inc.; 7.4a, © Frans Lanting/Minden Pictures; 7.6, Courtesy Marine World Africa USA/Darryl Bush; 7.8a, © Noel Rowe; 7.8b, © Noel Rowe; 7.8c, © Noel Rowe; 7.8d, Courtesy of the author; 7.9, Courtesy of the author; 7.10, © Noel Rowe; 7.13, © Noel Rowe; 7.14, © Noel Rowe; 7.15, © Noel Rowe; 7.16, © Noel Rowe; 7.17, © Noel Rowe; 7.18a, © Ron Garrison/Zoological Society of San Diego; 7.18b, Courtesy of the author; 7.18c, © Steve Turner/Animals Animals; 7.18d, © Ron Garrison/Zoological Society of San Diego; 7.19, © Jane Goodall/NGS Image Collection; 7.20, Courtesy of the author

Chapter 8 CO8, © Frans Lanting/Minden Pictures; 8.2, © T. W. Ransom/Biological Photo Service; 8.3, © Irven DeVore/Anthro-Photo; 8.4, © Zig Leszczynski/Animals Animals; 8.5, © Kennan Ward/DRK Photo; 8.6, © Frans Lanting/Minden Pictures; 8.7, © Noel Rowe

Chapter 9 CO9, © Enrico Ferorelli/NGS Image Collection; 9.1, Gorilla illustration by Enid Kotschnig. Cat illustration by Rudolf Freund.; 9.4, © Karen Huntt Mason/Corbis; 9.5, from "The Antiquity of Human Walking" by John Napier. © April 1967 by Scientific American, Inc. All right reserved. Illustration by Enid Kotschnig, 9.6a, Reprinted *from Identification of Pathological Conditions in Human Skeletal Remains*, Orter and Putschar (Washington, DC: Smithsonian Institution Press), pages 195, 198, by permission of the publisher. © 1985; 9.7, © E. E. Kingsley 1984/Science Source/Photo Researchers, Inc.; 9.8, © Enrico Ferorelli/NGS Image Collection; 9.9, From Price and Feinman, *Images of the Past*. Mayfield Publishing Company. Used by permission of McGraw-Hill; 9.11, © Stephen Alvarez/NGS Image Collection; 9.12, Courtesy Marsha Park Herman; 9.13, Reprinted with permission from J. J. Yunis et al., "The Striking Resemblance of High-Resolution G-Banded Chromosomes of Man and Chimpanzees," Science, 208 (1980), 1145–1149. Copyright 1980, American Association for the Advancement of Science.

Chapter 10 CO 10, © 1985 David L. Brill; 10.2b, Illustration by Rudolf Freund; 10.3, From R. D. Martin, *Primate Origins and Evolution: A Phylogentric Reconstruction*, p. 61. Kluwer Academic Publishers; 1.04, © David L. Brill, 1985; 10.6, Courtesy Dr. Ian Tattersall, American Museum of Natural History; 10.7, © 1985 David L. Brill; 10.10, ©

Index

Page numbers in **bold** indicate definitions of glossary terms. Page numbers in *italic* indicate illustrations, figures, or tables.

ABO blood group, 362–66, 396
  phenotypes and antibodies, *364*
absolute dating techniques, **198**
acacia wood, 276
Acheulian technique, 274, 283
acid rain, 123
Adapidae, *218, 219*
adaptation, **35,** 37, 39, 40, 42, 133
  human, 357
  natural selection and, 133
  species, 358
  to temperature, 359
  variation in, 358–62
adapted, **35**
adaptive fitness, 85
adaptive radiation, **97**
  speciation and, 96–100
adenine, 49
adolescent growth spurt, 372–73
Aegytopithecus, 220–21
Africa
  as the birthplace of modern humans, 300
  environmental fluctuations, 240–41
  fertility rates, 377
  general climatic and vegetation zones, *235*

hominid evolution, 326
increase in environmental variability, 248
sickle cell in, 86
African Americans
  hypertension and, 427–28
  IQ test results and, 405–10
  sickle cell and, 85, 86
  sports and, 408–9
African Burial Ground, New York City, 209
African Exodus: The Origins of Modern Humanity (Stringer and McKie), 334
aging, 72
AIDS. *See* HIV-AIDS
allele frequency, **71**
  calculating change over time, 343–46
  changes in, 71, 72, 75, 80
alleles, **55,** 56, 57, 59, 61, 86, 346
altitude, biological response to, 358
altruistic behavior, **167**
Ambrona, 274, 276
American Association of Physical Anthropologists, 428
American Sign Language (AMESLAN), 155
amino acids, **49,** 51, 52, 53, 96, 117, 207
amphioxus, *132*
analogies, *165,* **165,** 167, 206
analogous behaviors, 167–68

Anaximander, 26
Animalia, 132
animal rights, 156–57
Ankarapithecus, 221
anthropoids, 148, 149–55
anthropology, 10, **11**
  applied, **13**
  cultural, 12, **13**
  forensic, **13**
  linguistic, 12
  physical, 2, **11**
  subfields, 11–13, *12*
  See also biological anthropology/bioanthropology
antibiotics, overuse of, 369
antibodies, 364, **365**
antigens, 364, **365**
ants, 166, 168
apes, 149, 151
  bipedal, 231
  brain size, 154
  common ancestor with humans, 156, 182
  communication, 155
  dental, 221
  in the fossil record, 221–23
  genetic similarity of humans to, 156–57
  great, 152, *153,* 155
  southern, 225, 242
applied anthropology, **13**
arboreal, **99**
arboreal adaptation, 239, 241
archaea, 132
archaeological data, 322
archaeology, 12, **13**

Archaeopteryx, 101
  fossil remains of, 99
archaic hominids, 280–87
Ardipithecus ramidus, 228, 240,
  253
  foramen magnum, 228–29
  fossil tooth and a portion of
    jaw, *228*
argon/argon dating, **201**
argon gas, 201
Aristotle, 27
Armelagos, George, 368
art, in the Upper Paleolithic,
  302–4
arthropods, *120*
asexually, **117**
Ashkenazic Jews, 425–26
asteroids, 123, 124–25
Atapuerca, 285
athletic ability, racial differences
  in, 408–9
atoms, 115
Australopithecus, 225, 248, 261
  first specimen of, *223*
  foramen magnum, *224*
Australopithecus afarensis,
  229–32
  Lucy, 230, 241
  reconstruction, *233*
  side view of cranium, *231*
  upper jaws and tooth rows,
    230
  wrist joints, 235
Australopithecus africanus, 225,
  242
  as a continuation of A. *afaren-
    sis*, 243
  skull of, *242*
Australopithecus anamensis, 229,
  240
  mandible and maxilla of, *229*
  wrist joints, 235
Australopithecus bahrelghazalia,
  231, 241
Australopithecus garhi, 244

axolotl, *95, 96*
Aztecs, 367

Babitt, Bruce, 209
baboons
  on the African Savannas, *169*
  behavior, 143
  estrus, *158*
  hamadryas, 170, 171
  male protecting mother and
    young, *143*
  social structure among, 168–72
  threat, *170*
bacteria, *117,* 132
bald uakari, *142*
bases, 49, 51, 58, 397
Beall, C. M., 362
behavior
  of bonobos, 177–82
  chimpanzees, 172–77
  human, biological bases of,
    158, 180–81
  of primates, 141–45, 164–68
behavioral potentials, 166
belief systems, **19**
  science and, 18–21, 104–8
Bellantoni, Nick, 7, 8
The Bell Curve (Herrnstein and
  Murray), 405
berdache, 390
betaglobin gene, 331
Bible
  evolutionary theory and,
    27–28, 41
  literal interpretation, 27,
    104–5, 106
bifacial, 274, **275**
bifacially flaked Upper Paleolithic spear points, *303*
Big Bang, 114–15
Binford, Lewis, 253
biological anthropology/bioan-
  thropology, 2, 10, **11**–12
  applications of, 423–28

career opportunities in,
    428–29
  disease and, 425–28
  exercises in, 434–42
  fieldwork in, 2–9
  global issues and, 428–31
  of individuals, 371–77
  specialties, 12–13
biological change. *See* evolution
biology, and culture, 342
biomass, 96, 132
biostratigraphy, **198**
bipedalism, **137**
  anatomical changes and phys-
    ical evidence associated
    with, *194*
  apes, 231
  benefits of, 234–37
  carrying model, 237
  display model, 238
  energy efficiency model, 238
  explaining the emergence of,
    237–41
  as first hominid trait, 234
  foraging/bipedal harvesting
    model, 238
  heat dissipation model, 238
  hominids, 101, 136, 155, *224,*
    234
  humans, 139
  primates, 223–34
  vigilance model, 237
birds
  evolutionary relationship with
    dinosaurs, 124, 125
  prehensile feet, 235
birth control, 355, 376
birth rate, 376–77
births, 351
Black Death, 351–52, 368
  map showing the progression
    of, *352*
"Black Skull," *245*
blade tools, from Klasies River
  Mouth, South Africa, *303*

blank slates, 166
blood type
    and bacterial ailments, 365
    as clinal, 396
    distribution of, 362–66, *363*
    and noninfectious gastrointestinal diseases, 365
    and susceptibility to diseases, 364–65
body build, 359
bone tools, 243, 250
bonobos, 152, *153*
    behavior of, 177–82
    common ancestor with humans, 253
    food sharing, 239
    meat-eating, 154
    sexual behaviors, 239
    social structure, 177–82, *179*
    standing bipedally, *178*
    stimulus for bipedal locomotion, 237
    taxonomy of, 134, 137
    upright display posture, 238
    upright walking, 154
bony spine, 132
Border Cave, South Africa, 302
bottleneck, **79**
Bouri, Ethiopia, 243, 244
bovine spongiform encephalopathy (BSE), 371
Boxgrove, England, 284, 285
Boyd, Robert, 253
Brace, C. Loring, 400
brachiation, **139,** 152
brain, human structure/functions, *141*
brain size
    of *A. garhi,* 244
    of archaic hominids, 280
    of bipedal primates, 231
    compared with height, 373
    of great apes, 154
    of *H. erectus,* 277
    of *H. ergaster,* 267

of *H. habilis,* 250
of hominoids, 151
intelligence and, 140–41
of *P. boisei,* 247
Bräuer, G., 334
breeding populations, 76, **77**
brow ridge, **251**
    in fully modern humans, 319
    H. heidelbergenis, 284, 285
    Kabwe specimen, 286
    modern *Homo sapiens,* 298, *302*
    Neandertal, *288,* 289–90
Bruderhof, 3
Bryce Canyon, *32*
bubonic plague, 351–52, 364
Buchanan, Anne, 336
Buffon, Comte de, 30, 42
burins, *275*

Cambrian Explosion, 118
Cameron, Julia Margaret, 26
campylobacter, 370
canine fossa, 280
canine teeth, 231, 242
Canis familiaris, 69
Canis lupus, 69
cannibalism, 297
cape buffalo, 301
Carabelli's cusp, 422
carbon 14, 199–200, 417
carbon isotope, 242
caribou, 391, *392, 393,* 398
    North American populations of, 393–94
Carmill, Matt, 218
carnivore, **191**
    tooth mark, *254*
Cartmill, Matt, 335
carvings, 304
Cassidy, Butch, 419
Catarrhini, 149
catastrophism, **28**–30, 34, 35, 37, 42

catastrophists, **28**
Cavalieri, Paola, 157
Cavalli-Sforza, L. L., 332
cave bear, 295
cave paintings, 304, *305*
Celera Genomics, 62
cells
    division, 49, 58
    meisosis, *60*
    mitosis, *60*
    typical, *50*
cellulose, 235
Ceprano, Italy, 273, *274*
Cercopithecoidea, 150–51
Chad, 231, 241
Chaplin, G., 237, *238*
chimpanzees, 152, *153*
    behavior, 143, 172–79
    common ancestor with humans, 253
    dominance hierarchy, 173
    foreman magnum, *224*
    full open grin, *174*
    genetic similarity to humans, 206–7, *210*
    in Great Rift Valley, 241
    hunting behavior, 175, *176*
    meat-eating, 236
    mtDNA diversity, 327
    postnatal dependency, 156
    social structure, 154–55, 173–77
    stimulus for bipedal locomotion, 237
    taxonomy of, 134, 137
    upper jaws and tooth rows, *230*
    upright display posture, 238
    using tools, *154*
    vocal tracts, *279*
China, Zhoukoudian, 265–66, 275, *276*
Chinese white-handed gibbon, *142*
Chi-Square, 346

choppers, *275*
Chordata, 132
chromosomal mutations, **71**–72
chromosomes, **49,** 58
    comparison of human and
        chimpanzee, *207*
    number 22, 63
    twenty-three pairs, 59
chronometric techniques, **198**
cichlids, 94, 107
cladistics, **135**–37, 145, 306
    evolutionary tree based on,
        136
class, 131
cleavers, 274
cline, 394, **395,** 397
*Close Encounters of the Third
    Kind,* 84
Cocos Island, 97
codominant, 56, **57,** 82
codon, **49,** 51, 52, 53, 71, 208
Columbus's First Contact with
    Natives of the New
    World, *402*
common ancestor, 253, 327
    of apes and human, 156, 182
    of primates, 156, 164
communication
    bonobos, 181–82
    great apes, 155
    and grooming, among pri-
        mates, *144*
    primates, 145
    symbolic, 158
    touch as form of among pri-
        mates, 145
comparative anatomy, 30, **31**
competitive exclusion, 248, **249**
concealed ovulation, 157
continental drift, 18, 120–22
Coon, Carleton, 291, 335
cooperative hunting, 276
core tools, *248,* **250**
courtship behaviors, 92
cranial capacity. *See* brain size

cranial features
    of *Homo erectus,* 277, 284
    of *Homo erectus/ergaster,* 269
    of *Homo ergaster,* 284
    of *Homo heidelbergensis,* 284
    of *Homo sapiens,* 284
    human, sex differences in, *190*
    as indicator of brain size, 188,
        190
    Neandertal, 289–90
    Neandertal compared to mod-
        ern *Homo sapiens, 292*
cranial suture closure, *192*
creation stories, 27
*Cretacious/Tertiary (K/T) extinc-
    tion,* 124, 125
Creutzfeldt-Jakob disease, 371
Croatia, Vindija, 318, 319
crossbreeding, 48
crossing over, **61,** 68
crowned lemur, *148*
crust, of earth, 120
cultural anthropology, 12, **13**
culture, **11**
    biology and, 342
    as major adaptive mechanism,
        357, 400
    values, 158
    See also social structure
Cuvier, Georges, 28–30, 35, 37,
    42
cytosine, 49

Dart, Raymond, 197–98, 223,
    225
Darwin, Charles, 20, 34, 37–43,
    48, 73, 306
    delay in making natural selec-
        tion known to public, 75
    model of natural selection ap-
        plied to the evolution of
        long necks and tall bod-
        ies in giraffes, *39*
    natural selection, 42, 100

*On the Origin of Species by
    Means of Natural Selection*
    (Darwin), 40, 41, 75
    portrait of, *26*
Darwin, Erasmus, 35
Darwinian gradualism,
    100–102, *101*
Darwin's finches, 73–75, *74,*
    97–98, 102, 107, 333
dating
    argon/argon, **201**
    electron spin resonance
        (ESR), **201,** 285
    luminescence, **201,** 304
    potassium/argon (K/Ar),
        200–**201,** 271
    radiocarbon, **198**–99
daughter cells, 58, 60
death, twelve leading causes of
    in the United States, *367*
deaths, in population, 351
deduction, **14**–15
degenerative diseases, 368–69
demes, 76, **77,** 93, 342, 391
Democratic Republic of the
    Congo, 177
demography, **351**
dental apes, 221
dental eruption, *192*
dental remains. *See* teeth
deoxyribonucleic acid (DNA),
    49–53, 117, 323, 324
    from ancient remains, 326
    fingerprinting, 323
    "junk," 53
    molecule, *51, 52*
    samples from Neandertal
        specimens, 326–27
dermatoglyphics, **347**
    on the Hutterites, 347–50
developed nations, age-sex
    graph for, *355*
developing nations
    age-sex graph for, *354, 355*
    high mortality rates, 355

de Vries, Hugo, 68
Diamond, Jared, 425–26
diastema, 230
diet
    evidenced by teeth, 191
    of the Gran Dolina people,
        283
    herbivorous, 219
dinosaurs, 32, 75, 98
    mass extinction, 122–24
    painting of, *122*
discordant variation, diagram of,
    396
diseases
    bioanthropology and, 425–28
    degenerative, 368–69
    emerging, 429
    populations and, 366–71
    susceptibility to, and blood
        type, 364–65
    viruses, 366–68
display posture, 238
distance curve, **373**
    for height and age, *372*
    for height and age in males
        compared to females, *373*
    for height compared to brain
        growth, *375*
diurnal, **99**, 219
dominance hierarchy, **143**
    in bonobos, 177
    in primates, 173
dominant, 56, **57**
dominant male, 170
double helix, 49
Down syndrome, 71–72
Dubois, Eugene, 264–65

earth
    crust of, 120
    establishment of, 117
    history of life on, 28–34, *29*
East Africa, 241
Easteal, Simon, 327

East Turkana, Kenya, 267
Eaton, S. Boyd, 426
ecological opportunity, 97
Ehrlich, Paul, 392
Einstein, Albert, 17
eland, 301
Eldredge, Niles, 125
electrons, 115
electron spin resonance (ESR)
    dating, **201**, 285
endemic malaria, distribution of,
    83
endocasts, **277**
    from South African Australo-
        pithecines, *278*
endogamy, **333**, 350, 400
energy efficiency, of bipedalism,
    238
Entine, Jon: *Taboo: Why Black
    Athletes Dominate Sports
    and Why We're Afraid to
    Talk About It*, 408
environment
    body size and, 374–75
    skin color and, 358, 360–62
environmental, **57**–58
    fluctuations, in Africa,
        240–41, 248
    isolation, speciation through,
        94
enzymes, **49**
Eoanthropus, 252
Eosimiidae, 219
epidemics, 368
epidemiological, **369**
    transitions, 368–71
epiphyseal union, *192*, 268, 270,
    422, 442
Equatorius, 221
erosion, 31
essentialism, 27, 28, 34
estrus, 156–**57**, 171
    baboon in, *158*
    in bonobos and chimps, 180
ET, 84

Ethiopia
    Bouri, 243, *244*
    hominid fossils, 227–28
    Omo, 196
ethology, 168, **169,** 173
eugenics, 41
eukaryotes, 132
European explorers, 401–3
"Eve Theory," 325, 330
evolution, 12, 16, **27**
    in action, 106–7
    adaptive radiation and,
        96–100
    basic theory of, 68
    as a branching tree, 252
    changes in allele frequency
        through time, 71
    conceived of as ladder or
        chain, 252
    and concept of race,
        398–401
    definition of, 106, 343
    fact vs. theory of, 20
    future of, 84–85
    history of ideas about, 26–43
    hominid, 241–48
    human viruses and, 366–68
    models of, 100–103, *101*
    within populations, 346–50
    process of, 76
    progressive, 35, 40
    scientific creationism and,
        103–8
    technically defined, as change
        in allele frequency over
        time, 87
    timing of important events in,
        118–19
    units of, 68–71
evolutionary trees, 134–37, *135*
    for primates, *217*
exceptions, explanations for,
    15
extinction, 40, 75, 97
    mass, 122–25

family, 145
Fayum, Egypt, 220
Feder, Ken, 274
Fedigan, Linda, 13
fertility symbols, *304*
fertilization, 80
ferus (wild man), 403
fieldwork, 2–9
fingerprints, 347–48
  features, *347*
fire, use of by *Homo erectus*, 276
fission, 78, **79,** 86, 106
fitness, **37**
  adaptive, 85
  inclusive, 166, **167,** 175
flake tools, 248, **250,** 279, 283
folate, 358
folk taxonomies, 388, **389**
food sharing, 239
  bonobos, 177, 181
foramen magnum, **225**
  Ardipithecus ramidus, 228–29
  Australopithecus, 225
  wolves, *224*
forensic anthropologist, **13**
forensic anthropology, 416–23
Fore people, 371, 388
Fossey, Dian, 172
fossils, 12, **27**–28, 30, 34, 36, 42
  absolute dating techniques,
    202
  dating, 198–202
  formation of, 202–5
  locating, 194–97
  primate record, 216–17
  recovery, 197–98
fossil skull, cast of, *193*
founder effect, 78, **79,** 85, 106,
    348, 349, 350, 425
fox, 168
France
  cave paintings, *305*
  La Ferrassie, 296
  Le Moustier, *294*
  Moula-Guercy, 297

St. Acheul, 274
Soleihac, 273
Terra Amata, 273
Francois's langurs, 144
frontal sinuses, 289
frostbite, 361
fungi, 117, 132

Galápagos Islands, 73, 97
  finches, 98
galaxies, 114, 115, 116
Galdikas, Biruté, 172
gametes, 58–**59,** 60, 61, 72
gamete sampling, 80, **81,** 106
gender, **387**
  baboon social structure and,
    170, 171
  bonobo social structure and,
    177
  chimpanzee social structure
    and, 173
  identity, 387, 387–88
  and sex, 385–90
gene flow, 5, 75, 76–**77,** 85, 86,
    87, 93, 106, 331–32
  between archaics and mod-
    erns, 335
  Hutterite example of, 348,
    349–50
  as the norm for human
    species, 400
  simple example of, 78
  uneven, 391
gene frequency, **71**
gene pool, 72, **73,** 76
generalized, **97**
genes, 12, **49**
  evolutionary relationships
    and, 206–10
  functionally defined, 51
  how they work, 48–53, 58
  in populations, 343–46
  See also alleles
genetic code, 49, 57, 346

genetic drift, 5, 75, 76, 78–80,
    84, 87, 106
genetic family tree for forty-two
    populations, *399*
genetics, 39, 48
  basic laws of, 40, 43
  modern human origins and,
    322–31
genetic variation, and concept
    of race, 397–98
genome, **53,** 104, **397**
genotypes, 56, **57**
genus, 131
geological processes, history of life
    on earth and, 28–34, *29*
Geospiza fortis, 74
German shepherd, *70*
ghettos, 426
gibbons, 152
Gigantopithecus, 137, *138,* 222
giraffes, 35–36, 39
glaciers, **271**
global warming, 429–30
Goldstein, David, 329
Gombe Stream National Park,
    Tanzania, 173
Goodall, Jane, 172, 173, 175, 182
gorillas, 135, 145, 152, 172
  sagittal crest, 231
  skull of a male, *232*
  taxonomy of, 134, 137
  upright walking, 154
Gould, Stephen Jay, 16, 103, 206
Grand Canyon, strata of, *105*
Gran Dolina, 280, 282–83
Gran Dolina Cave boy, 283
Grant, Peter, 73, 74, 102, 107
Grant, Rosemary, 73, 74, 102,
    107
gravity, light bent by, *17*
gravity, theory of, 15, 16
The Great Ape Project (Cavalieri
    and Singer), 157
great apes, 152, *153*
great chain of being, 27, 30, 35

Great Rift Valley, Southern
Kenya, *240*, 241
Greene, John, 30
grid system, 109
diagram, *200*
grooming, 144, **145**, 173
grooming claw, 147, *148*
Grotte XVI, 322
guanine, 49
Gurche, John, 421

haft, **295**
half-life, **199**–200, *201*
hamadryas baboon, 170, *171*
hand axes, 274, **275**, 276, 285
bifacially flaked, *274*
hantavirus, 370
Haplorhini, 148
Harding, Rosalind, 331
Hardy-Weinberg equilibrium,
344, **345**, 440–41
harem, 170
harpoons, 302, *304*
Harsha, David, 423–24
health status, determining from
skeletal remains, 193–94
See also diseases
height
change in, 372–73
of Neandertals, 291
heliocentric (sun-centered) theory, 20
hematite "crayon," 304
hemisphere specialization, 278
hemoglobin, 53, 80–81
hemolyze, 364
herbivorous diet, 219
heritability, **405**
studies, 407
Herrnstein, Richard, 405
heterozygous, 56, **57**, 61, 82, 83,
344, 345, 346, 426,
437–38
Hijras, 389, *390*

Hippocratic Oath, 19
Hispanics, 404
HIV-AIDS, 366, 369–70, 377
as leading cause of death in
U.S., *367*
in the Year 2000, *370*
holistic, **11**
Holloway, Ralph, 277
Holm, Richard, 392
Hominidae, 133, 155
hominids, **93**
age of, 114
archaic, 280–87
bipedal primates, 223–24
brain size, 151
in cladistic analysis, 136–37
early fossils, *226*, 227–28
early fossil sites, *227*
evolution of, 241–48
fossil interpretations, 260–61
genera, 225
hyperrobust, 247
migratory activity, 332
orders, 133
origin of, 92, 100, 101, 149
phylogenetic relationships
among, *244*
robust, 245–47
scanning electron microscope
pictures of teeth surfaces,
243
Hominoidea, 150, 151
Homo, 225, 247, 248
arm-to-leg proportions, 252
debate between the single-
species model and five- or
six-species model, 313
evolutionary theory and,
262–63
first members of, 248–54
manufacture of stone implements, 250
possible set of relationships
for the six proposed
species of, *315*

social structure, 254
timeline of species within
genus, *262*
Homo antecessor, 280–83, 286
major fossils classified as, *281*
major fossil sites, *282*
Homo erectus, 85, 315
brain size, 267
change, 279
cranial features, *284*
European evidence of, 273–74
foraging, 277
fossil evidence of, 263–80
fossil evidence of, from
Africa, 268
fossil evidence of, major,
264–65
intellectual and linguistic
skills, 277
spread to China and Southeast Asia, 268–73
toolmaking, 274–76
use of fire, 276
vocal tract, 279
Homo erectus/ergaster
cranial features of, 269
major sites, *263*
skull of ER 3733, *268*
Homo ergaster, 263
cranial features, *284*
fossil record of, 266–68
intellectual and linguistic
skills, 277
major fossils, *264–65*
toolmaking, 274–76
Homo habilis, 250–51
Homo heidelbergensis, 284–85, 286
brain size, 284
cranial features, *284*
major fossils classified as, *281*
major fossil sites, *282*
skull of, *295*
toolmaking, 285
homologies, 164, **165**, *165*, 167,
206

Homo monstrosus, 403

Homo neanderthalensis. See Neandertals

Homo rudolfensis, 251

Homo sapiens, 69, 114, 261
  anatomically modern, 298
  archaic, 316, 318
  burials, 301
  chronological listing of important fossils of, *299*
  competing hypotheses regarding origin of, 312–17
  cranial features, *269, 284*
  evolutionary theory and, 331–36
  examples of early modern, *302*
  fossil evidence, and origin of, 318–22
  fossils, 298–300
  generalized models for origin of, *314*
  genetic evidence and origin of, 322–31
  "human" as term for, 306–7
  map of major early sites in Africa, Asia, Australia, and Europe, *300*
  migration to North America, 271
homozygous, 56, **57,** 61, 71, 82, 344, 346, 425
Hooke, Robert, 28, 34, 35, 42, 188
house sparrows, distribution of size variation in male, *394*
human ecology, **13**
human genome, decoding of, 62–63
Human Genome Project, 62
human growth hormone, 103
humans
  adaptation, 182
  behavior, 158
  forensic analysis of, 416–23

genetic similarity to chimpanzees, 206–7, 210, 336
  intelligence, 158
  lessons from the past, 423–28
  major parts and functions of brain, *141*
  meaning of terms used for, 306–7
  mobility, 398–401
  modern, upper jaws and tooth rows, *230*
  movement, 155
  origins, and race, 334
  production, 156–57
  senses, 155
  skeletal structure, 188–94
  vocal tract, *279*
hunter-gatherers, **13,** 426–27
hunting
  big-game, 305
  by bonobos, 177
  by chimpanzees, 175, *176*
  cooperative, 276–77
  by Gran Dolina people, 283
  by *Homo sapiens,* 301
Hutterites, 2–6, 347–50, 400
  age-sex graph of, *353*
  colonies, *348*
  colony, diagram of, *3*
  fission, 78–79
  genetic drift, 348–50
  high birth rate, 352–53
  marriages, 77
  population composition, 353–55
  women in typical dress, *5*
Hutton, James, 30–31, 42, 188
Huxley, Thomas Henry, 40
hybridization, 69, 333–35
hydrogen, 117
Hylobatidea, 152
hyoid bone, 298
hyperrobust hominids, 247
hypotheses, 14–**15,** 16, 17

Ice Ages. *See* Pleistocene
"Ice Maiden," 203, *204*
Ice Man, 416–19, *417*
  reconstructed face, *420–21*
iguanas, 220
inclusive fitness, 166, **167,** 175
independent assortment, **61,** 68, 73
individuals, recognition of, *142, 143*
induction, 14, **15**
infancy stage, 376, 377
infant mortality, 365
influenza, 367
infraorder, 145
inheritance, 58–61
  of acquired characteristics, **35**
  "blending" theory, 48, 56
  particulate, 48
  See also genetics; heritability
inorganic, **117**
insects, 145
Institute of Human Origins, 197
insulin, 103
intelligence, **141**
  claimed connection with race, 405–10
  human, 158
  primate, 140–41
interbreeding, 391, 393
  behavioral barriers to, 332, 333
  between nonhuman populations, 333
  between species, 92
interferon, 104
intersexes, 388
Inuit
  body build, *359*
  igloo, *357*
Irian Jaya, 385
Israel, 300
  Kebara, 294, 298
  Qafzeh, 301, 302, 318
  Skhul, 301, 302, 318

Jablonski, N. G., 237, 238
Java, 264, 271, 318
Java Man, 265
  skullcap and femur of, 266
Jebel Irhoud, Morocco, cranium
    from, 301
Jensen, Arthur: "How Much
    Can We Boost IQ and
    Scholastic Achieve-
    ment?", 405–6
Jinmium, 304
Johanson, Donald, 13, 230,
    234
Ju/'hoansi, 427
junk DNA, 53
Jurassic Park, 41
juvenile state, 376, 377

Kabwe (Broken Hill) specimen,
    286
kangaroos, 235
Kanzi, 181–82
Kebara, 294, 298
Keith, Sir Arthur, 253
Kennedy, John F., 419
Kennewick Man, 209
Kenya, 299
  East Turkana, 267
  Great Rift Valley, 240, 241
  Lake Turkana, 229, 240, 245
  Tugen Hills, 232
  West Turkana, 268
Kenyanthropus platyops, 479
Kenyapithecus, 221
Khoisan, 327, 328, 427
Kidd, Ken, 329
Kimbel, Bill, 197
Klasies River Mouth, South
    Africa, 301
knuckle walking, **235**
koala, 390–91
Konner, Melvin, 13, 426
!Kung San hunter, 328
kuru, 371

La Chapelle Specimen, 292
Laetoli, 232, 241
  footprints, 233
La Ferrassie, France, 296
Lake Turkana, Kenya, 229, 240,
    245
Lake Victoria, 107
Lamarck, Jean-Baptiste de, 39,
    42, 75
  model of evolution, 35–36
Langebaan Lagoon, 300
language
  genetic basis for ability, 181
  Homo erectus and, 277–78
Language Research Center, Geor-
    gia State University, 181
larval salamander, 95
larynx, of the Neandertals, 293,
    297
Lascaux cave paintings, 305
Lascaux II, 305
Laurasia, 218
law of parsimony, 260, **261**
Leakey, Louis and Mary, 194,
    232, 247, 248, 252
Leakey, Richard, 252
Le Moustier, France, unifacially
    retouched mousterian
    flakes, 294
lemurs, 147
leopards, 168, 204
lesser apes, 152
Levallois technique, **285,** 287
Lewontin, Richard, 397
life expectancy, 375
life history, 376–**77**
light, 115, 276
light skin pigmentation, evolu-
    tion of, 361–62
limb proportions, 244
linguistic anthropology, 12
linkage, **61**
Linnaeus, Carolus (Carl von
    Linné), 34, 42, 131, 134,
    306, 316, 403–4

lions, 168
Little Magadi, Kenya, 240
locomotion, 139
lorises, 218
The Lost World, 41
"Lucy," 13, 230, 241
  skeleton of, 230
luminescence dating, **201,** 304
lumpers, 261, 268, 306
Lyell, Charles, 31, 32, 33–34,
    42, 188

macromutations, 94–**95**
Madagascar
  lemurs, 147
  primates, 99, 148
  prosimians, 146, 221
mad cow disease, 371
magma, 120, 121
Malakunanja II, 304
malaria, 83–84, 86, 366, 368,
    430
  endemic, distribution of, 83
Mal'ta, 305
Malthus, Thomas: An Essay on
    the Principle of Population,
    376
mammals, 98–99, 123
  adaptation, 133
  adaptive radiation, 124
  orders, 133
mandibular foramen, 320
mandrill, 142
mangabey monkey, 369
manual dexterity, 140
Maples, William, 419
Marks, Jonathan, 157, 406, 407
marmosets, 96, 150
Masai, body build, 359
mass extinction, 122–25
Mauer, Germany, 284
McGrew, W. C., 176, 237, 238
McKenna, James, 424–25
measles, 366, 367

meat eating
  bonobos, 154
  chimpanzees, 236
  hominids, 242–44
meiosis, **59**, *60*, 61
melanin, **358**, 360, 361
melanocytes, **358**, 360
menarche, **375**
Mendel, Gregor, 40, 42, 43,
  48–49
Mendelian genetics, 54–58, **55**,
  59, 61
  exercise in, 434–35, 437–38
  independent assortment, 61
  segregation, 59
Mengele, Josef, 419
menopause, **375**
messenger ribonucleic acid
  (mRNA), **51**–53, 117
Mettler, Lawrence: *Population
  Genetics and Evolution*,
  394
Mexico, 354
microbes, 96, 132
microsatellites, **323**
migration, 351
Milky Way, 117
"missing link," 252–53, 264
Mississippi Delta, aerial view of,
  33
mitochondrial DNA (mtDNA),
  50, 322, **323**–24, *325*,
  326, 327, 329–30, 418
  nuclear DNA, different in-
    heritance patterns of,
    330
mitosis, 58, **59**, *60*
Modjokerto, 271
"molecular clock," 324
Molnar, Stephen, 403
monkeys
  colorful faces, *142*, 143
  fossil record, 219
  mangabey, 369
  New World, 149

New World, evolutionary theories of, 219–20
Northern Woolly Spider, *150*
Old World, 151, 219–20
Old World vs. New World,
  149–51
Rhesus, *151*
monogamous, 152
monogenic, **53**, 55, 56
Moreno Glacier, *272*
Morocco, 299
Morotopithecus, 221
mother-child units, 143
mother-infant bond, in chimpanzees, 173
Moula-Guercy, France, 297
mouse lemur, *138*, 218
Mousterian technique, 294–**95**
movement
  of humans, 155
  of primates, 139–40
mRNA (messenger ribonucleic
  acid), **51**–53, 117
mtDNA (mitochondrial DNA),
  50, 322, **323**–24, *325*,
  326, 327, 329–30, *330*,
  418
mules, 69
multicellular organisms, 117, 118
Multiregional Evolution (MRE)
  model, **313**, 315–23,
  326–32, 335, 400
  some representative fossils in-
    terpreted according to,
    317
mummies, 203
mumps, 366
Murray, Charles, 405
mutation, **57**, 61, 68, 71–72, 76,
  77, 84, 87, 106, 117, 324

Native American Graves Protection and Repatriation
  Act (NAGPRA), 208–9

Native Americans, skeletal remains, 208–9
natural selection, 20, **39**–40, 42,
  48, 72, 83, 85
  adaptation and, 87, 97, 133
  as a conservative force, 102
  evolution and, 73–76
  gradualism, 100
  observing in daily life, 106–7
  and population differentia-
    tion, 400
  variation and, 38, 61, 68
Neandertals, 191, 288–98
  adaptation to cold, 291, 293
  burial, 295, 296
  cannibalism, 297
  cave bear cult, 295
  coexistence with modern hu-
    mans, 318
  compared to modern *Homo
    sapiens* skeletal features,
    293
  cranial features, 289
  human status, 307
  linguistic abilities, 297–98
  major fossils of, *290*
  map of major sites, *289*
  original skullcap, *288*
  reconstructions, *291*
  short limbs, 291
  toolmaking, 294–95, 322
  use of to establish a definition
    of modern, 320
Neander Valley, 288
Necrolemur, *219*
neocortex, 158
neutrons, 115
Nevando Ampato, Peru, 203
New Guinea, 371, 385
Newton, Isaac, 26
New World primates, 149–50,
  219–20
Ngandong, 273
niche, **69**
Nicholas II, 419

nocturnal, 98, **99**, 219
nonadaptive traits, 320
noncoding DNA, 323, 346, 397
Northern Woolly Spider Monkey, *150*
noses, of New World vs. Old World primates, 149
notochord, 132, **133**
nuclear DNA, **323**, 324, 326, 327, 329, 331
nuclei, 117
nucleotide, **49**, 58
null hypothesis, 344
Nutcracker Man, 247

Ockham's razor, 260
"Old Man" of La Chapelle-aux-Saints, 295–97, *297*
Oldowan tools, 249–50, 252, 307
  flake and core, *248*
  process of removing flakes from a stone core, *249*
Olduvai Gorge, Tanzania, 194, *196*, *197*, 248, 249, 277
Old World primates, 149–50, 151, 219–20
olive baboons, 171
Olorgesailie, 277
omnivore, **191**
Omo, Ethiopia, 196
Omohundro, John T.: *Careers in Anthropology*, 429
Omomyidae, 219
On the Origin of Species by Means of Natural Selection (Darwin), 40, 41, 75
opposability, **139**, 147, 151, 155
optically stimulated luminescence (OSL), 201
Opukahaia, Henry, 7–10, 203, 209
  excavation of grave, *9*
  headstone of, *7*

orangutans, 152, *153*, 154, 157, 172
  behavior, 141
  taxonomy, 134
Orce, 283
order, 131, 145
organelles, 117
organic, **117**
The Origin of Races (Coon), 335
Orrorin tugenensis, 232–34
oscillating selection, 102, **103**
osteology, 12, **13**, **188**, 191
Ötztaler Alps, 416
Ouranopithecus, 221–22
Out-of-Africa model, **313**
overpopulation, 429

Pacific Islands, settling of, 398
pairwise comparison, 320–21
paleoanthropologists, 216
paleoanthropology, 12, **13**
paleomagnetism, 280
paleopathology, **193–94**
palmistry, 104
panda, 206
pangea, **123**
Papio, 168, 333
Papua New Guinea, 388
Paranthropus, 225, 227, 243, 244–46, 248, 261
Paranthropus aethiopicus, 245
Paranthropus boisei, 246–47, *247*
Paranthropus robustus, 246
parsimony, law of, 260, **261**
particulate, 48, **49**
Patagonia, *272*
pea plant traits, *55*, *57*, 61
Pearson, O. M., 334
pebble tools, 249
Peking Man, 266
  cast of skull, *267*
pelvis, human, sex differences in, *190*
Pennsylvania Dutch, 79

Permian period, 122
petrified, **197**
Pfeiffer, John, 276
phenetic taxonomy, 134, **135**, 136
  evolutionary tree based on, *135*
  of primates, *146*
phenotype, 56, **57**, 58, 63. *See also* traits
phenotypic variation, 68, 73, 357, *385*, 390
  among modern humans, 384
  and concept of race, 395–97
Philippine Tarsier, *149*
Philosophie zoologique (Lamarck), 35
photosynthesis, **117**
phyla, 132
physical anthropology, 2, **11**
pigeons, 37
Piltdown Man, 252–53
pipe-vine butterfly, *38*
Pithecanthropus erectus, 265
Pizarro, Francisco, 419
plague, 366
plankton, 123–24
plants, 132
plates, 120
plate tectonics, 18, **120**–*21*
Plato, 27
platyrrhine nose, 149, *150*
platyrrhines, 149, *150*, 219
Pleistocene, **269**, 271, 332, 333
  maximum worldwide glacial expansion during, *273*
pneumonia/influenza, as leading cause of death in U.S., 366, *367*
point mutation, **71**
points, *275*
polio, 366
pollution, 85
polygenic, **53**

polymorphisms, **357**
  adaptive significance of, 362–66
polytypic, **391**
Pongidae, 133–34, 136, 152–55
Pope, Alexander, 130
population crisis, 376–77
population genetics, exercise in, 435–36, 440–41
populations
  composition of, 353–55
  describing, 351–56
  disease and, 366–71
  evolution within, 346–50
  future projections, 356
  genetic changes in, 343–46
  size, 269, 351
  splitting, 348
Portugal, 321
postcanine teeth, 230
postnatal dependency, 140, **141**, 156
postorbital constriction, 284, **285**
potassium/argon (K/Ar) dating, 200–**201**, 271
Potts, Richard, 241, 248
predation, visually directed, 218–19
prehensile, **139**, 164, 218
  grip, *140*
  prosimians, 147
  tail, *150*
primates, **13**, 133–34
  adaptive radiation, 99, 124
  adaptive strategy, 145
  behavior patterns, 141–45
  brain sizes, 141
  characteristics in common, 137
  colorful faces, *142, 143*
  communication and grooming, *144*
  defined, 145

distribution of living nonhuman, *147*
  evolutionary tree, *217*
  human, 155–58
  intelligence, 140–41
  movement, 139–40
  origin and evolution, 216–23
  reproduction, 140
  rights of nonhuman, 156–57
  senses, 137–38
  simplified phenetic taxonomy, 145–46
  skeleton, 188–94
  skeleton, of modern human, gorilla, and domestic cat, *189*
  tailless, 151
primatology, **13**
Principles of Geology (Lyell), 34
prion proteins, 371
prognathism, **231**, 242, *245*, 284, 290, 298
progressive, **35**
prokaryotes, 132
prosimians, **99**, 146–48, 221
proteins, **49**, 63, 207
protein synthesis, **49**, 50, 51, *52, 53*, 58
protons, 115
provenience, **198**
pseudoscience, **104**–8
PTC (phenylthiocarbamide), 55–56
pubic symphysis, *192*
Puerto Ricans, 404
punch technique, 301
punctuated equilibrium, *101*, 102–3
Punnett Square, *61*, 437–38
pygmy chimpanzees. *See* bonobos

Qafzeh, Israel, 301, 302, 318
quadrupedal, **137**, 139

rabies, 370
Race and Human Evolution: A Fatal Attraction (Wolpoff and Caspari), 334, 335
races, **391**
  as biological concepts, 390–94
  as cultural categories, 334, 384
  as folk taxonomies, 401–4
  reason for nonexistence of, 395–401
  and social issues, 404–10
racism, 404, **405**
radiation, 115
radiocarbon dating, **198**–99
radiometric, **198**
RAD model, 324, 327
Rangifer tarandus, 391–92, *392*, 398
Recent African Origin (RAO) model, **313**–15, 318–19, 321–22, 324, 326, 327, 331, 333–36
recessive, 56, **57**, 71
recombination, **61**, 68, 73, 324
reconceptions, 17–18
red blood cells, normal and abnormal, *82*
reification, 406, **407**
reindeer, 391, 393, 398
relative dating technique, **198**
relativity, theory of, 15
religion, 41
repetition, 14
replacement model, 314
replication, **49**
reproduction
  human, 156–57
  primate, 140
  sexual activity separated from, 239, 241
reproductive isolating mechanism, 92–96, **93**
reproductive strategies, **167**, 175
  baboon, 171–72

RH blood factor, 151
Rhesus monkey, *151*
ribosomes, 50, 52, 53
rickets, 361
ridge count, 347, 350
Ridley, Mark: *Evolution*, 394
RNA. *See* messenger ribonucleic
    acid (mRNA); transfer
    ribonucleic acid (tRNA)
robust hominids, 245–57, 248
rootstock, 243

Sagan, Carl, 41
    The Dragons of Eden, 118
sagittal crest, **231**, 242, 267
    of male gorilla, *232*
    Paranthropus aethiopicus, 245
    Paranthropus robustus, 246
sagittal keel, **267**
salamander, 95, 96
Salem witch trials, 18
sampling error, 78, **79**
Sangiran, 271
Sarich, Vincent, 206, 207
savanna, 168, **169**, 172, 236
scalping, 194
scanning electron microscope,
    253, 277
scavenging, 236–37, 252, 253,
    274, 277
Schöningen, 285
science, **15**
    belief systems and, 18–**19**, 21,
        41, 104–8
scientific creationism, **104**
    theory of evolution and,
        103–8
scientific method, 14–18, **15**
    steps in, *15*
scientific names, 34, 42
scrapers, *275*
secular trends, 375
segregation, **59**, 61, 68, 73, 80
semispecies, **393,** 398

senses
    of humans, 155
    of primates, 137–38
sex, 386–**87**
    ambiguous, 388–90
    and gender, 385–90
sexual behavior
    of bonobos, 177–80
    human, 157
    of primates, 156–57
    separated from reproductive
        functions, 239, 241
sexual dimorphism, 190, **191,**
    385–86
sexual identities, *387*
sexually, **117**–18
shaft straightener, 302, *304*
Shanidar, Iraq, 295, 297
shared derived characteristics,
    135
Shea, John, 294
Shelley, Mary: *Frankenstein*, 41
Shipman, Pat, 253
shooting stars, 124
Shreeve, James, 271, 332
siamangs, 152
sickle cell anemia, 71, 80–86,
    331, 366, 425
    African Americans and, 85, 86
    allele frequency and, *81*, 343–46
    Punnett Square for, 85
sickle cell trait, 82
Silk, Joan B., 253
Sima de los Huesos, 283, 285–86
Simons, Elwyn, 13, 220
Singer, Peter, 157
single-celled organisms, 117
single nucleotide polymorphism
    (SNP), 346–**47,** 357,
    397–98
singularity, 114
sinus cavities, 293
sites, 194, **195**
Sivapithecus, 221, 223
    skull of, *222*

skeletal identification, exercise
    in, 436, 442
skeletal remains
    dating, 198–202
    determining ownership of,
        208–9
    information obtained from,
        188–94
    locating, 194–97
    major techniques used to de-
        termine the age of, *192*
    recovering, 197–98
    showing disease and injury,
        195
skeletal structure, human,
    188–94
Skhul, Israel, 301, 302, 318
skin color, 53, 54, 58, 360
    distribution, *360*
    environmental influences on,
        358, 360–62
    light, evolution of, 361–62
    variation, as a cline, 395
    and vitamin D production, 361
skull. *See* cranial features
slavery, in the United States,
    404
sleep behavior, 424
slender loris, *148*
smallpox, 366, 367, 368
Smilodectes, 218
Smith, Fred, 319
Smuts, Barbara, 13
Snow, Clyde, 13, 416, 419, 420
social interaction, use of fire
    and, 276
social selection, 408
social structure
    baboons, 168–72
    bonobos, 177–82
    chimpanzees, 154–55, 173–77
    early *Homo,* 254
    hylobatids, 152
    primates, 141–45
    wolves and wild dogs, 168

sociobiology, 166, **167**–68
socioeconomic status, and body size, 374–75
Soleihac, France, 273
South Africa, 299, 300
"southern apes," 225, 242
Spain, 273
sparrows, house, distribution of size variation in male, *394*
spear points, 301, 302
bifacially flaked Upper Paleolithic, *303*
specialized, **97**
speciation, **93**–94, 107
and evolutionary theory, 336
pattern of, 100–103
through environmental isolation, *94*
species, 10, **11**, 68–71, 131
adaptation, 358
classification, 130–34
defined, 69
generalized, 391
migration, 316, 332–35
new, 40, 92–96
specialized, 390–91
taxonomy of five familiar, *131*
transmutation of, 34–35
sperm whale, 141
splitters, 261–62, 268, 306, 321
spongiform encephalopathy, 371
"sports," 68
St. Acheul, France, 274
Steegmann, A. T. Jr., 362
Steno, Nicholas, 28, 42, 188
stereoscopic vision, *138*, **139**, 147, 218
Steudel, K., 238
Stinson, S., 374
"stone cache sites," 252–54
stone tools, 243–44, 248–50, 252, 274, 283
strata, **28**, **29**, 30, 31
stratigraphic sequence, hypothetical, *199*

stratigraphy, **28**, 42
Strepsirhini, 148
Stringer, Christopher, 313, 331, 332, 333, 334
stromatolites, *116*
Strum, Shirley, 13
subduction zones, 121
suborder, 145
subspecies, **391**–92
Sudden Infant Death Syndrome, 424–25
"Sue," 208
sulfuric acid, 123
Sundance Kid, 419
superfamily, 145
superposition, **198**
suspensory climbers and hangers, 139, 151
symbiosis, **323**
symbolic, **158**
symbols, 11
systematists, 70, **71**

tamarins, 150
tanning response, 358, 360
taphonomy, 204, **205**, 276
tarsier, 147–48, 218, 219
Philippine, *149*
taster trait, 56, 61, 71, 80
exercise in, 435–36
Tattersall, Ian, 306, 313, 321
Taung, 223
"Taung Baby," *223*, 225
taxa, 134, **135**, 137, 145
taxonomists, **70**, 71
taxonomy, **131**–34
cladistic, **135**–37, 145, 306
exercise in, 435, 439–40
folk, 388, **389**
folk, races as, 401–4
Linnaean, 34, 131, 134, 403–4
phenetic, 134, **135**, 136
Taylor, Zachary, 419

Tay-Sachs disease, 79, 85, 425–26
teeth
canine, 231, 242
dental eruption, *192*
diet evidenced by, 191
of New World and Old World anthropoids, 149–50
postcanine, 230
scanning electron microscope pictures of surfaces of hominids', 243
surfaces, of *A. africanus*, 243
surfaces, of *Paranthropus*, 243
tooth row of *A. afarensis*, 242
temperature, 358
Templeton, Alan, 326, 329, 333
temporalis, 232
termite sticks, 176, 249
Terra Amata, France, 273
testosterone, 387
test taking, 406
Thailand, 276, 377
theory, **15**–16, 17, 20
thermoluminescence (TL), 201
Thompson, Marcia, 423–24
thumbs, 250
thymine, 49, 51
tiger swallowtail butterflies, *38*
tools
blade, from Klasies River Mouth, South Africa, *303*
bone, 243, 250
choppers, 275
flake, *248*, **250**, 279, 283
flake and chopper, *275*
from Gran Dolina, 283
hand axes, 274, 275, 276
hominid, 285
of *Homo erectus*, 274–76
of *Homo ergaster*, 274–76
of *Homo heidelbergensis*, 285
of *Homo sapiens*, 301
marks, *254*
of Neandertals, 294–95, 322

Oldowan, *248*, **249**–50, 252, 307
  pebble, 249
  stone, 243–44, 248–50, 252, 274, 283
  in the Upper Paleolithic, 302–4
  use of by bonobos, 177
  use of by chimpanzees, 176
  wear-pattern analysis, 294–95
Torralba, 274, 276
torus, **267**
touch, as form of communication among primates, 145
traits
  in the ABO system, 364
  continuous, 395
  geographic variation, 384
  nonadaptive, 320
  pea plant, *55*, 57, 61
  phenotypic, 63
  polymorphic, *357*, 362–66
  sickle cell, 82
  taster, *56*, 61, 71, 80, 435–36
transfer ribonucleic acid (tRNA), *52*, **53**
transmutation of species, 34–35
trephination, 194, *195*
Trinil, 264
triradius, 347
Trisomy 21, 71–72
tRNA (transfer ribonucleic acid), *52*, **53**
troops, 170, 171
tuberculosis, 366, 369, 426
Tugen Hills, Kenya, 232
tundra, **271**
"Turkana Boy," 268, *270*
twins, 150
twin studies, 407
type A blood, 364
type O blood, 364–65
Tyrannosaurus rex, 208

ultraviolet radiation, 358, 359–60
ungulates, 235
uniformitarianism, 30–**31**, 34–35, 37, 40, 42
universality, 14
universe, history of, 114–20, *115*
Upper Paleolithic, 302–5
  artifacts, *304*
uracil, 51
Ussher, James, 27, 42
UV radiation, 361, 362

vampire finches, 97
"variability selection," 241
variation, 12, 37–39
  in adaptation, 358–62
  genetic, and concept of race, 397–98
  phenotypic, 68, 73, 357, 384, **385**, 390, 395–97
  in skin color, as a cline, 395
  in traits, geographic, 384
vegetarians, 157
velocity curve, **373**, *374*
Venus figurines, *304*
vertebrates, **118**
  seven classes within, 132–33
vertical clingers and leapers, 139, 148
Videan, E. N., 237, 238, 239
Vindija, Croatia, 318, 319
viruses, and evolution, 366–68
vision, primates and, 137–38
visually directed predation, 218–19
vocal tract
  of chimpanzees compared to modern humans, *279*
  of *H. erectus*, 278
  of Neandertals, 297–98
volcanic activity, 123

Wallace, Alfred Russel, 40, 42
Ward, C., 240
warm blooded, 133
Weiss, Kenneth, 336
Well-Known Skull 1470, *250*
West Highland terrier, *70*
West Nile virus, 430
West Turkana, Kenya, 268
White-Handed Gibbon, *152*
wild turkey, *125*
"will," 36
William of Ockham, 260, 351
Wilson, Allan, 206, 207
Wilson, Edward O., 93
Wolpoff, Milford, 307, 315, 319, 320, 329
wolves
  foramen magnum, *224*
  social structure, 168
woodworking, 276
woolly mammoth bones, 305
World Population Curve, 356

X chromosome, 59, 387
The X-Files, 84

Yali people, **385**
Y chromosome, 59, 387
Y-chromosome DNA, 324, 327
Y-5 cusp pattern, *221*
yeti, 222
Yucatán, 123

Zallinger, Rudolph, 122
Zhoukoudian, China, 265–66, 275, 276
Zinjanthropus, 247, 248–49, 251
zygote, **59**, 61

Brontë

Manuela Santoni

Translated by Matteo Benassi

Graphic Universe™ • Minneapolis

For Malpelo and Aida —M.S.

Story and art by Manuela Santoni
Translation by Matteo Benassi

First American edition published in 2021 by Graphic Universe™

Copyright © 2018 by Manuela Santoni
Copyright © 2018 by BeccoGiallo S.r.l. for the Italian edition.
Published in arrangement with Am-Book (www.ambook.ch)

Graphic Universe™ is a trademark of Lerner Publishing Group, Inc.

Graphic Universe™
An imprint of Lerner Publishing Group, Inc.
241 First Avenue North
Minneapolis, MN 55401 USA

For reading levels and more information, look up this title at www.lernerbooks.com.

Main body text set in DInkle.
Typeface provided by Chank.

Library of Congress Cataloging-in-Publication Data

Names: Santoni, Manuela, 1988- author, illustrator. | Benassi, Matteo, translator.
Title: Brontë / Manuela Santoni ; translated by Matteo Benassi.
Other titles: Sorelle Brontë. English
Description: First American edition. | Minneapolis : Graphic Universe, 2021. | Audience: Ages 13-18. | Audience: Grades 10-12. | Summary: "In the English countryside of the nineteenth century, Charlotte, Emily and Anne Brontë—coping with an elderly father and a brother dedicated to drinking—find themselves confronting their family's stormy economic forturnes. And they do it their own way: overcoming difficulties and first failures with pride and courage; transforming their creative talents into a source of sustenance; and finally living lives of freedom."— Provided by publisher.
Identifiers: LCCN 2019041801 (print) | LCCN 2019041802 (ebook) | ISBN 9781541581197 (library binding) | ISBN 9781541599482 (ebook)
Subjects: LCSH: Brontë, Charlotte, 1816-1855—Juvenile fiction. | Brontë, Emily, 1818-1848—Juvenile fiction. | Brontë, Anne, 1820-1849—Juvenile fiction. | Brontë family—Juvenile fiction. | Women authors, English—19th century—Juvenile fiction. | Graphic novels. | CYAC: Graphic novels. | Brontë, Charlotte, 1816-1855—Fiction. | Brontë, Emily, 1818-1848—Fiction. | Brontë, Anne, 1820-1849—Fiction. | Brontë family—Fiction. | Authors—Fiction.
Classification: LCC PZ7.7.S175 Br 2021 (print) | LCC PZ7.7.S175 (ebook) | DDC (Fic)—dc23

LC record available at https://lccn.loc.gov/2019041801
LC ebook record available at https://lccn.loc.gov/2019041802

Manufactured in the United States of America
1-47318-47945-7/8/2020

"My soul is awakened, my spirit is soaring
And carried aloft on the wings of the breeze"

—Anne Brontë, "Lines Composed in a Wood on a Windy Day"

"I am no bird; and no net ensnares me;
I am a free human being with an independent will"

—Charlotte Brontë, *Jane Eyre*

"I've dreamt in my life dreams that have stayed with me ever after,
and changed my ideas: they've gone through and through me,
like wine through water, and altered the colour of my mind."

—Emily Brontë, *Wuthering Heights*

Our house was very quiet...

Or so it seemed.

Early in the morning, the wind would rise...

A wind typical of our region...

Raging in from the four corners of the globe.

Stirring those wuthering heights.

But the fury inside never ceased...

That fury...

Blazing in their eyes.

So...

Who did it?

Who touched them?

Who touched my things!?

Why can't we have any peace in this house?

Emily, calm down!

I can't take much more of this...

I did it.

So...

Finally, the culprit confesses!

I didn't want to...Believe me.

Charlotte...

I don't understand you, sister.

You've been strange lately.

Ever since you returned from Belgium, in fact.

That Héger man scrambled your brains!

I...
I...

A married man. How could you let him put you in such a state?

Emily, I...

Enough!

Daughters, what's going on here?

Charlotte keeps sticking her nose into my affairs!

Charlotte, is what your sister says true?

I swear I wanted to stop...

But I couldn't restrain myself.

Charlotte.

Charlotte!

Aaaah!

Anne! Are you mad? You scared me!

Sorry, but I didn't want Emily to see me!

I need to show you...

Here.

These are the poems I've written in the last year.

Sometimes I don't understand Emily's reticence.

She's so secretive and proud...but so extraordinarily talented.

It's true.

My poems will never be as good as hers are...

But I want you to read them!

Dear sister, it would be an honor.

Wait!

In a foul mood, are we?

You look gloomier than Branwell...

Hello, Emily.

So you've decided to speak to me again?

Only a little.

I'm gloomy about the fate of the school we hoped to found.

I detest your lack of faith.

But you're right.

Come now. We always knew it was just a dream...

Months spent...

...on a dream.

There's another thing to consider...

Our family's never been poorer.

Father's getting older and sicker.

COUGH COUGH

And our only brother is leading himself to ruin.

You know I'm a private soul, Charlotte.

I'm not fond of people...

Woof!

I'm only fond of Keeper!

HA HA

Well, we must do something for this family!

I mean, about our finances.

As much as you might judge me for ending my time as a teacher...

I couldn't stay there...

CLANG!

You're really coming back at this hour? It has been morning for quite a while!

Fine! You're right! Must be time to leave!

SLAM!

Where did the Branwell of old go?

We should publish our poems.

Anne's latest are quite good...

And with you, Emily...

With you, we could find a house willing to publish us!

Let's use our talent to set ourselves free!

Free to support ourselves and not burden this family...

Emily, you owe something to this household and to our father. Don't you think?

That is truly enough!

Can't the two of you understand?

Emily...

You *must* respect that I *don't* wish to share my writings with others!

Writing is for me. Only for me.

Dear sister, I don't want to force you...

But you're well aware of our situation!

You left your position to be a writer...

Again with this story!

What are you afraid of, Emily?

You're afraid that others will judge you! Admit it!

You should let the world in...

You have more to give than you think.

He's not himself.

It's the drink that makes him do these things.

Did he beat you, Father?

Damn him!

He's lost control.

London

I'm sorry...

We've examined your writing...

We don't think it's suited to us.

What!?

You made me come here for a rejection?

We wrote you once already...

You insisted on coming in person.

GRR

Why? Why are my poems being rejected?

We don't find them compelling.

But that's hardly an explanation. Why?

What's wrong with them?

SCRATCH

SCRATCH

If you insist...

Well, well. Milord is back home.

Where the blazes did you go? We haven't seen you for a week!

Away on business.

In case you're interested...

Your father is fine. Despite what you did to him!

You have no respect for anything or anybody!

Emily, I didn't...

Go away.

The Branwell I knew would never had done what you just did.

SNIFF" SNIFF"

Haworth,
West Yorkshire

BLACK
BULL
INN

Branwell
Brontë?

Hic!

Hic!

In
the
flesh!

Who
the devil
are you?

I have
news
from the
Robinsons.

Lydia?
Lydia
sent
you?

Emily, what is it?

I don't know, Charlotte. I still have doubts...

Doubts about what?

About what we're doing.

Let me rephrase that...

About what *I'm* doing.

You both know me.

At home and outside it... I'm two different people.

The truth is that no one cares for me beyond these walls.

But, Emily...

GRRR...

We'll use our first initials...

Currer

Charlotte

Acton

Anne

Ellis

Emily

This... complicates matters. We simply don't have the money.

I may have a solution...

It's really them!

Anne, why didn't you say anything?

Nowadays, our soldiers might be worth a great deal.

You want to...

If Branwell finds out, he'll kill us.

Sisters, we're about to sell off the only fond memory of our brother...

Currer

Ellis

Acton

*I've always told you
**You must believe in yourself
***You are enormously talented, my dear

This is one of the love letters Willy sent me.

He wrote to me until the end. Even as the illness consumed him.

I had never had the heart to throw them away...

I decided to use them as inspiration for my novel.

The story of a passionate love...

You'll be scandalized, sister of mine!

HA HA

HA HA

Alone at last, Keeper.

I have all I need to write...

There was too much love in that house!

And in their stories too...

In mine, there will be hate and terror!

...And a pinch of passion, of course!

HA HA

They rejected it.

Charlotte, that's absurd!

Explain.

The two of you have nothing to worry about. Your novels are fine.

Mine not so much...

We said we'd do this together or not at all!

I only agreed because we were united.

Thank you, sisters.

I'll write another novel. And they'll accept it, I swear!

JANE EYRE
EDITED BY
CURRER BELL
VOL. I

JANE EYRE
EDITED BY
CURRER BELL
VOL. II

JANE EYRE
EDITED BY
CURRER BELL
VOL. III

WUTHERING HEIGHTS
by
Ellis Bell
———
———
VOL. I

WUTHERING HEIGHTS
by
Ellis Bell
———
———
VOL. II

AGNES GREY
by
Acton Bell
———
———
VOL. III

Charlotte, I believe you're famous now.

And you, Anne, how you've scandalized everybody...

So meek, yet so passionate!

HA HA HA

Charlotte...

I've been thinking about something for a while.

Maybe we should tell Father about our novels.

I think it would be a comfort to him, with the state that Branwell's in.

You know, sisters...

I read a review that said our novels seem to have been written by women.

It was inevitable... what a fool I am!

Better that Father hears it from us, or it'll land like a blow...

We owe him that.

At least he'll know he doesn't have to support us forever...

And I'm proud of our work. Even if I fear his judgment more than all the others.

These are dark times to be a woman...

Most people think literature isn't a woman's business.

When a man writes something, he's judged for what he writes.

When a woman does the same, she's judged for who she is.

I don't care about being judged. I only want to write!

Writing is my whole life...

It's the only thing that's mine, that makes me feel at peace when everything around me is going wrong.

Mr. Brontë...

You can't see Lydia anymore.

If she remarries...

She will lose her late husband's inheritance.

My dear Branwell...

You are banned from the Robinson house forever!

CRASH!

THUMP THUMP

SLAM!

Emily! Look at what your damn publisher has done!

Newby?

He took some pages of Anne's new novel thinking I wrote them!

And...?

We need to go to London to fix the mistake.

What!?

Don't even speak of that.

I don't want something I wrote attributed to someone else!

And I don't want my publisher to think I'm deceitful...

Or sell the book to the Americans this way!

Help us, Emily...

Come with us!

Such a
pity...

WOOF
WOOF

SLAM!

WOOF!
GRRR...

What on
earth...
WOOF!
Keeper,
what's
bothering
you?

What
have you
gotten
into...

WOOF WOOF

Wait, that's…

That's Lydia!

And those are her horrid daughters…

The ones I worked for.

The daughters are leaving…

Where's Lydia going?

It looks like she's entering the tailor's…

Our brother is an ingrate, but *she* is devious.

I must confess I always knew about their relationship...

But I did nothing to stop it.

I always felt like...

An accomplice.

Anne...

You had nothing to do with it!

You should know I'm still in touch with someone at the Robinson estate...

I've learned that our brother has been banished from their house!

Ah. So instead, she lost Branwell...

If Lydia remarries, she'll lose her late husband's fortune.

That's why he was in such a state last time.

Hurry, let's go!

I told you she saw us!

HA HA

HA HA

Ma'am, who are those two young ladies? Do you know them?

Oh, two harmless little fillies.

SLAM!

Emily…

Don't run off like that!

Emily, please, stop!

Don't tell him!

What? Is the apocalypse coming?

Worse.

Branwell.

What do you want, you madwoman?

I must tell you something...

No!

Here we go again!

Always pointing fingers...

Well, I don't want to hear it right now.

Is that opium you're smoking?

Yes. Top shelf!

It relaxes me.

Not in the house, I beg you.

I don't take orders from you. Is that clear?

At last, relief.

THUMP!

Father, let me take your place.

I'm not sick. Stop fussing over me!

You should show us more respect. Our father most of all.

You've never done a single good thing, but he's always loved you.

Oh, please!

Emily. So brave here at home...

Do you know what people say about you in town? That you're half crazed. Always silent and alone...

You and those other two. Always writing, nothing else...

It was fine enough when we were children, but I thought you would have grown out of your fantasies...

Now, what's the point?

131

You know that book you're reading?

This one?

I found it in our library. It came out not long ago.

I've read some negative reviews, but I quite like it.

What does that have to do with anything?

I wrote it.

HA HA

Don't talk nonsense!

This is a scandalous novel.

Someone like *you* couldn't have written it.

I wrote one of the story's characters with you in mind.

His name is Hindley.

He's a wicked man. Good for nothing. A parasite sucking the blood out of his family.

The reviewers often wondered where I got the inspiration for such a character...

But it was simple.

I've had such a character in front of my eyes constantly...when he's not out drinking or taking opium.

It must be difficult to live knowing that you've accomplished nothing...

That inside you is an unbridgeable emptiness.

While your sisters... strange creatures, it's true...

...are successful writers.

Emily, don't...

And another thing...

Lydia is going to remarry.

Anne and I saw her a few days ago...

HUFF HUFF

Ch-Charlotte...

Emily.

Emily, what are you waiting for? Hop on up!

COUGH
COUGH

SLAM!

I hate you!

Here we are.

Emily, don't lag behind...

Come in!

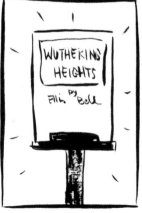

WUTHERING HEIGHTS

by Ellis Bell

THUMP THUMP

My God!

Everything all right, miss? Can I help you?

HA HA
HA HA

Emily!

Not so loud!

He started it!

Are you the man in charge?

No. Regrettably, he's occupied.

Could you call on him, please? It's an urgent matter.

Ma'am, he is occupied.

Please...

We traveled almost twenty hours to be here!

So sorry.

Listen, good sir...

We've said it's an important matter! Otherwise, we wouldn't insist so!

Now hurry up and fetch him!

To think she's the meekest of us...

Anne, how I love you right now!

You
three
are...

You're...

You're
exceptional.

My sisters revealed their identities and resolved the confusion...

I looked to Emily. She, at least, might have heard me.

Anne followed her a little later. She passed away with a pen in her hand.

But not before she wrote another novel.

Around the parsonage at Haworth, the wind ceased raging on the wuthering heights.

The Brontë sisters left this world.

Drawing the Brontës: Character Designs

Anne is the mildest, the sweetest of the sisters, so I designed her with soft lines. While I was drawing her, I was thinking of the actor Keira Knightley. I often do that—when I have to draw a character for a story, I think of some actor and then create my cast on paper.

Charlotte, the older sister, had to look even older than she was. She almost always wears dark clothes throughout the book. She also has large eyes and pronounced cheekbones, which I used to denote a strong and determined character. While I was drawing her, I thought of Charlotte Gainsbourg in Franco Zeffirelli's film adaptation of *Jane Eyre*.

Emily has hard, almost masculine facial features but long, sensual eyes. I drew her very thin and tall, almost as tall as Branwell. Given her androgynous characteristics, I thought of Tilda Swinton as I drew her.

Branwell was difficult to characterize. At first, I had drawn him with sloping, angular features. Then I changed my mind, and he became more beautiful, to destabilize the reader. In the final design, he looks nice on the outside but he's rotten on the onside. I took inspiration from *Corto Maltese* by Hugo Pratt.

Patrick Brontë, like Branwell, changed as I drew him, becoming more hunchbacked and stocky and definitely older. With this design, I didn't think about any particular actor.

A Brontë Timeline

April 21, 1816: Charlotte Brontë is born in Thornton, West Yorkshire, in England. She is the third child born to Maria (née Branwell) and Patrick Brontë, after siblings Maria and Elizabeth.

June 26, 1817: Branwell Brontë is born in Thornton, West Yorkshire.

July 30, 1818: Emily Brontë is born in Thornton, West Yorkshire.

January 17, 1820: Anne Brontë is born in Thornton, West Yorkshire.

1820: The Brontë family moves to Haworth, West Yorkshire.

1821: Maria Branwell Brontë dies of ovarian cancer.

1824–1825: The four eldest Brontë sisters, Maria, Elizabeth, Charlotte, and Emily, attend boarding school.

1825: The two eldest Brontë siblings, Maria and Elizabeth, die of tuberculosis. Their deaths deeply affect their younger sister Charlotte.

1835–1837: Anne attends boarding school.

1838: Emily begins work as a teacher in Miss Patchett's School for Girls at Law Hill, near Halifax, West Yorkshire.

1839: Emily leaves her position due to stress and exhaustion and begins to write at home.

1840: Anne begins work as a governess to the children of Lydia Robinson and the Reverend Edmund Robinson in North Yorkshire.

1842: Charlotte and Emily travel to Brussels, Belgium, and study under language teacher Constantin Héger.

Emily returns to Haworth after the death of the siblings' aunt Elizabeth.

1844: Charlotte returns to Haworth from Brussels.

1845: The four surviving Brontë siblings live at their family home in Haworth.

Branwell loses his position as a tutor for the Robinson family and becomes addicted to alcohol and opium.

Charlotte convinces her sisters to try publishing their poetry.

1846:	Charlotte, Emily, and Anne adopt literary pseudonyms. Aylott and Jones publishes the sisters' joint collection of poetry, crediting the works to the Bell brothers.
	Charlotte writes her first novel, *The Professor*, about Constantin Héger.
	Anne writes her first novel, *Agnes Grey*.
	Emily writes the novel *Wuthering Heights*.
1847:	Publishers reject *The Professor*.
	Charlotte writes her second novel, *Jane Eyre*.
October 1847:	Smith, Elder and Co. of London publishes *Jane Eyre*. The novel is credited to Currer Bell.
December 1847:	Thomas Cautley Newby publishes *Agnes Grey* and *Wuthering Heights*. The novels are credited to Acton Bell and Ellis Bell, respectively.
July 1848:	Anne and Charlotte travel to London and reveal their identities to their publisher.
September 24, 1848:	Branwell dies, most likely of tuberculosis.
December 19, 1848:	Emily dies of tuberculosis.
May 28, 1849:	Anne dies of tuberculosis.
June 1849:	Newby publishes Anne's second novel, *The Tenant of Wildfell Hall*. The novel is credited to Acton Bell.
October 1849:	Smith, Elder and Co. publishes Charlotte's third novel, *Shirley*. The novel is credited to Currer Bell.
1850:	Charlotte reveals the sisters' identities to the public.
January 1853:	Smith, Elder and Co. publishes Charlotte's fourth novel, *Villette*.
June 29, 1854:	Charlotte marries Arthur Bell Nicholls, a colleague of her father.
March 31, 1855:	Charlotte dies, most likely of tuberculosis and complications from pregnancy.
1857:	Smith, Elder and Co. publishes Charlotte's first novel, *The Professor*, for the first time.

About the Author

Manuela Santoni is an illustrator and a cartoonist from Rome, Italy. Born in 1988, she studied art at Rome's Liceo Artistico (High School of the Arts). In 2012 she received a degree in contemporary art history from Sapienza Università di Roma (Sapienza University of Rome). She also attended Scuola Romana dei Fumetti (the Roman School of Comics), and in 2013 she received a master's degree in illustration at Ars in Fabula in Macerata, Italy. Since 2017 she has been a teacher at the Pencil Art comics and illustration school.

Santoni has illustrated the young adult stories *Girl R-Evolution* by Alberto Pellai (De Agostini, 2016) and *Storie proprio buffe* by Paul Jennings (Il Castoro, 2016). In 2017 she published the graphic novel *Jane Austen* (Beccogiallo Editore, 2017), for North American readers as *Jane Austen: Her Heart Did Whisper* (2018). She lives in Fonte Nuova, a community in the countryside of Rome.

Acknowledgments

This second book was a much greater challenge than my graphic novel about Jane Austen. There were dark moments, blockages, and second thoughts that slowed down the early stages of my work. But the first experience taught me a lot, so I managed to recover lost time. Therefore, I want to thank again my publisher, which continues to believe in my work. I thank my friends for their enduring support. I thank my family, which has lovingly surrendered to the idea that this is the job I've always wanted to do.

Additional thanks to Serena Di Battista and Selene Chilla, who carry on their work writing about the Brontë sisters with exemplary passion and enthusiasm. They were my consultants throughout the work, always available although we never met. Thanks to the women who fought for what they loved in eras that kept them at a disadvantage. They are a constant example for me. And thanks to comics, beautiful comics, which are an escape from the ugliness in this world.